ORLANDO

and the Gibbons fa

ORLANDO GIBBONS

and the Gibbons family of musicians

John Harley

Routledge
Taylor & Francis Group

LONDON AND NEW YORK

First published 1999 by Ashgate Publishing

Reissued 2018 by Routledge
2 Park Square, Milton Park, Abingdon, Oxon OX14 4RN
711 Third Avenue, New York, NY 10017, USA

Routledge is an imprint of the Taylor & Francis Group, an informa business

Publisher's Note
The publisher has gone to great lengths to ensure the quality of this reprint but points out that some imperfections in the original copies may be apparent.

Disclaimer
The publisher has made every effort to trace copyright holders and welcomes correspondence from those they have been unable to contact.

A Library of Congress record exists under LC control number : 99031935

ISBN 13: 978-1-138-32717-7 (hbk)
ISBN 13: 978-1-138-32721-4 (pbk)
ISBN 13: 978-0-429-44939-0 (ebk)

CONTENTS

CONTENTS

ILLUSTRATIONS

PREFACE

Musical references and examples

Compositions published in the *Musica Britannica* series are identified by the volume and piece number, e.g. MB 20/2 means the second piece in volume 20. Similar references are made to works published in the series *Tudor Church Music* (TCM), *Early English Church Music* (EECM), and the *Byrd Edition* (BE).

Modern editions may halve the note values of the original sources. For the sake of consistency music examples and references in the text observe the original note values.

Many of the sources have no bar-lines, or bar pieces irregularly. Barring is therefore largely editorial, but for the convenience of readers referring to editions in the series *The English Madrigalists*, *Musica Britannica*, the *Byrd Edition* and *Early English Church Music*, their barring has been adopted. A few accidentals omitted by the sources, and a few 'reminders' (though not strictly necessary), have been inserted.

Spellings

Quotations from primary sources are given in the original spelling, but modern letter forms are used. Where necessary 'u' and 'v' have been exchanged, as have 'i' and 'j' (except where they occur together, e.g. in Roman numerals). Some contractions have been expanded in italics, but 'p̱' is often used for the crossed 'p' representing 'par', 'per' or 'pro'. A tilde is used for any superior mark indicating the omission of letters, and the ampersand replaces any sign for 'and'. The titles of compositions have usually been modernized, except when particular reference is made to an early printed edition, or when the title contains the word 'mask' (sometimes spelled 'maske' in the sources but never 'masque').

Dates and money

During Gibbons's lifetime the year began on 25 March. The date of an event falling in the period 1 January to 24 March is indicated by combining the old and modern styles, e.g. 1608/9.

Before the introduction of decimal currency in 1971, the English pound (£ or li., Latin *libra*) was made up of twenty shillings (s.), and a shilling consisted of twelve pence (d., Latin *denarius*). The mark was valued at two-thirds of a pound. The sums 6s. 8d. and 13s. 4d. were therefore equivalent to half a mark and one mark respectively.

Pitch notation

Where a note needs to be identifed by the octave in which it occurs, its pitch is indicated (from the bass) thus: C' to B', C to B, c to b, c' (middle C) to b', c" to b", etc.

Abbreviations

The following abbreviations are used:

BE   *The Byrd Edition*
BL   British Library
EECM   *Early English Church Music*
MB   *Musica Britannica*
OED   *Oxford English Dictionary*
PRO   Public Record Office
TCM   *Tudor Church Music*

A few other abbreviations are included in the bibliography.

Acknowledgements

It is a pleasure to acknowledge my indebtedness to Mr Richard Turbet, who has been generous in responding to repeated calls for advice and for help in obtaining printed materials. Others to whom I should like to express my gratitude for their assistance are Ms Humaira Erfan Ahmed (Administrator, Faculty of Music, Oxford), Dr Andrew Ashbee, Mr David Baldwin (Serjeant of the Vestry, Chapel Royal), Mr Allan Bicket, Miss Janet Clayton, and Mr Paul Vining. Thanks are due, too, to those having charge of the documents and books mentioned in the following pages; all have gone out of their way to help me locate and gain access to these materials, and I hope that the careful recording of the sources I have used will be accepted as an acknowledgement of my debt.

Illustrations are reproduced by kind permission of the following:

1, 2: The British Library; 3: The Guildhall Library, Corporation of London; 4: The Royal College of Music; 5: The Dean and Chapter of Westminster; 6, 8: The Faculty of Music, Oxford; 7: The Dean and Chapter of Canterbury.

PART I

THE GIBBONS FAMILY

Orlando Gibbons was the most notable member of a family which produced three generations of professional musicians. Its history can be traced from the middle of the sixteenth century. The arms on Orlando Gibbons's monument in Canterbury Cathedral indicate a belief in his descent ultimately from the Guybons of Norfolk,[1] though the earliest ancestor who can be identified with any certainty is his grandfather, Richard, who lived in Oxford.[2]

Richard Gibbons

Richard Gibbons may have been a glover, since a number of entries in the accounts of the City of Oxford record payments 'to Gybbons' for gloves.[3] Richard became a hanaster in 1549-50,[4] and by 16 September

---

1 The Guybon arms were: or, a lion rampant sable, over all on a bend gules three escallops argent. The crest was: a demi-lion rampant sable, armed or, charged on the body with three escallops in pale argent. The arms and genealogy given by Rye (1891, p. 141) derive from f. 61ʳ (modern 57ʳ) of BL Harleian MS 1552, compiled c.1620 by Richard Mundy from earlier visitations. The genealogy does not include Orlando Gibbons or his immediate forbears. Robson (1830, s.v. 'Gybbons') says the arms are those of Gybbons, or Guyon, of Stratchet, Norfolk. In depicting the arms on Orlando Gibbons's monument, Dart (1726, p. 51) errs in replacing the escallops with crescents.

2 William Gibbons, Orlando's father, was a freeman of Oxford (one with permission or liberty to trade in the city). As Richard Gibbons is the only earlier person with the same surname who is known to have been free of the city, it is fairly certain that he was William's father. No entry has been found for any member of the Gibbons family in the surviving subsidy rolls for Oxford.

3 From 1556 to 1562. Gloves were provided so that the council could present them as a token of regard for the recipients (Oxford City Archives, P.5.1, examples on ff. 10ʳ, 12ʳ, 30ʳ, 32ʳ; Turner, 1880, pp. 258, 260, 284, 299). Gloves were presented to Queen Anne and Prince Henry when they visited Oxford with King James in 1605 (Cambridge University Library, MS Mm.i.47, *olim* Baker 36, p. 450). William Piers mentions the 'Oxford courtesie' of presenting a pair of gloves (p. 65 below). The glovers' trade in Oxford was on a small scale, but prospered throughout the fifteenth and sixteenth centuries (McConica, 1986, p. 72). Crossley (1979, p. 109) refers to the position of the glovemakers on the city council. Richard Ball, a chorister of Magdalen College, had a brother and a nephew who were freemen glovers (McConica, p. 82).

4 Oxfordshire Archives, A.5.3 (not now bound in either date or folio order); Turner, 1880, p. 203. Hanaster: 'The name given (in the city of Oxford) to persons paying the

1557 he was one of the city councillors.[5] On 7 September 1562 he was excluded on account of his conduct:

> Item this Day it is also ordeyned that John Gorton[6] and Ryc. Gybbons shalbe dismyssed this house for beyng of the counselle & that they shall also be discharged of their imprisonm[t], but for the words that was spoken to aunswere thereto yf they be called.[7]

The ban was rescinded on 5 October:

> Richard Gybbons upon his umble submyssyon beinge sorye for his offence heretofore comytted in this howse/ was this daye Receyved agayne to be accouncyll wth the mayer And was pntlye Sworne to the mayers counseyll.[8]

He was sufficiently in favour on 8 October to be chosen, with Thomas Wylde, to 'take upp all the pore people and brynge thym this after none'.[9] In March 1563/4 he was chosen, with Sylvester Kytchyn, to report to the Council about the enclosure of a piece of ground called Sidelings.[10] In 1569-70 he was one of two chamberlains.[11] These were officers elected by the Council, whose duties included keeping the city's accounts and disbursing money after due approval.[12] Barnard Archdale and Richard Gibbons made up their accounts at Michaelmas 1570.[13]

Richard Gibbons was among the citizens who took an oath to observe the privileges of the university on 27 November 1561, and he did so again on 7 April and 26 October 1570.[14] In 1576, however, he refused to take the oath on 11 and 14 December.[15]

entrance-fee of the guild-merchant ... and admitted as Freeman of the City' (OED).

5   Oxford City Archives, A.5.5, f. 91[r]. (Turner, 1880, p. 268, is slightly in error.)

6   John Gorton became a hanaster in 1541-42. He was a chamberlain (see note 12 below) in 1559-61 (Turner, 1880, pp. 167, 280, 283).

7   Oxford City Archives, DC1/C1/A2/1, f. 18[v]; Turner, 1880, p. 293.

8   DC1/C1/A2/1, f. 27[r]; Turner, 1880, p. 300.

9   DC1/C1/A2/1, f. 29[r].

10   DC1/C1/A2/1, f. 36[r-v]; Turner, 1880, p. 307.

11   Oxford City Archives, A.5.5, f. 120[v]; Turner, 1880, p. 331.

12   Chamberlains alone originally handled the city's money, but they became subordinate to the keykeepers, instituted by an ordinance of 1448 (Salter, 1928, p. xviii).

13   Oxford City Archives, P.4.1, f. 20[r]; Turner, 1880, p. 332.

14   Clark, 1887-88, i, pp. 299, 301.

15   Ibid., 303, 304. Others refusing included Barnard Archdale and two aldermen.

Richard Gibbons appears to have died in 1577, in the parish of All Saints.[16] Letters of administration were granted to his widow, Alice, on 1 February 1577/8.[17] On 10 December 1594 the council determined to give sixpence weekly towards her relief.[18]

William Gibbons

Richard Gibbons's son William must have been born about 1540.[19] He cannot have been Richard's eldest son, or when in 1583 he gained the freedom of Oxford he would not have paid a fee.[20] His early life and musical training appear to have gone unrecorded. It is known that his wife was named Mary,[21] but neither her maiden name nor the place and date of their marriage has been discovered.

By 1566 William Gibbons was a wait in Cambridge — a member of one of the bands of musicians which had developed from the mediaeval night watch.[22] Over many years his name was entered frequently in the account books of the town and colleges. He is first mentioned as resident in Cambridge in 1566, in connection with payment for a tenor hautboy:

Quibus ut &c/ comparuit W gibbons ut petijt a mason xxiiij^s viij^d debitos pro instrumento musico vocato a teno^r hoeboye ut patet per billam obligatoriam dicti mason in presentia dicti mason confitentis predicta esse vera/ unde dominus decrevit ex consensu dicti gibbons xij^s iiij^d solvendos per mason in festo Sancti Iohannis bapt. proximo et xij^s iiij^d solvendos duodecimo die septembris proximo futuro post datum huius scripture et dictus mason fideiussores dedit pro dictis solutionibus χpoferum Russell burgenseum et[23] chandelor/ Michaelem Auger/ waferer/ et Ricardum gravers showemaker qui stipulatione legitima concepta promiserunt et c cum expensis[24]

---

16   All Saints' church is now the library of Lincoln College.

17   Oxfordshire Archives, will register of the Archdeacon of Oxford, 185, p. 522^v.

18   Oxford City Archives, A.5.6, f. 19^r; Salter, 1928, p. 90.

19   Early baptismal records for Oxford parishes are incomplete.

20   An eldest son could claim admission to freedom of the city by his father's 'copy' (Salter, 1928, pp. vi-vii). Further evidence that William had a brother is provided by his wife's will, which mentions her niece Elizabeth Gibbons (see p. 274).

21   See, for example, her will (p. 277).

22   The history of the Cambridge waits is traced by Nelson, 1989, pp. 738-741.

23   'ut' in original.

24   Cambridge University Library, University Archives, Collect. Admin. 13, f. 87^v, entry dated 26 March 1566; Nelson, 1989, p. 249.

In summary, William Gibbons sought from Mason[25] 24s 8d for a tenor hautboy.[26] With Gibbons's agreement, the court ordered Mason to pay 12s 4d on the feast of St John the Baptist next, and 12s 4d on 12 September next. His guarantors were Christopher Russell, burgess and chandler, Michael Auger, waferer, and Richard Gravers, shoemaker.[27]

When Gibbons arrived in Cambridge the town seems to have had five waits, led by John Hewarden (known as 'Blind John') with John Murton as his deputy.[28] A second group was known as the 'university waits'. The division between the town and university of jurisdiction over these groups is not absolutely clear, since besides performing a municipal function the town waits played in and about the colleges. In the Vice-Chancellor's court in 1590 Gibbons, who was then employed by the town, seems to have accepted the university's authority in his dispute with William Byrd, the university wait.[29]

William Gibbons appears at first to have assumed the role of university wait, for which he agreed to compensate Hewarden. On 23 November 1566 he undertook to make payments to Hewarden, 'as longe as blynd John should lyve/ and he the sayed Gybbons allowed accepted/ and not forbydden to be thuni*ver*sitie wayth'.[30] The town council admitted him by common consent as an 'histrio' on 3 November 1567, at an annual fee of forty shillings to be paid from the town treasury:

M*emorandum* qu*od* ad hunc diem Wille*lmus* Gibons ex co*mmun*i assensu admissus est histrio huius ville capiend*o* feod*um* xl[s] p*er* Annu*m* p*er* man*um* thezaur*ariorum* dict*e* ville Annuatim solvend*os*./[31]

---

25   The Town Treasurers' Books for 1567-58 record a payment of 26s 4d to 'masen for plaienge at y[e] guilde hall' and 'at the comaundment of m[r] maier & the counsell' (Downing College Library, Bowtell 2, f. 78[r]; Nelson, 1989, p. 253). It is not clear whether he was the Mason who appears in the records of Trinity College: 'to m[r] mason & organist for Violl strings — 5[s]' (Trinity College Archives, Box 19.280a, Liber Expensarum, 1612, p. 24; Nelson, 1989, p. 497). This Mason appears to have been an employee of the College: see, for example, p. 45 of the same document.

26   The hautboy was an instrument particularly associated with waits.

27   Gravers appears elsewhere as Greaves and Gravenes.

28   Nelson, 1989, pp. 740, 1004.

29   See pp. 12-13.

30   Cambridge University Library, University Archives, Collect. Admin. 13, f. 99[r]; Nelson, 1989, pp. 250-251. Gibbons promised that every year he would pay Blind John twenty shillings on each of four feast-days.

31   Cambridgeshire County Record Office, PB57, f. 262[r]; Nelson, 1989, p. 253. It is uncertain if forty shillings given to the waits in 1570 for liveries was their annual wage or a separate payment (Downing College, Bowtell 2, f. 116[r]; Nelson, 1989, p. 262).

A memorandum made three weeks later confirms that there were five municipal waits, and that Gibbons was their leader:

> *Memorandum* that at ye court holden the xxv[th] daie of november in the tenthe yere of the raign of our sov*e*raign ladie Quene Elizabethe M*aste*r maior did delyver to william Gibbons musition fyve sylver collers called the waites collers ponderynge xxvij ounces di*midium* And the said william Gibbons hathe founde suerties for ye delyv*e*rye of the same collers agayne when they be required vz william Barnes & Richard Gravenes.[32]

Two entries in the town records of 1567 read:

> Itm paid for mendinge the collers for y[e] wait*es* —— ijs
> Itm paid to Gibbons for his way*tes* —— xls[33]

There are many other entries concerning payments to waits in the town and college records of Cambridge.[34] It is evident from these that the waits played during ceremonies and processions, and in front of the gates of colleges on winter mornings. Some of the payments made by colleges were for performances on feast days, which were doubtless celebrated with a mixture of religious observance and institutional pageantry.[35] At times these performances probably merged into general revelry and entertainment. The waits certainly provided music for college plays. It is not always clear whether they were the municipal band or one sponsored by the university, but on occasion a reference is specific. In 1567 Jesus College made a payment of 6s 8d 'at candlemas to y[e] way*tes* of y[e] towne'.[36] Testimony that Gibbons led the waits is provided by payments such as that of two shillings, made by King's College in 1569-70, 'to gibbons/ and his companye'.[37]

It is possible that soon after William Gibbons settled in Cambridge he lost his first child. A boy named Richard Gibbons, perhaps after his grandfather, was buried at St Mary the Great on 11 July 1566. An entry in the burial register describes the father as 'goodman Gibbens', and if

32   Cambridgeshire County Record Office, PB57, f. 262[v]; Nelson, 1989, p. 254.

33   Downing College, Bowtell 2, f. 78[r] (sums of two shillings and forty shillings).

34   These musicians were not always from Cambridge. See, for example, under 'ffeoda et Regarda' in King's College Mundum Books, 19.2 (1588-89) 'Musicis de Nottingham'; 19.4 (1590-91) 'Tubicinibus Comitis Darbie'.

35   For example, 'It to the Wayt*es* at ash wedensdaye —— xxd' (Christ's College, Accounts B1/3, f. 213[v]; Nelson, 1989, p. 262).

36   Jesus College, Audit Book A/C 1.2, p. 224; Nelson, 1989, p. 254.

37   King's College, Mundum Book 16.1 ('ffeoda et Regarda'); Nelson 1989, p. 258.

this was indeed William it may mean that he was already the host of an inn, since the term 'goodman' was often applied to innkeepers.[38] He had four more sons (Edward, Ellis, Ferdinando and Orlando), and five daughters (Mary, Jane, Susan, Thomasine and Elizabeth).[39]

It may be surmised that William Gibbons moved from the parish of St Mary the Great, where his son Edward was baptized in 1567/8, to the parish of Holy Trinity, where his son Ellis was baptized in 1573.[40] His signature in the churchwardens' book of Holy Trinity in 1574 and 1578 indicates his agreement to resolutions of the parish.[41]

William Gibbons's interests were not confined to leading the waits. On the last day of July 1573 he sold Dr John Hatcher of Cambridge a messuage in St Edward's parish, which had been occupied by William Bright, an Alderman. At the Court of Pleas on 11 August following, Gibbons's wife Mary released her dower in the premises to Hatcher.[42] The messuage abutted on the south of another property held by Gibbons, which had lately belonged to Corpus Christi College.

On 29 September 1576 William Gibbons seems to have relinquished the leadership of the Cambridge waits, since John Murton received five silver collars, surety for which was given by John Scot and John Baker.[43] He may in fact have done so earlier: 'Morton' was paid by King's College in 1574-75,[44] and the accounts of Clare College for 1575 record a payment of 3s 4d 'to murton the musician for yᵉ fee of the way*tes*'.[45] In 1578 payment was made to 'one of Mortons men', named Richard Greaves or Gravenes.[46] Gibbons however continued some

---

38   He kept a dancing school in 1578, and his widow was hostess of the Bear in Cambridge when she died (see pp. 9, 14).

39   See pp. 269-270.

40   Susan Gibbons was however buried at St Mary the Great in 1576. Registers in Cambridgeshire County Record Office.

41   Cambridgeshire County Record Office, P22/5/2, ff. 4ʳ, 26ᵛ (leaves not bound in date order).

42   Cambridgeshire County Record Office, PB57, ff. 305ᵛ-307ᵛ; Cooper, 1842-1908, iii, p. 176.

43   PB57, f. 365ʳ; Nelson, 1989, p. 279. Murton also appears as 'Morton' and 'Martin'.

44   King's College, Mundum Book 16.6 ('ffeoda et Regarda): 'It mourton tibicini in festo purifcacīs — ijᵈ'. Other payments to Morton (under the same heading) were made in 1581-82 (Mundum Book 18.1), 1585-86 (18.5), 1586-87 (18.6), and 1587-88 (19.1).

45   Clare College Accounts, Safe A: 1/2 (unfoliated); Nelson, p. 273.

46   'Itm̄ the 28ᵗʰ of ffebruarie, to Richard Greaves on of Mortons men, for the way*tes* their stipend dewe at Candlemas' (Jesus College, Audit Book A/C 1.2, p. 642; Nelson, 1989, p. 280). 'Stipend' suggests the college employed the waits regularly.

musical activities, and on 1 June 1578 the proctors complained to the Vice-Chancellor that he did 'upholde, maintain, & kepe — or cause to be kept a dansing schole within ye Town of Cambr*idge*'. Gibbons confessed to the offence, and was fined forty shillings.[47]

William Gibbons returned to Oxford, where in 1583 he became a hanaster.[48] On 21 December of that year he took a lease of property owned by William Frere on the site of the Augustinian priory (now occupied by Wadham College).[49] And on Christmas Day his son Orlando was baptized at St Martin's church, part of which survives as the tower at Carfax. Under the heading 'Anno Dm̃ 1583 Baptized', the register reads: '25 December — Orlando Gybbins'.[50]

Gibbons still held the lease on 4 November 1586, when it was agreed that the Mayor and others should view the property, and discover the lowest price for which Frere would sell it. A document of 20 September 1587 states that the fair and tenements were occupied by Gibbons, John Rancken, John Webb and John Katheryne.[51] In that year the council bought the site from Frere's son William for £430.[52] Ten years later it granted Henry Dodwell and Isaac Bartholomew a lease in reversion for forty years of the part of the Augustine Friars leased by Gibbons.[53]

47   BL, Harleian MS 7030 (*olim* Baker 3), p. 413 (f. 214^r); Cooper, 1842-1908, v, p. 305.

48   Oxfordshire Archives, A.5.3; Turner, 1880, pp. 394, 434-435. The entry appears among those for the period Michaelmas 1582 to Michaelmas 1583, and reads 'Willm̃s Gybbons musition admiss est ... solvit iiij^s vj^d pro feod ...'. Among other entries relating to Gibbons is one for 4 August 1583. This refers to 'Willm̃o Gybbans de Comitat Oxoñ musitian ad artem suam de Musitions craft', and has 'et marie [—?—] eius' inserted above 'ad artem'. The word which is either deleted or illegible is probably 'uxor'. Gibbons was not the only musician to be a hanaster and councillor. Bartholomew Lant, the organist of Christ Church, became a freeman in 1546 and sat on the Common Council from 1549 to 1585, retiring at the age of seventy-two (McConica, 1986, p. 82).

49   Oxford City Archives, D.5.2, f. 190^r-v, a bond of £200 dated 21 December 1583 from Gibbons to Frere, to fulfill the conditions of an indenture of the same date. The lease was for twenty-one years at a rent of £10. The site of the Augustinian friary had been bought by Edward Frere in 1553. The history of the Frere family is outlined by Crossley, 1979, p. 138.

50   Register in Oxfordshire Archives.

51   Salter, 1926, pp. 359-360.

52   Salter, 1928, pp. 32-33.

53   Ibid., p. 113. Several documents relating to the site are in Oxford City Archives box D.6.1. It was bought in 1610 by Dorothy Wadham, née Petre (Crossley, 1979, p. 368; Davies and Garnett, 1994, pp. 10-14). One document is signed by Dorothy's brother John and his son William, the patrons of William Byrd of the Chapel Royal.

William Gibbons appears to have become the head of the Oxford waits soon after his return to the city.[54] The Keykeepers' accounts show that he had custody of the waits' scutcheons between Michaelmas 1583 and Michaelmas 1584 ('One bande of Willm̄ Gibbons and others for the Schutchins').[55] College records of the time contain several references to what may have been the band led by Gibbons, though none mentions him by name. St John's College paid musicians twice in the period from Michaelmas 1582 to Michaelmas 1583, and the accounts for 1583-84 contain the entry: 'To the musicians on Newyers day at night iiijs'.[56] New College paid ten shillings to two groups of musicians in 1583-84, and made another payment to some musicians in 1587-88.[57] The Disbursement Books of Christ Church record a payment made in 1584-85 'to ye musitians at my L. of Leycesters beinge here for theire paynes at supper and at ye tragedie, and whe^n ye comedie was first played'.[58] Christ Church again paid a group of musicians in 1588-89.[59] Magdalen College made a payment to some musicians in connection with a festival in 1585,[60] and musicians were paid by Merton College in 1587.[61]

Gibbons held his position as a wait in Oxford only until 14 September 1588, when it was recorded that

hit is also agreed that George Bucknall beinge appoynted to be the waite*s* of this Citie shall have the three scuttchins delyvered unto hym/ wch Mr Gybbons brought in/ and the said George shall make one at his owne charge*s* and whear Mr Gybbons is to make one more to be [delivered][62] to the said George/ the said George shall fynde two suerties for the redeliver*ance* of all

54   In a case heard in Cambridge in 1590 he was said to have been 'the waites or waighte player' in Oxford (Cambridge University Library, University Archives, Comm. Ct. II.4, ff. 45^v-46^v; Nelson, 1989, pp. 333-334).

55   Oxford City Archives, P.4.1, f. 47^v; Salter, 1928, p. 356. The Keykeepers' responsibilities included the city's plate.

56   Stevenson and Salter, 1939, pp. 243, 245, 253.

57   New College, Bursar's roll 7564 (1583-84), under 'Custos ad intra', payment of 10s to the 'waites et [musitians?] twelve day'; Bursar's roll 7572 (1587-88), 'Custos ad intra', 6s to the 'musicis'.

58   Christ Church, MS xii.b.27, f. 30^r, entry dated '23° Jan'. An entry on f. 31^r records expenses for the staging of the tragedy, including: 'To m^r Heyse [Henry Hayes] for ye musicians at m^r subdean*es* appoyntment — 3^s'.

59   Christ Church, MS xii.b.31, f. 28^r.

60   Magdalen College, Libri Computi (draft accounts), f. 20^r: payment of 6s 8d.

61   Merton College, Liber rationarius bursarum, Annunciation to St Peter in Chains 1587, under 'Liberata forinseca': 'Musicis ex consensu. xij^d'.

62   Conjectural reading. The passage is partly illegible and partly crossed out.

the same scutchyns at such tyme as they shall be demaunded by m^r mayor/ or any his successour.[63]

Gibbons evidently went back to Cambridge to resume the leadership of the town waits there.[64] The leader of the university waits was then one William Byrd.[65] Trinity College paid 'Byrd for Unive^{r}sitie Way*tes*' and 'Byrde the univ^{r}sitie musicion' in 1590 and 1591.[66]

Byrd had in fact been a university wait for a number of years. He was paid by Jesus College 'for ye wages of ye way*tes*' in 1582-83,[67] and on 7 September 1583 Dr John Bell, the Vice-Chancellor of the university, appointed him 'Lord of the Taps' at Sturbridge Fair:

... tyme owt of mynde/ it hath been a custome/ & alwaies used wthin ye fay^r/ y^t some musicõn (whom they have usuallie called the lorde of the tappes) should ... after sunne sett & likewaies before the sonne rysyng by sounde of some Instrumẽt gyve notize to shutt/ & open their shoppes; and y^t of la*te* one John pattyn wch for manye yeares had that roome is now departed this worlde; In cõsideracõn wherof manye of the Wourshipfull cytizens of london & other places have desyered one other to be placed in that roome/ and for that cause hath cõmended unto us Willm̃ byrde the bearer herof being a musicõn & now s^{t}vant & wayght of the said univ^{r}sitie. We the said vicechauncelo^r ... have gyven/ and graunted/ & by theis pñt*es* doth gyve & graunte unto the said Willm̃ Birde the said roome & place of the lorde of tappes, to cõtynue therin during o^r pleasuer/ upõ his good usage & honest behavio^r ...[68]

63 Oxford City Archives, DC1/C1/A2/1 (*olim* A.4.1), f. 162^r; Salter, 1928, p. 42. Had the resignation not been voluntary, the fact would almost certainly have been recorded. One of the Gibbons family may have practised as a wait in Oxford in the seventeenth century, for on 29 July 1627 Thomas Crosfield of Queen's College wrote in his diary: 'musicke up*on* wire strings [a cittern?] Mr Gibbons' (Crosfield, 1935, p. 15, where the editor's reference to Orlando Gibbons's fantasias is nonsense).

64 Nelson (1989, p. 740) says William Gibbons returned to Cambridge in 1588 or soon after with his complete Oxford band, taking on a new man, John Andrew, at Easter 1590. This appears to go further than the few known facts warrant, but he was certainly back in Cambridge by the latter year.

65 Not to be confused with William Byrd of the Chapel Royal. The name was surprisingly common in the sixteenth century.

66 Trinity College Archives, Steward's Books, 1590, f. 66^r, and 1591, f. 81^r; Nelson, 1989, pp. 325, 331.

67 Jesus College, Audit Book, A/C 1.2, p. 886; Nelson, 1989, p. 310.

68 Cambridge University Library, University Archives, Collect. Admin. 6a, p. 247; Nelson, 1989, pp. 309-310. Sturbridge or Stourbridge Fair 'was held in a field bounded

In 1590 ill-feeling between Gibbons and Byrd led to a hearing in the Commissary Court.[69] This took place before William Revell, acting as surrogate for the Commissary, Thomas Legge. It was for Legge's play *Ricardus Tertius* that a 'Mr Bird' wrote the song *Preces Deo fundamus*, and it is more than likely that he was the Cambridge wait.[70]

Evidence was given to the Court by Richard Walker, who had been a chamberlain at the sign of the Falcon in Petty Cury, close to where Byrd lived.[71] He said that 'a lytle before Midsomer day last past', about supper time, he had overheard Byrd tell 'William Gibbons his men or boyes' that Gibbons 'was banished oute of Oxford for his evell behaviour' and that 'the sayd Gibbons his boys or men were whipped oute of Oxford where he dwelte'. Among those 'then & there beinge present and hearinge the premisses [were] John Andrewe and others of the sayd William Gibbons his noyse or cumpanye, and Twoe Londoners sittinge at the ffalcon gate' together with 'mr Edward ffoxton and mr Harvye the grocer'. John Andrew's evidence was to the same effect.[72]

There was more trouble in November 1590. Byrd alleged that

> in the streate in Cambridge about or nighe the churchyarde wall and the churchyard gate of St Michaelles in Cambridge [Gibbons] did malitiouslie contumeliouslee and injuriouslie smite or strike the sayd Willm̃ Birde upon the head and upon the face wᵗʰ his the sayd Willm̃ Gibbons fiste And did then and there breake the staple[73] of one instrument of the said Willm̃ Birdes and

on the North by the Cam, and on the East by the "Stour", a tiny rivulet which runs under a bridge on the Newmarket road' (Skeat, 1901, p. 32). Taps: a signal sounded on a wind instrument or drum.

69   Cambridge University Library, University Archives, Comm. Ct. II.4, f. 42ʳ; Nelson, 1989, pp. 326-328. Gibbons's case seems partly to have been that Byrd claimed falsely to be the university wait: 'he hathe harde the sayde William Bird say ẏat he was and styll ys the weightes of the Universitye of Cambridge'. Nelson (1989, p. 1003) suggests that Byrd lost the mastership of the university waits to Gibbons by 1591-92.

70   A fragment of the song, with the attribution, is in BL Harleian MS 2412, f. 75ᵛ. The play was performed in 1573, 1579 and 1582 (Ward and Waller, 1910, p. 81).

71   Depositions are in Cambridge University Library, University Archives, Comm. Ct. II.4, f. 44ᵛ-45ᵛ; Nelson, 1989, pp. 327-329.

72   In evidence given in December, John Martin (i.e. Murton) of Newmarket said that Byrd's words were 'some of you were whipped oute of Oxford'. John Andrew is described in the documents as hailing from Walthamstow in Essex, and as having lived in Bradenham, Buckinghamshire, with Henry Windsor, Lord Windsor of Stanwell.

73   Staple: a tapering metal tube inserted into the top of the bore of a shawm, onto which the reed is fitted.

the reede of the same instrument w[ch] instrument was in the hand of John Chapman servaunt[74] of the sayd Willm̃ Birde And the sayd Willm̃ Birde by reason that the said instrument was so broken as is aforesayd and his companie colde play*e* no more on his waites[75] by the space of three dayes then next followinge ...[76]

Gibbons said on 14 December that in the previous July, when they travelled to Oxford to play for the commencement there, Byrd had been willing to come to an agreement with him, but Byrd denied this.[77] Byrd's name appears once more as a wait of Cambridge, on 12 October 1597.[78] He may have moved to Chester, for someone of the same name witnessed an agreement between two of the waits of Chester on 25 July 1599.[79] The name Gibbons appears in records of payments for the services of the Cambridge waits up to 1601-02.[80] But as William Gibbons seems to have been in failing health for some time,[81] it may be

74   A member of Byrd's band. Andrew was described as one of Gibbons's servants.

75   Waits, or wait: shawm or hautboy.

76   Cambridge University Library, University Archives, V.C. Ct. I.72(6) f. 9[r]; Nelson, 1989, p. 332.

77   Cambridge University Library, University Archives, Comm. Ct. II.4, f. 66[v]; Nelson, 1989, p. 335.

78   'To the wayt*es* —— vs' and 'More to Byrd —— ijs' (Emmanuel College Archives, Bursar's Long Book, BUR.8.1, p. 11; Nelson, 1989, p. 370).

79   BL, Harleian MS 2054, f. 101[r]; Clopper, 1979, pp. 194-195.

80   Payments apparently made to the waits before the death of William Gibbons include the following, among others. Jesus College, Audit Book A/C 1.2, p. 1106 (1592): 'It to Gibbons for his wages at Candlemas vj[s] viij[d]'; p. 1191 (1595): 'Imprimis to Gibbons the Musitian vj[s] viij[d]'. King's College, Mundum Book 19.6 (1592-93): 'Gibbons in festo Regine — ijs' (Michaelmas term), 'Gibbons in festo purificacionis — ijs' (Christmas term), 'Gibbons in festo Ann*uncia*tianis' (Annunciation term). Among payments made after his death are these. Jesus College, Audit Book A/C 1.2, p. 1244 (1597): 'Imprimis to Gybbons the Musition vjs viijd'. King's College, Mundum Books, under 'ffeoda et Regarda' except where indicated: 20.3 (1595-96) 'Item solut Gibbins in feste Regina ijs vjd'; 20.4 (1596-97) 'Gibbins p̱ musica in festo purific*ationis* ijs vjd'; 21.2 (1600-01, under 'Expense necessariae') 'Item solut Gibbins p̱ Musica in festo Dñe Regine — ijs vjd'; 21.3 (1601-02) 'Gibbon p̱ musica in festa Dñe Regine — ijs vjd' (Michaelmas term); 'Gibbons p̱ musica in festo Purific. — ijs' (Christmas term). Caution is however necessary in assuming that all these payments were made to the waits, for in 1594-95 payment was made to 'Magistro [i.e. Edward] Gibbons musico in festo Coronario D*omi*ne Regine' (Mundum Book 20.2); see p. 18 for the application of 'Magistro' to Edward Gibbons.

81   He wrote his name in the churchwardens' book of Holy Trinity in 1578 (see

that one of his sons assumed leadership of the band. Edward and Orlando were church musicians, while Ellis may have lived in London. It is therefore Ferdinando, who is known to have become a wait in Lincoln, who is most likely to have taken over.

A subsidy list compiled in 1595 shows William Gibbons as resident in the Market ward, where his widow, Mary, was later recorded.[82] He died shortly after declaring his will,[83] and was buried at Holy Trinity on 26 October 1595.[84] Mary lived on in Cambridge for nearly eight years, as landlady of the Bear.[85] Her son Orlando witnessed her will on 17 March 1602/3, and she was buried at Holy Trinity on 20 April 1603. The cause of her death is unknown, but the parish registers of Cambridge show that plague was rife in the town.

Orlando Gibbons's brothers

Nothing survives of the music played by William Gibbons and his band, though it is reasonable to suppose that each performance was tailored to a particular audience and venue. Their repertoire may have included arrangements, perhaps partly spontaneous, of dance tunes, songs and marches similar to those preserved in keyboard and other secular collections of the period. But some waits were highly skilled, and may sometimes have played pieces of considerable complexity, of the kind preserved in a manuscript entitled 'A booke of In nomines & other solfainge songes of v: vj: vij: & viij: p^ts for voyces or Instrumentes', containing music by Tye, Tallis, Robert Parsons, White, Byrd and others.[86] Orlando Gibbons seems to have known music of this sort early in his career.[87]

p. 8), but in signing his evidence to the Commissary Court in 1590 made only two complex marks. He may have become ill, and lost the ability to write.

82   William Gibbons is listed in PRO, E179/82/297 (30 September 1595). Widow Gibbons is listed in E179/83/306 (20 September 1598), E179/83/310 (28 September 1599), E179/83/313 (28 September 1600). Assessments in goods were £4 6s 8d (1595) and £3 8s 0d (1598 and 1599). The sum for 1600 is illegible.

83   See p. 273.

84   Cambridgeshire County Record Office, register of Holy Trinity: 'Mr Gibbins was buried the xxvj^th daye of October Anno dmi 1595 pd'.

85   Cambridge University Library, University Archives, V.C. Ct., I.4, f. 284^v, February 1599/1600; Nelson, 1989, p. 1004. A Robert Gibbons was an innkeeper and musician in Cambridge in 1625-27: see note 101 on p. 17.

86   BL, Additional MS 31390, perhaps copied by Clement Woodcock and completed in 1578. See Noble, 1955.

87   See p. 108.

Some Cambridge waits owned a variety of instruments.[88] Hautboys, sackbuts and cornetts were suitable for outdoor duties; viols, violins, lutes and citterns may have been used indoors. Regals and virginals were probably for the owners' domestic use. It can be guessed that in the Gibbons household the children learned to use a range of instruments.

Whatever the facts may be, the musical training received by William Gibbons's sons must have been thorough, for at least three of them pursued professional careers, and the other published two of his madrigals. Since Edward, the eldest of the brothers, achieved some distinction and played an important part in the training of Orlando, an account of his career will be given under a separate subheading (p. 17).

The second of the brothers, Ellis Gibbons, was baptized at Cambridge on 30 November 1573.[89] He was listed in the Cambridge subsidy rolls from 1598 to 1600, first as resident in the High ward, and then in the Market ward.[90] Anthony à Wood stated both that he was the 'Organist of *Bristow*' and that he was the organist of Salisbury Cathedral, but neither seems to be true.[91] His lease on property in St

88   Nelson, 1989, pp. 744-745.

89   Cambridgeshire County Record Office, register of Holy Trinity.

90   PRO, E179/83/306 (20 September 1598, High ward, 'Elias Gibbons' assessed in goods at £3 8s 0d), E179/83/310 (28 September 1599, Market ward, 'Elisms. Gibbons' assessed in goods at £4 10s 8d), E179/83/302 (28 September 1600, Market ward, partly illegible, but apparently 'E ... Gibbons' assessed on the basis of property). High ward consisted mainly of the present Trinity Street.

91   The first statement occurs in Wood, 1691-92, ii, col. 833 (1813-20, *Fasti*, ii, col. 277), contradicting another that Edward Gibbons was the organist at Bristol (1691-92, i, col. 768; 1813-20, *Fasti*, i, col. 258). Wood's manuscript notes on musicians, which form Bodleian Library MS Wood D19(4), refer (f. 56ᵛ) to 'Gibbons Ellis brother to Edw. Gibbons, and the most admired Organist of the Cath. ch. of Salisbury'. Thomas Forde, Chaplain of Christ Church, Oxford, who compiled manuscript notes on musicians after 1700 (Bodleian Library MS Mus. e.17), used Wood as a source (shown by the initials 'AW' after numerous entries) and repeated (and sometimes compounded) his errors. Burney and Hawkins, who also draw on Wood, are equally confused. The former says that Ellis Gibbons was the organist of Bristol (Burney, 1776-89, iii, p. 461; 1935, ii, p. 362); but elswewhere (iii, p. 328; 1935, ii, p. 264) he says that Edward Gibbons was organist of Bristol, and refers to Wood's designation of Ellis Gibbons as 'the admirable organist of Salisbury'. Hawkins says that Orlando Gibbons 'had two brothers, Edward and Ellis, the one organist of Bristol, the other of Salisbury' (Hawkins, 1776, iv, pp. 35-36; 1963, ii, p. 573). He adds that, besides being organist of Bristol, Edward 'was priest-vicar, sub-chanter, and master of the choristers in that cathedral'. The latter statement clearly applies to Edward Gibbons's career at Exeter. The succession of organists at Bristol and Salisbury is fully accounted for by Shaw (1991, pp. 36-37, 259-

Paul's churchyard suggests that he spent time in London, where he was to die.[92] His occupation seems to be unrecorded, but his acquaintance with Thomas Morley may mean that he had musical connections.

Morley's collection *The Triumphes of Oriana* (1601)[93] contains two madrigals by Ellis Gibbons.[94] *Long live faire Oriana*, in five parts, is semi-homophonic, and has the appearance of being written at the keyboard. It is rather dull, and exhibits little in the way of melodic, harmonic or rhythmic imagination, though Gibbons executes a neat stroke by duplicating the last line of the verse at the beginning, so that it starts with a reference to its end.[95] *Round about hir charret*, for six voices, is a more interesting piece, but still suggests that Ellis Gibbons was at best an unpractised composer. It is possible that the madrigals were first performed during the Maying of 1601 at Sir William Cornwallis's house at Highgate, with the intention of diverting the Queen from her melancholy after the execution of the Earl of Essex.[96] It is evident from *Long live faire Oriana*, set by both Ellis Gibbons and Thomas Hunt, that the Queen was conducted to the scene of a pastoral show by nymphs. Gibbons's second piece, *Round about hir charret*, with others by George Kirbye and John Lisley, ushered in a group of gods and goddesses, many of whom presented the Queen with gifts.[97]

On 14 May 1603, only three weeks after proving his mother's will, Ellis Gibbons made his own will. It was proved by his brother Edward on 18 May. A barely legible note on the back of a probate copy of his will indicates that he died in the parish of St Benet Paul's Wharf, just south of St Paul's Cathedral.[98] The cause of his death is unknown, but in 1603 the plague carried off nearly a quarter of London's population.

260) without reference to either Ellis or Edward Gibbons.

92   The lease is mentioned in Ellis's will (see p. 275). A plan of the churchyard area forms fig. 1 in Blayney, 1990, but the property in question has not been identified.

93   *Madrigales. The Triumphes of Oriana to 5. and 6. voices: composed by divers severall aucthors. Newly published by Thomas Morley.*

94   Wood (Bodleian Library MS Wood 19 D(4) 106, f. 57ᵛ), believed Ellis Gibbons also to have written 'other things wᶜʰ I have not yet seen', but he may have been thinking of Edward Gibbons.

95   The line is not repeated in Thomas Hunt's setting of the verse.

96   See Chambers, 1923, iv, p.113. On May Day 1604 there was a masque for the King and Queen at Cornwallis's house at Highgate (Jonson, 1925-52, vii, p. 136).

97   Strong (1959) suggests that the madrigals may have formed the background to a masque.

98   PRO, Prob. 10/216. The note would be quite illegible, had it not been deciphered by S. A. Smith (1901, p. 170). The parish registers and churchwardens' accounts of St Benet's for 1603 are not extant.

The information that the Christian name of Ellis Gibbons's wife was Joan comes from his mother's will; it is known from his own will that her maiden name was Dyer, so she was probably the sister of the James Dyer who married Ellis's sister Elizabeth in 1600.[99]

The third of the Gibbons brothers, Ferdinando, must have been born in 1581 or 1582, for he was not twenty-three when his mother made her will in March 1602/3, and a brother and sister were born in 1580 and 1583.[100] It is possible that he was a member of his father's band, and that for some time before and after his father's death he assumed responsibility for the Cambridge waits.[101] But all that is known is that he was employed at Lincoln by 8 June 1611, when the Common Council resolved 'That ffardinando Gibbyns & [102] Lockington musitians of this citie shall have two lyveryes of this cities charge'.[103]

Edward Gibbons

Edward Gibbons was baptized at Cambridge on 21 March 1567/8.[104] According to Anthony à Wood, he was a Bachelor of Music of Cambridge, and this is borne out by the description added to his name when he witnessed his father's will in October 1595.[105] As Wood puts it, he was 'incorporated in the same degree' at Oxford on 7 July 1592.[106] Wood's assertion that 'about this time' Edward Gibbons was the organist of Bristol Cathedral is however inaccurate.[107]

99 Wills: see pp. 273, 275. James Dyer: Cambridgeshire County Record Office, register of Holy Trinity.

100 See p. 274. The name Ferdinando, like Orlando, reflects a fashion for Italian names. It was also conferred on the courtier and composer Sir Ferdinando Heybourne, alias Ferdinand Richardson.

101 See p. 14. The family may have remained musically active in Cambridge. In 1634-35 payment was made to 'Gibbins ffor Musicke at heath Reach' (Downing College Library, Bowtell 5, f. 188ᵛ). Nelson (1989, p. 1004) suggests that this was Robert Gibbons, named in 1625-27 as an innkeeper and musician, who was in trouble 'ffor sellinge 4 pennyworth lesse then a quart' (Cambridge University Library, University Archives, V.C. Ct. I.11, ff. 29ᵛ, 74ʳ-76ʳ). Edward Gibbons had a son of this name.

102 Left blank for Lockington's Christian name, but never filled in.

103 Lincolnshire Archives, Common Council minute book L1/1/1/4.

104 Cambridgeshire County Record Office, register of St Mary the Great.

105 See p. 273.

106 Oxford University Archives, NEP/Supra/Reg L, f. 140ʳ; Wood, 1691-92, i, col. 768 (1813-20, *Fasti*, i, col. 258); Clark, 1887-88, i, p. 350. The information is repeated by Venn (1922-27, ii, p. 208) and Foster (1891-92, i, p. 560).

107 See note 91 above.

The first that is known of the musical career of Edward Gibbons (or 'Gibbins', as he liked to write himself) is his presence as a lay clerk at King's College, Cambridge. His name occurs regularly in the College's weekly accounts, beginning about the middle of March 1591/2.[108] His arrival at this time is confirmed by the College's Mundum Books, where 'Dño Edwardo Gibbons' is listed under 'Conduct*es* et Cl*eric*is'.[109] He must have married by 1596, for his first child was baptized at Holy Trinity in the following year.[110] His wife, Jane, is said to have been a relative of Lord Spencer.[111] He last appears in the records of King's at Michaelmas 1598.[112] His second child was however baptized at Holy Trinity in April 1599. He is not in the Cambridge subsidy lists, possibly because members of King's College were exempted from payment.[113]

Shortly after Gibbons's arrival at King's he began to receive payments for instructing the choristers, a job previously done by Thomas Hamond. Gibbons presumably learned the necessary skills as a chorister, but where he did so is unknown. He was paid an additional 20s a quarter '$\underline{p}$ informand chorist', and Hamond was paid as *informator* for the last time in June 1592.[114] Gibbons was then paid as *informator* until he left King's, when Hamond resumed his former responsibility.

From time to time 'Magistro' Edward Gibbons received other payments in connection with the choir. In 1593-94 he was paid for 'a sett of song book*es* ad usu*m* Coll*egij*', and for providing the choirboys with clothes and shoes.[115] In 1594-95 a payment of ten shillings was made to 'M$\bar{r}$o Gibbins for pricking 3 churche book*es* of ten part*es*', and another ten shillings was paid to 'Gibbons $\underline{p}$ 4^{or} grace book*es*'.[116]

Ellis Gibbons's will, made in May 1603, describes Edward as 'of Acton'. The county is not stated, but no record has been found of his residence at Acton in Middlesex. It is in fact possible that 'Acton' is an

108   King's College, Commons Books (weekly accounts, gathered annually, running from Michaelmas to Michaelmas) , under 'Com^{les} alij'.

109   King's College, Mundum Books (annual accounts, partly summarizing weekly accounts and partly containing new material), no. 19.5 onwards. He received 20s a quarter as a lay clerk. A number of entries about Gibbons are printed by Nelson, 1989.

110   See p. 270.

111   Walker, 1714, pt. ii, p. 32.

112   In the Commons Books and in Mundum Book 20.5.

113   PRO, E179/83/302, E179/83/327a and E179/83/328 refer to certain exemptions.

114   Mundum Book 19.5 and subsequently.

115   King's College, Mundum Book 20.1, under 'Expense necessariae' and 'Exhibitio choristarum'.

116   Mundum Book 20.2, under 'Custus Ecclesie' and 'Expense necessariae'. Concerning other payments to 'Gibbons' for music at King's, see note 80 above.

error for 'Exon', made when the original will, now lost, was copied into the probate register.[117] Edward was at Exeter by 1607, for his son William was baptized in the cathedral on 24 October of that year.[118] It would not be surprising to learn that he went there straight from Cambridge. John Walker, writing early in the eighteenth century, said that Edward Gibbons was tempted to the cathedral by Dr William Cotton, who was consecrated Bishop of Exeter on 12 November 1598.[119]

On 25 June 1608 the chapter 'decreed the choristers to be hereafter taughte by m^r Gibbons uppon suche condicõns as shalbe here after agreed on'.[120] It seems that, until this time, the instruction of the choristers was included in the duties of the organist, John Lugge. The fifty shillings a quarter hitherto received by Lugge was now divided between the two men.[121] It is evident that, with the agreement of the Chapter, Gibbons at times discharged his duties by means of a deputy. The Chapter resolved on 24 September 1608 'that Peter Chambers do teache the Choristers under m^r Gibbins yf he be founde fitte', and on 21 April 1610 that 'Greenwood Randall should have the place that Mr Chambers had under Mr Gibbins for teaching of the chorusters'.[122] Greenwood Randall was probably a relation of William Randall, who became a Gentleman of the Chapel Royal. Another Greenwood Randall, presumably a son, married Gibbons's daughter Mary at the cathedral on 4 May 1626. Their son Orlando was baptized on 14 September 1627.[123]

117 Suggested by Richard Turbet. As copies of wills vary so much from the originals in matters of spelling, etc., it is likely that the making of a copy involved one clerk reading to another. 'Exon' and 'Acton' might easily be confused in the process.

118 Register in Exeter Cathedral Archives; Reynell-Upham and Soper, 1910, p. 4. See p. 270 for Edward Gibbons's other children.

119 Walker, 1714, pt. ii, p. 32. Walker's account begins by repeating the erroneous information that Edward Gibbons was organist of Bristol, but his account of Gibbons's later life appears to be authoritative. It is worth remarking that the name Gibbons is found fairly often in the records of Exeter and the surrounding area. In 1647 a Major Gibbons was appointed Governor of Exeter Castle (PRO, SP16/515/82; CSPD, 1891, p. 563). One Gibbons of Exeter, to whom silk belonging to Sir John Greenfield was consigned, is mentioned in Committee for Advancement of Money, 1888, p. 1160, entry for 14 June 1650. Others named Gibbons are mentioned in documents preserved at the Devon Record Office, Exeter. No attempt has been made to establish whether Edward Gibbons was attracted to Exeter because of some family connection with the city.

120 Exeter Cathedral, D&C 3553, f. 4^r; Shaw, 1991, p.109.

121 Exeter Cathedral, D&C 3801, where a distinction was introduced between the posts of 'Organist' and 'Informator Chorus*tarum*'.

122 Exeter Cathedral, D&C 3553, ff. 8^r, 17^r.

123 Exeter Cathedral register; Reynell-Upham and Soper, 1910, pp. 7, 23.

Further appointments were granted to Gibbons on 25 March 1609:

Item they nominated m^r Gibbins to a vicars place now voide by the departure
of George Tucker late vicar of this Churche so as the saide m^r Gibbins by
reason of his degree in musicke or dispensacon from my Lo: Archebishoppe
be made capable of the same and by the Lo: Bishoppe of Exon to whome the
disposinge thereof is come by lapse the same shalbe approved & consented
unto.

Item decre^t a patente to be made to m^r Gibbins Bachelor of Musicke of xx^{li}
per annu*m* so longe to continewe as he shall teache the choristers and
secondaries of this churche in instrumentall Musicke.[124]

Some, at least, of Edward Gibbons's few surviving compositions had
probably been written by this time.[125] A short but competent keyboard
piece is described by Thomas Tudway as 'A Prelude upon ye Organ as
was then usuall before ye Anthem. By M^r. Edward Gibbons, Custos of y^e
College of Prist Vicars In Exeter 1611'.[126] It is not clear whether the
date is that of composition, or of Gibbons's election to the office of
Custos — or whether it can reliably be attached to either event.[127] The
prelude is followed by Gibbons's verse anthem headed 'How hath y^e

124 Exeter Cathedral, D&C 3553, f. 11^r-12^r. Another entry (in Latin) records that
Gibbons was assigned 'a place and stall in the choir, vacant by the cession and
deprivation of George Tucker'. The dispensation was necessary because Gibbons was a
layman. Royal approval was given under seal on 8 June 1609; the dispensation roll for
the year mentions Gibbons's virtue and the probity of his life, 'ac scientia in arte musica
& cantandi peritia singularis' (PRO, C58/13).
125 Wood says that Edward Gibbons 'made several compositions in his faculty,
some of which I have seen in the Musical Library reposed in the public School of that
profession in *Oxon*' (Wood, 1691-92, i, col. 768; 1813-20, *Fasti*, i, col. 258).
126 BL, Harleian MS 7340, ff. 193^v-194^r (modern numbering), dated 1715.
127 Election to the office of Custos was made from among the Priest-Vicars by
members of the College of Vicars Choral (disbanded in 1936), apparently annually on 20
September. (See Exeter Cathedral, D&C Vicars Choral Book I, ff. 11^v-12^r.) Mrs Angela
Doughty has kindly examined the extant records, which are confusing. Those of the
Vicars Choral have survived only patchily. Randomly placed entries in the unused
portions of the volume of ordinances from 1586 to the early eighteenth century name
Edward Gibbons as Custos in agreements dated 19 March 1613/14 and 29 September
1614 (Vicars Choral Book I, ff. 20^v, 23^v, 27^v). This is not however confirmed by entries
in the Act Book (D&C 3553), where from 19 December 1611 to 11 January 1613/14
Richard Wade appears as Custos. The Custos on 30 July 1614 is given as John
Mogridge, who resigned and was replaced by Robert Parsons on 23 September 1615.

City sate solitary'.[128] This is for two alto voices, chorus and instruments.[129] While the text is not wholly satisfactory in its surviving form, the setting of words adapted from the first book of Lamentations is genuinely moving. The date 1611 is again mentioned by Tudway,[130] but the adaptation was evidently made in the aftermath of an occurrence of plague, perhaps the severe outbreak of 1603. If one of the victims was Gibbons's brother Ellis the words have a highly personal application.

> How hath the city sate solitary, that was full of people. Elders are ceased from the gate, the young men from their music. The joy of our heart is ceased, our dance is turned into mourning ... O holy Lord God, which has wounded us for our sins, and consumed us from our transgressions, by the late heavy plague and dreadful visitation, and now in the midst of judgement hast showed mercy, and hast redeem'd our souls ev'n from the jaws of death. O give thanks to the God of Heav'n for His mercy endureth for ever.

The remainder of Edward Gibbons's church music consists of settings of the 'Commandements and Creed' and the Credo, for alto, two tenors and two basses. In the only source these pieces follow Mundy's Short Service (Te Deum and Benedictus), seemingly as an addition.[131]

A different side of Gibbons's musical character is shown by *Awake and arise*, for three voices.[132] Although the only copy lacks all but the first few words, this does not disguise the animation of the short piece. The two other surviving compositions by Gibbons are a workmanlike In Nomine for five viols,[133] and *What Strikes the Clocke?* for three viols.[134] In the second, the middle part consists of twelve groups of minims; each group is formed of notes of the same pitch, and the number of notes in a group increases from one to twelve as the piece progresses.

In 1614/5 Edward Gibbons was installed in the office of Succentor of Exeter Cathedral as a result of a mandate issued by Archbishop Abbot in

---

128   BL, Harleian MS 7340, ff. 194r-199v.

129   There are three instrumental parts, presumably for viols, but another instrument may have doubled the alternating solo voices. In editing the anthem, Payne (1993) found it desirable to add a fifth instrumental part to complete the texture.

130   The attribution is to 'Edward Gibbons Custos of ye College of Preists Vicars of the Cathedrall Church of Exeter, 1611'.

131   Christ Church, Mus. 1220-1224. Gibbons's pieces occur in a part of the manuscripts which perhaps dates from the earlier seventeenth century.

132   Christ Church, Mus. 43, f. 24r.

133   Bodleian Library, Mus. Sch. d.212-216.

134   Durham Cathedral, Dean and Chapter Library, Hunter MS 33.

January, to which the Chapter assented on 15 February.[135] He held the post until 15 December 1627, when it was recorded that 'm[r] Edward Gibbins relinquished all his interest in the Subchauntershipp of this Church, w[ch] he hath from the Lo Archbishopp of Cant'.[136]

By 1617 Gibbons, now aged about fifty, had in the view of some become lax in the performance of his duties. On 6 April he was required 'to frequent the service of the Quire', though two of the canons 'thought he did alreadie sufficiently performe his dutie in the Quire'.[137] The complaint was reiterated in 1634. Questions put during the visitation of Archbishop Laud received 'The answere of the Custos and Colledge of y[e] Preist vicars Chorall of the Cathedrall Church of Exeter', which included the observation that in 1563 there were six priest-vicars, but their number had been reduced to four '& one of them a leaman [layman], namely m[r] Edward Gibbins'. Two of the vicars choral, William Masters and Henry Trott, added that 'The forenamed M[r] Edward Gibbins doth not sitt in his place and read & singe at devine service tyme as the rest doth (but once a quarter (or ther about) doth sitt in his place, for two or three dayes but doth not usially do it as y[e] rest'.[138] Gibbons nevertheless continued to play some part in the business of the choir, and on 23 May 1640, when he was in his seventies, gave his opinion that Richard Carter was 'unfitt for his voice'.[139]

Walker recounts that Gibbons 'married Two Wives which were Gentlewomen of *Considerable Families* and *Fortunes*; the First a near Relation of the Lord *Spencer's*, and the Second of the *Ancient Family* of the *Bluets* in this County: By which means he had gotten a *very considerable Temporal Estate*'.[140] This is confirmed by a certificate of residence submitted to Exchequer officials in London:

135 Lambeth Palace Library, Archbishop Abbot's register, i, f. 415[r]; Exeter Cathedral, D&C 3554, ff. 11[v]-12[r]. Succentor: deputy to the precentor, who had control of the cathedral's musical arrangements.

136 Exeter Cathedral, D&C 3553, f. 134[v]. The entries continue with an admonition to the vicars to sing the psalms more distinctly.

137 Exeter Cathedral, D&C 3553, f. 68[v].

138 House of Lords archives, Main papers 1634, Laud visitations; Royal Commission on Historical Manuscripts, 1874, p. 137. The documents are annotated marginally, presumably by Laud himself. One note asks 'Why one a lay man?', and the complaint of Masters and Trott elicits the remark: 'Let this be remedyed'. Signatures on the documents include those of other musicians, e.g. John Lugge.

139 Exeter Cathedral, D&C 3557, p. 201. It should be noted that Edward Gibbons's name and signature occur more frequently in the records of Exeter Cathedral than is indicated here, and he signed a number of statutes and resolutions (D&C VC Book I).

140 Walker, 1714, pt. ii, p. 32. For Edward Gibbons's marriages, see p. 270.

These are to certefie you that Edward Gibbons of the parishe of S^t: Paules wthin the countie of the cittie of Exon Gent where he hath made his aboade and dwellinge for manie yeres last past is in the said parishe rated and taxed towardes the payment of the Third Subsidie of ffive entire Subsidies graunted to his Matie. in the late Session of Parliam^t. holden att Westm^r att Six poundes in landes aswell for his estate in Dandiland wthin the parishe of Dunsford in the hundred of wonford in the countie of Devon as for all his estate elswhere wch att the request of the said Edward Gibbons wee his Ma^{tes}: comission^{ers}: for the said Subsidie wthin the said cittie & countie of Exon have thought good to signifie yeven under o^r handes & Seales the Three & Twentieth daye of September Anno Dm̃: 1628.[141]

In 1636 Edward Gibbons was taxed for ship money above the level fixed for most of his colleagues. A document listing 'The names of such clergie men as are rated towardes the charge of shippinge for his Matie, wthin the said cittie of Exeter' includes the following entry:

M^r: Edward Gibbons clarke one other of the Priest vicars of the said cathedrall church of S^t: Peter in Exeter for his Ecclesiasticall possessions } xiij^s. iiij^d
And for his temporall estate —— xxvj^s. viij^d [142]

According to Walker, Gibbons and his family suffered severely during the Civil War. When he refused the Parliamentary Commissioners' demand for £500 his house was plundered and he, his wife and three grandchildren were turned out. Nevertheless, a little oratory at Dunsford (one of two he built on estates he had in the county) was still standing when Walker wrote.[143]

The last of Edward Gibbons's signatures as *informator* was made in the cathedral accounts about the end of 1644/5. Prior to that time payments to him were sometimes acknowledged by the signature of William Wake, who was a lay vicar and deputy organist. Several subsequent entries were left unsigned or marked with a cross.[144]

Edward Gibbons seems to have died in 1650. A decree by the Prerogative Court of Canterbury, granting the administration of his

---

141 PRO, E115/172/99. Certificates of residence were intended to prevent duplicate tax assessments of people moving from county to county.

142 PRO, SP 16/344/102.i; CSPD, 1867, p. 388.

143 Dunsford is a little to the west of Exeter.

144 Exeter Cathedral, D&C 3802. There is a gap in the accounts after 1645, lasting until 1660.

affairs to Rose Swanton, evidently a niece of one of his daughters, is dated 17 July of that year.[145] His place of burial is unknown.[146]

Orlando Gibbons

Orlando Gibbons grew up in a household where music was the family business. An ability to play a number of instruments and to write music when required was most likely taken as a matter of course. It is clear that he learned to play keyboard instruments, and his fluency as a composer for strings suggests that he learned the viol as well. He learned enough of composition to be able to write music of some complexity by his early twenties.

Gibbons became a chorister at King's College in February 1595/6, under his brother Edward. Assuming that his baptism on 25 December 1583 followed quickly on his birth, he entered King's shortly after his twelfth birthday.[147] He matriculated as a sizar (a student paying reduced fees and having certain menial duties) in Easter term 1598.[148] His name ceased to be entered regularly in the weekly lists of King's at Michaelmas 1598, but a few of the earlier lists for 1598-99 name 'Gibbins' irregularly as a chorister. Perhaps Orlando sang in the choir on odd occasions, or his name was copied from out-of-date lists. How he was occupied in the four or five years after he left King's College is unknown. This vitally important period of his life is a complete blank. He may have continued his training with Edward, but there is no evidence of this; nor is there any that he is the subject of references to 'Gibbons' in the records of Cambridge colleges at this time.[149]

However he was employed, he displayed abilities which, by May 1603, gained him a post in the Chapel Royal (his career in which is to be described in the next chapter). He was probably no more than nineteen years old. The beginning of 1603 must have been a time of great emotional strain for the young man, for besides obtaining a post that placed him on the upper rungs of the professional ladder, he lost both his mother and his brother Ellis.[150]

145   PRO, Prob. 6/25, f. 119ʳ (manuscript numbering). Rose Swanton is described as 'nept ex filia'.

146   He was not buried at Exeter Cathedral, and the registers of the parish of Dunsford are incomplete for the period, as are the Bishop's transcripts.

147   King's College, Commons Books, under 'Choristr'.

148   Venn, 1913, p. 279; Venn, 1922-27, ii, p. 209.

149   See note 80 above.

150   See pp. 14 and 16.

PART II

2

THE COURT MUSICIAN

The Chapel Royal is the body of priests, musicians and other officials serving the religious needs of the monarch and the royal household. At the beginning of King James's reign the musicians consisted of a group of singing men and organists (the 'Gentlemen' of the Chapel) whose number hovered around twenty-four (though there were often a few 'extraordinary' musicians waiting for an appointment in ordinary), and a dozen boy singers. The Chapel's musical traditions had been shaped by men of the calibre of Thomas Tallis and William Byrd. Its pre-eminence in English musical life can be attributed to its location at the centre of national power and culture, of which it was a visible manifestation, and in varying degrees to its function as an instrument of policy, to the quality of its musicians, and to a continuity of performance and repertory.[1]

A larger body of musicians served the king and his family in the provision of music for secular purposes. Subsidy lists of about 1608-10 name some fifty musicians in addition to those serving in the Chapel.[2] They include singers, and performers on brass, woodwind, bowed, plucked, keyboard and percussion instruments. Groups of these musicians played in the private apartments of the palace, on ceremonial occasions, and during the pageants and elaborate masques that were a feature of Stuart court life.[3]

---

1 See Baldwin (1990) on the evolution and duties of the Chapel Royal. The chapel building at Whitehall Palace is shown in drawings and on plans of the sixteenth and seventeenth centuries (see Thurley, 1998, pp. 37-38, 40-41, also the frontispiece and back cover). Nothing is now to be seen of it, but it was east of the Banqueting House in Whitehall and not far from the river (which then ran a little to the west of its present course).

2   PRO, E179/70/121, E179/70/122, E179/70/123a; Ashbee, 1986-96, iv, pp. 17-22, 25-27. A few musicians held posts in both the Chapel and the secular establishment.

3   The most complete survey of the musical resources of the court of James I is provided by Ashbee, 1986-96, iv and viii, and Ashbee and Lasocki, 1998. Further references to the latter work are not given, since it was published after the present book was completed.

Appointment to the Chapel Royal

King James VI of Scotland succeeded to the English throne as James I upon the death of Queen Elizabeth on 24 March 1602/3. He left Scotland on 5 April. His last stop on his way south was Theobalds, the Hertfordshire home of Sir Robert Cecil, from which he departed on 7 May.[4] He then spent time at the Charterhouse, the Tower and Greenwich before settling at Whitehall Palace in the latter part of June.[5]

Orlando Gibbons seems to have entered the Chapel very early in the reign of King James. He was not among those who were allowed mourning liveries for Queen Elizabeth's funeral on 28 April.[6] The first sign of his presence in the Chapel is his signature in the Cheque Book, where its boldness causes it to stand out among others at the end of a memorandum of 19 May 1603.[7] The oath of allegiance to the King was administered to the members of the Chapel at Greenwich on that day, and a Chapter meeting was held at the same time.[8] The memorandum records the agreement of the Gentlemen and other officers of the Chapel to submit themselves to the authority of the Dean and Subdean in carrying out their duties.

Gibbons must first have joined the Chapel as a Gentleman Extraordinary without pay, while he waited for a post to become vacant.[9]

4   Theobalds was surrendered to the Crown in 1607. For a history of the house see Page, 1912, pp. 447-450.

5   James's Queen, Anne of Denmark, followed later. The first entertainment provided for her on her journey south was at Althorpe, on 25-27 June, during which the name Oriana (Ori-Anna) was conferred upon her (Jonson, 1925-52, vii, pp. 119-131).

6   PRO, LC2/4; Ashbee, 1986-96, iv, pp. 1-4.

7   Cheque Book, f. 34ʳ; Rimbault, 1872, pp. 68-70. The Cheque Books provide a record of the Chapel's affairs from the sixteenth to the nineteenth centuries (originals at St James's Palace; microfilm at the Public Record Office). References here and below are to the 'old' Cheque Book (which is the volume transcribed by Rimbault; a new edition, by Andrew Ashbee and John Harley, of both the 'old' and 'new' Cheque Books is in preparation). Bodleian Library MS Rawlinson D.318 is a register of the Chapel Royal (1560-1643) which differs in some details from the old Cheque Book (it is transcribed in Ashbee, 1986-96, viii, pp. 316-333).

8   Cheque Book, f. 16ʳ; Rimbault, 1872, p. 107-108.

9   The memorandum of 19 May 1603 is signed by other Gentlemen Extraordinary. There were four Gentlemen Extraordinary at the time of Queen Elizabeth's funeral (PRO, LC2/4; Ashbee, 1986-96, iv, p. 4). One of them, George Green, was Sworn as a Gentleman Extraordinary without pay on 23 November 1601. Of the others, Edmund Hooper was sworn into a full place three weeks before Gibbons, but Peter Hopkins had to wait until John Bull went abroad in 1613 (see p. 31). The fourth, Edward Pearce,

Although there is no record of the fact, Gibbons presumably took part in the coronation of King James and Queen Anne at Westminster Abbey on 25 July 1603.[10] The ceremony was curtailed on account of the plague, but the surviving order of service refers to the singing of hymns, anthems and the offertory.[11] Gibbons's appointment as a Gentleman in Ordinary followed the death of Arthur Cock. The Cheque Book contains this entry for 1604/5:

> Arthur Cock died the xxvj[th] of Januar*ie* & Orlando Gibbons sworn in his roome the xxj[th] of Marche followinge.[12]

Gibbons was able to benefit straightaway from the King's grant of an increase in the stipends of Gentlemen of the Chapel, which raised them from thirty pounds a year to forty.[13] The precise capacity in which Gibbons was employed is not stated in the Cheque Book, but it is likely that he was appointed primarily as an organist with choral experience, and during his months of duty he probably rehearsed the choir and prepared pieces of music for performance. His work must have been akin to that of the organist in a cathedral.[14]

gave up his place in the Chapel in 1600, to become Master of the Children at St Paul's (Cheque Book, ff. 6[r-v], 24[v]; Rimbault, 1872, pp. 5-7, 38).

10   He is not included in 'A note of the names of the subdeane gent and others of the chappell at the tyme of the coronation of kynge James the first', which is bound into the Cheque Book as f. 87[r] (Rimbault, 1872, pp. 127-128), but this may have been copied or compiled from older lists, and in any case omits Gentlemen Extraordinary.

11   PRO, SP14/2/77 details the order of service, but does not specify the participation of the Chapel Royal. A reference to 'y[e] Quere' presumably means the singers of Westminster Abbey.

12   Cheque Book, f. 6[r]; Rimbault, 1872, p. 6. A parallel entry occurs in the duplicate cheque book (Bodleian Library, Rawlinson MS D.318, f. 29[r]; Ashbee, 1986-96, viii, p. 321).

13   The increase occurred at the end of 1604 (Cheque Book, f. 31[r]; Rimbault, 1872, pp. 60-61). The increase is mentioned in William Byrd's dedication of the first book of *Gradualia* to the Earl of Northampton, one of those who sued for it. It is recorded in Stowe, 1631, p. 1037, under the heading '*King* James *his Bounty*': 'The King enlarged the yearely Fee of the Gentlemen of his said Chappell, being thirty in number, from thirty pound a yeare, unto forty pound a yeare unto every of them ... The King also enlarged the Auncient allowance of six pence a day for every childe, unto the Master of the children of his Chappell, unto tenne pence a day for every of them, being 12. in number'.

14   The title-page of *XX. Konincklycke Fantasien* (Amsterdam, 1648), which contains Gibbons's three-part fantasias, describes him posthumously as 'Organist en

The senior organist of the Chapel was John Bull, who is invariably described as 'Doctor Bull' and heads lists of the Chapel musicians. Bull's Cambridge doctorate was incorporated at Oxford on 7 July 1592, the day on which Edward Gibbons's Cambridge degree was also incorporated.[15] A belief that the two men may have been well acquainted is inspired by the fact that, again in 1592, 'M[r]. Docto[r] Bull' and a 'M[r]. Gybbons' gave money towards the building of the steeple of St Mary the Great, Cambridge.[16] An acquaintanceship between them may have reinforced already close ties between the Chapel Royal and Exeter Cathedral, where it is possible that Edward Gibbons was employed as early as 1603. It could help to explain how Orlando Gibbons's talents

Zang-meester, van de Koninck van Engeland' (organist and choirmaster of the King of England). 'Orders for the Attendance of the gent: of his Maj[tes] Chappell', dating from the earlier part of King James's reign, include the provision that 'if ther be above two Organist*es* at once, two shall allwaies attend, if ther be but two in all, then they shall wayte by course one after an other weekly or monethly as they shall agree betwixt them selves, givinge notice to y[e] Subd*eane* & the Clark of y[e] check how they do dispose of their waytinge ...' (Cheque Book, f. 39[v]; Rimbault, 1872, pp. 71-72). The Dean of the Chapel Royal settled a dispute in 1615 by ordering that 'the auncient custom should be observed, w[ch] was and still must be, y[t] the most auncient Organist shall serve the Eeve & daye of ev[r]y principall feast ... the next Organist in place to serve the second daie; & soe likewise the third, for the third daie, if ther be so many Organist*es*: & for all other festivall daies in the yeare, those to be pformed by the Organist*es* as they shall fall out in their sev[r]all weekes of wayetinge; the feastes beinge ended, he y[t] did or shoulde begin the saterdaie before, shall finish up the same weeke, according to form[r] custom, & the other to followe: except the feast of Christmas, for then they change ev[r]y daye, as the Quier dothe duringe the whole twelve dayes'. Hooper and Gibbons agreed that All Saints should be deleted from the list of feasts on which the 'most auncient Organist' should serve, and on 2 November 1615 they signed a memorandum to that effect (Cheque Book, f. 33[v]; Rimbault, p. 74).

15   Oxford University Archives, NEP/Supra/Reg L, f. 140[r]; Clark, 1887-88, i, p. 350. See p. 17 concerning the incorporation of Edward Gibbons's Cambridge degree. There is no extant record of Bull's receipt of a doctorate at Cambridge. He supplicated for a BMus at Oxford on 8 July 1586 (assuming the date of the two preceding entries in the register applies to Bull's supplication), and was admitted the next day (Reg L, ff. 69[r]; Clark, i, p. 147). Another entry (Reg L, f. 157[r]), referring to 'Johanes Bald' (Clark reads 'John Bolde'), 'cant. mus.', has been struck through. A further musician to receive a degree at Oxford on 7 July 1592 was Giles Farnaby ('Egidius ffarnabye'), who was admitted BMus (Reg L, ff. 140[r], 157[v]; Clark, i, p. 147).

16   Cambridgeshire County Record Office, P30/4/1, f/ 196[r]; Foster, 1905, p. 227. There is no doubt about the identity of Bull, who gave 12d; the 'M[r]. Gybbons' who gave 6d seems likely to have been Edward, but this is not certain.

came to be recognized, and his appointment to the Chapel Royal made at so early an age.

Edmund Hooper was probably the next senior organist, though neither he nor Gibbons is named specifically as a Chapel Royal organist in any document earlier than 1615.[17] A little before Gibbons joined the Chapel Hooper had replaced William Randall, who had been at Exeter, and who was described as a Chapel organist in 1592 (though 'sworne pisteler' when he joined the Chapel in 1584).[18] Arthur Cock, whom Gibbons replaced, had been organist first at Canterbury Cathedral and then, from 1589 until his appointment to the Chapel Royal in 1601, at Exeter Cathedral, where he worked with Edward Gibbons.[19]

There is little evidence of Gibbons's participation in the day to day work of the Chapel Royal. It is to be assumed that, for twenty-odd years, he took part quietly in the annual liturgical cycle, sharing the organists' duties with his colleagues. After Bull fled the country in 1613 these responsibilities must have devolved principally upon Gibbons and Hooper. It was they who received the bulk of Bull's unpaid wages.[20]

While there is more information about ceremonies outside the usual run, it is rare for the music to be described in detail or for Gibbons to be mentioned. The Cheque Book contains an account of the Spanish Ambassador's visit to the Chapel in August 1604, but it says only that 'the Organs played'.[21] When Princess Mary was carried into the chapel at Greenwich in May 1605, to be baptized, 'did the Organest begine and continew playinge aloud' until she was placed in the traverse. He played

---

17   Cheque Book, f. 33ᵛ: 'the now Organist*es* Edmund Hooper & Orlando Gibbons'. They are again so designated in a document of 1619 (PRO, LC2/5 f. 44v; Ashbee, 1986-96, iv, p. 49).

18   Cheque Book, f. 5ᵛ, 6ᵛ, 20ʳ; Rimbault, 1872, pp. 4, 33; Shaw, 1991, pp. 4-5.

19   Shaw, 1991, p. 108.

20   John Bull left England in the late summer; the exact cause of his flight is uncertain, but see Royal Commission on Historical Manuscripts, 1940, pp. 261, 270-271, 346-347, 355, 411-412. The event is recorded twice in the Cheque Book. An entry on f. 1ʳ reads: 'Jo: Bull doctor of Musick went beyond the seaes & served the Archduke at Michãs & Peter Hopkins was sworne in his place the xvijᵗʰ of decembʳ following yᵉ wages in the meane tyme was disposed of ... in yⁱˢ sort. viz to mʳ Coton xxˢ To mʳ Gibbons iijˡⁱ vjˢ viijᵈ. To mʳ hooper iijˡⁱ vjˢ viijᵈ. To yᵉ Common servant ijˢ viᵈ & to yᵉ Clark of the Check the rest wᶜʰ was xljˢ ijᵈ.' This is paralleled by an entry (f. 6ᵛ; Rimbault, 1872, p. 7) which says the money was Bull's 'wages frõ michaelmas unto the daie of yᵉ swearinge of the said Peter Hopkins'.

21   Cheque Book, f. 69ᵛ; Rimbault, 1872, pp. 151-152. A closely similar description is given of an embassy in 1610/1 (Cheque Book, f. 70ʳ; Rimbault, 1872, pp. 152-153).

once more later in the ceremony, but there is no record of who he was.[22] The organist was again anonymous when the Queen was churched (probably at Whitehall) later in the month.[23] Quite possibly it was Bull who, as the senior organist, took charge on these occasions. It was he who played the organ throughout dinner when the Merchant Taylors' Company entertained King James on 16 July 1607. The Company's minute book records that in addition 'divers singing men and children of the said chappell did sing melodious song*es* at the said dynner', but no mention is made of Gibbons.[24]

Marriage and residence in Westminster

Less than a year after joining the Chapel, on 17 February 1605/6, Gibbons married Elizabeth Patten, the daughter of John Patten, a Yeoman of the Vestry in the Chapel Royal.[25] Since Elizabeth presumably lived with her parents in Westminster, the fact that the wedding took place in the City of London at St Mary Woolchurch Haw may mean that Gibbons lodged in the parish, though there is no other evidence that this was so.[26] Elizabeth was probably the 'Elizabeth Pattin' baptized at St Margaret's, Westminster, on 1 November 1590.[27] If she was baptized soon after birth, she was fifteen years old when she married.

22   Cheque Book, f. 32ᵛ-33ʳ; Rimbault, 1872, pp. 167-169.

23   Cheque Book, f. 33ʳ; Rimbault, 1872, pp. 169-170.

24   Guildhall Library, Merchant Taylors' records, minute book 5, pp. 261-268 and 283. Bull and Nathaniel Giles, Master of the Children of the Chapel, are mentioned by name; their admission to the Company is recorded on p. 279. Nichols (1828, ii, p. 139) drew his account from the Company's minutes, but his insertion of the names of Gibbons, William Byrd and others is without justification. Another account appears in Stowe, 1631, p. 891.

25   Guildhall Library MS 7644: 'Orlando Gibbons & Elizabeth Patten were maried the xviith of Februarie'; Brooke and Hallen, 1886, p. 348.

26   The church of St Mary Woolchurch Haw was demolished after the Great Fire. It may be coincidental that other people named Gibbons lived in the parish. They were William Gibbins of Sussex (buried 1595), Jane Gibbons (married 1595), and Elizabeth Gibbins (married 1608).

27   Westminster Abbey Muniment Room, register of St Margaret's church; transcribed by Burke, 1914. Many other people named Patten appear in the register, but their relationships have not been explored. John Patten's will mentions Elizabeth, her brother Richard (a Groom of the Vestry in 1615, and a Yeoman in 1620), and his son Oliver. The registers of St Margaret's list, as children of a John Patten, 'Joice Pattine' (baptized 27 March 1589), John Patten (baptized 18 August 1592), and 'An Pattin' (baptized 25 September 1593). The overseers' accounts of St Margaret's parish

John Patten had been sworn in as a Groom of the Vestry, at Chichester, during a royal progress in 1591. He became the 'yonger Yeoman' on Christmas Day 1592, and retired as 'eldest Yeoman' on 1 May 1608.[28] One of his earliest duties as Yeoman was to see that Queen Elizabeth's 'stuffe meete for her Chappell' was 'trussed upp at ev'ry remove, & sent to her highnes nexte house of waytinge'.[29] By 14 November 1607 he appears to have acquired a second post. This is evident from the records of 'A guift unto John Patten keep of his Ma[tes] Closet of the some of 200[li] lately ymposed by the L[d]: Archbyshop of Canterbury & other his h[s]: Comissioners in causes ecclesiasticall uppon Nicholas ffuller Esq.'[30]

In 1606, soon after his marriage, Gibbons obtained a degree at Cambridge. The entry in the Grace Book reads:

Bachalaurei in musica

Conceditur Orlando Gibbins Regius organista ut studium septem annorum in musica sufficiat ei ad intrandum in eadem: sic tamen ut canticum componat cantandum hora et loco per vicecancellarium designandis coram universitate in die commitiorum et ut presentetur per magistrum regentem in habitu Bacchalaurei in Artibus./[31]

Gibbons's Cambridge degree was incorporated at Oxford on 14 July 1607.[32] Writing of this, Wood said Gibbons was an MA of Cambridge, and the statement is repeated elsewhere, but it must be an error.[33]

By 1609 Gibbons was living in the Round Woolstaple, in the parish of St Margaret's, Westminster. The Woolstaple is shown on several maps of the period.[34] It was just north of New Palace Yard, which was

---

(Westminster Archives) list Thomas Patten, who was 'Clarke of y[e] Clossett' (PRO, LC2/5, f. 37[r]), as a near neighbour of John Patten.

28   Cheque Book, ff. 3[r], 21[v]; Rimbault, 1872, p. 131, 135.

29   Cheque Book, f. 23[r]; Rimbault, 1872, pp. 137.

30   PRO, SP38/8 and SO3/3.

31   Cambridge University Library, Grace Book E, p. 73; Carpenter, 1958, p. 206.

32   Oxford University Archives, NEP/Supra, Reg K reversed, f. 291[r]; Clark, 1887-88, i, p. 357; Foster, 1891-92, i, p. 580.

33   Wood, 1692-92, i, col. 843 (1813-20, *Fasti*, i, col. 406). The Cambridge graduates listed with Gibbons in the Oxford register were variously Bachelors and Masters.

34   William Morgan's *London &c. actually survey'd and a prospect of London and Westminster* of 1682 (part of which is reproduced on p. 34), shows the Round Woolstaple at the western end of the Long Woolstaple. *A new and exact plan of the*

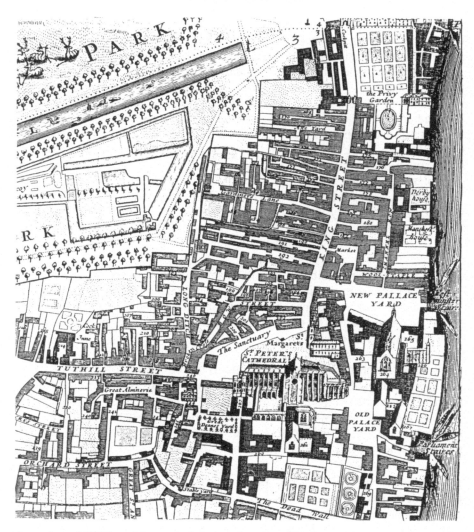

A section of William Morgan's *London &c. Actually Survey'd and a Prospect of London and Westminster* (1682). Just north of New Palace Yard is the Woolstaple, in the 'round' part of which Orlando Gibbons lived. His son Christopher Gibbons later lived between the Great Almonry and Orchard Street.

cities of London and Westminster (1738) by George Foster shows its position in relation to the new Westminster Bridge (still unopened when Foster's plan was published). For concise information about the Woolstaple see Walcott, 1849, pp. 78-80.

itself north of Westminster Hall. New Palace Yard is illustrated in Wenceslaus Hollar's engraving *Sala Regalis* of 1647 (see plate 3).

In the Woolstaple Gibbons was a neighbour of his father-in-law, who had lived there for a number of years. Gibbons is listed in the overseers' accounts for the parish of St Margaret's as resident in the Round Woolstaple in the years 1609-10 and 1610-11. He in fact appears in two sets of accounts dated 1609, and the incomplete first set may actually be a 'missing' set for 1608-9.[35] During the years 1611-12 to 1615-16 Gibbons's name is absent from the parish accounts. It is difficult to say why this should be so, without knowing the principles upon which residents were rated. The name of Gibbons's neighbour Arthur Agard[36] is also absent in some early years, so absence from the accounts may not imply absence from the parish. It is conceivable that Gibbons moved to the Woolstaple soon after his marriage to Elizabeth Patten, without being listed by the overseers. Gibbons's name reappears in the accounts for 1616-17, which show that he was rated at a penny a week. John Patten, originally rated at a penny was now rated at twopence. By the time Gibbons died, he too was rated at twopence a week.

Neither Gibbons nor Patten appears in the subsidy rolls covering the Woolstaples. Each is listed in a number of extant rolls for the royal household, but surviving Privy Seals show that members of the Chapel Royal and the royal musicians were regularly discharged from the payment of subsidies.[37] There are also two certificates of residence for Patten as a member of the royal household,[38] though none seems to have survived for Gibbons.

The first child of Orlando and Elizabeth Gibbons was James,[39] baptized at St Margaret's, Westminster, on 2 June 1607 and buried there two days later. It was not until 1613 that a second child, Alice, was

35   Westminster Archives. Residents of the Round and Long Woolstaples sometimes appear under the heading 'King Street East' in the overseers' accounts.

36   Replaced by Gregory Butler in 1618-19.

37   Documents all in PRO. Subsidy rolls: E179/70/122 (endorsed 19 April 1608, but compiled from an earlier list, with dead or retired musicians included and new names added), E179/70/121 (dated 1607-8 by PRO, but more probably 1608/9), E179/70/123a (endorsed 20 March 1609/10), E179/70/141 (1624-25); Ashbee, 1986-96, iv, pp. 19, 22, 27, 63. Privy seals discharging the Chapel Royal from paying subsidies, including Orlando Gibbons: E179/276/41B (12 October 1610, includes John Patten), E179/67/71 (30 June 1624, includes Richard Patten); Ashbee, iv, 28-29, 63-64. Records of the discharge of Chapel and other musicians occur also in the PRO's SO3 series (e.g. SO3/8, June 1624).

38   PRO, E115/295/134 (22 April 1607), E115/296/10 (November 1607).

39   Named after the King?

baptized. A son, Christopher, who was destined to carry on the family's musical tradition, was baptized at St Margaret's on 22 August 1615. Three more daughters (Ann, Mary and Elizabeth) and another son (Orlando) were baptized during the years 1618 to 1623.[40]

Patronage and publication

It seems to have been in 1611 that Gibbons sought the Queen's assistance in securing the gift of a lease. Papers of that time include an undated minute addressed to Salisbury, the Lord High Treasurer, which refers to 'The humble Petition of Orlando Gibbons Organist of his Ma[ties] Chappell', and summarizes the contents:

> Humbly shewing that the Petitioner hath bene an humble Sutor to the Queenes Ma[tie]: for her gracious furtherance in procuring him from his Highnes a lease in Revertion of 40 Mark a yeare of Duchy lands without fine. The consideracon whereof it hath pleased hir Ma[tie] to referre to yo[r] lo[P]: forasmuch as the Petitioner hath long depended upon this Sute in regard of her Ma[ties] gracious promise to him & by reason hereof hath neglected all other oportunities of benefitt by her Highnes favor ...[41]

The outcome of the petition is unknown.

Gibbons himself was instrumental in obtaining a grant for someone else. Docquets of 7-8 March 1611/2 among the Salisbury papers include a warrant to the Exchequer to pay 'to Thomas Dewxwell (at the suit of Orlando Gibbons, organist of his Majesty's Chapel) the sum of 63[l] 15[s] 11[d] as of his Majesty's free gift, which sum was due unto his Majesty by the conviction and execution of John Berrow for murder, and recovered and brought into the Exchequer at the charges of the said Dewxwell'.[42]

At this period Gibbons enjoyed the patronage of Sir Christopher Hatton.[43] It is difficult to say when their acquaintance began. The words of Gibbons's dedication of *The First Set of Madrigals and Mottets*, a collection of songs which he published in 1612,[44] suggest only that their

---

40   See p. 271.

41   PRO, SP14/67 no. 140; CSDP, 1858(a) p. 107; Ashbee, 1986-96, viii, p. 65.

42   Royal Commission on Historical Manuscripts, 1970, p. 338 (original document not examined).

43   Christopher Hatton (c.1570-1619) was a godson of his father's cousin, Christopher Hatton (1540-91), Queen Elizabeth's Lord Chancellor. For a family tree, see Wainwright, 1997, p. 4. Hatton was made a Knight of the Bath in 1603.

44   Probably very late in the year, which included the period 1 January - 24 March

connection was not new. It appears to have endured, and the first two of Gibbons's children to survive may have been named after Hatton and his wife, who were perhaps the children's godparents. The fact that Gibbons's first son was not given Hatton's name may mean either that he had to be baptized hurriedly because he was not expected to live, or that Gibbons and Hatton did not know each other well in 1607.

In his dedication of *The First Set of Madrigals and Mottets* Gibbons told Hatton that the songs 'were most of them composed in your owne house, and doe therefore properly belong unto you, as Lord of the Soile; the language they speake you provided them, I onely furnished them with Tongues to utter the same'.[45] None of the texts had previously been set, and it is to be assumed that some, if not all, were selected by Hatton. At least one of the authors must have been well known to Gibbons, for Joshua Sylvester, who wrote *I weigh not fortune's frown*, was a Groom of the Chamber to Prince Henry.[46]

Hatton owned Clayhall Manor, near Barking in Essex, and Kirby Hall, just outside Corby in Northamptonshire.[47] But Gibbons had no need to go so far afield to enjoy Hatton's hospitality. By 1606 Hatton was 'Commorant and resiant with his household and ffamily in the pishe of Great S^t. Batholomewes in the Ward of ffaringdon without London'.[48]

1612/3. See p. 133.

45   Hatton's name appears in other printed books. Each of the four extant copies of *Captain Humes Poeticall Musicke* (1607) by Tobias Hume has an individual printed dedication; that of the Henry Watson Music Library copy is 'TO ALL WORTHY AND RIGHT HONORABLE Lordes, Lovers of Musicke and favourers of all *Artes and Learning*. And to the truly noble knight of the high *Esteemed order of the BATH*. Sir CHRISTOPHER HATTON'. William Symson's *De accentibus Hebraicis breves & perspicuae regulae* (1617) is dedicated to Hatton, and he is listed among the subscribers to John Mishuen's *Ductor in linguas* (1617). Another subscriber to the latter work was 'Mr *Thom. Warricke*, Esquire one of the Gentlemen ushers or Presence waiters, to the *Qu. Maiestie*'. When Gibbons died Warrick succeeded to his place as organist in the Chapel Royal (see p. 228).

46   Joshua Sylvester (1563-1618) was made a Groom of the Chamber about 1606; he became Secretary to the Merchant Adventurers in 1613.

47   Hatton seems to have used Clayhall manor from about 1608, and a private chapel which he built there was consecrated by Thomas Morton, Bishop of Chester, in 1616 (Powell, 1966, p. 196). He simultaneously occupied Kirby Hall. He entertained Queen Henrietta Maria there as early as August 1605, and King James stayed there in 1612, 1616 and 1619 (Nichols, 1828, i, p. 525; ii, 453-454). For information about Kirby Hall, see Chettle, 1980. The house is known to have had an organ later in the century (BL, Additional MS 19571, f. 65^r, a letter dated only 'Monday ye 19th').

48   PRO, E115/211/15, E115/210/75, E115/207/92 (quotation from the last). These

In 1612 he was listed among the residents of New Palace Yard, near to Gibbons's house in the Woolstaple.[49] It is therefore possible that *The First Set of Madrigals* was composed in London, largely with the encouragement of Hatton, and since there are no pre-publication copies the songs it contains may not have been written very long before their appearance in print.[50] The part-books of *The First Set of Madrigals* in the library of Christ Church, Oxford, may have been presented to Hatton by Gibbons himself, since they are printed on fine large paper. Each book has the Hatton crest embossed in gold on its leather binding.[51] The original performers of the songs are unknown, but it may not be too much to conjecture that Hatton held musical gatherings at his house near St Bartholomew's, conceivably under Gibbons's direction. Is it possible that Gibbons ceased to write songs after 1612 because the gatherings were suspended when Hatton began living in Westminster?[52]

are certificates of residence prepared in connection with the subsidy granted by Parliament in the fourth year of the reign of James I. The only other surviving certificate of residence for Hatton (E115/218/98) was prepared at Alford Magna (Ilford, near Barking) in 1609-10. Although the Hatton family's house in Holborn had musical connections (the dedication to Sir Thomas Gerard of Michael East's *Second Set of Madrigales* of 1606 is written '*from* Ely *house Holborne*'), it was never owned by Sir Christopher Hatton. It was inherited by a nephew of the first Christopher Hatton: Sir William Newport, who took the name Hatton. When he died in 1597 the house remained in the hands of his widow Elizabeth until her death in 1646. It then passed to Christopher Hatton, first Baron Hatton (1605?-70), the eldest son of Gibbons's patron.

49   Westminster Archives, rate book of St Margaret's, Easter 1612 to Easter 1613. After being widowed, Lady Hatton remained in New Palace Yard until 1619 or 1620.

50   Thomas Hamond was virtually the only copyist who showed interest in Gibbons's madrigals (Monson, 1982, pp. 85, 140). Christ Church MS Mus. 21 contains variants of some songs, but it is not clear if they stem from pre-publication versions.

51   The books (Christ Church, Mus. 708-712) are illustrated in Wainwright, 1997, opposite p. 300.

52   The Hattons nevertheless retained the house near St Bartholomew's. Sir Christopher's name and that of his widow appear at the beginning of the parish register of St Bartholomew's, where they are included in a list of those who subscribed to the rebuilding of the church tower (Guildhall Library MS 6777/2: 'Alice Lady Hatton widdow', 'Sʳ Christopher Hatton knight of the bath'; the names were probably copied from another source, since the register covers the years from 1647). However, the rebuilding seems not to have been completed until 1628, long after Sir Christopher's death (Webb, 1921, ii, pp. 275, 535). Certificates of residence for Lady Hatton, as a widow, show her as resident in St Bartholomew's parish from 1622 to 1628 (PRO, E115 series, documents 184/8, 192/68, 204/40, 208/87, 211/16). These reveal some confusion. The ward in which Great St Bartholomew's lay is sometimes given as

A royal funeral and a royal wedding

On 16 May 1612 the first Act was signed for the marriage of King James's daughter, Princess Elizabeth, to Duke Frederick V, the Elector Palatine.[53] But the wedding was preceded by tragedy, with the death of the Princess's brother Henry, the heir to the throne.

Henry Frederick, King James's elder son, was born in 1594 and was created Prince of Wales in 1610. He seemed to recover from an illness in the spring of 1612, and was with his sister and prospective brother-in-law when the Children of the Chapel presented a play before them.[54] In October the Prince became seriously ill. His death on 6 November 1612, at the age of eighteen, was a devastating blow to those who saw great hope in the promise of his future rule. The King was inconsolable. Poets and musicians mourned the Prince's loss.[55] Ben Jonson wrote an epitaph. George Chapman, at much greater length, wrote *An Epicede*. Sir Walter Raleigh, whom the Prince had admired, asked:

What teares (Deare Prince) can serve to water all
The plants of woe growne in thy funerall?

John Coprario set seven poems by Thomas Campion, publishing them as *Songs of Mourning* in 1613.[56] The elderly William Byrd, the most senior and highly respected of the King's musicians, though retired, set the

Farringdon within, and sometimes as Farringdon without. In two documents (192/68 and 204/40) Lady Hatton is said to have dwelt in the parish of St Anne's, Blackfriars, but this may be an error, since the ward is given as Farringdon without. At the same time, she seems to have maintained her Northamptonshire home: a certificate of residence indicates her presence in the county in 1625 (E115/184/10).

53   PRO, E30/1197. The couple were very young: both were born in August 1596.

54   PRO, E351/544, m.14ʳ; Ashbee, 1986-96, iv, p.91. The warrant for payment to Philip Rosseter was not made until 24 November 1612, but it mentions 'the Prynce, the Ladie Elizabeth and the Prynce Palatyne'. A later warrant (31 May 1613) is 'for presenting before them [the Elector and his bride] two other playes by the Children of the Chappell'. E351/544 contains a good deal more information about the entertainment of the Elector.

55   Nichols, 1828, ii, pp. 504-512, lists thirty-two tracts on the death of Prince Henry, excluding 'numberless short elegies'. Godt (1982) lists musical tributes in which Absolom represents the Prince.

56   The volume was dedicated to Duke Frederick. The songs were dedicated separately to the King, the Queen, Prince Charles, Duke Frederick and Princess Elizabeth.

anonymous elegy *Fair Britain Isle*. Gibbons's *Nay let me weep* has every appearance of being another song of mourning.[57]

The Prince's body lay at St James's Palace until the day of the funeral. Cornwallis's account of events was written nearly thirty years afterwards, but appears to be authentic:

> The Time of the Funeral now approaching, on *Thursday* the third day of *December* the Coffin was removed from the Chamber where it stood all this while ... unto the Privy Chamber ... On the ... *Saturday* ... the Coffin ... was brought down Stairs towards the Chappell, where ... being lifted again the Gentlemen of his Majesty's Chappel singing mournful ditties before him, it was brought into the Chappel, and there placed under a Canopy set with great Arms of the Union at full ...[58]

An anonymous tract gives a closely similar account, but expands what is said about the music.[59] It tells how, at St James's Palace on Saturday 5 December, the coffin was carried from the Presence Chamber towards the Chapel, 'when being lifted up again, the Gentlemen of his Majesty's Chapel singing mournful Ditties ... the Corpse was solemnly carried into the Chapel of that House, and placed under a Canopy in the midst of the Choir, set with great Arms of the Union at full ... and the Gentlemen of the King's Chapel, with the Children thereof, sung divers excellent Anthems, together with the Organs, and other wind Instruments, which likewise was performed the Day following, being *Sunday*'. It is ironic that, in the funeral procession on the Monday, the Chapel should have walked to Westminster Abbey, where the Prince was buried, with the apothecaries, surgeons and doctors of physic who had failed to save the Prince's life. Whether Gibbons's *I am the resurrection*, a setting of words from the Order for the Burial of the Dead, was composed for the Prince's funeral cannot be determined, but it is possible.

Like other Gentlemen of the Chapel, Gibbons received an allowance of four yards of mourning livery, though the list of Gentlemen is headed by Edmund Hooper, who had served a year longer. Bull is listed separately as 'Doctor of Musicke to the Kinge', and was allowed seven yards of black cloth.[60] It is nevertheless probable that, in spite of their

57   This does not begin to exhaust the list of elegies.

58   Cornwallis, 1751 (written in 1641), particularly pp. 47-48.   King James had given St James's Palace to Prince Henry as his official residence.

59   *The Funeral of the high and mighty Prince Henry* (included in Cornwallis, 1751, pp. 55-57).

60   The same provision of four yards was made for sixteen singing men of Westminster Abbey. Nathaniel Giles, as Master of the Children of the Chapel Royal,

mourning dress, the Gentlemen presented a far from sombre appearance. A water-colour depicting Queen Elizabeth's funeral procession nine years earlier shows that over their cassocks and surplices they wore gold-embroidered copes of diverse hues.[61] They were among the most colourful figures in the procession.

On Christmas Day the King made his first appearance in public since the Prince's death. The banns for the wedding of Princess Elizabeth and the Elector Palatine were read in January and February, and the ceremony took place at Whitehall Palace on St Valentine's Day 1612/3. For weddings the Gentlemen usually received a fee of five pounds. The Cheque Book contains a detailed account of arrangements within the Chapel building, which was 'in royall sorte adorned', of those attending and their rich dresses, and of the procession and order of service.[62] 'Uppon the sides of the Chappell from the stales up to the Communion table weare a duble rowe of seates made for the Gent: of the Chappell arayed withe tapstery very comely'.

This Royall assemblie beinge in this sorte settled in y^{er} places, then began the Gent: of the Chappell to singe a full Anthem wch ended, the Bisshopp of Bathe & Welles deane of his Ma^{tes} Chappell went into ye pulpitt ... [After the sermon] the Quier began an other Anthem wch was the psalme: Blessed art thou that fearest God &c.[63] While ye Anthem was in singinge the Arch Bisshopp of Canterburie & ye deane of ye Chappell, went into ye vestery &

was allowed seven yards, but each of his twelve charges received only a yard-and-a-half (PRO, LC2/4(6), ff. 41^r-42^v; Ashbee, 1986-96, iv, pp. 36-38).

61   Howes (in Stowe, 1631, p. 1004) describes Prince Henry's funeral, and says 'the gentlemen of the K. chappell, being all in rich coapes attended the corps to Church, singing very solemnly as they marched'. They are pictured in BL MS Additional 35324, f. 31^v (frequently reproduced, e.g. in Woodfill, 1953, between pp. 48 and 49). The boys of the Chapel are dressed in black, but Lavina Teerlinc's miniature of the Royal Maundy service of 1565 shows that their normal dress was a red cassock and white surplice (Baldwin, 1990, p. 322).

62   Cheque Book, f. 77^{r-v}; Rimbault, 1872, pp. 161-166. Other descriptions of all the ceremonies and festivites are given in *The Magnificent Entertainments*, 1613, and in great detail in *Beschreibung der Reiss*, 1613. Further accounts occur in Jocquet, 1613, and *The Mariage of Prince Fredericke*, 1613. Much material is gathered in Nichols, 1828, ii, pp. 527-625. Howes (in Stowe, 1631, pp. 1005-1015) gives an account of the festivities and reprints *The Magnificent Entertainments*.

63   Gibbons set this text, but his verse anthem *Blessed are all they that fear the Lord* is described in Christ Church MS Mus. 21 (p. 262) as 'A Weddinge Anthem first made for my lord of Summersett'. The Earl of Somerset was not married to Lady Frances Howard until 26 December 1613.

putt on their Riche Coapes & came to ye Communion table, wher standinge
till the Anthem was ended: They two assended ye Throne wher these two
greate Princes weare married by the Bisshopp of Cant: ... When the Arch
Bisshopp had ended the Benedicčon, God the ffather, god ye sonne, &c the
Quier sange the same benedicčon in an Anthem made new for that purpose
by doctor Bull, this Anthem ended ... the versickles and prayers weare sunge
by the Arch Bisshop and answered by the Quier. The prayers beinge ended,
began an other Anthem ...

To celebrate the marriage, masques were given on the wedding night
and on the day following (14 and 15 February), and another, postponed
from the third day, was given on 20 February.[64] In order of presentation
they were Thomas Campion's *The Lords Maske*, George Chapman's *The
Memorable Maske of ... the Middle Temple, and Lyncolns Inne*, and
Francis Beaumont's *The Masque of the Inner Temple and Grayes Inne*.
It is probable that all three masques had scenery and costumes designed
by Inigo Jones. Some of the music occurs in William Brade's *Newe
Ausserlesene liebliche Branden* (Hamburg, 1617). Several pieces from
Chapman's masque can be ascribed to Robert Johnson.[65] As far as can be
determined, Gibbons had no hand in any of these entertainments, though
he made a keyboard arrangement of a tune from Beaumont's masque.[66]
Masque music, indeed, is one of the genres to which Gibbons made no
contribution. The notion that an instrumental piece derived from
Gibbons's song *The silver swan* may have been used in *The Lords
Maske* results from a misprint in the original edition of the words of the
masque.[67] This says that round about Orpheus were 'tamely placed
several wild beasts', one of which, it has been suggested, might have
been a swan.[68] But it is clear from the context that Campion wrote 'about
him tamely paced several wild beasts'.[69]

The newly married couple journeyed to Germany during April, May
and June, with an enormous entourage that included the Duke of Lennox

64   An idea of the sumptuousness of the masques can be gained from the King's
warrant to the Great Wardrobe (transcribed from BL MS Additional 5751, f. 106, by
Frederic Madden in *Archaeologia*, xxvi, 1836, pp. 383-394).

65   See Sabol, 1978. Sabol speculates (p. 33) that, as an English musician working
abroad, Brade could have accompanied Frederick to England.

66   MB 20/43: see p. 94.

67   Appended, as *The Description, Speeches, and Songs, of the Lords Maske*, to
Campion's *A Relation of the Late Royall Entertainment ... at Cawsome-House near
Reading* (1613).

68   Sabol, 1978, p. 615.

69   Emendation by I. A. Shapiro in Spencer and Wells, 1967, pp. 105, 120.

and the Earl of Arundel.[70] Among the Princess's attendants was 'Walter Ducker Bawberer', probably to be identified with 'Walter Tucker that playeth to her *grace* when she daunceth'.[71] 'M[r]. Coperario' and 'Daniel Callinder'[72] accompanied the Duke of Lennox, and among those who accompanied the Earl of Arundel was 'Gibbons'. The identity of the latter cannot be certain, since no forename is given and Gibbons is not known to have had any close association with the Princess — it was Bull who taught her to play the virginals — but it seems likely to have been Orlando Gibbons.[73] He can hardly have returned to England much before the end of July, when Bull may already have been preparing to leave the country.[74]

Parthenia

A by-product of the royal marriage was the publication of *Parthenia or the Maydenhead of the first musicke that ever was printed for the Virginalls*. This was a collection of keyboard music by William Byrd, John Bull, and Orlando Gibbons. The title-page stated that it was 'Ingraven by William Hole', 'print for M[ris]. Dor: Evans', and 'to be sould by G: Lowe print[r] in Loathberry'. The book was the first outside Italy to be printed from engraved copper plates. The method was particularly suitable for keyboard music, since the use of moveable type presented serious difficulties in printing notes simultaneously and aligning them on two staves.

70   Listed in the 'Cartel und Thurnier' section of *Beschreibung der Reiss*, 1613. Ludovic Stuart (1574-1623/4), second Duke and eighteenth Earl of Lennox (later fifteenth Earl of Richmond, and second Duke of Richmond and first Earl of Newcastle), held several high offices in Scotland, where he assisted King James's maintenance of political control, before becoming Deputy Earl Marshall and Lord Steward of the Household. Thomas Howard (1585-1646), second Earl of Arundel, carried the sword of state at the wedding ceremony; he was a collector and a patron of the arts, and a frequent performer in masques.

71   PRO, E407/57/2; Ashbee, 1986-96, iv, p. 207. The office of Bow Bearer is listed frequently in the records of the royal household.

72   Daniel Kalendar, the Queen's harper, perhaps identical with Daniel Cahill, the Queen's 'musician for the Irish Harp' (Ashbee, 1986-96, iv, p. 204, etc.).

73   Bull is described as the Princess's teacher in the dedication of *Parthenia*; see also PRO, E407/57/2 (Ashbee, 1986-96, iv, p. 207). The case for identifying Orlando Gibbons as the person who travelled with Arundel is argued by Dart, 1970. PRO documents E351/2801 and E351/2802 list the expenses incurred during the journey, but although Lennox and Arundel are mentioned by name their attendants are not.

74   See p. 31.

The dedication of *Parthenia* indicates that it was presented to the royal couple before their marriage on St Valentine's Day, 14 February 1612/3.[75] It is possible that the compilation was prompted by the signature of the marriage contract on 16 May 1612, but several factors cast doubt on this. Pavans and galliards by Byrd and Gibbons appear to have been included as memorials to the Earl of Salisbury, who died on 24 May, and other pieces were dedicated by Byrd to his friend Sir William Petre and to Mary Brownlow, who may have been his pupil and who was herself married in November 1613. It may be that the dedication to Duke Frederick and Princess Elizabeth was decided upon at a late stage.[76]

Many things about *Parthenia* neverthess proclaim its origin at the court of King James. The choice of Chapman to provide a commendatory poem is a reminder of his authorship of one of the wedding masques, and of the verses in his *Iliads* addressed to Prince Henry, Queen Anne, the Duke of Lennox, the Earl of Salisbury, the Earl of Arundel, and others. William Hole, *Parthenia's* engraver, had engraved the title-pages for editions of the *Iliads* published in 1608 and 1611. Chapman's *The Whole Works of Homer* (1614) again had a title-page engraved by Hole, and contained a sonnet to Prince Henry's memory. Hugh Holland, a friend of Ben Jonson and a member of the Mermaid Club, provided the other commendatory poem for *Parthenia*. Holland made a bid for royal favour early in James's reign, prefacing his *Pancharis* (1603) with verses to the King, the Queen and Prince Henry. His great patroness was said by John Aubrey to have been Elizabeth, Lady Hatton,[77] a performer in Jonson's *The Masque of Beautie* (1607/8) and *The Gypsies Metamorphos'd* (1621).

75   The dedication, found only in a copy in the Huntington Library, reads in part: 'The virgin PARTHENIA (whilst yet I may) I offer up to your virgin highnesses'. The title *Parthenia* ('virgin dances') puns on the ideas of virginal music, the first printing of such music in England, and the dedication to a newly betrothed couple. A copy of *Captain Humes poeticall musicke* (1607) in the British Library suggests how the presentation copy of *Parthenia* may have looked. It is lightly bound in vellum, with gold tooling on the back and front, and bears inside a short manuscript note from the composer, Tobias Hume, to the dedicatee, Queen Anne.

76   In a paper delivered to the International Musicological Society on 18 August 1997, Janet Pollack however suggested that the inclusion of references to 'honoured statesmen, beloved patrons, and revered saints' is typical of the epithalamion.

77   Barber, 1988, p. 73. She was a daughter of Sir Thomas Cecil, first Earl of Exeter, and the second wife of Sir William Newport, who took the name Hatton. In 1598, after Hatton's death in the previous year, she married Sir Edward Coke, but retained the name Hatton.

Parthenia was published under a royal privilege, and so was not entered in the registers of the Stationers' Company, which might otherwise have provided information about its date.[78] But the dedication refers to the royal couple as betrothed, and must either have been engraved after the convention on the marriage was signed and ratified in November and December 1612,[79] or engraved in anticipation of the event. *Parthenia* was included in a Frankfurt Fair catalogue for spring 1613. *Catalogus universalis pro nundinis Francofurtensibus vernalibus, de anno M.DC.XIII* lists it as follows, under the heading 'Libri Musici':

Parthenia sive virginitas protomusices primum impressa & clavecymbalis aptata. Composita à tribus nobilisimis Magistris, Guilielmo Byrdo, Doctore Ioanne Bullo, & Orlando Gibbono. Liber complectitur lectiones 21. Londini apud Billium in fol.[80]

The last phrase shows that it was offered for sale by the London printer, publisher and bookseller John Bill. He was someone whom those involved in the publication of *Parthenia* might easily have found willing to promote its sale. He had advanced money to enable Robert Barker, the King's Printer, to publish the Authorized Version of the Bible (1611), and became a shareholder in the King's Printing House. He was also a regular visitor to the Frankfurt Fair.[81] An intriguing aspect of his career is that he was associated with John Norton in St Paul's churchyard at about the time that Ellis Gibbons held a lease on property there.[82]

William Hole, the engraver of *Parthenia*, appears to have been the prime mover in its publication.[83] Hugh Holland's commendatory poem is addressed to 'his worthy frend W. H. & his Triumviri of Musicke', and

78   The title-page carries the words 'Cum privilegio'. Greg (1956, p. 93) states that books issued under a specific privilege had no need to be entered in the register.

79   PRO, E30/1180. The convention was signed at Westminster on 17 November, and ratified by the Count Palatine and Electress Palatine on 20 December.

80   Noted in Göhler, 1902, p. 5 of section headed 'Göhler 1'.

81   McKerrow, 1910, pp. 31-33. It is worth noting that pieces by Gibbons, apparently derived from *Parthenia*, occur in Continental manuscript anthologies such as Berlin, Staatsbibliothek, Stiftung Preussischer Kulturbesitz, Lynar MSS A1, A2.

82   Blayney, 1990, p. 54.

83   William Hole's career and engravings are described by Hind (1952-64, ii, pp. 316-340), but some additional information is given below, and more has been published elsewhere (e.g. by Challis, 1992). Further information is contained in documents which have not been published or calendared: for example, in January 1622 Hole was paid 'for makinge a seale of silver' (PRO, E351/544, m. 160r).

Hole signed the dedication to Duke Frederick and Princess Elizabeth. Little is known about Hole's family origins.[84] The only William Hole whose name occurs in the surviving London baptismal registers was the son of John Hole, and he was christened on 22 December 1588 at St Dunstan in the East.[85] It cannot be certain that this was the engraver, for the registers of many London parishes have perished, and the name William Hole occurs in those of parishes outside London. The notion that the engraver's father was named John is however encouraged by the fact that on 30 December 1619 the Wardens of the Mint were authorized to make a reasonable allowance to John Hole, 'graver of the Mynte, as well for patternes by him made for his Ma^{tes} gold moneys, as for his paines and travell & the paines and labo^{rs} of other gravers & workmen taken up for the expedic$\bar{o}$n of that service'.[86] John Hole may by then have retired. William Hole became Chief Engraver of the Mint in 1618, and he held the post until his death in 1624.[87] Letters of administration in respect of a 'William Holle', late of St Botolph Aldersgate, were granted to his widow Elizabeth in the latter year.[88]

William Hole seems to have modelled his style of engraving closely on that which Simone Verovio employed in a series of publications issued in Rome from 1586 onwards.[89] It recurs in his other engraved

84   He seems likely to have been related to Thomas Hole, a yeoman of His Majesty's Chamber (PRO, E179/70/123a, dated 20 March 1609/10).

85   The John Hole baptized at St Dunstan in the East on 1 June 1577 may have been an elder brother of William. The continued residence in the parish of members of the same family is indicated by the baptism there of another John Hole on 25 February 1609/10.

86   PRO, SP38/12; CSPD, 1858(b), p. 107.

87   1618 was the year in which Martin Billingsley's *The pens excellencie*, which Hole engraved, was dedicated to Prince Charles. A document of 29 May 1618 records 'A Grant to W^m. Holle Gent. of the office of head Sculptor of the Iron for Money ... dureing life' (PRO, SP14/141, p. 265, CSPD, 1858(a), p. 542; Challis, 1992, pp. 298-299). On 15 September 1624 'The office of cheife Graver of the Mynt wthin the Tower of London, and of Maker, and cheife Graver of all his Ma^{tes} Seales, Ensignes, and Armes', was granted, with survivorship, to John Gilbert and Edward Greene (SP38/11; CSPD, 1859, p. 340).

88   PRO, Prob. 6/11, f. 100^r, dated 17 June 1624. Although this is fairly conclusive evidence that the engraver's wife at the time of his death was named Elizabeth, the marriage of a William Hole to Alice Bennet on 30 January 1590/1 at St Mary Woolchurch Haw, the church where Gibbons was married in February 1605/6, arouses curiosity about whether Gibbons knew other members of the Hole family.

89   Verovio was the Italianized name of the engraver Simon Verovius, who had come to Rome from 's-Hertzogenbosch. His first musical publications, both issued in

music books, including *Prime Musiche Nuove* by Angelo Notari, a
musician who served Prince Henry and Prince Charles. The volume was
published with a dedication dated 24 November 1613. In 1616 Hole
adapted the title-page of Notari's volume for use by Thomas Myriell as a
title-page in manuscripts forming his compilation *Tristitiae Remedium*.[90]
Myriell, who became chaplain to George Abbot, the Archbishop of
Canterbury, and was appointed rector of St Stephen's Walbrook in 1616,
had a wide range of acquaintances in London musical circles.[91] He was
one of those, including Gibbons, favoured with dedications in *Songs of
3. 4. 5. and 6. Parts*, published by Thomas Tomkins in 1622.[92]

Other work undertaken by William Hole included *Parthenia In-
Violata* — at least, it has every appearance of being engraved by Hole or
someone closely associated with him. Like *Prime Musiche Nuove*, this
volume carries no date on its title-page, but its publication may have
occurred not long after Notari's book appeared. The music of *Parthenia
In-Violata* was 'Selected out of the Compositions of the most famous in
that Arte' by Robert Hole, whose relationship to William has not been
discovered. While it includes nothing by Gibbons, it is court-centred like
Parthenia, and many of the pieces it contains are from, or conjectured to
be from, court masques.[93] Another volume which seems to have been

1586, were the anthology *Diletto spirituale* and Jacob Peetrino's *Primo libro delle
melodie spirituale*. Concerning the figure of a woman playing the virginals which
appears on the title-page of *Parthenia*, see Deutsch, 1959. Hole copied the figure fairly
closely from an engraving of St Cecilia designed c.1588 by Hendrick Goltzius and
executed by his stepson, Jacob Matham. Later editions of *Parthenia* have title-pages with
a different picture, designed by Wencelas Hollar and engraved by Peter Stent.

90   BL, Additional MSS 29372-7; discussed by Monson, 1982, pp. 17-29.

91   Willetts, 1972. See Wainwright, 1997, p. 188 on Myriell's possible connection
with Gibbons's patron Sir Christopher Hatton.

92   Myriell was the dedicatee of *When David heard that Absolom was slain*.

93   *Parthenia In-Violata. Or Mayden-Musicke for the Virginalls and Bass-Viol
Selected out of the Compositions of the most famous in that Arte by Robert Hole*. A
publication date of c.1625 suggested by Dart (facsimile edition, 1961, pp. 42-46) derives
from his hypothesis that *Parthenia In-Violata* was produced for the wedding of Charles I,
who had learned to play the viol. If correct, this would have the merit of explaining why
it contains a viol part, but would mean that it was probably not engraved by William
Hole, who had died about a year before the ceremony. Dart's suggested date has,
however, been tentatively revised by later scholars. In a review of the facsimile edition
Jan LaRue (*Journal of the American Musicological Society*, xvii, 1964, pp. 406-407),
quoting Gerardy, 1963, argues that publication must have taken place much earlier than
Dart suggests, because the surviving copy is watermarked 1613 and printers did not keep
stocks of paper for a dozen years: 'an average of 77% of a given run of sheets was used

engraved by William Hole, or by a hand carefully following the models he provided, is Gibbons's *Fantazies of III. Parts* (c.1620). This is discussed below.[94]

For *Parthenia In-Violata* Robert Hole selected arrangements of currently popular tunes making few demands on the performer's technique. The music of *Parthenia*, on the other hand, generally requires an advanced technique, and some of the pieces seem to have been specially composed. The music was written by the leading Chapel Royal keyboard composers of successive generations, and consists almost entirely of the more elevated genres of instrumental music.[95] Assuming that William Hole took the lead in publishing *Parthenia*, it seems improbable that he had no help in choosing the music and preparing the copy from which it was to be engraved. Unless one is to believe that Robert Hole acted as the editor of both volumes of keyboard music, Dart's suggestion that Gibbons might have edited *Parthenia* is attractive, not only for the reasons he advanced but because there is no other obvious candidate.[96] It is not easy to imagine Bull, who never published anything on his own account, acting as editor, and Byrd, although he had extensive experience of publishing, was living in partial retirement.

within one year, the remainder in less than three years'. Pinto (1996, p. 98 fn. 26) plumps for early 1614 as a possible date of publication, i.e. soon after the publisher, John Pyper, gained the freedom of the Stationers' Company, and when the contents (some of which can be connected with masques of 1613) were still topical. He also floats the idea (pp. 99-100) that *Parthenia In-Violata* may have been produced for the wedding of the Earl of Somerset (see p. 50 below). The title might be thought to refer to the grounds on which Somerset's bride's previous marriage had been annulled, but the surviving copy contains no dedication and the suggestion of a connection with the Somerset wedding offers no explanation of why the publication included a part for bass viol. Nevertheless, in the absence of any further evidence, a date earlier than the one proposed by Dart appears convincing.

94   See p. 62.

95   Byrd was born in 1539 or 1540; Bull was born about 1562; Gibbons was baptized in 1583. The genres are described by Morley, 1597, p. 181 (1952, pp. 296-297).

96   Dart (1962, p. [41]) noted that the G-clefs in Gibbons's pieces, which he assumed the engraver to have copied exactly from the manuscript before him, take a consistent form, while those in Byrd's take two forms. (Bull's pieces use no G-clef.) He argued that Byrd's pieces with the Gibbons G-clef (a prelude to the 'Petre' pavan and galliard, and a second galliard to the 'Salisbury' pavan) are likely to have been copied by Gibbons. Whether this is so or not, it is quite possible that these pieces were written at the last minute and may have required recopying for the engraver.

Gibbons, while without Byrd's experience as a publisher, seems more likely to have assisted Hole in assembling the copy.

Whoever the editor was, he erred in attempting to Italianize as 'galiardo' the name of the dance generally known in England as 'galliard'. The word 'galiardo' occurs in no other English keyboard source.[97] If Gibbons was responsible, he may have been misled by his own Christian name and that of his brother Ferdinando. Of much greater consequence is the attention which the editor and his collaborators appear to have paid to the overall layout of *Parthenia*. Byrd's example may be seen in this, since his publications provided models for such care. The contributions of Byrd, Bull and Gibbons consist of eight, seven and six pieces respectively, and the order in which they are printed, as well as their number, reflects the composers' seniority.[98]

Mistress Dorothy Evans evidently put up the money for the publication of *Parthenia*, but neither her identity, nor how the book came to be 'sould by G: Lowe print' in Loathberry', has been discovered. A diligent search for Dorothy Evans in the records of the royal household and elsewhere has failed to reveal her name. It is possible that she held a post at court, but because women frequently held positions that attracted no remuneration, they are rarely mentioned in the surviving lists of payments made to members of the household. A 'Record Book of Parish Proceedings. 1571 to 1677' belonging to St Margaret Lothbury shows George Lowe to have been active in parish affairs.[99] His daughter Elizabeth was baptized at St Margaret's on 19 March 1609, and buried

---

97   The Italian is 'gagliarda', though there is also an Italian word 'gagliardo'. John Florio, in *Queen Annas New World of Words* (1611), gives the following definitions: 'Galiárda, *a dance called a galliard*', 'Gagliárdo, *strong, lusty, or nimbly disposed of body. Also frolike or blithe*'.

98   In the paper mentioned above (note 76) Pollack suggested that these numbers might be connected with the characters of stanzas of eight, seven and six lines, as described by Puttenham (1936, p. 65). She speculated that *Parthenia* might be modelled on the three-part form of the poetic epithalamion (Puttenham, p. 51), and that the title might signal a literary connection, since the character Parthenia appears in Sidney's *Arcadia*. She also considered that, in beginning and ending with a prelude, *Parthenia* displays a symmetry found in literary epithalamia.

99   Guildhall Library, MS 4352/1. There survive two certificates of residence, dating from 1620-21, for a George Lowe, citizen and Draper, living in the neighbouring parish of St Christopher le Stocks (PRO, E115/204/149 of 18 James I, and E115/239/136 of 5 May 19 James I). The Drapers' Company however has a note, compiled by W. R. Loosemore, which makes it clear that this Lowe was not the printer. A Peter Evans was also active in the affairs of the parish of St Margaret's, but there is no reason to suppose he was the husband of Dorothy Evans.

on 17 December 1610. A second daughter, Ellin, was baptized on 27 December 1610.[100] As a printer, Lowe is known only for *Parthenia* and a 'Map of New England' of 1614.[101] This suggests that he was equipped for printing from engraved plates, but he was apparently not a member of the Stationers' Company.

The Somerset wedding

On 26 December 1613 the wedding of the Earl of Somerset was celebrated in the chapel at Whitehall, in the presence of the King and Queen. He was married (scandalously in the opinion of many) to Lady Frances Howard, the daughter of the Lord Chamberlain, the Earl of Suffolk, soon after the annulment of her marriage to the Earl of Essex. 'And the gentlemen of the Chappell had for their fee as before had been used, the somme of five poundes'.[102] Gibbons may privately have had a further reward, if he composed the anthem *Blessed are all they that fear the Lord* for the service.[103] Shortly before the wedding, on 24 November, Angelo Notari dedicated to Somerset his *Prime Musiche Nuove*, which had been engraved by William Hole. In celebration of the marriage several masques were staged before the King, Queen and Prince Charles.[104] They included the 'masque of squires' by Campion,[105] *A Challenge at Tilt* and *The Irish Masque* by Jonson (who also wrote a poem beginning 'They are not those, are present wth theyre face'),[106] and

100   Guildhall Library, MS 4346/1.

101   McKerrow, 1910, p. 178.

102   Upon King James's accession, Robert Carr (1589-1645) accompanied him to England as a page; he was created Earl of Somerset on 3 November 1613. Samuel Calvert expected the wedding to be in Henry VII's chapel, Westminster, but the Cheque Book is quite clear that the Whitehall Chapel was used (Royal Commission on Historical Manuscripts, 1940, pp. 267-268; Cheque Book, f. 78[r]; Rimbault, 1872, pp. 166-167).

103   See note 63 on p. 41.

104   Samuel Calvert, clerk of the Virginia Company, wrote on 14 December 1613 that three masques were to be presented, 'one by the queen, the second by the Lords, the last [*The Maske of Flowers*] at S[r] Francis Bacon charge'. (Royal Commission on Historical Manuscripts, 1940, pp. 267-268, corrected by E. A. J. Honigman in Spencer and Wells, 1967, p. 153.)

105   Published as *The Description of a Maske: Presented in the Banqueting roome at Whitehall* (1614).

106   Jonson, who had written *The Masque of Hymen* for Frances Howard's first marriage, did not publish the poem and sought to expunge references to her marriages when he published the masques.

the anonymous *Maske of Flowers* presented by the gentlemen of Gray's Inn.

The happiness of the bride and groom was short-lived, and Gibbons may well have had qualms about his innocent involvement. In September 1613 Sir Thomas Overbury, who had vigorously opposed the marriage and attempted to deter Somerset from contracting it, died by poisoning in the Tower. His imprisonment had probably been contrived to enable the poisoning to take place. When, two years later, the circumstances of Overbury's murder were uncovered, Somerset and his wife were condemned for their part in it.[107] The sentence of death was commuted, but they were imprisoned in the Tower until 1622.

Sir Thomas Leighton

Another of Gibbons's acquaintances to suffer imprisonment, for an entirely different reason (and in his own view unjustly), was Sir Thomas Leighton.[108] He was a Member of Parliament and a Gentleman Pensioner in the reign of Queen Elizabeth. He was one of those knighted on the accession of James I, in whose honour he wrote *Vertue Triumphant, or a Lively Description of the Foure Vertues Cardinall* (1603). He fell into debt, and various actions were brought against him. He was outlawed, left the Gentlemen Pensioners, and in 1609 was ordered by the King's Bench to surrender to the Marshalsea Prison, where he is known to have been by 1612. It may have been there that he wrote his intensely religious poems, published as *The Teares or Lamentations of a Sorrowfull Soule* (entered at Stationers' Hall on 25 January 1612/3). Leighton must nevertheless have remained well-connected, for he somehow managed to persuade twenty leading composers to join him in making musical settings of fifty-three of his poems. He published the collection in 1614 under the original title.[109] Gibbons contributed short settings of *O Lord, how do my woes increase* and *O Lord, I lift my heart to thee.*

---

107 Simon Marson (Merson, Merston), one of the King's musicians, was an unwitting instrument of Overbury's death (PRO, SP14/82, no. 32; CSPD, 1858(a), p. 313; Ashbee, 1986-96, viii, p. 73).

108 Concise biographies of Leighton (c.1565-1622) are included in Grove, 1980, and Leighton, 1970.

109 But with the spelling 'Lamentacions'.

The Chapel Feast and the Scottish journey

It seems likely that, following Bull's departure, Gibbons occupied a more prominent place among the Gentlemen of the Chapel. One small sign of this may be his assumption of responsibility for an annual event enjoyed as a time-honoured custom. Although it is nowhere stated in the records, he may have been chosen as the senior steward of the Chapel Feast. A royal warrant of 26 June 1614 authorized the payment of sixty shillings 'To Orlando Gibbons one of the gent of his Ma^{tes} Chapple ... for himselfe and the rest of the gent of his Ma^{tes} Chapplle Royall given to them towardes their feaste by his Ma^{ty} as about this tyme in former tymes hath been accustomed'.[110] It is not known whether Gibbons exercised this responsibility in every succeeding year,[111] but in 1620 he again received 'in the behalfe of himselfe and his fellowes for his highnes guifte towards theire feaste as aboute this tyme in former yeares hath beene given unto them ... 60s'.[112] In 1623 the recipient was Thomas Day, who served successively as a musician to Prince Henry and Prince Charles, and also held a place in the Chapel.[113]

About the time of Gibbons's probable first stewardship, he received a mark of royal favour in the form of bonds of one hundred pounds and fifty pounds posted by Laurence Brewster of Gloucester, who forfeited them to the King by his failure to appear at Lambeth before the Court of High Commission. A document formally recording this was endorsed by Sir Francis Windebank at Theobalds on 19 July 1615.[114]

110   PRO, E351/544, m. 29^r; Ashbee, 1986-96, iv, p. 93. Money for the Feast was paid in 1605, 1606 and 1610 to Nathaniel Giles, Master of the Children since 1597, and in 1610 to George Woodeson, who had joined the Chapel Royal from St George's Chapel, Windsor, in 1602 (see Ashbee, iv, pp. 76, 78, 85, 91). Very often the recipient is unnamed.

111   In 1662 Henry Cooke, Master of the Children, agreed to be a steward for the feast of 1663, on the condition that it should not form a precedent binding him or his successors to accept the office in later years.

112   PRO, E351/544, m. 119^r; Ashbee, 1986-96, iv, p. 106. Gibbons was among the Gentlemen who subscribed their names to a memorandum of agreement 'by generall consent that alwaies heerafter, ther shalbe allowed unto the steward*es* of the chappell ffeast of ev^ry gent: attendant, the some of Three shilling*es* fower pence' (Cheque Book, f. 36^r; Rimbault, 1872, pp. 122-123). This was in addition to the allowance traditionally made by the King.

113   PRO, E351/544, mm.160^v-161^r; Ashbee, 1986-96, p. 112. Day was sworn in as a Gentleman of the Chapel on 30 September 1615 (Cheque Book, f. 6^v; Rimbault, 1872, p. 8).

114   PRO, SP39/5 m. 38 (modern numbering); CSPD, 1858(a), p. 295; Ashbee,

Such glimpses of Gibbons's life are unaccompanied by any record of his musical duties. Even in the case of an event so well documented and so much remarked upon as King James's visit to Scotland in 1617, Gibbons's presence among those who attended him has to be inferred. In all the many accounts of the visit, and the many comments upon it, there is no mention of Gibbons or the music he wrote for the occasion.

The reason given publicly for the journey to Scotland was stated in the proclamation of a Parliament which was to meet in Edinburgh: 'the Kingis Majestie hes thir mony yeiris bigan had a [grite] and naturall longing to see this his ancient kingdome and native soile, and hes resolvit, God willing, to make a jorney thither this approtcheing sommer'.[115] 'The king was much laboured to defer his journey to the next year, whenas he should find things better prepared', wrote John Spottiswoode in 1655.[116] But he would not be swayed, despite — or perhaps because of — less than fond memories of his boyhood. 'How they used the poore Lady, my mother', he had cried in 1604, 'is not unknowne, and with griefe I may remember it ... And how they dealt with me, in my *Minority*, you all know; it was not done secretly, & thogh I would, I cannot conceale it'.[117]

Regardless of the logistical problems of the progress, the King took pleasure in it. In the words of a modern historian, 'He hunted, hawked and feasted, warming the country as he went with the glories of his court'.[118] He crossed the border on 13 May, and travelled by way of Castle Douglas and Seton to Edinburgh, which — with the barely concealed misgivings of its citizens — was to sustain the main burden of his visit. The King had ordered the refurbishment of the chapel at Holyrood.[119] Thomas Dallam was commissioned to build 'a faire double Organ' for the chapel, with a case designed by Inigo Jones, and this was sent by sea from London and installed by English workmen.[120] Jones was

1986-96, viii, p. 73. The Signet Office record of the grant is PRO, SO3/6; Ashbee, 1986-96, iv, p. 43 (where 'his Majesty's organist' should be deleted).

115 Privy Council, Scotland, 1894, p. 36; see also p. 121, where reference is made to 'The Kingis Majesteis vehement and unchangeable desyre these mony yeiris bigane to visite this his native kingdome'.

116 Spottiswoode, 1847-51, iii, p. 238.

117 Barlow, 1604, pp. 79-82.

118 Wilson, 1956, p. 390.

119 The Scottish Chapel Royal had ceased to be a centre of serious musical activity in the 1560s. Shortly after James's baptism 'the Earl of Mar had stripped the three organs and everything else deemed papistical from the Chapel Royal' (Purser, 1992, pp. 100-101, 116).

120 Dallam was paid £300 initially, and a further £50 later. References to the organ

also the designer of gilded images of apostles and patriarchs. As the restoration work progressed a rumour went round 'that the organs came first, now the images, and ere long the mass'. To those who complained, the King retorted: 'you can endure lions, dragons, and devils to be figured in your churches, but will not allow the like place to the patriarchs and apostles'.[121]

On 16 May James rode on horseback into the city by way of the West Port. He was greeted by the Provost and other dignitaries, heard speeches of welcome, and (doubtless more pleasing) was presented with a purse containing 'five hundreth double angellis laid in a silver basing double overgilt'.[122] At St Giles's the King heard a sermon by John Spottiswoode, the Archbishop of St Andrews, before going on to Holyrood, where at the gate of the Inner Court he received a book of Greek and Latin verse from the College of Edinburgh. At some point in these proceedings Gibbons's welcome song, *Do not repine, fair sun*, must have been performed. The words are thought to have been written by Joseph Hall, who was in the King's party. Gibbons probably knew Hall well, since by 1608 he was in Prince Henry's service, where he remained until the Prince's death.[123]

Whether the song was sung before or after the King had entered the building must remain a matter of conjecture.[124] It is not mentioned by any contemporary, and when Calderwood came to write his account he briskly dismissed such matters: 'The solemnities, which were used at his passing through the Town, I passe by, as not pertinent to the Historie'.[125]

occur in PRO documents SO3/6 (July 1616, July 1617, July 1619), SP39/6 no. 38 (July 1616), SO39/8 (July 1617), E403/1721 (July 1616), E403/1723 (July 1617). Printed references occur in Devon, 1836, pp. 189, 325; CSPD, 1858(a), pp. 379, 476; Ashbee, 1986-96, iv, 44, 46, 168 and viii, pp. 74, 76.

121   Spottiswoode, 1847-51, iii, pp. 238-239.

122   Nichols, 1828, iii, p. 317ff, from an anonymous account.

123   Joseph Hall (1574-1656), Dean of Worcester 1616, Bishop of Exeter 1627-41, Bishop of Norwich 1641-47. Reasons for ascribing the words to him are summarized in Hall, 1949, p. 276.

124   The surviving source, New York Public Library MSS Drexel 4180-5, does not specify the accompanying instruments. If, as appears to be the case, they were viols, the song would not have been suitable for open air performance. It may have been sung inside the building, but not in the chapel. Brett, in his article of 1981 and in notes to his edition, observes that the words of the song would not have been appropriate for performance in church, and that the choir of the English Chapel Royal would not have been welcome outside Holyrood.

125   Calderwood, 1678, p. 674.

'Upon Saturday the seventeen of *May*', Calderwood continued, 'the English service, singing of Quiristers, and playing on Organs, and Surplices were first heard and seen in the Chappel Royal'. The English Chapel Royal had travelled to Scotland by sea: 'there were deliv'ed unto the Deane of the Chapell then being for us towards o' charges for that journey 400¹', it was later recalled. 'Then was also allowed us a good shipp well victualled for o' passage & carriage of the Chappell stuffe and o' owne necessaries'.[126] The celebration of the Anglican rite at Holyrood, throughout the King's visit, was clearly intended to assist in the implementation of his policy towards the Scottish church. The King's finest organist is hardly likely to have been left at home, and it can confidently be assumed that Gibbons played on the newly installed instrument. He had written the anthem *Great King of Gods* specially for the King's visit, and it is likely that he had done so before setting off from England.[127]

Queen Anne's funeral

On 2 March 1618/9, eighteen months after the King's return from Scotland, Queen Anne died.[128] Her last illness had not been painful, and it was said that she had too long delayed the settlement of her affairs.[129] The King also had been ill, on and off, for some time. Now he suffered a 'fit of the stone', and his death was anticipated. He himself made 'a very religious and wise speech' to the Prince and Privy Councillors.[130] Although he and the Queen had not lived together for some years (she spent much of her time at Denmark House[131] or at Greenwich, while James was constantly on the move), the severity of his illness looks very like a reaction to the Queen's death. He was out of danger, though still very weak, by the beginning of April, and public thanks were given at St

126   The Gentlemen of the Chapel in a petition to King Charles I about May 1633 (SP16/237 no. 77; CSPD, 1863, p. 38; Ashbee, 1986-96, viii, p. 109).

127   In Christ Church MS Mus. 21 (p. 230) the anthem is headed: 'This anthem was made for ye kings being in Scottland'.

128   The King had reached London on 15 September 1617.

129   Sir Thomas Edmonds writing to Sir Dudley Carleton (PRO, SP14/107, no. 38; CSPD, 1858(b), p. 25).

130   Sir Edward Harwood writing to Sir Dudley Carleton (PRO, SP14/107 no. 60; CSPD, 1858(b), p. 28).

131   Somerset House was renamed Denmark House in 1606 in honour of the Queen's brother, Christian IV of Denmark, who was staying with her.

Paul's for his recovery.[132] It is very likely that Gibbons wrote the anthem *O all true faithful hearts* for the service on that occasion.[133]

The Queen's funeral was postponed until 13 May 1619. The Master of the Wardrobe, Sir Lionel Cranfield, refused to pay excessive prices for mourning cloth, as ready money was in short supply. John Chamberlain reported that 'the Quenes funerall is put off till the 29th of Aprill, and perhaps longer unless they can find out monie faster, for the master of the ward-robe is loth to weare his own credit thread-bare'. The Queen's body lay at Denmark House, watched over by her ladies, who not surprisingly grew weary of waiting.[134] When at last she was buried at Westminster Abbey, King James remained at Greenwich.[135] 'The President of the Funerall of o[r] late Soveraigne Lady Queene Anne' lists the many who at last received mourning liveries, including the Gentlemen of the Chapel Royal (among whom Gibbons and Hooper were named specifically as organists) and twelve Children of the Chapel, the Abbey choristers, twenty-eight trumpeters, and a dozen other musicians.[136] John Chamberlain considered the procession very dull; Nathaniel Brent pronounced it better than Prince Henry's, but thought it fell short of Queen Elizabeth's.[137] When the King returned to Whitehall, he surprised the ambassadors who came to condole with him by being gaily dressed, while they were in mourning.[138]

Patrons and friends

Five months after the Queen's funeral, on 10 September 1619, Sir Christopher Hatton died, and Gibbons lost a patron.[139] It may have been

132   Harwood to Carleton, 4 April 1619 (PRO, SP14/108 no. 15; CSPD, 1858(b), p. 33).

133   'A thanks Giving for the kings happie recoverie from a great dangerous sicknes' (Christ Church MS Mus. 21, p. 210).

134   From letters of Sir Thomas Edmonds and John Chamberlain to Sir Dudley Carleton (PRO, SP14/107 nos. 38, 54; CSPD, 1858(b), pp. 25, 27; Chamberlain, 1939, ii, p. 224).

135   John Chamberlain, writing on Friday, 14 May 1619, said the King went to Greenwich 'last Tuesday' (Chamberlain, 1939, ii, p. 224).

136   PRO, LC2/5, ff. 32[v]-45[v] (Gibbons and Hooper on f. 44[v]); Ashbee, 1986-96, iv, pp. 48-50.

137   Letters to Sir Dudley Carleton (PRO, SP14/109, nos. 32, 34; CSPD, 1858(b), p. 45; Chamberlain, 1939, ii, p. 237).

138   Chamberlain to Carleton (PRO, SP14/109, no. 75; CSPD, 1858(b), p. 51; Chamberlain, 1939, ii, p. 242).

139   Hatton and his wife (d. 1638) were buried in Westminster Abbey.

about this time, or a little earlier, that Gibbons was commissioned by another patron or friend to write the anthem *Sing unto the Lord*. A copy at Christ Church has an inscription which says it was 'made for Do^r: Marshall'.[140] There is no further clue to Marshall's identity, but it seems possible that he was Hamlett Marshall, who obtained his doctorate in 1615, and was one of the King's Chaplains in Ordinary by 1616.[141]

Another with whom Gibbons was probably acquainted at the same period was Dr Godfrey Goodman, who was a Chaplain to the Queen before 1616. It was he who wrote the words of Gibbons's anthem *See, see, the word is incarnate*.[142] A third anthem, *This is the record of John*, was composed for Dr Laud, apparently during his term as President of St John's College, Oxford, which began on 10 May 1611.[143] Laud, who was consulted on church affairs by the King, would have known Gibbons by reputation, and perhaps in person.[144]

Henry Eveseed

The most bizarre event of Gibbons's career in the Chapel Royal involved Henry Eveseed, a very troubled, and most troublesome, Yeoman of the Vestry. Eveseed was first admitted as a yeoman extraordinary, and about 1611 was admitted in ordinary, 'since wch tyme he hath misbehaved him selfe continually'.[145] He was 'infected wth a fowle disease in his groine, to the great offence of all, but cheifely of those that were constrained by meanes of their service to lye neere him, uppon wch the late Lo: Deane thought him unfitt to serve his Matie in his progresse into Scotland'. But

140 Christ Church MS Mus. 21, p. 190.

141 The record of the institution of Hamlett Marshall to Alresford on 11 July 1616 refers to him as Chaplain in Ordinary to James I (Lambeth Palace Library, register of Archbishop Abbott, I, f. 283^r).

142 Godfrey Goodman, 1583-1656. He became a canon of Windsor on 20 December 1617, Dean of Rochester on 4 January 1620/1, and Bishop of Gloucester on 6 March 1624/5. In Christ Church MS Mus. 21 (p. 176) the words are attributed to 'Doctor Goodman De: of Rochester', but Thomas Myriell copied the anthem into his *Trisitiae Remedium*, which he dated 1616.

143 'This Anthem was made for Dr Laud presedent of Sant Johns': 'Oxford' added in a later hand (Christ Church MS Mus. 21, p. 200).

144 William Laud (1573-1645), Dean of Gloucester, 1616; a prebendary of Westminster,1620/1; Bishop of St David's, 1621; Bishop of London, 1628; Archbishop of Canterbury, 1633.

145 A long and detailed account of his misdeeds is given on ff. 37^{r-v} of the Cheque Book (Rimbault, pp. 101-104). In the list of those receiving mourning for Prince Henry, Eveseed is named as one of the vestry to the Prince.

his difficult behaviour sprang from recurrent drunkenness, so that 'at his Ma^{tes} last beinge at Greenw^{ch}, he soe still contynuinge his drounkennes, that the porters complayned of his continuall late cominge in drounke, at wch tymes he tak*es* occasion to quarrell & beate the servant*es*'. The Cheque Book adds:

> Againe uppon St Peters day[146] last [1620] being ye day of o^{r} feast, unto wch were invited many officers of the house & other o^{r} good friend*es*, ye sayd Eveseed did violently & sodenly w^{th}out cause runne uppon m^{r} Gibbons, took him up, & threw him doune uppon a standard, wherby he receaved such hurt, y^{t} he is not yett recov^{r}ed of the same, & w^{th}all he tare his band frō his neck to his p^{r}judice & disgrace. then he pceading from m^{r} Gibbons, mett o^{r} fellow m^{r} Cooke in the Chappell, wher he gave him three blowes in the face, & after y^{t} he abused o^{r} fellowe m^{r} Crosse, and Richard Patten, and was not satisfied wth those abusing*es* but challenged the field of some of them: wch abuse did tend to o^{r} great discreaditt contemning ye Subd*eane* or anything he could say or doe therin.

A complaint to this effect was read at a chapter held at Hampton Court on 29 September 1620. Gibbons had by then recovered sufficiently to join other members of the Chapel in signing a memorandum of the swearing in of the younger Thomas Pierce.[147]

Prince Charles's household

On 3 November 1616, four years after Prince Henry's death, his younger brother Charles was created Prince of Wales, at the age of fifteen.[148] Charles's musical establishment was thereafter to include seventeen musicians, together with trumpeters and drummers, the majority of whom had previously served Henry.[149] Most of the seventeen musicians were lutenists and singers, though among them were Thomas Lupo, a violinist, and Robert Taylor and Alphonso Ferrabosco, who played the viol.[150] Gibbons, while retaining his place in the Chapel

146   29 June, the feast of St Peter Apostle.

147   Cheque Book, f. 37^{r}; Rimbault, 1872, p. 47. Eveseed was first suspended and eventually dismissed. He was presumably a son of the Henry Eveseed who was a child of the Chapel, and succeeded to Thomas Tallis's place in 1585 (Cheque Book, f. 5^{v}; Rimbault, 1872, p. 4).

148   Prince Charles was born on 19 November 1600 at Dunfermline.

149   Ashbee, 1986-96, iv, p. 216.

150   Six singer-lutenists had served Prince Henry. They were Thomas Day, a Gentleman of the Chapel Royal who became Master of the Children, Angelo Notari, who

Royal, was the only specialist keyboard player in the group. The musicians may on occasion have been joined by the Prince. Many years after Charles's death John Playford wrote that '*his late Sacred Majesty ... could play his Part exactly well on the* Bass-Viol', and in the next century Burney added that Charles, 'during the life of his father, had been a scholar of Coperario, on the viol da gamba'.[151]

Gibbons must have entered Charles's service shortly after he became Prince of Wales. This is evident from the declared accounts of Adam Newton, the Prince's Receiver General.[152] A warrant dormant drawn up under a Privy Seal dated 5 November 1617 is for the payment to Gibbons of nine months' portion of his wages of forty pounds a year.[153] On 24 February 1617/8 Gibbons signed for the receipt of ten pounds for his quarter's wages due at Christmas 1617.

Receaved by me Orlando Gibbons one of his Highnes Musicions, of Adam Newton esquir Treasurer or Receavo[r] generall to his said highness, the some of tenne pounds current money of England for my quarters pensio*n* due to me from his Highnes a*t the* feast of the Nativitie of o[r] *Lord* god last past. I say rec*eaved*

Orlando *Gibbons*[154]

was no doubt valued for his mastery of Italian styles, Jonas Wrench, Thomas Forde, Robert Johnson, and John Sturte. Six of the new appointees were also singers and lutenists: John Daniel, Alphonso Ball, Richard Ball, John Coggeshall (Coxall), John Drew and Robert Marsh. The remainder of the group consisted of Thomas Lupo (violin) and John Ashby (instrument unknown), both of whom had served Prince Henry, Alphonso Ferrabosco (viol), who had taught music to Prince Henry, Robert Taylor (viol) and Gibbons. Some of Prince Charles's musicians were also composers. The group's make-up remained fairly constant, but small changes can be traced in the accounts (Ashbee, 1986-96, iv, p. 217ff; Holman, 1993, p. 198).

151 Playford, 1683, Preface (also in later editions); Burney, 1776-89, iii, p. 361; (1935, ii, p. 287). Hawkins mentions that in a lost manuscript of Hingston's, 'one of Gibbons's songs has this memorandum, "Made for Prince Charles to be sung with 5 voices to his wind instrument"' (Hawkins, 1776, iv, p. 44; 1963, p. 577). See also note 202 on p. 69.

152 Newton had been Prince Henry's schoolmaster. He was created a baronet in 1620.

153 PRO, SC6/James I/1680; Ashbee, 1986-96, iv, p. 217.

154 Royal College of Music, MS 2187, reproduced as plate 4. Manuscript damaged; editorial readings in italics.

Records of similar payments exist from subsequent years.[155]

In January 1619/20 Gibbons added to his income by gaining another place at court:

> Orlando Gibbons one of his Ma^{tes} Musicõns for the virginalles to attend in his highnes privie Chamber wch was heretofore supplyed by Water Earle deceased at xlvj^{li} per ann during his life.[156]

Walter Earle had begun his career as a page in ordinary in the household of Anne of Cleves, whom Henry VIII married in January 1539/40.[157] He was employed in the household of her successor, Catherine Parr, and in the Privy Chambers of Queen Mary and Queen Elizabeth.[158] He would have been well into his eighties by 1619, and the continued payment of his salary was clearly a reward for long service. His replacement by Gibbons can be seen less as an indication of Earle's musical abilties than as the diversion of money to a new purpose.

Gibbons could now feel that he was extremely successful. His method of bettering his position is in contrast to that of his predecessor in the Chapel Royal, William Byrd, who collected leases on properties but whose only court post was one of organist. New times demanded a new approach to advancement, and Gibbons took advantage of his opportunities by acquiring appointments. He held the post of organist in

155 A receipt similar to RCM MS 2187, bearing Gibbons's signature but otherwise not in his hand, is in the library of the Fitzwilliam Museum, Cambridge. It is dated 10 April 1619, and acknowledges the payment of £10 'for my quat^{rs} pencion due to me from his highnes at the feast of the Annunciation ... last past'. BL Additional MS 33965, no. 42A, a document of 1 February 1619/20, is signed by Gibbons in acknowledgement of receipt of his quarterly pension of ten pounds, due at the previous Christmas, from 'Adam Newton esq^{er} Treasurer or Receavo^{r} generall to the Prince his Highnes'. Other records of payments to Gibbons as one of the Prince's musicians (all in PRO) are: SC6/James I/1681 (1618); SC6/James I/1682, duplicated in E101/434/15 (1619), SC6/James I/1683 and E101/435/5 (1620), SC6/James I/1684 and E101/435/9 (1621); SC6/James I/1685 and E101/435/12 (1622), SC6/James I/1686 (1623); SC6/James I/1687 (1624), SC6/James I/1630 (1625). Periods covered are summarized by Ashbee, 1986-96, iv, pp. 220, 222-226, 228-229.

156 PRO, E351/544, m. 112^{r}; Ashbee, 1986-96, iv, p. 106. Subsequent payments are recorded in E351/544: m. 128^{r} (1620-21), m. 142^{r} (1621-22), m. 154^{v} (1622-23), m. 169^{r} (1623-24), m. 182^{v} (1624-25, half a year's payment only) ; Ashbee, iv, pp. 108, 110, 112, 114 and iii, p. 133.

157 *Letters and papers*, 1896, p. 9, no. 21. See also Pinto, 1993.

158 PRO, LC2/2, f. 44^{r}, LC2/4/2, f. 26^{r}, 33^{r}, and E101/427/5, f. 58; Ashbee, 1986-96, iv, pp. 1, 2, vii, p. 131, and viii, p. 7.

the Chapel Royal, at a salary of forty pounds a year, a place worth another forty pounds among Prince Charles's musicians, and his new post in the Privy Chamber.

The records are not always clear about whose Privy Chamber it was in which Gibbons served. The words 'his Highness' were not reserved for the Prince. When Gibbons received bonds forfeited to the King by Laurence Brewster in 1615 he was described as 'his highnes Organist'; and when in 1620 he received a contribution towards the cost of the Chapel Feast, which must have been given by the King as in earlier years,[159] it was 'his highnes guifte'. The balance of probability is however that Gibbons, already a member of Prince Charles's musical establishment, was now appointed additionally to serve in the Prince's Privy Chamber.[160] The assumption is supported by Gibbons's subsequent association with a select group of musicians led by John Coprario.

The name of the violist John Coprario at first appears separately from the names of other musicians in Newton's accounts, where in March 1617/18 he was described as 'for his highness speciall use and service'.[161] But by 1622 he was 'one of his Highnes musicians in ordinary'.[162] 'Coprarios musique' seems to have been a distinct unit formed about this time. When, in 1625 the violinist John Woodington unsuccessfully sought a place which had become vacant on the death of John Sturte, he was described as 'Musition to K. James 6 yeares, and to his Ma[tie] [the former Prince Charles] in Coperarios musique 3 yeares'.[163]

Under a warrant of 1634/5 Woodington was paid for providing 'a new sett of books ... by his Ma[tes] speciall coṁannd'. The wording of the warrant is expanded in the Audit Office accounts, where the books are described as 'prickt wth all Coperaries & Orlando Gibbons theire Musique'.[164] The books may have been a set copied by several hands, perhaps under Woodington's supervision, and are now divided between

159 See p. 52.

160 After Gibbons's death, when Thomas Warwick was granted the two salaries Gibbons had received as one of Prince Charles's musicians and as a musician in the Privy Chamber, he was described as one of 'his Ma[tes] musicians in ordinary' (see p. 228 but this is explained by the fact that Charles had then become King.

161 PRO, SC6/James I/1680; Ashbee, 1986-96, iv, p. 217.

162 PRO, SC6/James I/1686, the wardrobe accounts for 1623 recording a payment made under a warrant of 4 April 1622.

163 BL, Additional MS 64883, f. 57[r]; Royal Commission on Historical Manuscripts, 1888, p. 195; Ashbee, 1986-96, v, p. 299. Woodington eventually obtained a supernumerary place when Adam Vallet died in October 1625 (PRO, SO3/8; Ashbee, 1986-96, iii, p. 12).

164 PRO, LC5/134, p. 43, AO1.394/72; Ashbee, iii, pp. 81, 150.

Christ Church, Oxford, and the British Library.[165] They contain music by Coprario for one or two violins, a bass viol and an organ, and fantasias by Gibbons for the double bass. As Coprario did not long survive Gibbons, all the music is likely to have been written by 1625. The violin parts may have been played by Thomas Lupo and Woodington, while the viol part may have been played by Robert Taylor or Alphonso Ferrabosco. Gibbons must have played the organ.[166]

Fantazies of III. Parts

At about the time of his latest appointment, Gibbons published *Fantazies of III. Parts*. This collection of pieces for viols was engraved by William Hole (or, less probably, by someone following as closely as possible the style Hole had adopted from Verovio). Gibbons must have recognized the elegance of Hole's engraving, and chosen to make further use of his services for that reason. There was no practical need for Gibbons to have the fantazies engraved, since moveable type would have presented no difficulties in the setting of separate parts. Gibbons dedicated the fantazies 'To the patterne of virtue & my ho^ble freind Mr Edward Wraye one of ye Groomes of his Ma^ts bedChamber'.[167] The dedication helps to date printing to the period July 1618 to February 1621/2, for Wraye was appointed groom of the bedchamber with effect from 24 June 1618;[168] and was banished from court in March 1622 as the result of his marriage to Elizabeth Norris.[169] It is fairly certain that Wraye owed both his post and his loss of it, directly or indirectly, to the King's favourite, George

165 The string parts are Christ Church MSS Mus. 732-735. Grey paper covers are incorporated into the vellum binding, and inside that of Mus. 732 is written the name 'John Wodenton'. The back cover of Mus. 734 bears the name 'Woodington' in a different hand which seems to be Woodington's own (see Lefkowitz, 1965, pl.1, no. 5). The organ part is BL MS R.M. 24.k.3. For a succinct summary of research on the compilation of these books, see Wainwright, 1997, pp. 61-64.

166 On the part played by this group in the development of English music, see Holman, 1993, pp. 213-224.

167 Wraye lived from 1589 to 1657. His life is traced by Pinto, 1996, pp. 95-98. Wraye is among the surprisingly numerous, and often notable, residents of the parish of St Margaret's, Westminster, who (principally in the year 1618-19) paid for licences to eat flesh in Lent (Westminster Archives, Overseers' accounts; see also Smith, 1900, p. 94).

168 PRO, SO3/6, entries for February and March 1618/9. Pinto (1996, p. 96) says Christmas 1618, but the appointment ran from the feast of John the Baptist, i.e. 24 June. It was the feast of St John, apostle and evangelist, which fell on 27 December.

169 PRO, SP14/128 no 96; CSPD, 1858(b), p. 366; Chamberlain, 1939, ii, p. 429.

Villiers.[170] When Elizabeth Norris eloped with Wraye plans were being laid for her marriage to Villiers's brother Christopher, an earlier appointee to the Privy Chamber who became Master of the Robes in 1618.[171]

Wraye may have shared a love of music with his elder brother John, who later employed an organist in his household,[172] but any other reason advanced for Gibbons's dedication can be no more than speculative. One possibility is that, while Wraye was in a position to help, Gibbons dedicated the *Fantazies* to him in the hope of securing a post. This would mean that he did so before January 1619/20, when he obtained a post in the Privy Chamber. Alternatively, the dedication may be an expression of gratitude for a post already obtained, in which case it would have been made after January 1619/20.[173]

According to the preface of *XX. Konincklycke Fantasien* (Amsterdam, 1648), in which Gibbons's pieces were reprinted, they were composed for 'the greatest monarchs in Europe', and were intended to celebrate a proposed marriage between Prince Charles and the Spanish Infanta.[174] This, however, seems improbable. James I had entertained the notion of a marriage between the heir to the English throne and a Spanish princess even when Prince Henry was alive, but the writer must surely have been mistaken if he believed the pieces to have been composed in anticipation of a successful outcome to negotiations which were begun in 1617 and dragged on until their final collapse in 1623 (by which time the *Fantazies* were already in print).[175]

170   George Villiers (1592-1628): cup-bearer, 1614; Gentleman of the Bedchamber, 1615 (appointed by King James in defiance of Somerset); Master of the Horse, January 1615/6; Order of the Garter, April 1616; Viscount Villers and Baron Waddon, August 1616; Earl of Buckingham, January 1616/7; Marquess of Buckingham, January 1618/9; First Duke of Buckingham, May 1623.

171   Her uncle, Henry de Vere, eighteenth Earl of Oxford, was committed to the Tower for his part in the elopement.

172   Edward and John were sons of Sir William Wraye of Glentworth, Lincolnshire. John succeeded to the baronetcy on the death of Sir William in 1617. The organist was named Goodwin; he left Sir John's employment in or before January 1632/3, before his indenture expired (Hulse, 1996, pp. 83, 86-87, quoting Huntingdon Library MS EL 6502).

173   The suggestion made by Pinto (1996, pp. 100-102), that the *Fantazies* were engraved as a wedding gift for Wraye, is highly speculative.

174   'om datse tot vermaeck der grootste Monarchen van *Europe* gestelt zyn, en weerdigh gevonden om de Bruylofts-staetsi van *Spenje* en *Engeland* te verheerlycken; dewelke mislukt zynde ...'

175   See p. 62

It is evident that the *Fantazies* were initially printed for presentation to Wraye and other selected individuals, as two surviving copies bear no imprint. The imprint was added later by the alteration of the plate bearing the dedication, presumably when copies were placed on public sale. At some time, probably shortly after Gibbons's death, copies with the imprint were further altered by the addition of a title-page printed from moveable type.[176]

Gibbons was himself the subject of a dedication in Thomas Tomkins's *Songs of 3. 4. 5. and 6. parts* (1622).[177] Tomkins, the organist of Worcester Cathedral, was sworn in as a Gentleman of the Chapel Royal on 2 August 1621, as a replacement for Edmund Hooper, who had died on 14 July.

Gibbons's supposed doctorate

It is often said that in 1622 Gibbons obtained the degree of MusD at Oxford. There is much confusion about this, however. The writer of a note on the back of Gibbons's portrait at the Faculty of Music in Oxford believed him to be a Doctor, but the note probably dates from the nineteenth century and reflects a common misconception. Wood was the first to investigate the matter, and wrote: 'On the 17 of *May Orlando Gibbons* one of the Organists of his Majesties Chappel, did supplicate the venerable Congregation that he might accumulate the degrees in Musick; but whether he was admitted to the one, or licensed to proceed in the other, it appears not'.[178]

Wood drew his information from the University's Registers of Convocation and Congregation. The former records the supplications of 'Richus Heither' (correctly William Heyther) on 17 May 1622 for a BMus, and for permission to accumulate the degrees in music. Each entry is followed by another of the same date, recording a supplication by Orlando Gibbons 'sub eadē forma'.[179] Under the heading

---

176 See pp. 283-286. The sequence of events outlined here accords closely with that postulated by Holman, 1993, p. 220.

177 *Chloris, whenas I wooe* was dedicated 'To Mr. Orlando Gibbons'.

178 Wood, 1691-92, i, col. 842 (1813-20, *Fasti*, i, col. 406). In his manuscript notes on musicians Wood writes of Gibbons as 'D^r of Musick quere' (Bodleian Library MS Wood 19 D(4) 106, f. 58^r). Venn (1922-27, ii, p. 209) states that Gibbons 'Supp. for MusD at Oxford 1622'; Foster (1891-92, i., p. 560) says that Gibbons 'Suppl. B. and D. Mus. 17 May 1622'.

179 Oxford University Archives, NEP/Supra/Reg N, f. 144^v; Clark, 1887-88, i, p. 148. William Heyther or Heather (c.1563-1627) was a lay clerk of Westminster Abbey from 1568 to 1615, when he became a Gentleman of the Chapel Royal. He

'Admissiones Baccalaureorū in Musica', the Register of Congregation contains the entry: 'Richūs Heyther maij 17° 1622'. A second entry, under the heading 'Admissiones Doctorū in Musica', indicates Heyther's receipt of a doctorate on the same day.[180] The next entry records the award of a doctorate to Nathaniel Giles, Master of the Children of the Chapel Royal, who had supplicated for it in 1607 after receiving a BMus on 26 June 1585.[181] This entry is dated 5 July, but there is reason to believe that Giles received his degree on the same day as William Heyther (see below). There is no further mention of Orlando Gibbons.

A letter written to William Camden by William Piers on 18 May 1622, the day after Heyther received his doctorate, seems at first glance to put beyond doubt the question of whether Gibbons received a doctorate.[182] Camden, who was friendly with Heyther, lived in the parish of St Margaret's, and must have known Gibbons as well. Piers was the Vice-Chancellor of the University of Oxford, and his letter reads:

Worthy Sir,

The University returns her humble thanks to you with this Letter. We pray for your health and long life, that you may see the fruits of your bounty. We have made *Mr. Heather* a Doctor in Musick, so that now he is no more Master, but Doctor *Heather*. The like honour for your sake we have conferred upon Mr. *Orlando Gibbons*, and made him a Doctor too to accompany Doctor *Heather*. We have paid Mr. D. *Heather*'s charges for this journey, and likewise given him the *Oxford* courtesie, a pair of Gloves for himself, and another for his wife. Your honour is far above all these things. And so desiring the continuance of your loving favour to the University, and to me your Servant, I take my leave.

Oxon. 18 May.   Yours ever to be commanded,
1622.   William Peirs.

A footnote to the second edition of Boyce's *Cathedral Music* (1788), evidently written by Hawkins, refers obliquely to Piers's letter and says that Boyce heard it reported that Gibbons was a Doctor, but doubted the truth of it because he was not so styled on his monument. John Chamberlain, writing to Sir Dudley Carleton on 13 July 1622, said it

---

consistently appears as 'Richard' in the University's records quoted here.

180   Oxford University Archives, NEP/Supra/Reg Sa f. 298^v.

181   Ibid., ff. 49^v, 52^r; Clark, 1887-88, i, p. 146.

182   Camden, 1691, p. 329; postscript omitted here. The letter is quoted by Burney, 1776-89, iii, p. 359 (1935, ii, p. 286), and by Hawkins, 1776, iv, p. 31 (1963, p. 572). It appears to be behind the information in Williams, 1893, p. 122.

was Nathaniel Giles who received a doctorate with Heyther.[183] It may be that Piers wrote something like 'G——s', which his editor interpreted as 'Gibbons', but as the original letter seems to have perished this cannot be verified.

The likelihood that Gibbons never received a doctorate is supported not only by the inscription on the monument, but by several other pieces of evidence. In recording the amount of black cloth allocated for the funeral of King James I, the Cheque Book of the Chapel Royal refers to both Nathaniel Giles and William Heyther as 'doctor', but describes Gibbons as 'senior Organist'. The title-page of the third state of Gibbons's *Fantazies*, probably issued after his death, still describes him as a Bachelor of Music. Tenbury MS 791, compiled c.1633-35, distinguishes the titles of 'Mr Gibons' and 'Dr Giles'. The word books of the Chapel Royal (compiled after 1660, but presumably relying on earlier sources) refer simply to 'Orlando Gibbons', while Giles and Bull invariably receive the title 'Dr'.[184] Christ Church MS Mus. 21 distinguishes Orlando Gibbons from his son Christopher, whose name is inserted (by a hand later than that which began the manuscript) as 'Dr Gibbons'.

Whatever may be the truth of the matter, it is probable that Gibbons wrote the anthem performed in the Act for Heyther. Wood says that 'one or more eminent musicians then living have several times told me' that this was the case. In the 'Gostling' part-books the anthem *O clap your hands*, for eight voices, is described as 'D^r. Hether's Commencem^t Song sett by M^r. Orl. Gibbons'.[185]

Two patents

Gibbons's association with Heyther at this time extended to their attempt, with others, to obtain a monopoly for the manufacture of strings for musical instruments. An entry of May 1622 in the Signet Office docquet books is written as though it had been granted.

A Privilege to Orlando Gibbons, Adam Vallett, Thomas Daye, Willm̃ Heather, and John Clarke, and their Assignes, for the sole making of all strings for musicall Instruments, called Venice, or Romish minikin, and Catlin strings, for fourteene yeares; wth a prohibicõn for importacõn of any

183   PRO, SP14/132 no. 38 (small manuscript numbering); Chamberlain, 1939, ii, p. 447; CSPD, 1858(b), p. 424, which omits the reference to Giles.

184   BL, Harleian MS 6346; Bodleian Library, Rawlinson MS Poet. 23.

185   York Minster Library, MSS 1/1-8, thought to date from c.1675.

such strings. paying to his Matie the yearely rent of 16^{li}. Subscribed by m^r Sollicitor, by order from m^r Secretary Calvert, and by him procured [186]

The grant must however have been withheld at the last moment, for a marginal annotation says 'staid'. This was almost certainly a result of the attack on monopolies begun by the Parliament which met in January 1620/1, when the King averted the threat of a Monopolies Bill by promising to cancel monopolies which existed and scrutinize petitions for new ones.[187]

Around this time Gibbons was invited to write tunes for biblical paraphrases and religious verse by George Wither, who may have provided the texts for some of Gibbons's anthems.[188] Wither initially published a collection under the title *The Songs of the Old Testament* (1621). He revised and enlarged this as *The Hymnes and Songs of the Church*, which appeared with Gibbons's music and a dedication to King James in 1623.[189] Wither obtained a royal warrant requiring that 'no copy of the psalm book in metre shall be bound up without the said Hymns being annexed thereto'.[190] It had therefore to be printed in formats from 32mo up to folio, and owing to the requirements of the printers' guilds the music had to be reset on each occasion.[191] Wither's patent caused him a good deal of bother.[192] On 10 March 1622/3 the Stationers' Company appointed a committee to talk to him about it, and an entry of 21 February 1626/7 in the Company's records states: 'It is ordered that if mr withers will deliv^r to mr weaver acertaine number of his hymnes of every volume, That mr weaver shall deliv^r them out to the bookesellers who are to binde them wth the Psalmes and preferr them to Costomers and he is every quarter to account wth mr withers and allowe him for so many of the same as shalbe sold as shalbe agreed upon betwixt him and the Company'. Another entry, of 27 March 1633, reads: 'The now Stockkeeps m^r Islip and the rest are requested by the Table to treat with M^r. Withers about his proporcōns concerning his

186   PRO, SO3/7; Ashbee, 1986-96, iv, p. 55.

187   The device of raising money by charging for monopolies was to be used more widely by Charles I.

188   See note 49 on p. 153.

189   For a brief account of Wither's life and *The Hymnes and Songs of the Church*, see Gibbons, 1978, pp. ix-xii. See also Scholes, 1934, pp. 156-158.

190   PRO, C66/2270, no. 11.

191   The stemmatic relationship of the different editions is described by Wulstan, in Gibbons, 1978, pp. 203-204. See also *A short-title catalogue*, 1976-86, nos. 25908-25910a.7.

192   Greg, 1967, pp. 62, 69, 72-73, 90, 93, 212-218, 230-231.

himnes & to Certify the Table of their doeings'.[193] A year later Wither petitioned the Privy Council for aid against the Stationers,[194] and when he published *The Psalmes of David* in 1632 he sent them to the Netherlands to be printed.

Westminster Abbey

Gibbons gained a new source of income when, in addition to the posts he already held, he was appointed organist of Westminster Abbey in succession to John Parsons, who had filled the post from 1621 until his death in August 1623. Prior to that the post of organist had been held for many years by Gibbons's Chapel Royal colleague Edmund Hooper.[195] During Gibbons's tenure, the post of master of the choristers was filled by another Chapel Royal musician, Thomas Day.[196]

Gibbons marked his appointment with a gift to the Abbey of two books. An entry in the Abbey's Benefactors' Book records that 'Mr Orlando Gibbons Organist of S^t: Peters Church at Westminster gave as followeth / John Speedes *Chronicle of the Kings of England: Fol: Together wth: another Volume of the Mapps of all the Shires, & Townes*

---

193   Jackson, 1957, pp. 156, 192, 247.

194   PRO, SP16/263 no. 80; CSPD, 1863, p. 533.

195   le Huray (1978, p. 73) notes: 'The links between Westminster Abbey and the Chapel Royal certainly grew very close — so close, in fact, that by 1625 well over half the Abbey choirmen were Gentlemen'. Wither's dedication of *The Hymnes and Songs of the Church* was evidently printed before Gibbons obtained his Abbey post, and refers to him only as 'your MAJESTIES servant, and one of the Gentlemen of your honourable Chapell'.

196   Westminster Abbey, WAM 33681, f. 2^r, covering the period up to Michaelmas 1624, has the entry: 'Ma͠gr chorist Et in denar hoc anno sol Orlando Gibbons et Tho͠m Daye p̱ an͠n — x^{li}'. The next entry reads: 'Chorist. Et in denar hoc anno sol Tho͠m Daye pro decem chorist ad lxvjs viij^d pro quolt cop p̱ an͠n — xxxiij^{li} vj^s viij^d'. The entries are repeated in WAM 33682, f. 34^v, covering 1625-26. Shaw (1991, pp. 329-330) notes: 'the stipend of the master of the choristers has the names of both Gibbons and Thomas Day entered against it ... Day, however, is credited with the allowances for the choristers and the "regard" for teaching them. One cannot believe that Gibbons shared a stipend with Day; clearly, he succeeded Parsons in his capacity as organist, and what we see in the accounts is the continuing inability of the treasurer to express how matters stood since the division of the two offices under Hooper, their reunion under Parsons, and now their separation once again'. WAM 33682, f. 34^v, also records a payment 'To Thomas Dalh͠m for tuneinge the Organes for one whole yeare — } xls'.

of England, & Wales: Lond. 1622'.[197] The copies now in the Abbey's library are unfortunately not those donated by Gibbons.[198]

Gibbons's appointment to his new post coincided with the death of his father-in-law, John Patten, who was buried at St Margaret's, Westminster, on 15 September 1623. Gibbons was his executor, and on 17 September proved his will, which had been witnessed by Thomas Tomkins's brother Peregrine.[199] Patten left two hundred pounds to Elizabeth Gibbons, his daughter, and to Gibbons's children. After bequests to his son Richard and his grandson Oliver, and other smaller gifts, Patten left the remainder of his possessions to Gibbons.

The Chapel at Whitehall Palace and the Abbey were close to each other, and each was within a stone's throw of Gibbons's home, but if he continued to fulfil his responsibilities in the Chapel, he must occasionally have deputed someone to play the Abbey organ. Anthony à Wood's manuscript notes on Richard Portman say 'He was bred up under Orlando Gibbons', so it is possible that he acted as a deputy.[200] He succeeded to the post of organist at the Abbey upon Gibbons's death.[201]

Another to receive instruction from Gibbons was John Hingston, said by Hawkins to have been his 'scholar'. Hawkins also recounts an anecdote, 'communicated by one of Hingston's descendants now living, to wit, that the Christian name Orlando, for reasons which they have hitherto been ignorant of, has in several instances been given to the males of the family'.[202] Hingston, who had been a chorister at York Minster, was apprenticed as an organist to Francis Clifford, the Fourth

197 Westminster Abbey Muniment Room, Benefactors' Book, f. 48[r]. The entry is not dated, but evidently belongs to 1623 or 1624.

198 The book by Speed was probably the second edition of *The Historie of Great Britain*, published in 1623. The Abbey's present copy (shelfmark L.4.38) carries the bookplate of Edward Stanley (the father of Dean Stanley), and the title-page is signed 'William Holland N°. 50 Oxford S[t]. 1797'. The Abbey's book of maps (T.4.22) has the date 1676 stamped on the modern binding, though the date on many of the maps is 1610, which has in some cases been altered in manuscript to 1666.

199 See p. 277.

200 Bodleian Library, Wood MS D.19(4), f. 103[v].

201 Westminster Abbey, WAM 33682. The records are slightly confused, but their import is clear. See Shaw, 1991, p. 330.

202 Hawkins, 1776, iv, p. 44 (1963, p. 577); the information is confirmed by Hulse, 1983, p. 25. Hawkins refers to a lost manuscript in Hingston's hand, entitled 'My Masters Songs in score with some Fantazias of 6 parts of my own'. He says: 'The Fantazias stand first in the book, and are about six in number, some subscribed Jo. Hingston, Jan. 1640, and other dates; the songs are subscribed Orlando Gibbons'. See also note 151 on p. 59.

Earl of Cumberland. Clifford was well acquainted with musicians who worked at or for the court, and it was to him that William Byrd dedicated his *Psalmes, songs, and sonnets* (1611). Thomas Campion, in a verse dedication of *Two books of ayres* (1613?), wrote of Clifford as one 'Whose House the *Muses* pallace I have knowne'. It is probable that when, in 1621, Hingston was sent to London 'to learne to play', Clifford chose Gibbons to train the young man, which he continued to do at least until October 1623. By February 1624/5 Hingston had returned to Yorkshire.[203] The period of instruction was short, but in his will, made in 1683, Hingston referred to Gibbons as 'my ever Hono^rd. Master'.[204]

Hawkins believed the younger Randall Jewett also to have been 'a scholar of Orlando Gibbons'.[205] He would have been of the right age, since he is thought to have been born about 1603, but the possibility cannot be confirmed beyond doubt. Jewett's grandfather, William, was sworn in as a Gentleman of the Chapel Royal on 18 June 1569,[206] and therefore belonged to the same generation of Gentlemen as William Byrd. Jewett's father, Randall, who died at Chester in 1619, is reputed to have sung in the Chapel. This notion seems to derive from British Library Harleian MS 2163.[207] The entry for the older Randall has the words 'marchant' and 'a singer [in?] kyng*es* chappell' inserted above the line by a later hand, which also added a marginal entry written in 1619 or after. It may, however, be that the writer confused the older Randall Jewett with his father, William.

Gibbons appears in his own person as the organist of the Abbey in a holograph note of 1625, assuring William Ireland that a bill submitted by the organ-maker John Burward can safely be paid:

Mr Ierland I know this bill to be very resonable for I have alredy Cut him off ten shillings therfore I pray despathe him for he hath delt honestly wth ye Church soe shall I rest y^r serfant

Orlando Gibbons[208]

203 Hulse, 1983, p. 25.

204 PRO, Prob. 11/375, ff. 134^r-135^r (probate copy).

205 Hawkins, 1776, iv, p. 64 (1963, ii, p. 584). The name appears in various forms, e.g. Randle or Randolph, Juet or Jwett. For an account of Jewett's career, see Shaw, 1991, as indexed.

206 Cheque Book, f. 5^r ; Rimbault, 1872, pp. 2, 55. The year is mistakenly given as 1568, but also correctly as 11 Elizabeth, i.e. 1569.

207 f. 76^r (now 82^r), apparently quoted by Bridge, 1913, p. 83.

208 Westminster Abbey, WAM 53317, dated on the back 'Midsom^r q^tr 1625'. See plate 5. The note was first reproduced in an exhibition catalogue (Musicians' Company, 1909, p. 334), and was believed at the time to provide the only surviving example of

The marriage and coronation of Charles I

One of the most ill-conceived projects of King James's reign was the intended marriage of Prince Charles to the Infanta of Spain. Its collapse, and the Prince's return from Madrid in October 1623 as a bachelor and a Protestant, was greeted with rejoicing in England. The feeling was evidently shared by Gibbons, who is credited with marking the occasion by writing a catch that begins: 'Orlando was his name that first did make this same in honour of his highnesse coming out of Spain'.[209]

The joy of the English was somewhat tempered when Charles embarked, with the encouragement of Buckingham, on a scheme for an alliance with Henrietta Maria, the Catholic sister of Louis XIII of France. A treaty for the marriage was concluded in Paris in 1624.[210] The formal betrothal took place on 15 December,[211] and was celebrated in London by an entertainment for the French ambassadors, given with the King's approval by the Lord Keeper.

The King's Will signified, the invitement at a Supper was given and taken. Which was provided in the College of *Westminster*, in the Room named *Hierusalem* Chamber;[212] but for that night it might have been call'd *Lucullus* his *Apollo*. But the Ante-past was kept in the Abby, as it went before the Feast, so it was beyond it, being purely an Episcopal Collation. The Embassadors, with the Nobles and Gentlemen in their company, were brought in at the North-Gate of the Abby, which was stuck with Flambeaux everywhere, both within, and without the Quire, that strangers might cast their Eyes upon the stateliness of the Church. At the Door of the Quire the Lord Keeper besought their Lordships to go in, and to take their Seats there, for a while, promising in the Word of a Bishop that nothing of ill Relish should be offered before them; which they accepted; and at their Entrance the Organ was touch'd by the best Finger of that Age, Mr. *Orlando Gibbons*.

Gibbons's handwriting. Ireland, who was related to William Heyther, held several minor posts at the Abbey. See Harley, 1997, pp. 27-28, although it now seems likely that William Byrd's nephew was not William Ireland of Westminster, but William Ireland of the parish of St Andrew by the Wardrobe, a member of the Haberdasher's Company (Harley, 1998, p. 482).

209   Duffin, 1993.

210   PRO, SP108/544.

211   Christmas Day according to the Gregorian calendar used in France.

212   Added to the mediaeval house of the Abbots of Westminster by Nicholas de Litlyngton (Abbot 1362-86). The entertainment of the French Ambassadors was commemorated by John Williams, at the time Dean of Westminster and Lord Keeper of the Great Seal, who erected the present overmantel.

While a Verse was plaid, the Lord Keeper presented the Embassadors, and the rest of the Noblest Quality of their Nation, with our Liturgy, as it spake to them in their own Language; and in the Delivery of it used these few Words, but Pithy: *That their Lordships at Leisure might Read in that Book, in what Form of Holiness our Prince Worshipp'd God, wherein he durst say nothing savour'd of any Corruption of Doctrine, much less of Heresie, which he hoped would be so reported to the Lady Princess* Henrietta. The Lords Embassadors, and their Great Train took up all the Stalls, where they continued about half an Hour, while the Quire-men, Vested in their Rich Copes, with their Choristers, sung three several Anthems with most exquisite Voices before them. The most honourable and the meanest persons of the French Attended all that time uncover'd, with great Reverence, except that Secretary *Villoclare* alone kept on his Hat. And when all others carried away the Books of Common Prayer commended to them, he only left his in the Stall of the Quire, where he had sate; which was not brought after him (*Ne Margarita*, etc.) as if he had forgot it.[213]

Marriage articles were signed in Cambridge three days later.[214]

King James's health now declined sharply. He became seriously ill on 24 March 1624/5, and died at Theobalds on 27 March. For embalming his body, William Walker, a surgeon, received a gift of fifty pounds from the new King. The burial at Westminster Abbey did not take place until 7 May. This meant that Charles could not journey to Paris, as he had planned. He was instead married by proxy on 1 May, in a ceremony before the doors of Notre Dame at which he was represented by Buckingham.[215]

The Cheque Book of the Chapel Royal contains a long account of the funeral of King James, and the preparations for it.[216] The King's body was first carried from Theobalds to Denmark House, where it lay in a temporary chapel attended by all his officers except the members of the Chapel Royal. They waited on King Charles at Whitehall, until two days before the funeral. Then, at Denmark House,

the corps were brought into y[e] sayd Chappell in greate solemnitie w[th] an Anthem, & sett under an hearse of velvett, and the gent: of the chappell frõ that tyme wayted there, & pformed solemne service w[th] the Organs brought thither for that purpose, they also wayted w[t]h the corps by course night and

213   Hacket, 1692, p. 210.
214   PRO, SP14/176 no. 65; CSPD, 1859, p. 411.
215   11 May in France. PRO, SP16/2 no. 27; CSPD, 1858(c), p. 19; Chamberlain, 1939, ii, p. 614.
216   Cheque Book, ff. 70[v]-71[r]; Rimbault, 1872, pp. 154-156.

day, by night first Decany syde, and next Cantoris syde, & twise in the night, viz at nine of the clock & at midnight they had prayers wth a first & second Chapters, & ended wth an Anthem ... Kinge Charles resided all the tyme that the corps lay at denmark house at Whithall beinge attended by his officers & servant*es* as he had while he was Prince, & there the gent: of the Chappell wayted: the Chappell there was also hunge as that at Denmark house ... all these afforesayd h333333hanging*es*, tafata traverse, Chayer, ffootestoole, cusshions, Carpett*es*, pulpitt clothe, deske cloth, &c, were fees to the gent: of the Chappell, and divided amongest them, wherin the officers of the vestery had also their ptes accordinge to their Places ... Kinge Charles was him selfe in pson the cheife mourner, & ffollowed the Corps of his ffather on foote from Denmark house unto Westminster churche: and the wardrop being unprovided of a traverse & other necessaries for Westminster church, wch could not sufficiently be provided, a warrant frõ the Lo: Chamberlaine to the deane of the Chappell was pcured to borrow the traverse in the Chappell at Whitehall, some of the Cusshions & carpetts: all wch were restored back againe by the Lo: Chamberlaines comaund unto the gent: of the Chappell as their propper fees & duties ...

The Cheque Book records that 'Orlando Gibbons, senior Organist' was among those who each received an allowance of nine yards of black cloth for themselves, with an allowance of two yards apiece for their servants.[217] A document entitled 'The president of the Funerall of our late Dread Soveraigne of Blessed Memory King JAMES' confirms these allowances, and shows that Gibbons received another four yards as organist of Westminster Abbey.[218]

It is to the Cheque Book that we have to turn again for an account of the coronation of Charles I.[219] The ceremony took place on Candlemas Day, 2 February 1625/6:

Upon which day all the Chappell mett at the Colledge hall in Westminster wher they had a breakfast at the charge of the Colledge, from thence they went by a back way into the Church & so into the vestrie, where together wth the Quier of Westminster they putt on surplesses & Copes, & went into

217   Cheque Book, f. 71^r; Rimbault, 1872, p. 156.

218   PRO, LC2/6, ff. 42^v, 55^r; Ashbee, 1986-96, iii, pp. 2-3. Gibbons's name bears the annotation 'privy organ' when it occurs with those of the Gentlemen of the Chapel Royal, and 'organiste' when it occurs with those of the singing men of Westminster Abbey. A further document concerning the funeral sets out the order of precedence, mainly by office, but lumps together 'The whoole Chappell and vestry in there Copes' (PRO, SP16/2, no. 29; CSPD, 1858(c), p. 20).

219   Cheque Book, f.71^v; Rimbault, 1872, pp. 157-160.

Westminster hall, & there wayted untill the Kinge came thither, who came
from Whitehall by water ... The Chappell followed the knights of the privie
Counsell who went next after the knights of the Bath, the Sergeant Porter w[th]
his black staff, & Sergeant of the Vestry wth his virge goinge before them,
next the Quier of westminster, then the Chappell, who went singinge through
the Pallace yard, & round about the church through the great Sanctuarie till
they came to the west dore of the church, when all the Chappell were within
the church, they began the first Anthem.

The Cheque Book lists all the anthems sung during the ceremony, but
none is among the surviving works of Gibbons. It was in fact Thomas
Tomkins who composed 'many songs against the Coronacōn of Kinge
Charles'.[220]

After all y[e] ceremonie in the Church was ended, the Kinge returned back
againe into Westminster hall in the same manner as he went, the Chappell
goeinge in their former order & singinge all the waye, till they came to
Westminster hall dore, & their they stayed makeinge a lane for y[e] Kinge &
all the lord*es* to passe betwixt them, & continued singinge till the Kinge was
w[th]in the hall: & frō thence they returned back into the church, where, in the
vestry they putt of their Copes & surplusses, & came to White hall, wher
they had some allowance of diett for their suppers.

220   Cheque Book, f. 1[v].

3

ORLANDO GIBBONS'S PERSONALITY AND MUSIC

Although so much is known of Gibbons's family and his life, there are two important gaps. One concerns his activities after he left King's College and before he joined the Chapel Royal. Unless his name is found in some so far undiscovered document, the gap will not be filled. The other lack is of a contemporary statement about the sort of man he was. The posts he held at court and at Westminster Abbey testify to the regard in which he was held as a musician, as do references to him as 'the best Finger of that Age' and 'the best hand in england',[1] but there is little to cast light on his personality and social relationships.

Gibbons achieved professional success at a remarkably early age,[2] and as far as we know his career then proceeded smoothly until his premature death. Compared with the lives of his Chapel Royal predecessors William Byrd (who was constantly in the courts on account of his Catholicism and battles over property) and John Bull (who found it expedient to flee the country), Gibbons's life was decidedly dull. In the absence of evidence to the contrary, it must be assumed that he gave satisfaction to his employers and their representatives, and was on good terms with his fellow musicians. He collaborated with Byrd and Bull in *Parthenia*, and received Thomas Tomkins's dedication of *Chloris, whenas I wooe*; he seems at least once to have been chosen as senior steward of the Chapel Feast; and he is said to have helped William Heyther by providing music for him to submit in connection with the award of a doctorate by Oxford University. Otherwise the records contain very little of a personal nature. His patrons Sir Christopher and Lady Alice Hatton appear to have become his friends, as does Edward Wraye, a groom of the King's bedchamber. The facts that he was a near neighbour of his father-in-law in the Woolstaple, and evidently maintained warm relations with his brother Edward, who seems to have accepted some responsibility for him when he was young and to have taken charge of his children when he died, suggest a solid family background — his monument claims that he was a 'most admirable

---

1   Hacket, 1692, p. 210; PRO, SP16/3, no. 60 (CSPD 1858(c), p. 43; Chamberlain, 1939, ii, p. 622.

2   His appointment to the Chapel Royal, probably at the age of nineteen, is even more impressive than William Byrd's appointment, in his early twenties, as organist and master of the choristers at Lincoln Cathedral.

husband' — but in documents he appears only as a son and brother carrying out the duties that follow a death.

The inscription on Gibbons's monument tells us, too, that he was of upright character and possessed charm — but it would be an unusual inscription which said otherwise. Almost the only clues to his personality lie in his music, and that cannot tell us if he was habitually agreeable and even-tempered, for excellent music has been written by men who were neither. It is not even clear how far the somewhat sober personality reflected in much of his music represents his customary mien. There was certainly more to him, for although the music is often inclined to be subdued and serious, he had access to a span of emotion from the pensive to the intensely passionate, without excluding the romantic and pastoral spirit that often appears in the painting, literature and drama of his time. *The Cries of London* and his catch *Orlando was his name* suggest that he had a sense of humour, even if it was usually kept in check. Probably he knew where his strengths lay, and confined himself chiefly to exploring the areas of composition that most fascinated him, and in which he could achieve most.[3]

It is plain that Gibbons had a precocious musical talent, and though he was probably recruited to the Chapel Royal primarily as an organist, he was a young man able to turn his hand to any task that might be required of him. It is impossible to be sure quite how early and how quickly his talent flowered, because we cannot accurately date his early compositions. The first truly reliable point of chronological reference is provided by groups of pieces published in or about 1612, almost certainly a good many years after he had achieved mastery as a keyboard player and composer.

The compositions that are apparently among Gibbons's earliest show him working with materials developed by Byrd and others whose music he must have grown up singing and playing. His first instrumental compositions are likely to have included some unremarkable if competent keyboard fantasias and preludes, and other pieces for viol consort, all in a style that was becoming dated by the time Gibbons was born. One keyboard fantasia, so unlike his later work as to cause its authenticity to be in doubt, and one piece for viols (perhaps an arrangement of a pavan by someone else) may belong to his Cambridge years. A series of consort In Nomines shows him maturing rapidly. The greater maturity of two of them may be the fruit of contact with the

---

3 He seems to have made no attempt to compose for the lute, either as a solo or accompanying instrument, or for a broken consort made up of instruments of different kinds — or, unlike several of his contemporaries, to set Latin words, though this may have been because a commission never came his way.

experienced composers he met at court. It is possible that *Deliver us, O Lord*, which may be Gibbons's earliest surviving anthem, was written shortly before or after he joined the Chapel Royal, for it incorporates a substantial passage lifted from a piece which Weelkes published in 1601. Another probably early anthem, *Hosanna to the Son of David*, seems to show not only the influence of Weelkes, but of Byrd as well.

Byrd was Gibbons's senior by more than forty years, and had been retired from the day to day work of the Chapel Royal for over ten years when Gibbons joined it, yet he continued to write and publish music of supreme quality. It would have been difficult for a young composer of Gibbons's perception and aspirations not to be influenced by him, and Gibbons's so-called 'Second' Preces and his Short Service display an acute awareness of works by the older composer. Byrd's influence is there, too, in the more mature of Gibbons's In Nomines. The songs Gibbons published in 1612, and the *Salisbury* pavan and galliard published around the same time, show a deep indebtedness to Byrd, though there is no question that these works disclose a distinct personality, and that when they appeared Gibbons was at the height of his powers. Although Gibbons made important advances in new directions, he never totally abandoned the style he formed in early life, and it was very largely his facility in employing it that kept his reputation alive. Two things need to be said about this, however.

The first is that 'facility' is a word which often comes to mind in describing Gibbons's work. His music is invariably skilled, and much of it bears comparison with the work of his great predecessor William Byrd and his great successor Henry Purcell, but it is not without signs that he found composition almost too easy. Technical devices such as imitation, inversion and augmentation caused him no difficulty; but he did not possess the self-critical tenacity of a Byrd — or, if he possessed it, he did not always exercise it. Some assignments failed to engage his interest, and it shows. He never wrote anything that is perfunctory, but there are a number of pieces which might have benefited from greater attention. His major sets of keyboard variations are astonishingly brilliant, in the manner of Bull's, and like Bull's variations their construction does not stand up to close inspection. He was never casual, but one feels that he experienced no difficulty in surpassing most of his contemporaries, and sometimes saw no need to extend himself over a few details in order to improve music that easily went beyond the demands of the moment.

The inner compulsion that fired Byrd was evidently not always as strong in Gibbons. Time and again he was content to build passages from a series of notes that form a rising or falling scale, as though this was a tested formula, and there was no point in struggling to devise something different when a piece might be performed only once or twice, and would subsequently have a restricted circulation. This was natural enough for a hard-working musician of the seventeenth century, employed principally as a reliable and superior craftsman, and such lapses should not be unduly overemphasized. Often, no doubt, they result from works being written to fulfil special commissions, or hastily composed to meet unexpected demands. The prospect of publication inspired him to polish his work to a high degree. What is more, the strength of his personality and vision emerges on infinitely more occasions than any indication that he was too easily satisfied. So does the fecundity of his invention, never more clearly than in his response to a new text for setting to music.

The second thing to be said about the above statement is this: to judge Gibbons solely on the basis of the skill and ease with which he handled traditional methods of composition is to misjudge him. Although he continued until the end of his life to exhibit the influence of composers of a previous generation, the impression left by his work as a whole is of a bold and fertile innovator. He lived in an age of intellectual and geographical adventure: Bacon's *Advancement of Learning* was published two years after Gibbons joined the Chapel Royal, and the King to whom it was dedicated gave his name to the first permanent English settlement in America two years after that. Gibbons's music reflects something of the restlessness of his time. If a thorough grounding in traditional methods of composition gave him anything, it was the power to proceed confidently with his innovations. His vocal works and string fantasias contain much that reveals his training, but the evolution of his work shows a mind that was at once enquiring and imaginative, and richly equipped to deal with the problems he encountered. He increasingly cultivated forms and means of expression that were new and personal.

Although Gibbons's later music shows the influence of current musical tastes and styles, as well as being highly individual, his early demise must have meant that, without his presence, some of the more experimental aspects of his work were not taken up by others, and were ignored or unappreciated for that reason. This state of affairs was compounded by political upheavals that put a temporary end to the court and church for which his music was written and where it was chiefly performed. A few pieces — primarily those printed by Barnard and Boyce — kept Gibbons's memory alive, but he tended to be admired as a successor to Tallis and Byrd, working in a style not essentially different from theirs.[4] It was not until well into the twentieth century that the

---

4 It has to be admitted that evidence about the knowledge of Gibbons's music among

whole corpus of Gibbons's music became accessible in modern collected editions, and not until the second half of the century that a different picture of him began to emerge. He can still be seen as a composer trained in, and with a deep appreciation of, the music of his predecessors. But he was able to incorporate what he learned from them into music that was fashioned for a new age. It is now easier to view him also as a pioneer, whose work was cut short by his untimely death.

amateurs is slim, and it may have been greater than at first sight appears. The existence of a substantial amount of his music in print helped it to survive. Thomas Crosfield, writing on 20 April 1631, noted that 'Pitcher sould me a sett of choise MS. Song bookes 5 & 6 parts, also Allisons 5 parts, and Gibbons 5 parts' (Crosfield, 1935, p. 52; 'Allisons 5 parts' is Richard Allison, *An Howres Recreation in Musicke*, 1606). 'Gibbons Madrigals, 5 parts' and 'Gibbons 3 part fantasies, graven upon Copper' were listed by John Playford in *A catalogue of all the musick-bookes that have been printed in England, either for voyce or Instruments* (1653), which suggests that he may have acquired copies for sale. Several editions of *Parthenia* meant that some of Gibbons's keyboard music continued to be played for a considerable time.

4

KEYBOARD MUSIC

The body of Gibbons's keyboard works comprises fewer than fifty pieces, many of them short. It is not, perhaps, a great number for an outstanding keyboard player, whose career at the centre of English musical life lasted for twenty-two years, even bearing in mind his compositions of other kinds, and his duties as organist, choir master and performer in chamber ensembles. The supposition must be that Gibbons was a skilled improviser, and that much of what he played was never written down. A few of his extant pieces look as if they were composed early in his career, but there is nothing obviously from his student years, unless a fantasia (MB 20/48) based on an unidentified cantus firmus is to be accepted as genuinely by Gibbons.[1] Probably most of what survives was composed after he joined the Chapel Royal.

Twenty-nine keyboard compositions which can, with some confidence, be accepted as Gibbons's are found in sources compiled in his lifetime (see the table opposite).[2] These give little help in dating

1 It is excluded from the canon by Hendrie (in Gibbons, 1967). It is attributed to Gibbons in two of the six manuscripts in which it occurs: those of Cosyn (BL, R. M. 23.1.4) and Tunstall (BL, Additional 36661). Elsewhere it is anonymous, though Tomkins, who entitles it 'Kiri Eleyson' in his text, indexes it with Bull's In Nomines (Bibliothèque Nationale, Paris Conservatoire MS Rés. 1122). Cosyn, too, mistakenly calls it an In Nomine.

2 The problem of conflicting or questionable ascriptions in the sources can be further illustrated by a piece entered by Cosyn on f.100ʳ of BL MS R. M. 23.1.4, where it is attributed to Gibbons. It is a short version of a piece given the title 'Dorick' or 'Dorick musique' in Bibliothèque Nationale, Paris Conservatoire MS Rés. 1185 (p. 178), which Cosyn acquired and indexed without attributing the piece to Gibbons or anyone else, and in Christ Church MS Mus. 1113 (p. 201), compiled by William Ellis, who attributed the piece to Bull. The two versions are printed as nos. 57 and 57a in Bull, 1967 (MB 14), where Steele and Cameron cast doubt on Bull's authorship of either piece. Cunningham (1984, pp. 79-80) suggests MB 14/57 may be an arrangement or transcription of a consort work by an older or more conservative composer than Bull, but regards the attribution of MB 14/57a to Gibbons as convincing. Hendrie (in Gibbons, 1967, p. 103) thinks MB 57a could be by Gibbons, but that the related piece MB 57 is uncharacteristic of him, and so excludes both pieces from the Gibbons canon, though printing the incipit of the short version as no. 51. In the space available here it is clearly impossible to review every case in which an attribution to Gibbons gives rise to doubt, but brief notes are included in Section E of the list of Orlando Gibbons's works (see pp. 298-301).

Gibbons's keyboard music in sources compiled in his lifetime

Pieces are listed in the order in which they appear in the sources. For a complete list of Gibbons's keyboard works see pp. 292 and 296-298.

Parthenia

Galliard in C MB 20/25
Fantasia in a MB 20/12
Pavan in a (Lord Salisbury)
    MB 20/18

Galliard in a (Lord Salisbury)
    MB 20/19
The Queen's Command MB 20/28
Prelude in G MB 20/2

Cosyn

The Hunt's Up MB 20/30
A Mask MB 20/45
Galliard in a MB 20/24
Galliard in d (Lady Hatton)
    MB 20/20
Prelude ('Fancy') in d MB 20/3
Coranto ('A Toy') MB 20/40
Galliard in d MB 20/21
Almain in C MB 20/35
French Almain MB 20/41
Pavan ('Almain') in d MB 20/15
Fantasia in a MB 20/10

Galliard in d MB 20/22
Fantasia in d MB 20/8
Prelude in a MB 20/1
Fantasia in d MB 20/6
Almain in G (The King's Jewel)
    MB 20/36
Almain in G MB 20/37
Fantasia in d MB 20/7
Fantasia in g MB 20/9
Fantasia in C MB 20/13
Fantasia in C MB 20/14
Fantasia in a MB 20/11

Fitzwilliam Virginal Book

The Woods so Wild MB 20/29
Coranto MB 20/40

Pavan in a (Lord Salisbury)
    MB 20/18

the pieces, although the printing of *Parthenia* about December 1612 provides a terminal date for six of them. The *Fitzwilliam Virginal Book*[3]

MB 20/51 (MB 14/57a) is consigned to this section on the grounds that the problem of its authorship cannot be resolved satisfactorily, and that the attribution to Gibbons is too insecure to accept.

3   Fitzwilliam Museum MS Mu 168 (*olim* 32.G.29).

contains three pieces, including a version of the *Salisbury* pavan which differs slightly from the one published in *Parthenia*. It is no longer possible confidently to accept that this manuscript was written during the years 1609-19 (although an alternative period has yet to be suggested), so a convincing terminal date for another piece it contains — *The woods so wild* — cannot be deduced from its occurrence in the earlier part of the manuscript.[4] The most one can say is that *The woods so wild* probably came into the copyist's hands before the *Salisbury* pavan. A third source, British Library manuscript R.M. 23.1.4, was compiled by Benjamin Cosyn, who indexed it in 1620. This provides a terminal date — albeit a late one — for twenty-three keyboard pieces by Gibbons, including the 'toy' which occurs also in the *Fitzwilliam Virginal Book*.[5] As little is known about the compilation of Cosyn's volume, it is impossible to say whether the pieces near the beginning were copied much earlier than those that occur later, but the probability is that they were not.[6] Nevertheless, an earliest date can be suggested for one piece copied by Cosyn (MB 20/45), since it is an arrangement by Gibbons of a tune from Ben Jonson's masque *Lovers Made Men*, performed in February 1617/18. This is not much to go on, and the most convenient method of discussion will therefore be by genre rather than chronology.

But a word should first be said about the instruments for which Gibbons's keyboard music was composed. Only rarely does a source distinguish music as specifically for the virginals or the organ. Many sources mix pieces which seem most suited to one type of instrument with pieces which seem more suited to the other. Even though the sole printed source, *Parthenia*, is said to contain 'the first musicke that ever was printed for the virginalls', it includes a few pieces which are not incompatible with performance on the organ.[7] The bulk of Gibbons's

4   The period 1609-19 was proposed by J. A. Fuller Maitland and W. Barclay Squire in the preface to their edition (*The Fitzwilliam Virginal Book*, Leipzig, 1894-99). Thompson (1992) and Cuneo (1995) have cast doubt on long-accepted theories about the manuscript's compilation.

5   Ignoring some pieces of doubtful authenticity. Cosyn included nothing from *Parthenia*, probably because it had been published before he started copying. The version of MB 20/28 which he included appears to be his own work.

6   On the compilation of Cosyn's manuscript, see Harley, 1992-94, i, pp. 10-11, 27-28; Willetts, 1993.

7   The term 'virginals' embraces plucked keyboard instruments of all kinds, from compact instruments suitable for a small room to larger models with two keyboards and stops enabling different sounds to be selected. Examples of the latter appear to have been available in England in Gibbons's time, but are not essential for the performance of any of his music. Those pieces which seem best suited to the organ can also be played on a

keyboard music, however, assumes an instrument with a compass from C (or occasionally A') to a"; and it can be played on an instrument which is chromatically incomplete below F. Instruments of this type were evidently general in England in Gibbons's time, though two of his pieces reflect makers' gradual extension of the compass. MB 20/22 rises a semitone above Gibbons's customary top note, and MB 20/44 rises to c'''. Matthew Locke and some of those who contributed to his *Melothesia* (1673) wrote for instruments (both virginals and organ) with a compass extending to c''', which was by then more common; but while it is unusual to find an English composer of Gibbons's generation demanding notes above a", his pieces with the greatest compass may not have been written particularly late in his career. MB 20/22 is a galliard that is not radically different in style from another galliard (MB 20/25) which he included in *Parthenia*, and MB 20/44 is an arrangement of a tune used in a masque performed in 1611. Probably Gibbons had access to the most up-to-date instruments.

Pavans and galliards

Starting in the 1570s, the keyboard pavan and the keyboard galliard underwent a remarkable development in the hands of William Byrd, who continued to produce outstanding examples in the second decade of the seventeenth century. Bull and Gibbons took Byrd's pieces as models for their keyboard pavans and galliards, each imposing on the dances the stamp of his own personality and technique. Since Gibbons belonged to the generation that came after Bull, who was a generation younger than Byrd, his work shows in some degree the influence of both older men.

Most of Byrd's pavans consist of three sixteen-semibreve strains, though a few have strains of eight or twelve semibreves. His galliards usually have strains of eight bars, with three minims to a bar. Following what seems to have been a common practice, found as early as the *Dublin Virginal Book* of about 1570,[8] Byrd extended the dances by repeating the strains in a varied form. In many cases he joined a pavan with a galliard to form a larger composition, in which a careful and adventurous use of tonality helps to shape and link the dances.

Gibbons rarely follows Byrd's procedures closely. His dances, like Bull's, consist largely of irregular strains.[9] Touch has been lost with dancers' need, noted by Morley, for pavans with strains of eight, twelve

---

on a single-manual instrument, but see the comments on pp. 104-105 below concerning *A Fancye for a double Organ*. Pedals were not provided on organs of Gibbons's time.

8   Trinity College, Dublin, MS D.33.30/1.

9   For a table of Bull's strains, see Harley, 1992-94, ii, p. 52.

or sixteen semibreves, and galliards with strains of comparable length.[10] Gibbons's pieces have become separated from their social origins, and are governed by purely musical considerations. Strings of rapid notes retard the once lively dance tempo.

Only one of Gibbons's pavans (MB 20/15) has three sixteen-semibreve strains; the others have strains of different lengths, embodying odd numbers of semibreves or even numbers that are not multiples of four. The galliards are equally irregular. Even a 'regular' strain may be deceptive. The first strain of a pavan in d (MB 20/15)[11] is sixteen bars long, but the final cadence is reached in bar 15 and is prolonged for a further bar. The strain starts regularly enough with two two-bar phrases; the second, however, introduces a bass ostinato, one bar in length, that persists for five bars. As the treble melody continues the first four bars with three phrases one bar in length, everything has shifted by bar 7, where a dominant chord a minim in length is the nearest Gibbons comes to marking the central point of the strain with an unambiguous cadence. The compression of what might have been four bars into three is clear in the decorated reprise of the strain, where in bars 5-6 an imitative semiquaver figure starts to be repeated more closely.

The writing of a sixteen-bar strain with an intermediate cadence in bar 7 and a final cadence starting in bar 15 is something Gibbons may have learned from Byrd. In proceeding a step further, and creating strains of irregular length, he follows Bull. His method is either to elide or overlap phrases, or to insert phrases with an odd number of bars, sometimes combining them with one another or with phrases made up of an even number of bars, as in MB 20/15. The seven-bar second strain of a galliard in C (MB 20/25) is composed of two-bar phrases until bar 6, when the second and third beats of the bar are replaced by what, in an eight-bar strain, would be bar 7. The pavan in g (MB 20/16), based on Dowland's *Lachrymae*, begins with a phrase that seems destined to reach a cadence on the second beat of the second bar, but as it reaches that beat the phrase begins again, a minor third higher (Ex. 3 on p. 89). This overlapping is present in Dowland's original lute piece, but Gibbons changes the value of the notes, delays the repetition of the phrase, and instead of Dowland's slightly pedestrian strain of eight bars writes a more interesting strain of seven bars. Dowland's third strain is nine bars

10   Morley, 1597, p. 181 (1952, p. 296).

11   Upper and lower case letters are a convenient means of indicating 'major' and 'minor' tendencies in Gibbons's still essentially modal writing. Although the major and minor keys were in the process of formation (see p. 238), Gibbons can only rarely be said to have adopted them.

long, due to the extension of the final cadence. Gibbons takes it as the starting point for his second strain, but by condensing his material he produces a strain of seven bars.

Gibbons, though less inclined than Byrd to explore to the full the possibilities of tonality in his pavans and galliards, shows more understanding of them than Bull. His first and third strains are usually centred on the tonic, and his second upon the dominant, but this simple plan may accommodate a more complex design. The pavan in d (MB 20/15) is a case in point. The first strain is restricted very largely to chords on the tonic, dominant and subdominant. The last strain, too, is centred on the tonic, but it introduces chords on the mediant and submediant, and the rate of harmonic change is quicker.

Harmonic variety in Gibbons's pavans and galliards frequently results from or gives rise to sequences. He is particularly fond of those which descend by steps. Since he often allows sequences to run on until they reach a point from which he can proceed to a desired cadence, they may contribute to the irregularity of strains (as in strain 3 of the *Salisbury* pavan). But this is not always so. Both outer strains of one of his earlier pavans (MB 20/17 in a) contain sequences, but each is eight bars long. The fact is that there is nothing haphazard about Gibbons's sequences, which are carefully structured. A sequence in the second strain of a galliard in d (MB 20/22, bars 20-24) is based on chords whose roots progress purposefully by fourths (A D G C F). The third strain has two sequences in its first five bars (Ex. 1). Each bar contains two chords, so that there is a pattern of two sets of roots moving conjunctly (A G F G A combined with D C D E F).

Ex. 1. Orlando Gibbons, galliard in d (MB 20/22), bars 37-41

Gibbons commonly uses two methods of varying the strains of pavans and galliards when they are repeated. One is to add passages of quick notes. The other is to enrich the figuration, either by developing the initial pattern (galliard in d, MB 20/21, bars 5-7 and 13-15) or by introducing new figures. The figures may be derived from the type of imitative writing employed by Byrd (Gibbons's galliard in a, MB 20/24, bars 35-40) or be indebted to Bull (*Salisbury* galliard, MB 20/19, bars 24-31). The *Salisbury* galliard and another from *Parthenia* (MB 20/25) show the full development of Gibbons's skill in varying his strains.

The more elementary variation of repeats in two galliards in d (MB 20/20 and 20/23) suggests earlier composition (though it could also indicate simple writing for teaching purposes), but there is no way of deciding what this means in anything but general terms. Although Lady Hatton's name is attached to the first, we cannot be sure when Gibbons's association with the Hattons began.[12]

The enhanced figuration of a pavan in g (MB 20/16) frequently takes the form of groups of semiquavers, which easily combine with freely flowing streams of notes of the same value. Since the pavan may have been written late in 1612 (see below), it suggests an approximate period of composition for a galliard in a (MB 20/24), with repeats that possess similar characteristics. The conjectural date is supported by comparable stylistic traits in another galliard, already mentioned: the one in C from *Parthenia* (MB 20/25). Indeed, it can be surmised that during a few months of 1612 Gibbons wrote a group of dances in his most advanced manner. While special circumstances may surround the composition of the pavan in g and the *Salisbury* pavan and galliard, it is possible that the other dances are connected with Prince Frederick's entertainment at court prior to his marriage to Princess Elizabeth.

Although the *Salisbury* pavan and galliard in a (MB 20/18-19) were perhaps included in *Parthenia* to mark the death of Lord Salisbury in May 1612,[13] variant readings in the *Fitzwilliam Virginal Book* suggest the possibility that an earlier version of the pavan was in circulation.[14] There may also be a hint in the published version's full title, *The lord of*

---

12   Gibbons may have become friendly with the Hattons between 1607 and 1612 (see pp. 36-37). The occurrence of MB 20/23 only in a Continental source (Berlin, Staatsbibliothek, Stiftung Preussischer Kulturbesitz, Lynar MS A2) led Dart (1970, p. 31) to suggest that it might be connected with Gibbons's supposed journey to Germany in 1613 (see p. 45). The manuscript's compiler clearly had access to various pieces by Gibbons, however, since he included nine others, of which five seem to derive from *Parthenia*.

13   See p. 46.

14   Gibbons, 1967, pp. 37-38, 97.

Salisbury his Pavin, that the piece was dedicated to Salisbury while he was still alive.[15] The galliard alone may have been composed specially for publication. In any event, the *Salisbury* pavan reuses and expands material tried out in the apparently earlier (because simpler and less accomplished) pavan in the same key (MB 20/17).[16] Although the correspondence between the pieces is not close enough to qualify the later pavan as a reworking of the earlier, it does suggest a reformulation of Gibbons's ideas in the light of experience (Ex. 2 on p. 88).

A motive which appears in both the pavans in a is the series of descending notes that occurs in John Dowland's *Lachrymae* pavan. All Gibbons's keyboard pavans tap the vein of fashionable melancholy worked by Dowland, and all incorporate the *Lachrymae* motive.[17] Somewhat similar figures were in common use, and begin four of Dowland's ten pavans for lute, other than the *Lachrymae* pavan, but the piece was so well and so widely known, and so frequently arranged or quoted, that there can be little doubt that Gibbons's references to it are deliberate. His intention may have been to evoke the 'passionate' nature of Dowland's piece — the word was applied by Dowland himself to his set of pavans for viol consort incorporating the famous theme, published in 1605 as *Lachrimae, or Seaven Teares Figured in Seaven Passionate Pavans*. But quotations also serve as a shorthand for expressions of grief. This is clear in Gibbons's pavan in g (MB 20/16). As observed above, the opening bars of its first and second strains echo those of the first and third strains of Dowland's pavan (Ex. 3, on p. 89), the solo lute version of which may have prompted Gibbons's choice of key.[18]

Gibbons's particular purpose in his pavan in g may declare itself in the third strain. This resembles his song *Ne'er let the sun* (the second

15 Did Byrd know of Gibbons's piece before he wrote his own, and decide to deliver one of his commentaries on the work of younger contemporaries? (There are some similarities of figuration in the pieces.) Or do the 'Salisbury' pavans of the two composers reflect only their personalities and ages? In either case, nothing could differ more from the luxuriance of Gibbons's piece than the simple economy of Byrd's, born of long experience.

16 MB 20/17 is at present known only from a version published in 1907 by J. E. West (no. 31 in his series *Old English Organ Music*). He described it as a voluntary, though it is clearly a pavan. West took it from a manuscript then owned by W. H. Cummings (see West, 1910-11, p. 4), possibly no. 488 in Sotheby's catalogue of the sale of Cummings's library, May 1917. West's notation is slightly modified in Ex. 2.

17 The motive appears too in Gibbons's 'De le roye' pavan for viols. See p. 107.

18 There is in fact a wider similarity between the pieces than is apparent from the short extracts given here. See Poulton, 1982, p. 127, concerning Dowland's choice of keys for his original lute version and his later version for viols.

Ex. 2.

(a) Orlando Gibbons, pavan in a (MB 20/17), first strain

(b) Orlando Gibbons, *Salisbury* pavan (MB 20/18), first strain

Ex. 3.

John Dowland, *Lachrymae* pavan (lute version), first and third strains

Orlando Gibbons, pavan in g (MB 20/16) first and second strains

part of *Nay let me weep*), which may well have been written as a memorial tribute to Prince Henry, who died on 6 November 1612.[19] It is thus possible that the pavan was occasioned by Prince Henry's death, and that references to Dowland's piece would have been recognized and understood: 'let's ha' Lachrymae' is in fact demanded of the musicians in Beaumont and Fletcher's *The Knight of the Burning Pestle* (II, viii), printed in 1613. The disciplined writing and the confidently decorated repeats mean that the pavan in g cannot have been written much earlier

19   The strain begins by quoting Gibbons's setting of the words 'With whom my mirth, my joy, and all is done'. See Pinto, 1996, pp. 90-93.

than 1612, though caution is necessary in making too ready an assumption about the circumstances of its composition. It could be the song that quotes the pavan, which might have been written before Prince Henry died. The third chorus of Gibbons's anthem *Behold, thou hast made my days*, thought to date from 1618, resembles the third strain of his keyboard pavan MB 20/17, probably composed before 1612.[20]

If the pavan in g was written at the end of 1612, it may slightly post-date the *Salisbury* pavan, and possibly the *Salisbury* galliard too. Nevertheless, the *Salisbury* pavan and galliard are the greater achievement, because they jointly form a work that is not only noble and deeply moving, but larger and more elaborate. It seems as if, to produce a composition of the highest quality of which he was capable, Gibbons sometimes needed an external stimulus. (This need will be remarked again in later chapters.) There can be little question that in this case he was stimulated by the publication of *Parthenia* to create an extended composition that is unique among his dance-based works.

The relationship between the *Salisbury* pavan and its galliard is complex, as even a cursory examination of their joint plan reveals.[21] Some aspects of the relationship are easily apparent. The first strain of each dance, broadly speaking, is in a, the second is in e, and the third is again in a. There is an obvious common thread, too, in the quotations from Dowland's *Lachrymae* which can be detected in both dances at the beginning of every strain. The source of the quotations may well be the first of Dowland's consort pieces incorporating his descending motive — the *Lachrimae Antiquae* — though Gibbon's second strain is closer to Dowland's third, and vice versa (Ex. 4).[22] The consort piece may also have suggested the key chosen by Gibbons.

Other aspects of the relationship between the pavan and the galliard are more detailed, and often quite subtle. For example, each strain of the pavan builds to a melodic peak, from which it then descends. The peaks rise progressively higher, from d" in the first strain to g" in the third, but it is left to the galliard to reach a" in its second and third strains.

20   See p. 87.

21   Salter, 1979, gives a brief analysis of these pieces.

22   Since references to Dowland's piece were so common, Gibbons's inclusion of quotations with sorrowful associations does not contradict the suggestion that the *Salisbury* pavan might have been composed while Lord Salisbury was alive. Melancholy was not exclusively connected with death.

Ex. 4.

John Dowland, themes from *Lachrymae Antiquae*, cantus part

Orlando Gibbons, themes from (a) *Salisbury pavan*, (b) *Salisbury* galliard

   The powerful strains of the pavan should be played without repeats, to avoid overwhelming the galliard.[23] The galliard, however, has decorated repeats, and the imitative figures in those of its first and third

23   Hendrie (in Gibbons, 1967) and Dart (in his edition of *Parthenia*, 1962) both insert repeat signs in the pavan. The original edition of *Parthenia* divides the strains only by double bar-lines, not by repeat signs of the type it includes in Byrd's pieces.

strains echo both the *Lachrymae* motive and the descending lines of notes occurring throughout each dance. In particular they develop, and sometimes invert, the short descending figures that fill much of the third strain of the pavan.

The first of several long continuous descents (from e" to d♯') occurs in the second strain of the pavan (bars 12-14). The third strain of the pavan contains two more such descents, which help to relate it to the second strain. The highest voice falls from e" to f♯' (bars 20-22), and the descent is continued to d' by another voice. More spectacularly, the highest voice descends (with one interruption) from the peak of g" to e' (bars 24-26). The first strain of the galliard is firmly associated with the pavan, by the descent of the upper voice from g" to g♯' (bars 2-5) and the descent of the lower voices combined from e' to B (bars 2-5).

Despite his success in creating an extended, unified work from a pair of dances, Gibbons seems to have felt no inclination to follow it up. Perhaps he was aware that music of that sort had run its natural course.[24]

Variations

Gibbons's variations on the popular tune *The Woods so Wild* show him to have been the possessor of a formidable keyboard technique. Although Byrd had written a set of variations on the same tune,[25] it was Bull's most dazzling variation style which Gibbons adopted as his model. Manual dexterity and brilliance are given precedence over the careful structural planning exemplified by Byrd's variations.[26] One senses a young composer trying to surpass a master without fully comprehending the master's achievement. The same remarks can be applied to Gibbons's longer set of variations on *The Hunt's Up* (or *Peascod Time*),[27] for he again pursues keyboard virtuosity at the expense of musical architecture, and again seems to pit himself against Byrd. But

24   Some of Thomas Tomkins's pieces in the same style, which (if his own dates in Bibliothèque Nationale, Paris Conservatoire MS Rés. 1122 are to be believed) were written as much as twenty-five years after Gibbons's death, are an isolated phenomenon.

25   Dated 1590 in *My Ladye Nevells Booke*.

26   The simple plan of Gibbons's set is: (1) contrapuntally elaborated statement of the theme, mostly in quavers, (2) running semiquavers in the right hand, (3) running semiquavers in the left hand, (4) continuous quaver figuration in both hands (5) running right-hand semiquavers against a left hand octave ostinato, (6) triplets, (7) running right-hand semiquavers turning into semiquaver figuration, over continuous left-hand quavers and repeated bass notes, (8) continuous quavers in both hands, turning into (9) a similar final statement of the theme.

27   The tune was known by both titles, and each is attached to Gibbons's variations.

whereas Byrd, in his early variations on *The Hunt's Up*, had used the bass alone, treating it as a ground, Gibbons made use of both the bass and the tune.

The Queen's Command is based on another ground. In the first section, the first half of the ground is played and varied before the other half is played and varied; the second section consists of a variation of the whole of the first.[28] The piece is very like a type of coranto with variations of which Byrd and Bull left examples. Several variations in the different versions of Bull's *Jewel* provide obvious comparisons with those written by Gibbons. *The Queen's Command* has something of the style of Gibbons's *The Woods so Wild* and *The Hunt's Up*, but makes many fewer demands on the player, as do short sets of variations on *Whoop, do me no harm good man*, and *The Italian Ground* (called 'Almain' in some sources). *The Italian Ground* was a popular basis for keyboard variations,[29] and in Gibbons's setting (as in *The Queen's Command*) the first half of the ground is played and varied before the second half is played and varied. Most sources give the second section of the piece as an uninterrupted variation on the complete ground, but one copy separates the halves with repeat marks, in accordance with the clear division Gibbons makes between them.[30]

The ground on which Gibbons based another set of variations (MB 20/26) is also one with a long history: a version of the *passamezzo antico*, known in England as the 'passing measures'. The variations are made up of elements familiar in Elizabethan and Jacobean keyboard music — the imitation of short motives, and strings of semiquavers — but the original statement of the theme has a quality that connects it with a newer style being developed in music for court entertainments. It is direct, uncluttered and bass-oriented. This style is found, to a greater or lesser degree, in a whole group of dance and masque tunes composed or arranged by Gibbons (MB 20/32-45). They have much in common with the contents of Anne Cromwell's somewhat retrospective virginal book, dated 1638.[31] Whereas Gibbons's pavans, galliards and virtuoso variations are founded on the work of his distinguished predecessors, in these short pieces he was associating himself with composers who wrote

28 The plan was not wholly exceptional. Peter Philips adopted it in his keyboard almain, and Sweelinck did so in arranging a pavan by Philips.

29 It appears as *Revenant* by Bull, as *Aria detto balletto* in *Il secondo libro di toccate* by Frescobaldi, and as *More Palatino* in variations by Sweelinck, Steenwick and Buxtehude.

30 Bibliothèque Nationale, Paris Conservatoire MS Rés. 1185, where the piece was entered by Benjamin Cosyn.

31 Cromwell Museum MS 46.78-748.

to satisfy the current taste. Four of the pieces are corantos, but the rest are almains or almain-like.[32] A number bear titles in some sources that suggest they have come from masques, though only three of Gibbons's arrangements (MB 20/43-45) have been connected with specific entertainments.[33] Some of these pieces are in binary form, the strains of others are equipped with variations. Some are distinctly diatonic in character, and it is significant that two almains in G (MB 20/36-37) have a sharp in the key signature, not to indicate modal transposition (as is apparently the case in Preston's Mass, quoted in Ex. 5a on p. 95), but because to all intents and purposes they have abandoned the almost defunct modal system and are in the key of G major.[34]

Preludes and fantasias

The sources of two of Gibbons's keyboard pieces betray uncertainty about the difference between a prelude and a fantasia. A piece in a (MB 20/1), which Cosyn calls 'Prelludem' or 'A Prellude', has the title 'A Running fantazia' in Christ Church MS Mus. 47. Another (MB 20/2), in G, is called 'A Voluntary' (a synonym for 'fantasia') in British Library Additional MS 22099, but in *Parthenia* it is called 'Preludium', presumably by Gibbons himself.[35] Gibbons probably regarded the distinction as of little consequence, if he thought about it at all. Both preludes and fantasias (or fancies, to use another common term) retain in some measure the freedom and spontaneity of the improvisations from which the genres developed, though pieces of some length and falling into sections with different subjects were generally regarded as fantasias.

32   Elizabeth Rogers's virginal book (BL Additional MS 10337) however contains a version of *Nan's Masque* (one of the title's given to MB 20/41) that begins in triple time and changes to duple time. It is thus transcribed in Sabol, 1978, p. 293.

33   MB 20/43 comes from Beaumont's *The Masque of the Inner Temple and Grayes Inne* of 1613 (see p. 44, and Sabol, 1978, p. 584, note to no. 155). MB 20/44 is from Jonson's *Oberon*, of 1611 (Sabol, p. 589, note to no. 188). MB 20/45 comes from Jonson's *Lovers Made Men*, of 1617/18. The title 'The Temple Mask', attached to it in Bibliothèque Nationale, Paris Conservatoire MS Rés. 1185, appears to be erroneous. The tune, with the main and exit dances, appears in BL Additional MS 10444, ff. 35[r,v] (see also Sabol, 1978, pp. 220-221, 413, 577, 606, nos. 120-122, 296). Another piece arranged by Gibbons (MB 20/34) is called 'A Toy' or 'An Aire' in keyboard sources, but appears as an anonymous piece for strings entitled 'The first of the Lords' in BL Additional MS 10444 (ff. 26[r], 78[v]). This could refer to a number of masques.

34   The principal source for both is Cosyn's manuscript (BL, R. M. 23.1.4).

35   See the Textual Commentary in Gibbons, 1967, for a full list of sources of these pieces and those discussed below.

The nature of MB 20/1 and MB 20/2 reveals a good deal about their ancestry. Each consists of long, flowing lines of semiquavers played by one hand against harmonies outlined by the other hand. This type of keyboard writing can be traced at least as far back as the music of John Redford, who died in 1547. A setting for organ of the plainsong for the Easter Mass, by Redford's (probably slightly younger) contemporary Thomas Preston, illustrates not only the origin of Gibbons's running semiquavers, but how such cantus firmus settings encouraged the use of sequential or quasi-sequential figures like those that crop up repeatedly in Gibbons's music (Ex. 5a).[36] While this manner of writing occurs in the music of Byrd and Bull, it seems possible that, as a youth, Gibbons got to know an organ repertoire composed long before he was born.

The prelude in G is more interesting than the one in a, as Gibbons acknowledged by choosing it for inclusion in *Parthenia* (assuming both preludes to have been written by 1612). It may therefore be the later, although an early version appears to have been in circulation.[37] Its brilliance is due partly to the unceasing flow of rapid notes, underpinned by firm harmonies which give rise in the central section to strands of crotchets and minims ascending and descending by steps (Ex. 5b, on p. 96).[38] But it is also due to a strong major key feeling, which belongs to a new age, and is hardly diminished by traces of modal writing.

Ex. 5(a). Thomas Preston, *Missa in die Paschae*, bars 369-376

continued

36 Preston's Mass occurs in BL MS Royal Appendix 29996, f. 62ᵛ ff. It is edited by Denis Stevens in *Early Tudor Organ Music: II. Music for the Mass*, London, 1969 (EECM, 10), pp. 20-37.

37 Christ Church MS Mus. 89 is the earliest extant source of variant readings given in Gibbons, 1967, but is later than *Parthenia*. A prelude or fantasia by Bull (MB 14/16 in g) uses figuration similar to that of Gibbons's prelude, but as it appears only in a Continental source (Vienna, Österreichische Nationalbibliothek MS 17771) it may have been written after Bull left England in 1613.

38 The prelude in G can be regarded as falling into three main sections: bars 1-9, 10-24, 25-39.

Ex. 5(a) *continued*

Ex. 5(b). Orlando Gibbons, prelude in G (MB 20/2), bars 10-20

As was pointed out above, keyboard sources dating from Gibbons's time suggest that music was not, on the whole, categorized as appropriate for just one kind of keyboard instrument. The inclusion of the prelude in G in *Parthenia* indicates that Gibbons thought it suitable for performance on the virginals, but it is just as well suited to being played on the organ, even if it loses some of its sparkle. Four of his works (MB 20/3-6, in d, a, d and d respectively)[39] have the appearance of short pieces of the kind an organist might often have had to improvise, and a post-Restoration source actually calls MB 20/4 'versus'.[40] But the titles given to these pieces by copyists reveal different ideas about their exact purpose. In sources compiled before the Civil War, MB 20/3 and MB 20/6 are called 'fantasia' (or 'fancy' or 'voluntary'), and MB 20/5 is called 'preludium'.[41] All four pieces are nevertheless short, contrapuntal, and at times imitative, and all illustrate Gibbons's frequent recourse to melodic lines that embody rising scale passages.[42]

Eight longer pieces (MB 20/7-14) are described in the sources as fantasias (or fancies, or voluntaries). These have a claim to be Gibbons's most important group of keyboard compositions, not solely because they are more numerous than any other type, but because in his fully developed fantasias he reached a high level of originality and accomplishment. He seems to have been most at home in the kind of contrapuntal writing which they exemplify, and he was supremely resourceful in employing it.

All Gibbons's fantasias have the time signature ₵,[43] and none includes the change of time found in most of Byrd's fantasias and in several of Bull's. Yet there is great diversity in their movement. The variety of their invention and spirit defies all but the most elementary generalization. While each fantasia is based upon a succession of subjects, usually (if briefly) treated imitatively, later examples are less clearly sectionalized than Byrd's fantasias, and are less apt than Bull's to depend on new motives or on more rapid movement as a substitute for development. Bull's fantasias often convey the impression that he had not entirely shaken off a training in setting plainsong, or an admiration for Tallis's two settings of *Felix namque*, with their rather rigid series of

39   Any intended difference in mode between MB 20/3 (no flat in the key signature) and the other pieces in d (one flat in the signature) is not strictly maintained.

40   'Versus' ('verse'): a short organ piece of the type sometimes substituted for a verse of a hymn, etc.

41   Titles are given in BL MSS R. M. 23.1.4 (MB 20/3 and MB 20/6), Additional 31403 (MB 20/3), and Additional 36661 (MB 20/5); and in Bodleian Library MS Mus. Sch. f.575 (MB 20/4). MB 20/49, though anonymous, may be by Gibbons; it follows MB 20/5 in the source, and is similar in style to this group of pieces.

42   MB 20/5 is distinguished by having the same point of imitation as a longer piece in a, ascribed to Thomas Tomkins in Christ Church MS Mus. 1113. The resemblance between the pieces is close enough to suggest that one composer knew the work of the other (assuming the attribution to each composer to be correct).

43   'The imperfect of the less': duple or common time, neither too fast nor too slow.

figures filling out a plan dictated by the cantus firmus. While Gibbons tended to rely on a constant supply of fresh ideas rather than the amply worked points found in Byrd's fantasias, his mature fantasias largely avoid the mechanical aspects of Bull's style, and seem to develop spontaneously, creating a virtually seamless fabric of a sort not previously (or subsequently) found in English keyboard music.

Subject to reservations about the validity of any opinion where the detailed chronology of Gibbons's music is concerned, it is possible to discern the steps by which he progressed towards his highly individual later fantasias. It is remarkable that he travelled such a distance in what must have been a comparatively short period. Although, as has already been observed, Gibbons appears at times to have needed an incentive to produce his best work, the problems of the fantasia seem to have come to interest him for their own sake. Central to these was the construction of a unified work from a succession of different elements.

Gibbons had clearly given little thought to the nature of the fantasia when he wrote what may be the first of the series. It is an uncomplicated and light-textured three-part piece in a (MB 20/10), consisting of two easily identifiable sections. The first is constructed largely from one five-note figure, and has a motion determined mainly by notes of crotchet or quaver value. Most of the second section consists of running semiquavers like those in the long preludes in a and G, although the looser stringing together of sequences suggests earlier composition.

Another fantasia in the same key (MB 20/11), this time in four parts, also falls into two large sections. But it is a more concise piece, and more tightly constructed. Gibbons again progresses from longer notes (minims) in the first section to shorter notes (crotchets) in the second, and in the second section produces a growing sense of urgency by piling one short rising scalar figure on another. The figures occur in parallel or overlap closely to create a density of texture often found in Gibbons's choruses, for example 'Glory be to God on high' in the anthem *Behold, I bring you glad tidings*. Under the fingers the fantasia feels rather like the earlier of Gibbons's pavans in a (MB 20/17).

Two Restoration sources present an abbreviated version of a four-part fantasia in C (MB 20/13), ending it with a tonic cadence in bar 43.[44] Earlier sources add a second part to the piece, continuing it for twenty-four more bars.[45] If the later sources derive from a short original version to which a second part was afterwards added, the second part is nonetheless carefully integrated with the first.

44   Christ Church MSS Mus. 47 and 1176, which slightly prolong the cadence.
45   BL MSS R. M. 23.1.4 (Cosyn) and Additional 31403. For other sources see Gibbons, 1967.

Ex. 6. Orlando Gibbons, points from fantasia in C (MB 20/13)

Each of the first three points, on its initial occurrence, marks the beginning of a section, though overlapping of the sections obscures the joins. Similarities between the points make clear that the sections are formed from common material. The relationship between the first two points is plain enough. The third point draws on a few notes from the middle of the first point. In addition to that, it appears in combination with the second point before it makes an independent appearance. The second part of the fantasia is introduced by a point (number 4 in Ex. 6) which is related to each of those contained in the first part. Because of this it knits the two parts of the fantasia together. The formation of sections from similar material and the blurring of divisions between them, though features that occur in fantasias by Byrd and other earlier composers, are important steps in the evolution of Gibbons's keyboard fantasias.

The running together of sections is carried further in a group of four fantasias: MB 20/8 in d, MB 20/9 in g, MB 20/12 in a (the *Fantazia of foure parts*), and MB 20/14 in C. They also share another characteristic, namely the inclusion of rhythmically complex passages. These result from the unsynchronized occurrence in different voices of figures with dotted notes, or comprising groups of long and short notes. It is possible that such passages show the influence of Bull, and derive from his keyboard In Nomines. There is no doubt that Bull composed his In Nomines before he left England in 1613, so the hypothesis that they influenced a group of Gibbons's fantasias is not inconsistent with the publication of one of the latter (MB 20/12) in *Parthenia*, about the end of 1612. There are nevertheless differences between Gibbons's four fantasias. MB 20/8, MB 20/9 and MB 20/12 all begin with imitative points in the customary manner, whereas MB 20/14 does not (it is described below). MB 20/8, however, differs from MB 20/9 and MB

20/12 in containing a good deal of figuration in the style of Bull, together with passages of flowing semiquavers.

Of the latter two fantasias, MB 20/9 is the one in which separate points and transitions from one section to another can more easily be identified. Thematic relationships can be discovered throughout the piece, often involving material near the beginning. For example, the fifth point, which makes its appearance in bar 41, is an inversion of a group of notes heard in bars bars 3-4 (Ex. 7).

Ex. 7. Orlando Gibbons, fantasia in g (MB 20/9)

It would be simplistic to suggest that all the unifying relationships in MB 20/9 are so easily recognizable. There is no elementary melodic connection between the last point of the fantasia, which enters in bars 67-68, and anything occurring earlier. This final point ushers in a long concluding section consisting essentially of a series of chords, embellished with decorations that grow increasingly ornate beneath the composer's fingers. It is easy to sense Gibbons's powers of extemporization here, as in many other passages of his fantasias, but although there is a strong feeling that Gibbon's improvising hands may already have conjured up the music his pen committed to paper, one is always conscious that behind these flights of fancy there is a controlling mind. The last section of MB 20/9 is not something added merely in a frenzy of inspiration; it is an integral part of an overall plan, and the chordal writing connects it with the largely chordal second section beginning at bar 19 (Ex. 8).

Ex. 8. Orlando Gibbons, fantasia in g (MB 20/9)

(a) bars 19-22

(b) bars 67-69

A striking feature of MB 20/12 is the extent to which material from the first four bars recurs as the piece unfolds (Ex. 9). Melodic fragments lend thematic unity as one section slips into another, and the piece grows in complexity and intensity of feeling. How much of this is intentional, or due to Gibbons's intuition, is impossible to say. The sobriety of MB 20/12 complements that of the *Salisbury* pavan, and some short figures call to mind similar figures in the pavan. Quite possibly the pieces were composed about the same time.[46]

Ex. 9. Orlando Gibbons, fantasia in a (MB 20/12)

46   Significant variants suggest that, like the pavan, the fantasia was revised for publication (Gibbons, 1967, p. 24).

MB 20/14 depends very little on easily perceived thematic relationships. This is clear from the outset. A free voice is the first to enter, and although the next voice is only a beat behind with the point of imitation, strict imitation does not extend beyond its first three notes (Ex. 10a). None of the sections into which the fantasia falls is longer than a few bars, and one melts imperceptibly into another. A very strong harmonic framework is needed to prevent the disintegration of a structure that is so loose thematically, and that is what Gibbons provides. It is not difficult to reduce the polyphony to writing of the kind encountered in Ex. 8a above (Ex. 10b).

Ex. 10. Orlando Gibbons, fantasia in C (MB 20/14)

(a) bars 1-4

(b) reduction of bars 1-4

The material of MB 20/8 is as diverse as that of MB 20/14, and is treated more brilliantly and at greater length. For the purposes of the present discussion it will be convenient to regard MB 20/8 as comprising three main sections (bars 1-15, 15-37, and 37-63), each introduced by a point of imitation. It is evident that the points come from a common inspirational source, and certain correspondences spring to the attention, but there is little to suggest a conscious attempt to develop one point from another by any process of melodic transformation. The points seem rather to be shaped by what Gibbons felt instinctively to be needed melodically and rhythmically in a particular place. Amid the heterogeneous contents of the fantasia, the points of imitation provide a means of orientation, and a number of symmetries in the fantasia's layout serve a parallel purpose.

One such symmetry occurs in the first section, which is centrally divided by the delayed entry of the third voice in bar 7. Another is found in the second section, where an extended semiquaver flourish ends at the section's mid-point. This is effectively the middle of the fantasia, and is marked by a cadence on F, the furthest Gibbons's broad tonal scheme departs from the tonic.

Like the previous main sections, the third is divided into two subsections. The division occurs at the end of a flourish, echoing the one at the centre of the fantasia. But this simple statement hardly does justice to the section's complexity. Although it starts with an imitative point, it quickly introduces figures recalling (and at times derived from) some of those in the previous sections, and generates new ones of its own. The point is clearly heard in the bass as far as bar 47, but the section depends heavily on Gibbons's powers of invention in producing a series of short figures that are repeated over the space of one or two bars, either sequentially or in the course of close contrapuntal imitation, before being overtaken by new ideas. The ingenuity with which these are moulded into a unified whole is striking. Whether or not Gibbons actually thought of the four notes d-f-B-d in bar 53 as a reinterpretation of part of the point that begins the section, they confirm that the ideas welling up in his mind were all of a piece, and conferred unity on what he was writing. He can hardly have failed to notice that he repeated these notes in bar 61, having preceded them with six notes forming a pattern resembling one in bars 21-24.

Reference was made above to the broad tonal scheme of MB 20/8. The large-scale tonal plans of Gibbons's fantasias are invariably simple, and (in modern terms) he rarely strays from the tonic or closely related keys for very long. Nevertheless, an overall tonal tranquility may cloak considerable local harmonic animation. The varied harmony resulting from Gibbons's counterpoint in MB 20/8 is associated with fluctuating emotional intensity (Ex. 11a). Comparable features occur in MB 20/9 (Ex. 11b).

Ex. 11(a). Orlando Gibbons, fantasia in d, MB 20/8, bars 15-22

continued

Ex. 11(a) *continued*

Ex. 11(b). Orlando Gibbons, fantasia in g, MB 20/9, bars 25-36

Neither Gibbons nor any other keyboard composer followed up the experiments he conducted in the four fantasias just discussed. Gibbons himself seems to have transferred his interest to the consort fantasia. He did, however, write one more fantasia for keyboard. This piece (MB 20/7 in d), which Cosyn described as 'A Fancy for a double Orgaine', is the most likely of Gibbons's fantasias to date from later than around 1612, since it is based on a fresh constructional principle in which the bass assumes a prominent role. It is generally closer to, though more accomplished than, the fantasias which Christopher Gibbons was to write. The new departure may, as Cosyn's title suggests, have been prompted by the availability of an organ with two keyboards, though there must be uncertainty about this.

Because Cosyn's copy is the only one known, it is impossible to confirm that the fantasia was originally intended for performance on an instrument with two manuals. Two facts cast doubt on the notion: first,

Cosyn's indications of register towards the end of the piece are unsatisfactory; and second, Cosyn tried also to insert indications of register in the next piece in his manuscript, MB 20/9, but found he could not do it and was forced to abandon the attempt. MB 20/7 can in fact be played perfectly well on a single-manual instrument, either an organ or a harpsichord, and colour is inherent in Gibbons's use of all ranges of the keyboard, from the lowest (bars 49-52) to the highest (bars 72-74).

Not the least of the differences between MB 20/7 and Gibbons's other fantasias is that it is more extroverted and lighter of mood. While such lightness is not altogether absent from his earlier fantasias, the customary tinge of gravity is less pronounced in MB 20/7. There is a temptation to think that the piece may be connected with the refurbishment of the organ at St James's Palace in 1621, but as the notion cannot amount to more than speculation it is idle to pursue it.[47] The new spirit of the piece can be attributed more certainly to the new way the bass functions in a generally three-part composition. The first and last sections of the fantasia (bars 1-14 and 66 to the end) are thoroughly imitative, but elsewhere the bass is the shaping force. Gibbons's adoption of a plan with clearly defined outer sections may indicate that the piece was influenced by his work on the later three-part fantasias.[48] In between the outer sections of the fantasia, instead of progressing from one point of imitation to another, the music is articulated by the entries of a series of bass motives (Ex. 12) and by unequally spaced cadences.

Ex. 12. Points and motives from Orlando Gibbons's fantasia in d (MB 20/7)

continued

47   Entries in the accounts of Sir Adam Newton for 1621 record payments 'for Painting and guilding of the Organes at Sᵗ James' and 'for altering and new making of his Highnes [Prince Charles's] Organes at Sᵗ James'; it is uncertain whether the instrument was Prince Henry's 'greate Organ bought of mr Hamlett placed at St. James', and mended on purchase (PRO, SC6/James I/1685, E101/435/12, E351/2794, and AO1/2021/21; Ashbee, 1986-96, iv, pp. 215, 225).

48   See pp. 124-125.

Ex. 12 *continued*

There are numerous similarities between the bass motives, and many of the elements they contain evolve — sometimes by means of inversion or retrogression — from the opening point of the fantasia. Above the bass the other parts, played by the right hand, pursue a dialogue, either freely or imitatively, often ignoring, but occasionally borrowing from, figures played by the left hand (Ex. 13).

Ex. 13. Orlando Gibbons, fantasia in d (MB 20/7), bars 20-24

1. Oxford as Orlando Gibbons knew it, based on a drawing by Joris Hoefnagel
(from *Civitates Orbis Terrarum*, 1575)

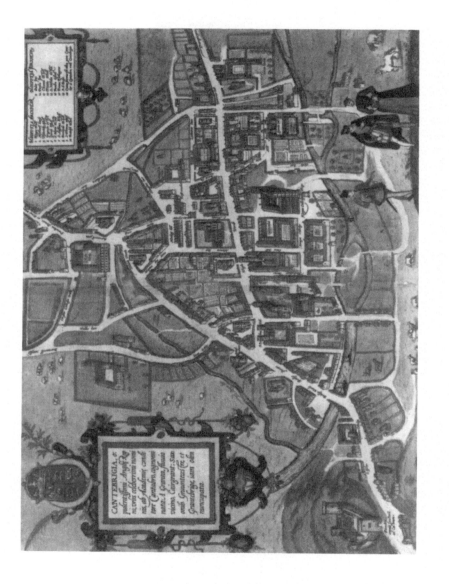

2. Cambridge in Orlando Gibbons's time (from *Civitates Orbis Terrarum*, 1575)

Sala Regalis cum Curia Weſtmonaſterij vulgo Weſtminſter hall

3. New Palace Yard, shown here in Wenceslaus Hollar's engraving *Sala Regalis* of 1647, was a familiar sight to Orlando Gibbons

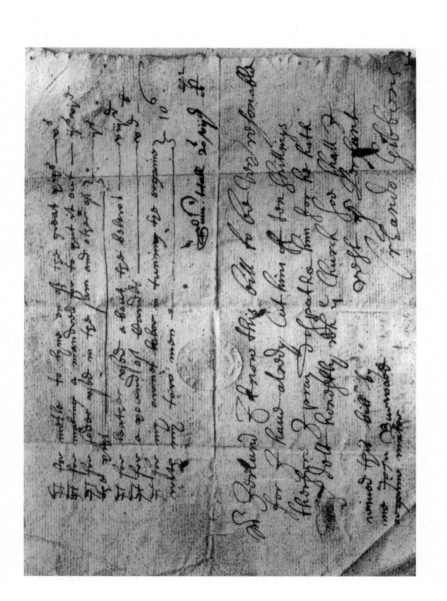

5. A note written by Orlando Gibbons in 1625

6. The Oxford portrait of Orlando Gibbons

7. The monument to Orlando Gibbons made by Nicholas Stone

8. The Oxford portrait of Christopher Gibbons

CONSORT MUSIC

Early works

A pavan and two In Nomines for viols appear to be among Gibbons's earliest surviving compositions. The incomplete pavan 'De le roye' (MB 48/30) may date from Gibbons's Cambridge days. Indeed, it occurs in a set of part-books which contain music with university and East Anglian connections.[1] It is attributed simply to 'mr Gibbons', but there is no strong reason for assigning it to anyone except Edward or Orlando Gibbons, and since its third strain contains the 'Lachrymae' motive which crops up in all Orlando's keyboard pavans it is probably by him (compare Ex. 14 with Ex. 4 on p. 91).[2]

Ex. 14. Orlando Gibbons, pavan 'De le roye', third strain (two parts lost)

1   See Payne 1988; Payne, 1989; Harper, 1982, p. 122. The surviving three parts of Gibbons's pavan (evidently the second treble, second tenor and bass) occur in BL Additional MSS 30826-8, which may have been copied by Thomas Statesmore, whose name was recorded at Trinity College in 1620/1 and at King's College in 1623. The books include three pavans by 'Wilkinson', who is identifiable with Thomas Wilkinson, perhaps a lay clerk of King's College 1579/80-1595, and organist and master of the choristers at Trinity College 1609-12.

2   It is likely that Dowland's *Lachrymae* pavan was circulating by 1595. See Poulton, 1982, p. 126.

The pavan may be an arrangement of a popular tune — perhaps, as the title suggests, one believed to have taken the fancy of a king. Alternatively, the title may mean that it is an arrangement of a piece by the lutenist and publisher Adrian Le Roy, though no model has so far been identified. The loss of two parts is a hindrance in judging the nature of Gibbons's contribution, but the higher surviving parts, largely in semibreves or minims and with indications of open writing and occasional imitation, place the piece round about the time of his four-part In Nomine (see below). The regular eight-bar strains may be attributable to the original; so may the fact that, contrary to Gibbons's mature practice, the first two strains end with a cadence on the same note (A), while the third ends with one on a different note (E). Gibbons's lowest part, which in the first two strains consists entirely of breves and semibreves, may be a youthful essay in providing a bass for a primarily melodic piece.

Two In Nomines by Gibbons, one in four parts and one in five, are found in the original layer of a single source, where they occur with pieces predominantly by Elizabethan composers.[3] This alone would suggest that they cannot have been written much later than 1610. But since each reflects familiarity with a sixteenth-century repertoire, and is in a loose-textured style in vogue before Gibbons was born, they may have been composed a good deal earlier, prior to his exposure to the more modern pieces he is likely to have encountered in court circles.

The four-part In Nomine (MB 48/26) is the one which more strongly suggests older models. In Nomines of four parts were commoner in the early days of the genre than they later became (though it may have been Gibbons's inexperience which caused him to restrict the number of parts). Like many composers of In Nomines Gibbons made minor adjustments to the plainsong cantus firmus, and in the four-part In Nomine he omitted one A from the group that usually occurs as breves 30 to 33. Whether he copied the cantus firmus from Tallis, in whose two four-part In Nomines the same alteration occurs, it is impossible to say. Gibbons's obligation to older composers is in any case wider. Insofar as there is a specific debt, the open writing and melodic shapes of Gibbons's piece often recall passages from the In Nomines of Tye.

---

3   Bodleian Library MSS Mus. Sch. d.212-216. The In Nomine as a type sprang from the Benedictus of a mass by John Taverner (d. 1545), based on the *Gloria tibi trinitas* chant and containing a setting of words beginning 'In nomine Domine'. This part of the mass includes the whole chant melody. It circulated independently, and was an important influence on English consort music, generating many pieces based on the same cantus firmus. See Dart and Donington, 1949; Reese, 1949.

Another consideration which places the four-part In Nomine early in Gibbons's career is its uncertain sense of direction. In the first, most clearly defined, section, ending at bar 16, the free parts begin with a strongly characterized figure incorporating the rising minor third with which the cantus firmus begins. The second section forms a satisfactory contrast, but the progress of the quietly meditative sections which follow is slightly indecisive.

The five-part In Nomine (MB 48/27) is more tightly knit, and is clearly the result of greater experience. It may well have been influenced by Byrd's most popular piece of the kind (BE 17/22). The resemblance, although not precise, is close enough to indicate a possible ancestry. The first few notes of Gibbons's piece make use of a common formula,[4] but a specific relationship with Byrd's In Nomine is suggested by a rising sixth in Gibbons's fourth bar. This occurs too in the seven-part In Nomine by Robert Parsons (MB 44/75) from which Byrd may well have derived it (Ex. 15). Gibbons also follows Byrd in constructing the last section of his piece from variants of a short figure, which the different instruments play in parallel or close imitation.

Ex. 15.

Robert Parsons, 7-part In Nomine (MB 44/75)

William Byrd, 5-part In Nomine (BE 17/22)

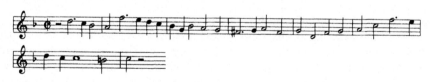

Orlando Gibbons, 5-part In Nomine (MB 48/27)

4   See, for example, In Nomines by Alfonso Ferrabosco (MB 44/50), William Mundy (MB 44/54) and Nicholas Strogers (MB 44/61).

Later In Nomines

Two further five-part In Nomines (MB 48/28-29) are plainly more mature than the works discussed above. Although they are included in the set of part-books containing Gibbons's early In Nomines, they are in a later layer, which contains works by Jacobean contemporaries. MB 48/28 was among the most popular of Gibbons's consort pieces, and occurs in eight more seventeenth-century sources.[5]

The scheme of MB 48/28 is exceptionally clear, recalling Byrd's apparent practice of mapping out an overall design in his mind before embarking on detailed composition. Gibbons's plan is superimposed with some skill on the cantus firmus. Although the result is a little mechanical, and he seems at times to be stretching his material to fill a given space, he maintains a fine sense of ebb and flow.

The long first section of the work contains one of its most notable features: a virtually uninterrupted series of descending tetrachords, played in minims at different pitches.[6] The tetrachords are incorporated into longer stretches of melody, and combined in counterpoint with additional, often closely related, material. They may be the ultimate source of numerous falling or rising groups of notes occurring throughout the piece (for example, the rows of crotchets in bars 85-94). Gibbons relieves any monotony resulting from the repeated tetrachords by punctuating the first section at its midpoint. He does so with three bars (23-26) in which the bass plays two breves in time with the cantus firmus, while the two tenor parts play descending tetrachords in parallel. The next section maintains a nearly continuous motion in quavers, echoing earlier quaver passages. In the final section Gibbons contrives to increase the emotional level, with a series of rising sequences based on a short figure of a quaver and two semiquavers. Here, perhaps, there may be a recollection of Byrd's five-part In Nomine BE 17/21, in which the final section is similarly built around rising sequences.

Quite as striking as the plan of MB 48/28 is its inclusion of a series of dissonant syncopations, announced by the first of the descending tetrachords (Ex. 16a). There is a possibility that this feature was suggested to Gibbons by the five-part consort pavans of Dowland's *Lachrimae, or Seaven Teares* (1605), with their falling motive, in which 'one of the main characteristics is the exploitation of continual momentary dissonance'.[7] Gibbons did, indeed, borrow from Dowland on

5   The sources of Gibbons's consort music are described in Harper, 1983(a).

6   This feature recalls the 'four-note' pieces of the time. See those by Daniel Farrant and Alfonso Ferrabosco II printed by Dart and Coates, 1955, pp. 101-103.

7   Poulton, 1982, p. 347.

other occasions, although his contrapuntal writing is so much superior to Dowland's that any influence can hardly have been very profound. Dissonant syncopations were in any case widely used, and could have been suggested to Gibbons by any number of sources. Similar passages occur frequently in Claudio Monteverdi's first book of madrigals (1587), and the 'e pur si more' passage of *Baci soavi e ceri* is based on four descending notes like Gibbons's In Nomine. We shall never know whether Gibbons actually saw *Il Primo Libro de Madrigali*, but Monteverdi's madrigals were certainly known in England.[8] Whatever his source, Gibbons employs the same device elsewhere. There are examples in the song *What is our life?*, where it likewise appears in a passage built around sequences (Ex. 16b on p. 112), and in the anthem *O Lord, in thy wrath* (Ex. 31 on p. 166). *What is our life?* was certainly written by 1612, and the beginning of the anthem is reminiscent of *O that the learned poets*, another song of the same period.[9] All this suggests that a conjectural date of around 1610 for the In Nomine may not be too wide of the mark.

Ex. 16.

(a) Orlando Gibbons, In Nomine (MB 48/28) bars 1-18

continued

8   The sources indicating this are probably later than Gibbons's In Nomine. Tregian's anthology (BL Egerton MS 3665), for example, includes most of Monteverdi's fourth book of 1603, but it is uncertain when it was copied. See Thompson, 1992, and Cuneo, 1995.

9   See p. 134.

Ex. 16a *continued*

(b) Orlando Gibbons, *What is our life?* bars 83-88 (transcribed as a solo song)

The last of Gibbons's In Nomines (MB 48/29) occurs in three sources, always in conjunction with MB 48/28, but it differs from that piece in its instrumentation. Two sources indicate that it is for a viol consort of two trebles, one tenor and two basses, instead of the more usual two trebles, two tenors and bass. It also differs from MB 48/28 in method, but both pieces rely heavily on sequences, and their melodic material is often closely similar. MB 48/29 may therefore have been written as a companion piece to MB 48/28, though the small number of surviving copies suggests that it never achieved the same popularity.

Of the two works, it is MB 48/29 which provides the more skilful solution to Gibbons's problem of how to give rein to his natural instincts within the constraints imposed by the cantus firmus. Its plan is executed with less rigidity than that of MB 48/28, and it is more densely filled with material that evolves with greater freedom. Every point is related to every other, and each is capable of unlimited sequential extension. The multiple forms in which the points appear mean that they can be illustrated only by typical examples, but an indication of their relationship is given below (Ex. 17). The first point (a) is composed of descending fourths and fifths; initially it consists of four such intervals, but for the next entry it is extended to seven. The second (b) is derived from the first, largely by a process of inversion and diminution, and like the first it is extended as required. The third point (c) is again an extensible descending sequence, now including semiquavers; it is, in fact, an inversion of the point which closes MB 48/28. The next point (d) reverts to the quavers of the second point, and in one of its forms combines an ascending scale with descending sequential fourths and fifths derived from the first point. Gradually it changes into a new motive (e), while retaining a sequential structure.

Ex. 17. Orlando Gibbons, In Nomine (MB 48/29)

(a)

Bass II, bars 1 - 8

(b)

Bass II, bars 26 - 28

Bass II, bars 31 - 35

continued

Ex. 17 *continued*

Variations and dances

A set of variations, and a pavan and galliard, each in six parts, occur in sources connected with the Hatton family.[10] Whether they are a product of Gibbons's work for Sir Christopher Hatton is a matter for surmise; but they seem to belong to the period of Hatton's patronage, and the pavan begins with a point reminiscent of one at the beginning of *O that the learned poets*, which appeared among the songs dedicated to Hatton.

Gibbons's writing for six instruments displays all the mastery he had acquired by the time he published his songs. There is, however, something slightly superficial about these pieces. It may be doubted whether without a commission of some kind he would have chosen to write in genres unsuited to gifts whose natural outlet was the fantasia, and he seems not to have been wholly absorbed in the job assigned to him. Byrd would have been stimulated by the challenge and risen to the occasion; in failing to engage fully with his task, Gibbons appears as the composer of lesser stature.

10   All are in Christ Church MSS Mus. 2 and 403-408. The variations are also in Christ Church MS Mus. 21. The Hatton connections are discussed by Pinto, 1990, and Wainwright, 1997. Other sources of the pavan and galliard are listed by Harper, 1992, p. 124, and Harper, 1982(a), pp. 7-8.

The variations on *Go from my window* (MB 48/40) are anonymous in the sources, though strong evidence of Gibbons's authorship is provided by their position relative to other pieces by him in Christ Church MS Mus. 21.[11] They display the same qualities as Gibbons's keyboard variations: great technical ability and not a little imagination in handling the medium, and a considerable lack of interest in working out and executing a comprehensive design. His urge to write pieces with a forward movement conflicted with the static tendency inherent in a set of variations as he conceived it. A fermata and double bar-line after the fourth variation may indicate that Gibbons extended a short composition. If so, he can have had no concern but to increase its length, for there is no sense of a plan slowly unfolding, or of a purpose gradually being revealed. The variations which contain similar ideas are separated — numbers 4, 6 and 8, composed largely of quavers, are alternated with contrasting material — but Gibbons evinces no anxiety to carry planning beyond this rudimentary level. He begins as though his intention is to rotate the tune through each part in turn, but its allocation to the instruments is unequal, and it is never given to the second tenor. This is a little odd when he is intent on providing all the performers with something satisfying to play, as though he is writing for a group of amateurs, and ensures that the running semiquavers of variation 9 are shared between the two basses. Gibbons is nevertheless adept at creating contrasts of texture: the trebles are silent in the distinctive third variation, and in the eighth the four upper parts play in quavers while the basses are restrained before their moment of glory in the ninth variation.

Looseness of form is still more marked in the pavan and galliard (MB 48/41-42), and an apparent absence of concern for structure is matched by the same indifference to the the social and musical roots of the dances as appears in Gibbons's keyboard pavans and galliards. Each piece consists of the usual three strains, which are repeated without variation; but the strains are irregular, and the underlying nature of the dances is sometimes obscured. The pieces appear as a pair in all the sources containing them, but although they contain similar motives there is little to suggest that Gibbons attempted to link them, either by the familiar expedient of deriving the galliard from material used in the pavan, or by the more complex methods he employed in the Salisbury pavan and galliard.[12] Gibbons treats each strain as a separate entity, constructed from a single motive or from two or more motives (the initial strain of the pavan, for example, falls into three overlapping but

---

11   Harper, 1982, pp. 123-124; Harper, 1983(a), p. 11.
12   See pp. 90-92.

distinct sections). The chief link between the two pieces is their genial disposition. Compared with Gibbons's keyboard pavans, the consort pavan is unexpectedly sunny. It shares with the galliard and the variations on *Go from my window* a character found in his other Mixolydian pieces, which often contain a popular component.[13]

Six-part fantasias

Whatever Gibbons may have felt about writing consort variations and dances, his interest in the composition of fantasias could hardly be illustrated better than by the number and quality of those he wrote for strings. While these are not immune from the Italian, often madrigalian, influence apparent in other Jacobean consort fantasias,[14] his methods in many of the consort fantasias are quite as individual as in those for keyboard. In composing for each medium he came to employ a highly personal procedure for maintaining the flow of ideas, frequently treating a new point as a means of articulation rather than as material for prolonged formal development. The result, in his mature pieces, is a succession of rapid melodic and textural contrasts, differing from the more fully worked sections often favoured by contemporaries. Stability is maintained by a strong underlying tonal structure, for which Byrd's works surely provided the model, while a flow of fresh ideas carries the music forward and gives it variety.

Christ Church MS Mus. 436 contains a reduction of Gibbons's six fantasias in six parts which reveals how intimately his consort writing is at times related to his writing for keyboard.[15] But it is not always easy to connect the fantasias for keyboard closely with those for strings. In composing for consort he was less apt to be guided by the recollection of his fingers on the keys, and responded to the contrapuntal opportunities provided by separate stringed instruments, and to the variety of attack, dynamics and sustaining power they offered. Furthermore, the fantasias for keyboard are not fully synchronous with those for strings. Advances in Gibbons's thinking mean that, whereas his mature keyboard fantasias have the character of skilfully developed improvisations growing in intensity, in his later consort fantasias he returned to the clear sectionalization which he earlier abandoned. These pieces often have the

13   The Mixolydian mode occurs in *The King's Jewel*, *The Hunt's Up* and *Whoop, do me no harm*, which all include a popular element; but Gibbons did not reserve the mode entirely for such pieces, as the First Preces show.

14   See Neighbour, 1983, p. 352; Wess, 1986, p. 3.

15   The reductions are in the nature of slightly simplified adaptations, rather than literal transcriptions on to two staves.

character of an argument proceeding with varied pace — though the difficulty of bringing it to a conclusion was one which caused him some trouble. The question of how to end a fantasia was one which he attempted to answer in different ways.[16]

Gibbons seems to have concentrated on the consort fantasia mainly after he had composed most of his keyboard fantasias, and to have brought to it an increasing awareness of music written for court entertainments. It appears, too, that the majority of Gibbons's consort fantasias were composed after he became engaged more with the verse anthem than the full anthem. Although there is no exact parallel between his later consort fantasias and his verse anthems, he found in each an opportunity to explore new procedures and to extend his emotional range. The six-part fantasias seem, however, to belong to a period when he was still occupied with the ideas that inform his full anthems. He may have begun writing them about the same time as his six-part variations and dances for consort.

The six-part fantasias (MB 48/31-36) occur as an anonymous group in each of three connected sources.[17] Although not ascribed to Gibbons, they are associated with works by him in the major source, which also places together works by other composers. Partial confirmation of Gibbons's authorship is provided by a further source, which attaches his name to the second fantasia.[18] The six fantasias were evidently planned as a set, and the sources (presumably adhering to Gibbons's intention) order them by key: 1-2 in g (one flat), 3-4 in d (no flat) and 5-6 in a. It will be better to identify them by their position in the set than by their numbers in the *Musica Britannica* edition.

Gibbons	1	2	3	4	5	6
MB	31	32	33	34	35	36

16   See p. 125.

17   Christ Church MSS Mus. 403-408 (the major source); also Christ Church MSS Mus. 2 and 436. See Harper, 1982, pp. xvii-xviii; Harper, 1983(a), pp. 6-7, 11-12. For the connections of the manuscripts with the Hatton family see Pinto, 1990, and Wainwright, 1997.

18   Bodleian Library MSS Mus. Sch. E.437-442. Harper (1982, p. 123) notes that the fifth of the six-part fantasias includes an extended use of rising chromaticism (bars 27-54), unlike anything else in Gibbon's work, but balances any doubt this may create about Gibbons's authorship with the presence of a passage echoing one in another piece by Gibbons (see note 20 below).

On the whole, the six-part fantasias lack the distinctive characteristics of the three-part fantasias and double bass fantasias that Gibbons seems to have composed after the end of 1616, when he became a member of Prince Charles's musical establishment. But indications of chronology are not altogether clear-cut. On one hand, the six-part fantasias exhibit a preference for regularly spaced entries in the opening exposition, also found in the earlier of the three-part fantasias which Gibbons eventually published; and all but number 5 include (though they do not begin with) points containing repeated notes, of a type found in the earlier fantasias of the published set, and in some of the keyboard fantasias Gibbons had probably written by about 1612.[19] On the other hand, the brevity of six-part fantasias 3 and 4 matches almost exactly the brevity of 5 and 6 of the published set; while dance-like elements in numbers 5 and 6 of that set are matched by a similar passage (bars 59-67) in the second six-part fantasia. Perhaps the conclusion to be drawn is that Gibbons worked on the six-part fantasias over an extended period, completing them before he wrote the later three-part fantasias.

Indications of chronology within the set of six-part fantasias are also ambiguous. Numbers 5 and 6 are contrapuntally less complex than their companions, but this may not be a sign of early composition,[20] especially since Gibbons's method in the initial exposition of fantasia 5 is comparable to his procedures in numbers 3 and 4 (see below). The relative order of the pieces is however less important than the features that mark them out as a set. All the six-part fantasias contain a variety of the contrapuntal devices and textures that appear not only in Gibbons's full anthems but in his songs, and his use of them is often strikingly similar.

Fantasia 1 begins straightforwardly with three entries of a point at two-bar intervals, but Gibbons delays the fourth entry for an extra half-bar before resuming entries at two-bar intervals. This disruption of regularity is paralleled in several anthems — *I am the resurrection*, for instance. Other parallels with Gibbons's method in his anthems often occur in the body of a fantasia. The first fantasia illustrates how, just as

19   Points of this type occur in a number of pieces composed for masques, and their occurrence in Gibbons's music may indicate the influence of masque music upon him before he joined the Prince's musicians. Examples can be found in Sabol, 1978, nos. 154, 168, 177, and the second strain of 275. Compare also tunes such as 'Mundesse', in Playford, 1651, p. 90.

20   Neighbour (1983) suggests it may be sign of anxiety to complete the set. Baines (1968) notes that six-part fantasia 5 (he refers to it as no. 4) contains a passage (bars 70-75) curiously like one in the earliest of Gibbons's five-part In Nomines (MB 48/27, bars 53-58); but it seems hardly probable that the pieces can date from the same time.

in an anthem, he may briefly reduce the number of parts to three or four, so as to achieve a change of texture or colour.

Fantasia 2 starts, not unlike the song *Nay let me weep*, with the three lower instruments playing in free counterpoint while the upper instruments play more or less imitatively. The opening of number 3 combines two short points, and groups adjacent parts in pairs like the song *'Mongst thousands good* and the anthem *O Lord, in thy wrath*. A similar procedure is adopted in numbers 4 and 5, though in the latter case the pairing of voices is different. The beginning of fantasia 6 returns to straightforward imitation, rounding the set off as it began.

Fantazies of III. Parts

The *Fantazies of III. Parts* were published at some time between July 1618 and February 1621/2.[21] They also appear in a remarkably large number of seventeenth-century copies.[22] No manuscript source is known to predate the original printed edition, but five manuscripts contain features that may indicate derivation from an earlier text.[23] Since none of the five presents the complete set of nine fantasias, some tentative deductions can be made about the order in which the pieces were composed.[24] It will be convenient to use Gibbons's numbering instead of that of the *Musica Britannica* edition.

Gibbons	1	2	3	4	5	6	7	8	9
MB	7	8	9	10	11	12	13	14	15

The nine three-part fantasias for viols can be grouped in three different ways:

(1) Fantasias 1-3 are in g (with one flat in the signature); numbers 4-9 are in d (no flat).

21   See p. 62. They were reprinted in Amsterdam in 1648.

22   Harper, 1982, p. 119; Harper, 1983(a), pp. 6-7. Ashbee observes that 'The large series of three-part fantasias by Lupo may in part have been inspired by Gibbons' collection − and initially were presumably played by the same group of musicians − but there can be little doubt that Jenkins, too, was encouraged by this example to begin both his splendid series of three-part fantasias'. He adds that Gibbons's pieces 'seem to have reached a wide public and to have been instrumental in shaping a good many pieces by his successors in the field, including Jenkins' (Ashbee, 1982, pp. 133, 276).

23   Harper, 1983(a), p. 9.

24   The contents are given by Harper, 1982, p. 119, and Harper, 1983(a), pp. 7-10.

(2) Although Gibbons labelled the parts for all the fantasias 'Altus', 'Tenore' and 'Basso', 1-4 are apparently for treble, tenor and bass viols, and 5-9 for two trebles and a bass.[25] The middle parts of 1-4 have a lower tessitura than the middle parts of the remaining fantasias.[26]

(3) With the partial exception of 3, fantasias 1-4 are stylistically related. Fantasias 5-9 are in a different common style.

Fantasias 8 and 9 are omitted from two of the manuscripts, so may have been written after 1, 2, 4, 5, 6 and 7, which are included. As fantasia 3 is omitted from all but one of the manuscripts, where it is grouped with 8 and 9, it may have been the last to be composed. The sources differ about the order of 5, 6 and 7, but one which omits 8 and 9 also omits 7, so it may be later than 5 and 6. The numerical order in the printed edition therefore seems to indicate the order of composition of all the fantasias except 3.

If this conclusion is valid, how is it to be accounted for? A possible explanation is suggested by Gibbons's practice of composing his string fantasias in sets of six. It may be that, having already written three-part fantasias 1-2 and 4 (two in g and one in d, but for the same combination of instruments), he embarked on a set for a different instrumental combination, beginning with number 5. Then, before completing six new pieces, he determined on publication, and decided that a set of nine, incorporating those he had previously composed, would be more impressive.[27] It may have been to satisfy his sense of proportion that he wrote the last piece in g and inserted it near the beginning of the set, so that three pieces in g precede six in d. Caution is however necessary in advancing this hypothesis. If it is accepted that Gibbons did write the third fantasia after the others, it has also to be accepted that he went to some lengths to disguise the fact.

---

25   Harper (1982, p. xxi) however observes that 'Within the viol family the wide range of tuning enables many of the parts to be played on more than one instrument'. Dart was the first to suggest that the second group may have been intended for two violins and a bass, with organ (Dart, 1956, pp. 345-347; see also Holman, 1993, p. 221). This must be reckoned only a stimulating suggestion, though some manuscripts contain indications of Gibbons's consort pieces being adapted to changing tastes.

26   In 1-4 the 'tenore' part has a C clef on the second line up; in 5-9 it has a G clef on the second line up.

27   Pinto (1996, pp. 105-106) considers possible reasons why Gibbons decided to publish nine fantasias, and to group them as he did, but concludes that the matter remains obscure.

Gibbons's appointment to Prince Charles's musical establishment in 1616 cannot be connected certainly with differences between the earlier three-part fantasias and the later, but the idea of a connection is plausible. The first two fantasias may in fact have been written some years before that appointment. While they are more mature than Gibbons's three-part keyboard fantasia MB 20/10, they share with two somewhat later keyboard fantasias (MB 20/8 and 20/13, both likely to date from before 1612) the characteristic of points which repeat one note.[28] The first string piece contains sequential imitation of a kind found in Gibbons's first keyboard pavan (MB 20/17) and in the keyboard galliard named after Lady Hatton (two more works likely to have been written before 1612), though its more closely knit construction seems to place it slightly after the keyboard pieces.

A curious feature is found in the later three-part fantasias, which may indicate that they were written over a comparatively short period. It may also indicate that the third is part of the later group. Brief phrases which are closely alike occur in the first few bars of numbers 3 and 5-9. Although there is a somewhat similar phrase in number 4 (Ex. 18), it contains no quavers and does not occur quite so early. There is a danger that, once such a phrase has been spotted, others will be found everywhere. They may in any case be no more than part of the common idiom of the time, but it is possible that they expose a facet of Gibbons's mind at the time he was working on the fantasias. [29]

Ex. 18. Phrases from Orlando Gibbons's three-part fantasias

continued

28   See note 19 above, however.

29   Pinto (1996, pp. 103-105) suggests that the phrases may derive from the tune used by Byrd in *The Queen's Almain* (MB 27/10), but similar tunes occur in music for Stuart masques (see Sabol, 1978, nos. 89, 107 and 213). Pinto's hypothesis that words attached to versions of Byrd's tune may have suggested its suitability for a collection dedicated to Edward Wraye depends on the further, rather unsafe, hypothesis that Gibbons published the fantasias as a wedding present for his friend (see pp. 62-63).

Ex. 18 *continued*

The first two fantasias begin with the instruments entering in turn at two-bar intervals (number 1 has seven such entries in succession), and they continue to progress in phrases which, though generally less regular, are clearly defined.[30] The fourth fantasia (probably the third to be written) forms a bridge between the earlier and later groups of the collection. It shares the instrumentation of the earlier, but is in a new key, and it relaxes the two-bar regularity of numbers 1 and 2. Although its initial point begins with a two-bar phrase, it is continued by one of three bars; and while the second entry occurs after two bars, the third entry is delayed for another three bars.

Fantasias 5 and 6 introduce a group with a different instrumentation, in which Gibbons starts to explore new possibilities. Number 5 begins, like its precursors, with entries at two-bar intervals, but the initial point is less strait-laced than those of the earlier fantasias. While a popular component is not entirely absent from numbers 1, 2 and 4 — the repeated notes with which they begin are paralleled in several dance tunes of the period[31] — fantasia 5 has a more immediate appeal. The first and last sections suggest the outer strains of a dance, an impression nourished by the repetition of the last section (bars 40-47, 48-56). The new element occurs also in Gibbons's series of fantasias for the great

30   Neighbour (1983, p. 352) draws attention to an eight-bar phrase in fantasia 2 (bars 59-66), consisting of two matching four-bar periods.

31   See note 19 on p. 118.

double bass, and it will be suggested later (p. 130) that the two groups are connected.

If fantasia 5 discloses Gibbons's decision to return to a type of composition in which the sections are clearly defined, fantasia 6 develops its mood and plan. Here again the outer sections of the piece are of special importance in the overall design. The eight-bar strain with which number 6 begins not only has a popular character — it seems to be based on a tune known in England for at least half a century — but is, with minor changes, the eight-bar strain with which it ends.[32] There is another respect in which fantasia 6 elaborates the plan of fantasia 5. In the first of these pieces a short rising motive of two quavers and a crotchet, occuring in the opening ten-bar section, reappears in the central sections and again in the repeated eight-bar section at the end. The outer sections of fantasia 6 also contain melodic and rhythmic motives which provide material for the middle.

Gibbons was now thinking on new lines, and conceived the fantasia in terms that differed from those formulated in his keyboard fantasias. Both 5 and 6 are short in comparison with others of the set, as though he was trying out new methods in pieces fashioned on a relatively small scale. Yet, despite his exploration in new directions, he remained a traditionalist in many ways. The shape and rhythm of his melodies in his fantasias mean that they could not be mistaken for Byrd's, but he retains much of the modal language of composers of Byrd's generation, and in this respect his fantasias are not nearly as up to date as, say, the music Robert Johnson provided in 1613 for *The Memorable Maske of ... the Middle Temple, and Lyncolns Inne* (Ex. 19 on p. 124).

Features of fantasia 6 are adopted, and at times accentuated, in fantasia 7. The earlier piece includes passages that are either wholly or nearly homophonic; so does the later. The first three entries of number 6 occur at half-bar intervals; the opening point of number 7 makes its first three entries at the distance of a crotchet (it is inverted in the second treble part). In other respects number 7 is associated with the fantasias that follow it. The contrasts between successive passages are more emphatic in numbers 7-9 than in the preceding fantasias, and each piece includes a clearly defined section in triple proportion (something used elsewhere by Gibbons only in his double bass fantasias). Gibbons's experiments with form may conceivably owe something to Byrd's six-

---

32   The tune is identified by Holman (1993, p. 221) as one forming the basis of no. 19 in the *Dublin Virginal Book* (c.1570). Ward (in *Dublin Virginal Manuscript*, 1983, pp. 51-52) traces its history to Tylman Susato's *Het Derde Musyck Boexken* (Antwerp, 1551), and gives other instances of its occurrence, sometimes under the name 'Almande Bruynsmedelijn'.

Ex. 19.

(a) Orlando Gibbons, three-part fantasia no. 5 (MB 48/11), bars 40-48

(b) Robert Johnson, *Baboons' Dance*, first section[33]

33   From William Brade's *Newe Ausserlesene liebliche Branden* (Hamburg, 1617). See Sabol, 1978, pp. 33, 78, 263.

part consort fantasias (BE 17/11-13), with their repeated sections and rhythmic changes.[34] But a more immediate influence is suggested by Gibbons's association with Coprario, the leading member of Prince Charles's music and a seasoned masque composer. Masque music provides many examples of sectionalized pieces with changes of rhythm and tempo.[35]

Gibbons makes another formal experiment in fantasia 8, where he treats the last two sections, in triple and duple time respectively, as a single unit to be repeated.[36] Fantasia 9 combines two procedures from earlier fantasias: that of finishing with a section balancing or recapitulating the beginning of the piece, and that of repeating the ending. The long point at the beginning of the fantasia provides a motive which, in reverse, is a principal element in the penultimate section, and which in its original form yields the material of the final section. Gibbons's concern with the endings of these fantasias seems to reveal his awareness of a difficulty. Instead of following up the success achieved with a clearly sectionalized structure in the *Salisbury* pieces, he had sought the uninterrupted forward drive offered by the more flexible fantasia, but had still to create a satisfyingly complete form.

Without the evidence provided by the omission of the third fantasia from most manuscript sources, it might still be felt that the piece is not quite at home in the position allotted to it. Although fantasia 3 is related to the first two fantasias by key and instrumentation, and its opening eight-bar melody consists of four two-bar phrases which parallel the two-bar spans in fantasias 1 and 2, Gibbons may have sought deliberately to create a relationship with the first two fantasias of the set — something which would lend credence to the notion that the development of his ideas about the form of his fantasias was largely a conscious one and the result of careful reflection. Even though number 3 does not exhibit the most obvious formal features of numbers 5-9, the length and character of its opening melody suggest a chronological relationship with the opening bars of the ninth fantasia.

34   BE 17/13 was published in Byrd's *Psalmes, Songs, and Sonnets* of 1611.

35   See Sabol, 1978, nos. 129-134, 137-138, 140-142, 144-145, etc. Some of Sabol's attributions to Coprario are amended by Charteris, 1982, pp. 17-19.

36   A repeat sign in the 'altus' and 'basso' parts of no. 8 is mentioned on p. 120 of the *Musica Britannica* edition, but omitted from the score. Furthermore, triple time is not introduced as abruptly in the original print as the edition suggests. Minims (dotted minims in bars 47-59 of the edition) are played at the same speed throughout the piece; mensuration signs occur before groups of notes transcribed as crotchets in bars 47-59.

Two-part fantasias

The unique source for Gibbons's fantasias for two treble instruments presents them as two groups: MB 48/1-2 and MB 48/3-6.[37] This may mean that the first two were at one stage circulating alone. But while they are in a common key (F) which is not shared by the other four, there is no reason to regard the six fantasias as anything but a set. It may be that they were written for the players who performed the two treble parts of numbers 5-9 of the three-part fantasias, although they have a character of their own.

Numbers 1-3 of the two-part fantasias consist of a series of overlapping but easily discernible sections. There is contrast between the sections, but there are none of the changes of tempo and rhythm found in the three-part fantasias, and the contrasts are not as pronounced as those in the double bass fantasias discussed below. The writing is broadly canonic throughout, with the parts crossing frequently.

The fourth fantasia differs from its companions. It carries to extremes the tendency of the other two-part fantasias to begin with points incorporating intervals of anything from a third to a sixth. And in spite of its comparative brevity it is the only two-part fantasia to be divided into two distinct parts. Since the fifth and sixth two-part fantsias are cast in the mould of the first three, these differences may mean that the fourth was the last to be written. Its brevity and its frequent four-bar phrases suggest comparison with numbers 5 and 6 of the three-part fantasias.

Fantasias with double bass

A group of Gibbons's fantasias (MB 48/16-19 and 24-25)[38] demand a bass instrument with a compass down to A'. The 'great bass viol', or *violone*, appears to have been in use among Prince Henry's musicians, for 'Thaccompte of Sir David Murray knight keaper of the saide late Princes privie Purse' records a payment for 'Voyalls twoe greate ons xl^{li}'.[39] Later records point to the instrument's continued use at court,[40]

37   King's College, Cambridge, Rowe Music Library MSS 112-113, where the groups are separated by a number of pages.

38   MB 48/20-22 are probably by Coprario. MB 48/23 is a galliard of uncertain authorship. See p. 131 below.

39   PRO, E351/2794, covering the period 1610-12; also AO1/2021/2 ('Vyolles twoe greate'); Ashbee, 1986-96, iv, p. 215.

40   Under a warrant of 24 January 1624/5, Jerome Lanier was paid twenty pounds for 'a greate base Vyall' (PRO, E351/544, m. 194^r; Ashbee, 1986-96, iii, p. 134).

where the earliest part-books to contain Gibbons's fantasias with the great double bass seem to have originated.[41]

Part-books at Christ Church present the fantasias as a set, apparently in the order of composition,[42] and they may be numbered accordingly.

Ch. Ch. MSS	1	2	3	4	5	6
MB	16	17	18	19	24	25

The set falls into three pairs: 1-2, in three parts, in the key of g (one flat); 3-4, in three parts, in d (no flat); 5-6, in four parts, in C. Some sources of 1 and 2 (but not of the other fantasias) contain fragments of an additional part. These may be relics of an organ accompaniment, but if so it is impossible to say at what stage the accompaniment was added, or by whom. It may reflect the taste of a slightly later time, when the organ accompaniment of string consorts had become common.[43] Another puzzle about the performance of the double bass fantasias concerns the instrument for which the highest part was written. The case for believing that it may have been the violin, rather than the treble viol, is persuasively set out by Holman.[44]

Quite apart from their unusual instrumentation, the double bass fantasias seem as if written to a specific brief. All are long by

Instruments of this sort were clearly very expensive. Another payment of twenty pounds was made to Alfonso Ferrabosco, for 'a greate Base Vyall, and greate Lyra' under a warrant of 17 February 1626/7 (E351/544, m. 223ᵛ; Ashbee, iii, p. 138).

41   Christ Church MSS Mus. 732-735. See Harper, 1982, p. xvii; Harper, 1983(a), p. 13; Lawes, 1991, p. xvi; Wainwright, 1997, pp. 61-64, 396-400. Use of the great double bass was not confined to the court, and Robert, 3rd Lord Petre, owned a similar instrument (though it was valued at only 15s.) in the 1630s (Essex Record Office, D/DP F224, an inventory of 1638; facsimile in Grieve, 1954, plate XXVIII).

42   Christ Church MSS Mus. 419-421 and 732-735; the order in which the fantasias appear is confirmed by other sources. See Harper, 1983(a), p. 15.

43   Neighbour (1983, p. 353) and Holman (1993, pp. 215-216; 1996, pp. 368-369) take the view that the fragments may well stem from Gibbons's own practice. Holman writes that 'Gibbons clearly intended an organ accompaniment', and discreetly provides one in his recording of the fantasias (Hyperion CDA66395, recorded in 1991). A manuscript describing the fantasias as 'Fancyes ... to the Organ' (formerly King's College, London, MS 3) probably dates from the Restoration period. It is sometimes stated that BL MS R. M. 24.k.3, an organ book, is associated with Christ Church MSS Mus. 732-735, but this is doubtful, and the organ book contains none of Gibbons's double bass fantasias (Wainwright, 1997, pp. 61-64; Field, 1998, pp. 243-244).

44   Holman, 1993, pp. 217-218. See also Harper, 1982, p. xxi.

comparison with the published three-part fantasias. All are in distinct, contrasting sections, some of which are repeated. Contrasts between the sections include those generated by changes of rhythm and speed. And tunes of a popular type are introduced, linking them with the later fantasias of the published set. The common characteristics of the double bass fantasias are however embodied in plans of considerable variety.

Gibbons proclaims at the outset his intention of creating contrasts. The four-bar phrase with which the bass viol begins the first fantasia consists of contrasting pairs of bars, the first bar of each pair containing descending semibreves, while the second is more lively (Ex. 20).

Ex. 20. Orlando Gibbons, double bass fantasia no. 1 (MB 48/16), bass viol part, bars 1-8

The whole phrase is repeated by the bass viol, and taken up by the other instruments. The importance of the semibreves is emphasized by the treble, which includes seven of them in its first nine bars. In combination with the livelier second half of the opening phrase, played in turn by the bass and double bass, the treble's semibreves anticipate the contrast between two sections at the centre of the fantasia, one in a sprightly triple time and the other in the original duple time and with longer note values.

The second double bass fantasia elaborates the layout of the first, so that the contrasts are more extensive. It embraces two sections in triple time, and there are two sections in long notes, the second of which contains pairs of descending semibreves forming a thematic connection with fantasia 1. Another thematic link is found in the resemblance between part of the initial point of number 2 and part of the point with which number 1 begins. The possibility that these pieces were the first of the fantasias to be written, and for a time were circulating as a solitary pair, is suggested by the fact that they are the only members of the set to survive with the vestigial 'organ part' mentioned above.

Gibbons retains a semi-formal opening in the third double bass fantasia, but in the course of the piece the popular element is made quite explicit, when the sole section in triple time gives way to a genuine popular tune in common time.[45] The four bars it occupies are repeated

45   Identified by Meyer (1982, p. 177) as a Dutch tune called 'de Rommelpot'. It occurs as a medius part in Ravenscroft's *Pammelia* (1609), with words beginning 'The

exactly, and may have stimulated two eight-bar sections which occur successively in bars 109-124 (both sections are marked 'soft' in the Christ Church part-books). In other regards double bass fantasia 3 exhibits a slight change from the plan of the first two fantasias. Instead of an interior section in long notes, there is a section in which one instrument at a time plays a series of minims while the others play shorter notes (mainly quavers). And the fantasia closes with a slow section combining long and short notes, where Gibbons seems to be musing on the Tudor origins of his contrapuntal craft. Its mysterious, enigmatic mood is but one example of the highly personal quality Gibbons was able to convey into 'entertainment' music.

The next fantasia, number 4, develops ideas which were introduced in number 3. Two sections, one of four bars and one of eight bars, are now repeated, and the slow ending is elaborated into a section thirty-three bars long.

Gibbons's double bass fantasias 5 and 6 are in four parts, and once more form a pair linked by key — unusually, among his consort pieces, the 'major' C mode. The addition of a part for tenor viol suggests that he may have become dissatisfied with the frequently wide open texture almost unavoidable in the three-part double bass fantasias.

In one respect the fifth fantasia introduces a new procedure, by beginning with a less formal point. In other respects it persists with the type of structure established in fantasias 1-4. Gibbons's method of assembling contrasting sections is, indeed, more clearly manifest in number 5 than in the previous double bass fantasias. The liveliness of the beginning may be one reason why there are several sections with longish notes (or, conversely, their presence may make a solemn beginning inappropriate). Directions for playing 'Soft' or 'Long', found in some sources of numbers 3 and 4, are multiplied in number 5, and supplemented by 'Away'.[46] To distinguish it from slower sections marked ₵, the quicker 'Away' section is marked by the same sign reversed. This section, as has often been remarked, is based on the third strain of the tune *Rufty tufty*.[47] There is, perhaps, an echo of *Rufty tufty* earlier in the fantasia, for bars 27-30 bear some resemblance to the tune's second strain. Though this may arise simply from Gibbons's adoption of a popular idiom and his fondness for strings of descending

crampe is in my purse full sore'. See Pinto, 1996, p. 103.

46   Christ Church MSS Mus. 419-421 (incomplete) and 732-735.

47   *Rufty tufty* appears on p. 70 of John Playford's *English Dancing Master* (1651). Its use by Gibbons is noted by Baines, 1970, p. 37; Neighbour, 1983, p. 354; Pinto, 1996, p. 102.

notes, there is no doubt that the melodic shape exercises an influence on the remainder of the fantasia.

In the last double bass fantasia of the series, Gibbons makes another new departure. The exposition of the lively initial point lasts for twenty-eight bars, and is succeeded by a further thirty-five bars in which he introduces and combines a succession of motives, as though revisiting the style of his mature keyboard fantasias. An ample slower section in long notes then follows, and is itself followed by what amounts to a quick dance with three repeated strains. Gibbons must have felt that a section in triple time would be superfluous.

The characteristics of the double bass fantasias suggest that they were specially commissioned, and that the popular element which Gibbons introduced into them may have been part of the commission. If this was indeed the case, it is possible that the element found its way into others of Gibbons's later fantasias via these pieces, first giving rise to the same feature in number 5 of the three-part fantasias which Gibbons published. The repetitions occurring at the ends of some of the published fantasias seem also to be associated with those in the double bass fantasias. At the very least the two groups of pieces must be contemporaneous. The triple time sections in the double bass fantasias, and in fantasias 7 to 9 of the published set, seem likely to have originated in the former, where they assume a natural place in a series of dance-like episodes. The eight-bar periods of the third double bass fantasia could well be connected with the eight-bar structure of the melody which begins the third (and probably last) fantasia of the published set. Again, the opening points of double bass fantasias 5 and 6 may have given rise to the opening points of numbers 9 and 3 of the published fantasias.

Consort pieces of uncertain origin

Three three-part fantasias requiring a double bass appear anonymously in a single source, where they follow the three-part double bass fantasias known to be by Gibbons.[48] They are therefore printed with Gibbons's consort music as MB 48/20-22. Apart from their instrumentation, they are connected with Gibbons's pieces by their inclusion of 'popular' material and of contrasting sections, some of which are written wholly or partly in long notes. Two include sections in triple time, and all three have endings broadly comparable to those added by Gibbons to MB 48/17-19. More particularly, MB 48/22 begins with an inversion of

48   Dublin, Archbishop Marsh's Library, MS Z2.1.13, compiled c.1666-78. Gibbons's name is attached only to the first and last of the four double bass fantasias acknowledged to be his.

the point which opens Gibbons's MB 48/18. A manuscript leaf discovered in the 1970s, however, bears a fragment of MB 48/22 with an attribution to Coprario, while the reverse side of the leaf bears part of another piece attributed to him elsewhere.[49]

There are two possible explanations of the origin of the anonymous fantasias. Either they are superseded works by Gibbons, or they are by Coprario, and written in association with Gibbons in response to a shared commission. Neighbour favours the latter interpretation, on grounds of style, and suggests that the pieces represent a first step towards Coprario's fantasia-suites. It would be difficult to disagree with this: the anonymous pieces do not seem like Gibbons's work.[50]

Along with the double bass fantasias, the *Musica Britannica* edition prints a three-part galliard (MB 48/23). It is ascribed to Gibbons in the single source, where it follows his double bass fantasias 1 and 4.[51] The bottom part nevertheless descends only to C, no further than the lower bass viol part of Gibbons's six-part pavan and galliard, while the middle part is within the compass of a tenor viol. The editor's labelling of the lower parts 'bass' and 'double bass' may therefore be questioned.[52] So may the source's ascription of the galliard to Gibbons. Attractive as the piece undoubtedly is, it is very slight, and consists of only two strains, whereas Gibbons's galliards usually have three. There is no denying that Gibbons could have written the sequential scalar phrases of which the piece largely consists, but if he did it must have been early in his career, well before he wrote any of the three-part fantasias he published.

In Christ Church MS Mus. 21, between the three-part fantasias and textless versions of Gibbons's songs, are a fragment of his variations on *Go from my window*, and three six-part instrumental pieces (printed as

49   Charteris, 1977, pp. 36, 94-95; Charteris, 1982.

50   Neighbour, 1983, p. 355-356. Neighbour's argument is, briefly, that the 'Coprario' pieces are more consistently imitative than those by Gibbons; points tend to be kept in play for longer, sometimes with more than one exposition; expositions on later points are as amply spaced as initial ones; duet interludes are more frequent and longer; and in freer passages the parts are less closely coordinated. It might be added that the anonymous pieces often contain motives that Gibbons is unlikely to have written. Neighbour notes, too, that the indication of an organ part places the instrument in the lead at the beginning of MB 48/20-21, consistently with Coprario's later practice.

51   Dublin, Archbishop Marsh's Library, MSS Z3.4.1-6, compiled c.1666-78. The manuscripts include (considerably later in the volumes) Gibbons's In Nomine MB 48/28 and his pavan and galliard MB 48/41-42.

52   Dart and Coates (1955, p. 22) also label the parts treble, tenor and double bass. On the grounds that the double stops of the bottom line are unplayable on the viol, they interpret it as a continuo part for organ or harpsichord doubled by a bass viol.

MB 48/37-39). The manuscript attributes the latter group to Gibbons, and they have generally been accepted as his work, though they have been regarded as vocal in origin.[53]

At first sight, MB 48/37-38 look like textless versions of anthems. It is easy to imagine some passages of the first being sung by small groups of voices, with others being sung by the full choir. Writing of a similar kind can be found in two anthems likely to belong to the second decade of Gibbons's career at court: *Lord, grant grace* (the section 'Glory, honour and power'), and *O clap your hands* (the second part). Comparison with Gibbons's anthems may, however, be misleading. MB 48/37-38 have an overall compass (G-g") greater than that customary in Gibbons's anthems (F-d" at written pitch, sometimes extending down to E and up to e"). It is, in fact, the one found in Gibbons's secular songs. The usual compass of the songs in *The First Set of Madrigals and Mottets* is G-g"; only occasionally is it extended downwards to F. The welcome song *Do not repine, fair sun* has a bass viol part which descends to D, but the compass of the vocal parts is once more G-g". The notion that the MB 48/37-38 might be transcriptions of secular vocal pieces finds support in the ABB form of the first, which suggests a song with repeated chorus.[54]

The overall compass of MB 48/39 again goes up to g", but it goes down to F and even E flat, as though the lowest part was originally played by or shared with a bass viol. The piece is far longer than either MB 48/37 or MB 48/48, and only a little shorter than *Do not repine*. The original may well have had some of the characteristics of that work. An introduction played by viols was evidently followed by a vocal duet, and though the exact nature of the piece is subsequently less clear, the manuscript indicates an entry for chorus at bar 85 and the beginning of a verse at bar 109. These facts, combined with the qualities which MB 48/37-39 have in common, and their occurrence together, suggest that all three may be transcriptions of secular songs, and possibly of works celebrating events in the reign of James I.

53   Some doubt about this is expressed by Harper, 1983(a), p. 12.

54   When bars 42-66 are repeated, an exchange is made between the treble parts, and between the parts marked tenor II and tenor III in the *Musica Britannica* edition.

6

SONGS

The First Set of Madrigals and Mottets of 5. Parts: apt for Viols and Voyces bears the date 1612. It contains Gibbons's settings of verses from thirteen poems, printed as twenty pieces. No doubt following the example set by Byrd in his publications, Gibbons organized his pieces by key. He may perhaps have intended also to bring together those with the

---

Key plan of *The First Set of Madrigals and Mottets*

1	F	13	d (one flat)
2	F	14	d (one flat)
3-6	G[†]	15	d (one flat)
7-8	a[†]	16	d (one flat)
9	a	17-18	g (two flats)*
10-11	a[†]	19	g (one flat)*
12	a	20	g (one flat)

[†]Each group of songs sets one poem. *17-19 set one poem.

---

same combination of clefs, although number 15 breaks the pattern.[1]

The title-page describes the songs as 'newly composed'. This might be taken to mean 'not previously printed', but no pre-publication copies survive, and the songs may have been too recent to have achieved anything but a limited circulation before their appearance in print.[2]

If, as seems probable, *Nay let me weep* was one of the many songs written as a lament for Prince Henry, who died on 6 November 1612, the part-books must have been printed about the end of that year (which ran up to 24 March 1612/3). There is little to date most of the songs more closely, although it is possible that the words of *Lais now old* were

---

1 See Kerman, 1962, p. 63, for a table illustrating Nicholas Yonge's arrangement of pieces by clef combination in *Musica Transalpina ... The Second Booke* (1597).

2 Copies in Christ Church MS Mus. 21, made in the 1620s, include important variants, though whether they present an early text is uncertain. For an example see Harper, 1983(b), p. 770.

not written until after 1606, when the Greek original was rediscovered.[3] And there could be some significance to the fact that in *A Pilgrimes Solace*, published in the same year as *The First Set of Madrigals and Mottets*, John Dowland drew on sources which supplied the words for Gibbons's *O that the learned poets*[4] and *Ah, dear heart, why do you rise?*[5] Although Dowland's songs may have been written earlier (he had not published a collection for nine years), it may equally well be that he and Gibbons were prompted to make settings of poems that were popular about the time of publication.[6]

Character of Gibbons's songs

The First Set of Madrigals and Mottets appeared near the beginning of a decade in which, to judge by printed collections, the madrigal experienced a revival of popularity after a period in which the solo lute-song had been more in vogue. But only one of Gibbons's songs much resembles a madrigal of Italian ancestry: he seems to have used the word 'madrigals' as a general term for his lighter songs, and to have thought of any serious vocal piece as a 'motet'.[7]

3 *Lais now old* imitates an epigram attributed to Plato. This is included in the *Palatine Anthology*, and so in the *Greek Anthology* (vi.1). The manuscript of the former was rediscovered at Heidelberg by the French scholar Claude de Saumaise (Claudius Salmasius) in 1606. The results of Saumaise's discovery did not appear in print until many years later, but the interest it stimulated may have led to the verse set by Gibbons.

4 From *The passion of a discontented mind* (1601, further editions in 1602 and 1621), published anonymously but attributed to Nicholas Breton. The poem's authorship is discussed in Corser, 1867, pp. 42-45 (where the poem is printed) and Breton, 1952, pp. xciii-xcviii. Gibbons set stanza 5. Dowland set three stanzas, beginning with the words 'From silent night'.

5 The poem resembles one beginning ''Tis true, 'tis day', by John Donne, and is ascribed to him in some manuscript sources. A version is prefixed to ''Tis true' in the edition of Donne's poems printed in 1669; but the couplets concluding Donne's stanzas are pentameters, not tetrameters as in the verses set by Gibbons and Dowland. Gibbons set one stanza of the poem; Dowland's song has two stanzas, and begins 'Sweet stay awhile, why will you rise?'

6 *The Second Booke of Ayres* by William Corkine, also published in 1612, contains a setting of Donne's ''Tis true, 'tis day' (see the note above).

7 Gibbons's 'madrigals' approximate to the 'sonnets and pastorals' of Byrd's *Psalmes, Sonets & Songs* of 1588. Thomas Morley wrote of the 'madrigal' as requiring 'an amorous humour', and the word 'motet' as comprehending 'all grave and sober musicke' (Morley, 1597, p. 179; 1952, p. 294). Martin Peerson published a collection with the title *Mottects or Grave Chamber Musique* in 1630.

The poems set by Gibbons, of which some at least may have been chosen by Sir Christopher Hatton,[8] show a preference for 'philosophical' verse, though none is in any way complex, in the sense in which the poems of John Donne (Gibbons's senior by ten years) are complex. A number display the slightly self-indulgent sorrow or pessimism associated with Dowland.[9] Few of the songs are unaffected by this trait, and it would be difficult to distinguish in every instance the lighter 'madrigals' from the more serious 'motets'. In their solemnity Gibbons's texts are reminiscent of many set by William Byrd. There is a particularly close similarity between the words of Gibbons's *I weigh not fortune's frown* and those of two songs in Byrd's *Psalmes, sonets, & songs* of 1588: *My mind to me a kingdom is* and *I joy not in no earthly bliss*.[10] Gibbons, however, never looked quite as far back as Byrd did for some of his texts, even if they are not altogether up to date.[11]

Gibbons's songs are decidedly individual, not to say idiosyncratic, and demand to be accepted on their own terms. But it is not hard to see that he took Byrd's songs as his point of departure, either because of his own inclination or because he was writing for a patron or performers with conservative tastes. A passage in the dedication of *The First Set of Madrigals and Mottets* to Sir Christopher Hatton in fact echoes one in Byrd's address to 'all true lovers of Musicke' in his last publication, *Psalmes, Songs, and Sonnets* (1611). Byrd asks connoisseurs to 'be but as carefull to heare them well expressed, as I have beene both in the Composing and correcting of them'. Gibbons asserts that 'Songs of this Nature are usually esteemed as they are well or ill performed'.

Kerman has observed that, 'Like Byrd, Gibbons is not altogether untouched by the madrigal aesthetic or by Italianate techniques'.[12] Indeed, the changing sense of the words of *How art thou thralled* is matched — quite in the madrigal manner — by changes in the texture, movement, motives and feeling of the music. Yet the majority of

8   See p. 37.

9   See Jacquot, 1954, and Mellers, 1954.

10   The words of the first of Byrd's songs are attributed to Sir Edward Dyer. Those of the second are anonymous, but may be associated with Dyer's verses. *I weigh not fortune's frown* is a poem by Joshua Sylvester, first printed by Grosart, 1880, ii, p. 340.

11   The words of Gibbons's most popular song, *The silver swan*, nevertheless have a traditional element. They were inspired by *Il bianc' e dolce Cigno*, a poem often set to music. In a setting by Vecchi it is translated in the second book of Nicholas Yonge's *Musica Transalpina* (1597) as 'The white delightful Swanne sweet singing dyeth'. *Now each flowery bank of May*, too, seems to look back to an Italian model: Petrarch's 'Zefiro torna'.

12   Kerman, 1962, p. 125.

Gibbons's songs could hardly differ more from the kind of piece attempted by his brother Ellis when, in 1601, he contributed to *The Triumphes of Oriana*.[13] For the most part, they give musical expression to the words more through their general mood than through attention to the minutiae of the text; and their musical structure adheres more closely to the larger pattern of the verse than to its details.

Gibbons is not indifferent to the pattern or meaning of the poems he sets — despite making nonsense of a stanza from Spenser's *The Faerie Queene* by breaking it in the middle of a sentence.[14] But he seems often to be more interested in creating a broad impression than in illustrating particulars. He rarely attempts word-painting, even when it is invited by a phrase like 'thunder's crack'. He only occasionally emphasizes a word with an unexpected harmony, and is likely to define a verbal phrase chiefly by a change of speed or rhythm, as he does in setting 'I sound not at the news of wrack' in *I tremble not at noise of war*.[15] Another example is found in *What is our life?*, where the phrase 'That sits and marks still who doth act amiss' is set to crotchets and quavers, and the succeeding phrase 'our graves that hide us from the searching sun' is set to semibreves and minims. *Farewell all joys*, the second part of *How art thou thralled*, provides an exception. It is one of the most madrigalesque of Gibbons's songs. Here, phrases such as 'She smiles, she laughs, she joys at my tormenting' and 'tossed on despair's black billow' are illustrated harmonically, rhythmically and melodically, while a suitable gloominess is lent to 'Break then poor heart' by its allocation to the three lower voices.

Original form of the songs

Although Gibbons sanctioned the performance of all his songs by five singers, many are easily adapted to other modes of performance. The title-page of *The First Set of Madrigals and Mottets* implies the possibility either of *a cappella* performance or performance by a consort of viols (the songs do in fact appear without texts in Christ Church MS Mus. 21). This is more than the mere convention of the time.[16] The

13   See p. 16.

14   *Fair ladies, that to love—'Mongst thousands good* (dashes are used here to join the incipits of consecutive songs which set verses from a single poem).

15   'sound': swoon.

16   During the period 1600 to 1624, sixteen out of thirty printed collections of songs for several voices had title-pages declaring their contents 'apt for voices and viols' (or using some similar phrase). The first was Thomas Weelkes's *Madrigals Of 5. and 6. parts* (1600).

adaptability of these pieces to a variety of circumstances is a mark of Gibbons's skill as a song-writer. Several lend themselves to performance by a solo singer (or two singers) and viols, and it may be that, like Byrd in *Psalmes, Sonets, & Songs*, Gibbons in some cases adapted solo songs by adding words to parts written initially for instruments. While Gibbons did not mark a 'first singing part', as Byrd did, it might be argued that several of the songs show signs of having been conceived for a treble voice (the 'cantus' in the part-books) and a viol consort.[17] But a difficulty in accepting this argument without reservation is the absence of early copies which support it. Moreover, all the parts are written with the possibility of *a cappella* performance in mind. In no song does the lowest part descend uncomfortably low, as it might if written for a bass viol. The most one can say with certainty is that many of the songs leave room for choice in deciding how to perform them.

If Gibbons ever adapted existing solo consort songs when he was preparing pieces for publication, he did not do so in every case. It is fairly clear that a few songs (for example, the madrigal-like *Farewell all joys*) were intended primarily for *a cappella* performance. Yet — rather strangely, in the work of someone trained as a singer — much of the writing in *The First Set of Madrigals and Mottets* has an abstract cast, especially in parts other than the cantus. Although the words of most, if not all, the songs must have been Gibbons's starting point, the musical lines often develop as if they were composed with instruments in mind and the words were fitted to them later. This may be a factor — though not the only one — contributing to the verbal repetition in Gibbons's songs. (It is unusual for him to set a syllable to more than one note, and often when he does so it is not simply to stretch the words to fit the music.) There is extensive word-repetition in *Fair ladies—'Mongst thousands good* and *O that the learned poets*, where the style is very close to that of Gibbons's fantasias (Exx. 24 and 27 on pp. 141 and 146). In some instances it appears as if Gibbons had to amend the lengths of notes to accommodate the words. An expected crotchet in *Fair is the rose* is often divided into a pair of quavers (see the untexted parts of Ex. 25 on p. 143). Not infrequently the association of words with quasi-instrumental writing results in a less than comfortable partnership.[18]

17   All the songs have cantus parts within the written range c'-a", the extremes of which are for the most part avoided. The note c' in fact occurs only once, in *Yet if that age*.

18   McGuiness (1995, pp. 27-28) discusses infelicites in *Now each flowery bank of May*.

The silver swan is a song which works well when performed by a solo singer accompanied by four viols. In the cantus part the repetition of words is avoided and nearly every syllable is sung to a single note. (This is not proof that it was written for solo performance, for the whole song is economical in these respects.) A few songs have the appearance of requiring five viols, one of which sometimes alternates with and sometimes doubles a solo voice. (Justification for performance in this way may lie in the distinct possibility that, prior to preparing fully-texted copies of his songs for printing, Gibbons himself did not write out separate vocal and instrumental parts, but wrote texted and untexted parts on the same staves, with imprecise underlaying and the repetition of words indicated only by a sign, leaving copyists and performers to decide how things should be managed in practice. Copies of his anthems in Christ Church MS Mus. 21 and the only surviving copy of *Do not repine, fair sun*, in New York Public Library MSS Drexel 4180-5, are so written, and may reflect Gibbons's own habits.)[19] In some songs, a viol alone may originally have played the opening bars of the cantus part. It has been suggested that the vocal part of *What is our life?* did not begin until bar 12, and that the voice did not enter until bar 13 of *Yet if that age.*[20] This would account for some of the repeated words. It is difficult, however, to accept that repetition in *Fair is the rose* could be explained in this way, and word-repetition must be recognized as an intrinsic feature of Gibbons's style. It was, after all, a familiar feature of madrigals, not to mention more austere songs such as the three-part psalms Byrd published in 1589.

The cantus of Gibbons's 'solo' songs is generally the only part with a G clef, while in his polyphonic songs he uses the same clef in both the cantus and quintus parts.[21] One would not wish to be absolute about this (and might hesitate to deny that *Dainty fine bird*, with two G clefs, works well either as a solo song or as a duet for two trebles), but the test does help to identify songs which may have been written primarily for five voices. They are *O that the learned poets, I weight not fortune's frown—I tremble not—I see ambition—I feign not friendship, How art thou thralled?—Farewell all joys,*[22] *Fair ladies, that to love—'Mongst thousands good* and *Trust not too much.*

19   Manuscript sources of the time include the works of other composers written in a similar manner.

20   Kerman, 1962, p. 123; McGuiness, 1995, p. 21. A viol can be substituted selectively for the voice in *Now each flowery bank of May* and *Lais now old*.

21   McGuiness, 1995, p. 31; noted also by Kerman, 1962, p. 124. The part-books of Gibbons's songs are designated 'cantus', 'quintus', 'altus', 'tenor' and 'bassus'.

22   McGuiness points out that *How art thou thralled*, which employs C clefs for the

A few pieces in *The First Set of Madrigals and Mottets* are suited for performance as solo songs with chorus. *Nay let me weep—Ne'er let the sun—Yet if that age* shares with *What is our life?* the time signature ¢ instead of the C usual in Gibbons's songs.[23] A change to C3[24] in the third part introduces what appears to be a choral finale. *Ah dear heart* is another which may end with a choral passage, beginning with the fifth line of the verse ('O stay ...').[25] This matches the piece's ABB form.

Word-setting

The repetition of words in Gibbons's songs has already been mentioned, but the adaptability of these pieces complicates any further discussion of his approach to word-setting. The insertion of bar-lines, where the part-books have none, can also lead to misconceptions, for the melodic lines are often rhythmically free and independent of one another. In general, it can be said that Gibbons plays off the rhythms of speech against his musical rhythms as a poet plays them off against the metre of his verse. There is a tension between the length of syllables in the words and the length of the notes given to them, and between the movement of the verse and that of the melody. On occasion it is plain, just from the cantus parts of songs which lend themselves most readily to solo performance, that Gibbons has allowed musical considerations to take precedence over verbal considerations. The iambics of *Ne'er let the sun* become almost uniformly spondaic in Gibbons's setting (Ex. 21).

Ex. 21. Orlando Gibbons, *Ne'er let the sun*, cantus part, bars 6-21

cantus and quintus parts, could conceivably be performed as a solo song.

23   Later in the century ¢ indicated a slightly quicker tempo than C, but whether Gibbons intended this distinction is open to question.

24   'The imperfect of the more', indicating that three minims are to be played in the time of a semibreve.

25   Suggested by Kerman (1962, p. 124) and Dart (in his Reviser's Note of 1963 to Fellowes's edition of *The First Set of Madrigals and Mottets*). Dart suggests that *What is our life?* also may have *a cappella* sections at 'Our graves' and 'Only we die', but it is hard to see where the first such section might end and the second might begin.

The cantus part of *Yet if that age*, a setting of the third verse of the same song, is closer to speech rhythms, but it is far from naturalistic (Ex. 22).

Ex. 22. Orlando Gibbons, *Yet if that age*, cantus part, bars 13-38

This does not mean that Gibbons is careless or inept in setting words. He possesses a controlled variety of tone. In the song *How art thou thralled* he responds sensitively to the verse, conferring on each verbal phrase its own musical shape. He gives the words 'How art thou thralled' and 'O traitorous eyes' the character of exclamations, and dramatically lengthens the note values in setting the words that follow them (respectively, 'poor despised creature' and 'to gaze so on her eyes'). He can, when he wishes, capture the rhythms of natural speech in a graceful tune, and the abiding popularity of *The silver swan* may owe something to his success in this direction (Ex. 23).[26]

Ex. 23. Orlando Gibbons, *The silver swan*, cantus part, bars 1-7

Gibbons's frequent intention, however, unlike that of his contemporaries who were pioneering a declamatory style, was not to create a melodic parallel to everyday speech. His songs emphasize different compositional values from those of the continuo-accompanied songs developed in the

26   The popularity of the song in the seventeenth century is evidenced by the inclusion of the treble and bass in a book of string parts compiled after 1623 (BL Additional MS 10444: treble f. 5ʳ, bass f. 60ʳ), and by Playford's publication of an arrangement in *Catch that Catch Can* (1663). It was afterwards reprinted a number of times as a glee. The only other song by Gibbons to have been reprinted before the 1840s is *O that the learned poets* (Turbet, 2000).

masquing hall by Alphonso Ferrabosco, Nicholas Lanier and others.[27] It is seldom that the verse he sets, or his treatment of it, is colloquial. Gibbons's songs are, in the true sense, artificial.

Gibbons rarely writes treble melodies that are unbroken. None of his songs, except perhaps *The silver swan*, has a cantus part able to live outside its contrapuntal context. The treble voice usually has many long notes, and in solo performance seems to float upon the instrumental sound; and it alternates with passages played by viols alone. The treble parts of songs tend to adopt recurring characteristics of the lower parts, which frequently include passages based on sequences or on a rising or falling scale (Ex. 24).

Ex. 24. Orlando Gibbons, '*Mongst thousands good*

continued

27   See Spink, 1974, pp. 38ff.

Ex. 24 *continued*

These characteristics are prevalent, too, in all the parts of Gibbons's
most obviously *a cappella* songs. Gibbons was evidently aware of his
fondness for scalar motives, and in *Fair ladies, that to love*, he
contrasted ascending motives with those that descend. Although such
passages are invariably handled with great skill, their constant
occurrence in Gibbons's works of all kinds engenders a feeling that he
found them too easy to write, and that they sometimes result from an
insufficiently self-critical approach to the problems of composition.

Structure

Some of the poems set by Gibbons are almost completely neutral with
regard to musical pattern. The four verses of *I weigh not fortune's
frown—I tremble not—I see ambition—I feign not friendship* show no
progression of thought, and there is no logical requirement for them to
be in the order in which they appear. Although Gibbons tends to set the
words line by line, he distinguishes the verses of this otherwise
unstructured poem by treating each of them in an individual way. Apart
from writing the settings in one key, all he does to unify them is to
round them off by repeating the last two lines of the fourth verse.

The verses of *I weigh not fortune's frown* are not only static in the
ideas they express, but there is little metrical difference between them.
In fact, there is very little variation of metre or length of line in most of
the poems Gibbons set.[28] This does not seem to have worried him. It is

---

28   The most frequently used metre is iambic pentameter. Numbers 3-6 and 15 are in
iambic tetrameter; and so is 12, though each of its lines omits the initial weak stress. The

usually only in the broadest terms that the sense and pattern of the poems dictates the musical shape of his songs, and details may be overlooked. The three couplets of *The silver swan* give rise to a setting with the form ABB, but it seems that Gibbons wrote the two B sections with the words of the second in mind. He employs an affective diminished chord on 'death',[29] which is out of place in the first B section, where it occurs on the second syllable of 'against'. In other instances, however, Gibbons follows the structure of his text more carefully in setting it to music. In *Fair is the rose*, thesis and antithesis in the verse are reflected in the musical phrases (Ex. 25).[30]

Ex. 25. Orlando Gibbons, *Fair is the rose*, bars 1-31 (transcribed as a solo song)

continued

poem forming numbers 7 and 8 includes some shorter lines among the pentameters.

29   The full effect is reduced if words are sung to the four lower parts.

30   Aston, 1980, analyses the pattern of *What is our life?*, which he describes as 'one of the great masterpieces of Jacobean secular song'. He notes the question in the first phrase, the reply in the second, and the subsequent modification and inversion of the opening phrase, etc.

Ex. 25 *continued*

Gibbons's attention to the broader aspects of the meaning and pattern of the verses he sets is often reflected in the contrapuntal structure of his songs, and in his use of tonality as a structural element. He was a skilled, though never rigid, contrapuntist, and had an armoury of musical devices at his fingertips. It may have been from Byrd's music that he learned to employ the artifices described by Morley:

> If you would compose well the best patterns for that effect are[31] the workes of excellent men, wherin you may perceive how points are brought in, the best way of which is when either the song beginneth two severall points in two severall parts at once, or one point foreright and reverted ...[32]

Gibbons uses 'one point foreright and reverted' (by which Morley means 'inverted') in *Now each flowery bank of May* (Ex. 26).

31   Morley has 'or'.
32   Morley, 1597, p. 167 (1952, p. 176).

Ex. 26. Orlando Gibbons, *Now each flowery bank of May*, bars 1-15

At the beginning of *O that the learned poets* Gibbons indulges in 'learned' writing (which might be regarded as a form of rhetoric, or a musical equivalent to poetic 'wit'): he combines two simultaneous points, and a voice which has sung one proceeds to the other (Ex. 27).

Ex. 27. Orlando Gibbons, *O that the learned poets*, bars 1-12

It seems probable that Gibbons studied Byrd's use of tonality, though he is not as adventurous as Byrd, and seldom moves very far from the tonic key, unless for some special purpose. *O that the learned poets* illustrates Gibbons's use of both tonality and counterpoint, and though no brief analysis can do justice to the song's complexities it is worth looking at some aspects of it more closely.

Some aspects of *O that the learned poets*

The rhyme-scheme, ababcc, is matched by a setting in three sections.[33]

O that the learned poets of this time,
  Who in a love-sick line so well can speak,

The setting of the first line combines two points (Ex. 27). In bar 15 a cadence on D coincides with the end of the first line in the cantus and quintus parts. The second line introduces several imitative or partly imitative figures; some resemble points used in setting the first line, but their free treatment anticipates a total absence of imitation in lines 3-4. The second line ends at bar 28, having moved from F to C (tonic to dominant) without straying further from the tonic key than the subdominant. This is established by a languishing plagal cadence (bar 23) where the tenor and bassus sing of 'a love-sick line' (the attention given to the lower voices is confirmation of composition for five singers).

Would not consume good wit in hateful rhyme,
  But with deep care some better subject find [seek]

Imitation plays no part in this section (bars 28-48, ending on the tonic). The line-break is again clear in the cantus, and is again marked by a cadence on D (bar 39), but Gibbons creates continuity by overlapping the parts: although the cantus ends line four at bar 48 the tenor continues it into bar 49, while the altus begins line five in bar 47.

For if their music please in earthly things,
  How would it sound if strung with heavenly strings?

Imitation is resumed in the third section, where the fifth and sixth lines are distinguished by separate points. Since the cantus is silent when the break between the lines occurs in bar 60, the division is marked by the quintus, the highest voice then singing. In bar 67 the non-key note E♭ makes a second appearance (the first helps to illustrate 'love-sick' in bar 23). This time it forms part of a C minor chord where the altus and quintus sing of 'heavenly strings'.

---

33   The rhyme scheme requires that 'find' in line 4 should be amended to 'seek'.

Appreciation of Gibbons's use of different combinations of voices or instruments as a constructional and expressive element in *The First Set of Madrigals and Mottets* is somewhat obscured by the mixing of songs intended for *a cappella* performance and songs easily adapted to solo performance. The subject is also difficult to discuss without very long examples, but a short quotation from *Yet if that age* illustrates Gibbons's facility in disposing the several voices (or, as transcribed here, the members of the viol consort) to lend colour to the setting (Ex. 28).

Ex. 28. Orlando Gibbons, *Yet if that age*, bars 35-62 (transcr. as a solo song)

continued

Ex. 28 *continued*

Gibbons seems to have made little or no attempt to combine into one large structure his separate settings of the stanzas of one poem. This was noted earlier in connection with *I weigh not fortune's frown—I tremble not—I see ambition—I feign not friendship.*[34] Even his setting of four lines beginning 'Fair ladies, that to love captived are' has no strong thematic links with that of the remaining five lines of Spenser's verse, beginning "Mongst thousands good'. Such links as might, by some stretch of the imagination, be perceived, are as likely to spring from Gibbons's general style as from any deliberate design. The same can be said of other settings of two or more related verses, and the statement is borne out by Gibbons's evident indifference to clef combinations and key signatures in composing them. The two songs *How art thou thralled—Farewell all joys* have different clef combinations. In *Nay let me weep—Ne'er let the sun—Yet if that age*, where the three songs have the same clef combination, the last has a different key signature from the other two (one flat instead of two). This appears to be of little significance, however. E flat in the key signature of the first two settings is frequently cancelled by a natural, while E is as frequently flattened in the third setting.

The Teares or Lamentacions of a Sorrowfull Soule

Sir William Leighton's *The Teares or Lamentacions of a Sorrowfull Soule* appeared in 1614, and consists of settings of verses from the religious poems he published under the same title in the previous year.[35] The first part of the collection contains songs accompanied by a broken consort, but Gibbons provided nothing for this. Like Byrd, he showed

34   See p. 142.
35   See p. 51.

no interest in writing for a group of mixed instruments. The other two parts contain songs for four and five unaccompanied voices. It was to these that Gibbons contributed a four-voice setting of *O Lord, how do my woes increase* and a five-voice setting of *O Lord, I lift my heart to thee*.[36] Each is a concise setting of the initial four-line stanza of each poem, but Leighton advises performers to sing the subsequent stanzas included in his book of poems.

Gibbons's pieces have much in common with his songs in *The First Set of Madrigals and Mottets*. Their style is not far removed from that of the second section of *O that the learned poets* (bars 28-48), and they are framed in a counterpoint where imitation plays little part. The resemblance to Gibbons's secular songs in fact goes further, for it is easy to imagine the cantus parts being sung as solos. It is they which illustrate the ideas conveyed by the words: rising melodic peaks denote mounting troubles in *O Lord, how do my woes increase*, and in *O Lord, I lift my heart to thee* the idea of lifting is represented by the lower notes of the melody to which the words 'I lift my heart to thee' are set (f♯' g' a'). Just as the cantus parts of songs printed in *The First Set of Madrigals and Mottets* frequently include rests which are filled by the other voices or the accompanying viols, so lengthy rests punctuate the cantus parts of *O Lord, how do my woes increase* and *O Lord, I lift my heart to thee*. And, as in the secular songs, the happy match of words to music in the cantus part of the pieces written for Leighton is not always equalled in the other parts.

Uncollected secular vocal works

Apart from the songs collected in *The First Set of Madrigals and Mottets*, only three secular vocal works by Gibbons are known. They are *The Cries of London*, *Orlando was his name*, and *Do not repine, fair sun*.

The Cries of London belongs to a small group of compositions into which the composers introduced the cries of watchmen, street vendors and beggars. The group includes *The Cries of London* by Thomas Weelkes, *The City Cries* and *The Country Cries* by Richard Dering, *New Fashions* by William Cobbold, and *The Cry of London* by an anonymous composer.[37] The earliest surviving copy of Gibbons's piece is to be found in Thomas Myriell's *Tristitiae Remedium*, dated 1616,[38]

---

36   Gibbons, 1925, fails to mark the repetition of the last two lines of *O Lord, I lift my heart to thee*.

37   Bridge, 1919-20; Johnson, 1972; Brett, 1974, pp. 158-171, 189.

38   BL, Additional MSS 29372-7. See p. 47.

but it could easily have been written a few years earlier. It consists essentially of two five-part consort In Nomines, and may well belong to the period in which Gibbons composed the more mature of his purely instrumental pieces of that kind.[39] The In Nomine chant forms a cantus firmus in the alto part, and is played through once in each piece, mostly in long notes but with occasional decorated passages. The free viol parts are intermittently doubled by voices singing the cries. These begin the first piece with 'God give you good morrow, my masters, past three o'clock and a fair morning', and end the second with 'Twelve o'clock, look well to your lock, your fire, and your light, and so good night', thus forming a parallel to Edward Gibbons's *What Strikes the Clocke?*[40] The second piece may, however, have been an afterthought, since the first exists in two forms, one concluding with 'Lanthorn and candle-light, hang out maids for all night', and another with words neutral as to time of day, perhaps substituted when the second piece was added.

Pieces composed of such disparate elements could easily become fragmented and directionless. Gibbons manages to avoid this danger, thanks in part to the controlling influence of the cantus firmus. Many of the cries he introduces are in any case brief, and can be inserted without disrupting his harmonic and melodic plan — in addition to which, some of them have probably undergone a slight modification to suit his purpose.

Little needs to be said about *Orlando was his name*. The piece is a catch of the sort published by Thomas Ravenscroft, and the circumstances of its composition in 1623 have been outlined above.[41] It survives uniquely in a manuscript in the Special Collections Library at Case Western Reserve University,[42] but although it is unlike anything else Gibbons is known to have written there is no reason to doubt that it is genuine. There is a hint in the words, which end with the behest 'call in the quire & with a chearfull noise give thanks unto our god, that hears both men & boyes', that it was written with the singers of the Chapel Royal in mind.[43]

The words of *Do not repine, fair sun* suggest that it was composed for King James's visit to Scotland in 1617. The text set by Gibbons

39   See p. 110.

40   See p. 21.

41   See p. 71. Ravenscroft's collections were *Pammelia* (1609), *Deuteromelia* (1609), and *Melismata* (1611).

42   It is one of the fragments bound into a copy of Ernest David and Mathis Lussy, *Histoire de la notation musicale depuis ses origines* (Paris, 1882).

43   As written, the catch is entirely in the treble range, but was no doubt sung at whatever pitch was comfortable for the singers.

consists of two of three associated poems ascribed to Joseph Hall.[44] Although Hall never rises to great heights, the irregular pattern of his poems calls to mind the verse Jonson wrote for court masques, and from that point of view they are more interesting than most of the texts Gibbons had to deal with.[45] But, in setting them, Gibbons could not quite shake off his solemnity, even for a supposedly joyful occasion, and the first half of his work is surprisingly sober for a celebratory song.

The piece is on an altogether bigger scale than the songs in *The First Set of Madrigals and Mottets*, and though it shares many of their attributes it is really a secular counterpart of the verse anthem *Great king of gods*, also written for the royal visit. Each piece is scored for solo voices (singing the 'verse' sections) and chorus, and each survives in a source that suggests the possibility of an instrumental accompaniment.[46] Unfortunately, neither *Do not repine* nor *Great king of gods* survives elsewhere, and neither source makes clear the nature of the accompaniment.[47] In both cases texted and untexted parts are written on the same staves. The untexted parts of *Great king of gods*, which was probably sung in the newly refurbished chapel at Holyrood, may have been derived from an organ accompaniment,[48] but it is possible that viols participated in the secular *Do not repine*. These may or may not have doubled the voices, but although the chorus is in five parts, the passages in which instruments may have played alone are in only four parts.

Despite similarities between *Do not repine* and *Great king of gods*, each piece represents an individual response to the pattern of its words. The first two verse-and-chorus sections of *Do not repine* set the first of Hall's poems; the brighter second half of the piece sets the second poem.

44   See p. 54. The verses are printed in Hall, 1949, pp. 150-152.

45   This is to some extent apparent in Gibbons's musical phrases, though somewhat masked by the repetition of words. Although the words are not fully written out in the source, it is evident that, as in his shorter songs, Gibbons sets few syllables to more than one note.

46   The top voice of *Do not repine*, however, rises to g", compared with the d" which is the usual limit in Gibbons's anthems (though these occasionally rise as high as e").

47   *Great king of gods* is in Christ Church MS Mus. 21. *Do not repine* is in New York Public Library, Drexel MSS 4180-5, compiled by John Merro. Monson (1982, p. 143) remarks: 'How this work, so intimately connected with life at court, should find its way into Merro's provincial collection, which otherwise seems so isolated from both London and courtly circles, is puzzling'. He suggests that Hall, who was Dean of Worcester 1616-1627, is 'the most obvious link between this courtly composition and Merro in the western counties'.

48   See pp. 53, 55 and 196ff.

The instrumental interlude between the sections is longer than is customary in Gibbons's anthems. Each of the choruses repeats all the words of the preceding verse, but does not in any straightforward manner repeat the verse's music. It seems to have been Gibbons's intention that the second poem should be sung by the chorus, though not entirely by the full chorus. The choral setting treats separate passages of the text in different ways (homophonically or contrapuntally, with or without imitation), and creates different combinations of voices to produce changes of colour.

The possibility that three pieces (MB 48/37-39) preserved as works for viols were originally secular songs, perhaps similar in nature to *Do not repine*, is discussed on p. 132.

Hymns

Gibbons provided music for a number of the pious verses which George Wither published as *The Hymnes and Songs of the Church* (1623).[49] Wither's epistle dedicatory claims that he had 'laboured to sute them to the Nature of the Subject and the common Peoples capacities, without regard of catching the vaine blasts of Opinion. The same also hath beene the ayme of Master *Orlando Gibbons* ... in fitting them with Tunes'.

The Hymnes and Songs of the Church has been described as 'the first hymnal proper of the Church of England, designed from the outset for congregational use'.[50] There is little doubt that Wither hoped that his words, and the tunes he included in his publication, would take a place in church alongside those of Sternhold and Hopkins.[51] This is clear from his provision of a long hymn to be used during the administration of the sacrament, '*the better to keep the thoughts of the* Communicants *from wandering after vaine objects*',[52] and is implicit in the terms of the royal

49   See p. 67. It is clear from Wither's dedication to King James that the verses had been produced over a longish period: 'what I delivered unto your Princely view at severall times, I heere present againe, incorporated into one Volume'. It is possible that Wither may also have written the words to some of Gibbons's anthems which survive in fragmentary form: *So God loved the world, Thou God of wisdom, This is the day*, and *Teach us by his example* (Gibbons, 1978, p. xii; Vining, 1979).

50   le Huray, 1978, p. 392. Wulstan, on the other hand, contests the idea 'that Wither's book was intended for congregational use, and that the organist would have supplied the inner parts' (Gibbons, 1978, p. xv).

51   The first complete edition of *The Whole Booke of Psalmes*, a metrical rendering of the psalter compiled by Thomas Sternhold and John Hopkins, appeared in 1562. Many more editions followed.

52   Song 83, sung to the tune supplied by Gibbons for song 3, *Sing praises Israel to*

patent dictating that *Hymnes and Songs* should be bound up with copies of the metrical psalms. But whether the collection was so used, even in churches which had an organist to fill out the harmonies and a parish clerk and congregation prepared to sing unfamiliar words to unfamiliar tunes, seems impossible to establish. It is equally difficult to prove — although it seems altogether probable — that the book had a place in domestic music-making, along with other volumes containing settings of pious verse. Wither's own words may be held to suggest that he hoped for this as well.[53]

Gibbons provided Wither with fourteen tunes, each printed with a bass.[54] The words are placed between the staves, and fit both parts, so that vocal performance of each is possible.[55] The songs may also have been performed domestically in other ways, including those described by Martin Peerson: 'to either the Virginall or Lute, where the proficient can play upon the Ground, or for a shift to the Base Viol alone'.[56]

The metre of Wither's verses is uniformly iambic. His lines usually contain four feet, but some verses have lines of three or five feet, or of four and three feet alternately. Gibbons's craftsmanship is visible in his

the Lord.

53   In his address 'To the Reader', at the end of the *Hymnes*, Wither says: 'That such as have skill and are delighted with Musicke, may have the more variety, to stirre up the soone cloyed affections, these *Hymnes* ar fitted with many new tunes; nevethelesse all (but some few of them) may be sung to such tunes as have bin heretofore in use; For the benefit therefore of those who have no experience in musicke, I have here set downe which Songs they be; and to what old tunes they may be sung'. Wither's preface to *The Songs of the Old Testament* (1621) refers, without further explanation, to 'the laudable custom of singing now in use'. His thoughts about stirring up the affections concur with those expressed by Ravenscroft in the preliminary matter of his version of *The Whole Booke of Psalmes* (1621).

54   The tunes are for songs 1, 3, 4, 5, 9, 13, 14, 18, 20, 22, 24, 31, 41 and 47. The tunes to 34 and 44 seem to be variants of 9, and that to 46 is a variant of 47. It is possible that Wither was responsible for the variant versions. A further tune (67) was taken from Edmund Prys's *Llyfr y Psalmau* (1621), and may have been written by Gibbons. Vining (1979) suggests that Gibbons may also have provided some of the music for Wither's earlier book, *The Songs of the Old Testament* (1621). Wulstan (in Gibbons, 1978, pp. x-xi), while remarking that the composers of the 1621 set 'remain, with some justification, anonymous', agrees (p. xi) that Gibbons may have based at least one tune on a piece published in 1621, and says 'Song 4 has striking similarities with that in the earlier book'.

55   Performance of any kind requires the correction of a number of errors scattered through the various editions.

56   Title-page of *Private Musicke* (1620).

method of dealing with this simple material. The barring of his tunes is irregular, and differs from edition to edition, but they generally have an implied four beats to a bar. Sometimes, however, he varies the metre. *Who's this, that leaning on her friend* (no. 18) is in triple time throughout.[57] *Thy beauty Israel* starts with an implied four-beat bar and immediately changes to three in a bar. *Come, kiss me with those lips of thine* begins with four bars of four beats, switches to three to a bar, and has a penultimate six-beat bar.

Gibbons sets the verses line by line, in the customary manner of psalm tunes, with a cadence and a rest at the end of each line.[58] The verses are short, and Gibbons is often content to restrict his cadences to the tonic and dominant, but at times cadences occur on a surprising number of different notes. *Sing praises Israel to the Lord* has cadences on D (the tonic), A, F, G and C. Even where cadences are formed on only two or three notes, Gibbons rings the changes by varying his stepwise approach to the melody note of the final chord, and his approach by step or leap to the bass note.

The phrases of Gibbons's tunes balance one another without being alike in duration. He sets metrically identical lines of verse to notes of different values, and shows the sensitivity to melodic shape that is evident in his larger compositions. The tunes enhance poetry which seldom rises above the pedestrian. Wither at his worst could inspire Gibbons to produce a small gem in *O, my love* (Ex. 29 on p. 156).

The first phrase of *O, my love* rises from a' to d" and returns to a', the second rises to from c" to f" and returns to c". The third phrase begins like the first, but sinks to g', and the fourth, beginning like the second on c", drops down to f'. The six-line verse leads Gibbons to repeat the last two musical phrases. The song's subtleties include the alternation of bars of four and six beats, and the modest ornamentation of the tune. *O, my love* is not far removed from the melodic continuo-accompanied pieces by professed song writers of the time.

57   It is one of only three tunes with time-signatures, the others being 14 and 41. Wulstan notes the inferiority of 14 and 41, and suggests that the time-signatures may indicate that they were not obtained directly from Gibbons (Gibbons, 1978, p. xi).

58   This assumes that Gibbons wrote his tunes with specific words in mind, though it is not sure that he invariably did so. Rests at the ends of lines are not usually explicit in *The Whole Booke of Psalmes* of Sternhold and Hopkins, but Gibbons does write them into his settings. The nature of such rests is to break up the verse, and (perhaps because Wither added words after the tune was written) song 22 contains a glaring example of the unfortunate effect this can have: 'O Lord of hosts and [rest] God of Israel'.

Ex. 29. Orlando Gibbons, *O, my love, how comely now*

O, my love, how come - ly now, and how beau - ti - ful art thou. Thou of

dove - like eyes a pair, Shi - ning hast with - in thy hair, And thy

locks like kid - lings be, which from Gil - ead hill we see.

7

ANTHEMS: INTRODUCTION

The Anglican liturgy of Gibbons's time permitted the singing of an anthem towards the end of Matins and Evensong, though it was not until 1662 that the provision was incorporated into the *Book of Common Prayer*, with the words 'In Quires and places where they sing, here followeth the Anthem'.[1]

Many of Gibbons's anthems are settings of biblical texts. Only one of these (*Sing unto the Lord*) comes from the Authorized Version of the Bible, published in 1611, although he is thought to have written at least three anthems with biblical texts after that date. For some reason — perhaps because of a rooted conservatism — Gibbons, or those who commissioned work from him, chose not to use the new translation. In one instance (*Hosanna to the Son of David*) he seems to have gone back to the Geneva Bible (1560).[2] But usually he turned to the Bishops' Bible, first published in 1568, or to one of the editions of the *Book of Common Prayer* which included the psalms in the same translation.[3] His few departures from the wording of the Bishops' Bible are invariably slight, and can often be put down to adaptation (enabling part of a text to stand alone, or two or more texts to be joined together), or to musical needs. A few apparent changes may be due to modernization during copying.[4]

Some departures are more curious. The words of *O Lord, in thy wrath* differ from those given by the editions of the Bishops' Bible, the

1 A definition of the term 'anthem' is included, by implication, in Thomas Morley's definition of the word 'motet': 'a song made for the church, upon some hymne or Anthem, or such like ... under which I comprehend all grave and sober musicke' (Morley, 1597, p. 179; 1952, pp. 292-294).

2 *Hosanna to the Son of David* consists of passages from the gospels. These were taken into the Bishops' Bible from the Geneva Bible with only minor changes, but the older text is the source of Gibbons's 'Blessed be he' (the later text has 'Blessed is he').

3 There were a number of editions of the Bishops' Bible. The British Library has a copy of the 1588 edition, which belonged to Gibbons's patron Sir Christopher Hatton (shelf mark G.12228). The cover is embossed in gold with the Hatton arms, beneath which is the date 1591. Gibbons can sometimes be shown to have used one of the later editions of the Bishops' Bible. For example, his text of *If ye be risen again with Christ* agrees with the Bishops' Bible of 1598 in its translation of Colossians iii.2 ('things which are on the earth'), but not with earlier editions (which read 'things on the earth').

4 It seems possible that 'highly exalted' in *O clap your hands* is a modernization of 'very high exalted'.

Geneva Bible and the Authorized Version examined for the purposes of this chapter. *This is the record of John*, besides small deviations from the Bishops' Bible text, introduces words from the Authorized Version ('the voice of him that crieth in the wilderness' is substituted for 'the voice of a crier in the wilderness'). It may be that this results from the instability of printed texts in the sixteenth and seventeenth centuries,[5] and that Gibbons's text occurs in some edition which has escaped notice, or it may be that he sometimes received texts from men who made their own versions, or muddled the published translations.

Apart from biblical texts, Gibbons's anthems set passages from the *Book of Common Prayer*, or specially written texts in prose or verse. The authors of the latter are for the most part anonymous. Only Godfrey Goodman is known, as the author of *See, see, the word is incarnate*.[6]

Eight of Gibbons's anthems which survive in a complete form are full anthems, sung throughout by the whole choir.[7] Twice as many are verse anthems, alternating choral passages with 'verses' for a soloist or a small group of singers, and including an organ accompaniment.[8] So, probably,

---

5   Scot (1997) deals with differences between copies of the *Book of Common Prayer*, but his findings probably apply to the Bible as well.

6   See p. 57.

7   This total includes *Hosanna to the Son of David*, though it is possible that it should be counted as a verse anthem (see p. 164 below). Two anthems printed in Gibbons, 1964(b), are probably by other composers. *The secret sins* may be by William Mundy (see le Huray, 1978, pp. 313-314). The six-part setting of *Out of the deep* is almost certainly by Byrd. The reasons for believing this are as follows. (1) A work with this title is attributed to Byrd in a collection of texts (Bodleian Library MS Rawlinson Poet. 23) and the indexes of two part-books which belonged to John Barnard (Royal College of Music MSS 1049 and 1051). (2) Manuscripts compiled by John Merro include two settings, in six parts and five parts, to each of which he attaches Byrd's name (New York Public Library, Drexel 4180-4185, which contains both settings, and BL, Additional 17792-17796, which contains the five-part setting). The text of the six-part setting is the one given by the Rawlinson word-book. (3) The six-part version occurs, anonymously, in a bass part-book from the Chapel Royal (St John's College, Oxford, MS 180), which is the richest source of Byrd's anthems. (4) The six-part version is ascribed to Gibbons in the index of Christ Church MS Mus. 1001, but this manuscript is the most complete source of organ parts for Byrd's anthems. (5) On grounds of style, one would be reluctant to attribute the six-part setting to Gibbons, or the five-part setting to either composer (Byrd, 1983, pp. vi, xiii). (6) In the *Annual Byrd Newsletter* (no. 1, 1995, p. 4) Turbet draws attention to similar passages in the six-part setting of *Out of the deep* and the Venite of Byrd's Short Service (also in six parts).

8   'Verse anthem' may be a later coinage. Barnard (1641) refers to 'anthems with verses'. The Chapel Royal's New Cheque Book (p. 9) has 'verse anthem' in 1726.

are nine more surviving mainly in the guise of organ parts. Seven out of eight to which dates can be attached with a modest degree of confidence are verse anthems, and appear to have been composed after 1611. (This assumes information given in Christ Church MS Mus. 21 to be accurate, though it is not confirmed independently.) While the evidence tends to suggest that Gibbons concentrated chiefly on verse anthems after his first decade in the Chapel Royal, it is slightly suspect because there is nothing outside the music to date most of his full anthems. One, *O Lord, in thee is all my trust*, may belong chronologically with the verse anthems which precede it in Christ Church MS Mus. 21. But *O clap your hands* is the single full anthem coupled to a date; Anthony à Wood and the scribe of the 'Gostling' part-books believed it to have been used in 1622, although its exact date of composition is open to question.[9]

The table on pp. 160-161 shows that, of Gibbons's two dozen anthems that survive completely or in a form complete enough to permit restoration, at least seven are occasional pieces. Most of his other anthems probably fall into the same category, since they have verse or prose texts which suggest that they were specially commissioned. Gibbons's muse seems often to have responded to an external stimulus.

Gibbons's anthems are notable for their variety of plan. and frequently for their intensity of emotion. Gibbons's music, like Byrd's, generally has an underlying sobriety, but in his anthems — especially those in the verse style — this often gives way to a passion that is all but operatic. The puritanical souls of the early seventeenth century who inveighed against the use of music in church had good cause to be suspicious. Like the religious poetry of Donne, Gibbons's anthems are a remarkable blend of intellect and ardour, and sometimes anticipate the poetry of Crashaw in expressing religious fervour with an amatory sensuousness.[10] This may or may not reflect Gibbons's religious attitude — we have no means of knowing — but it represents a generational shift in musical sensibility. An affective quality sometimes present in Byrd's work is commoner in Gibbons's, and was to become stronger in the work of Humfrey and Purcell. There is also an intimacy of feeling in many of the anthems, and some have survived in sources with a domestic origin (a few of them only in such sources), prompting the question of whether they were sometimes sung recreationally. Indications that the verse anthems might, in such circumstances, have been performed as consort songs with choruses are discussed below.[11]

9   See pp. 168-169.

10   Richard Crashaw was born c.1612; his *Steps to the Temple* was first published in 1646.

11   See pp. 200-201.

Gibbons's anthems: indications of date

1611
or
later
This is the record of John. 'This Anthem was made for Dr Laud presedent of Sant Johns'(Christ Church MS Mus. 21). The anthem's text seems to connect it with the Oxford college, and the inscription refers to Laud's position there between 10 May 1611 and 17 November 1621. It does not mention the posts he gained at Westminster and St David's (both in 1621). This suggests composition and copying in the period 1611-1620.[12] Laud may have marked his appointment as President by commissioning an anthem, though his diary mentions another occasion which might have led to a commission: the setting up of the college's new organ in 1618.[13]

1613
Blessed are all they that fear the Lord. 'A Weddinge Anthem first made for my lord of Summersett' (Christ Church MS Mus. 21). The Earl of Somerset married Lady Frances Howard in December 1613 (see p. 50).[14] An anthem with these words was sung at the wedding of Princess Elizabeth and the Elector Palatine in February 1612/3 (see p. 41), though whether it was Gibbons's is unknown.

Before
1616
See, see, the word is incarnate. 'The words were made by Doctor Goodman De: of Rochester' (Christ Church MS Mus. 21). Godfrey Goodman became Dean of Rochester on 4 January 1620/1 (see p. 57), but the anthem is included in Thomas Myriell's *Tristitiae Remedium* of 1616 (BL Additional MSS 29372-7).

1615
or
later
Sing unto the Lord. 'Psalme 30: Anthem of 5 voc: was made for Do^r: Marshall' (Christ Church MS Mus. 21). The text, from the Authorized Version, was published in 1611. The anthem may have been commissioned by Hamlett Marshall, who obtained his doctorate in 1615, and by 1616 was a Chaplain in Ordinary (see p. 57).

continued

12   Laud became a prebendary of Westminster on 20 January 1620/1 and Bishop of St David's on 29 June 1621. The note about the anthem's being composed for Laud is repeated in BL Additional MS 31821. Several pieces in that manuscript bear similar notes, with additional inscriptions acknowledging derivation from 'Dr Philip Hayes's copy', which may in turn have drawn upon the Christ Church manuscript.

13   Laud, 1695, p. 4: 'The great Organ in St. *John*'s Chappel set up: It was begun *Febr.* 5. 1618.'

14   BL Additional MS 31821 repeats the note on the anthem's origin.

Gibbons's anthems: indications of date *continued*

1617   *Great King of Gods.* 'This anthem was made for ye kings being in Scottland' (Christ Church MS Mus. 21).[15] (See pp. 53-55.)

1618   *Behold, thou hast made my days.* 'This Anthem was made at the entretie of Doctor Maxcie Deane of Winsor the same day sennight before his death' (Christ Church MS Mus. 21). Dr Anthony Maxey died on 3 May 1618.

1619   *O all true faithful hearts.* 'A thanks Giving for the Kings happie recoverie from a great dangerous sicknes' (Christ Church MS Mus. 21). Thanks were given at St Paul's for the King's recovery in April 1619 (see pp. 55-56).

1622   *O clap your hands.* 'D^r. Hether's Commencem^t Song sett by M^r. Orl.
?   Gibbons' (York Minster Library MSS 1/1-8(S)). Heyther gained his doctorate on 17 May 1622. The anthem may, however, have been written earlier (see pp. 168-169).

Note   *Grant, Holy Trinity* is headed 'The Kings Day' in the Durham manuscripts.[16] The surviving words give the impression that it is a prayer for Charles I, who became King on 27 March 1624/5, but 'Charles' may have been substituted for 'James'. (Byrd's anthem *O Lord, make thy servant Elizabeth*, appears as *O Lord, make thy servant Charles our King* in the Chapel Royal word-books.)[17]

---

15   BL Additional MS 31821 repeats the note on the anthem's origin.

16   For a list see Gibbons, 1964(b), p. 211.

17   BL MS Harleian 6346; Bodleian Library MS Rawlinson Poet. 23. The date of another anthem, *Glorious and powerful God*, may be hinted at in James Clifford's note that it is 'An Anthem for the Consecration of a Church or Chappel' (*Divine services and anthems*, 1664), but the occasion of its composition has not so far been identified. However, see p. 203 for an account of a consecration in 1622/3.

8

FULL ANTHEMS

Gibbons's full anthems have been much admired by later ages. In the latter part of the eighteenth century Burney wrote: 'though the *purists*, on account of the confusion arising from all the parts singing different words at the same time, pronounce the style, in which the full anthems are composed, to be vicious; yet the lovers of fugue, ingenious contrivance, and rich, simple, and pleasing harmony, must regard them as admirable productions, *alla Palestrina*, a style in which Tallis and Bird acquired so much renown'.[1] This opinion was maintained at the expense of Gibbons's verse anthems, which for long were ignored or regarded as inferior works.[2] Gibbons's skill in using the methods of older composers, on whose works he was nurtured, was what Burney admired. Gibbons began by writing in their manner, and he never wholly abandoned it. Gibbons's choral writing, whether in full anthems or verse anthems, shows him adapting the style of his predecessors to meet his current needs. As far as Byrd is concerned, it seems often to have been his later anthems and motets which influenced Gibbons. Confusion arising from his ability to approach Byrd's style is apparent in the still common attribution to Gibbons of a six-part setting of *Out of the deep*, which is much more probably by Byrd.[3]

It is not, however, Byrd's influence which is most plainly evident in Gibbons's *Deliver us, O Lord*, for the final 'Amen' is appropriated from Weelkes's setting of the words 'Long live fair Oriana', in his madrigal *As Vesta was from Latmos hill descending* (published in 1601).[4] *Deliver us, O Lord* is likely to be the earliest of Gibbons's surviving anthems. Its failure to match up to the standard of his other anthems — even allowing for its survival in a possibly incomplete state — has caused mild doubt about its authenticity, but no source ascribes it to anyone else.[5] Melodic lumpishness might be expected in the writing of an inexperienced composer, as well as wholesale borrowing, and in spite of

1   Burney, 1776-89, iii, pp. 329-330 (1935, ii, p. 265).

2   See pp. 170-171.

3   See note 7 on p. 158.

4   Noted by Vining, 1975. Weelkes's madrigal appears in *The Triumphes of Oriana*, to which Gibbons's brother Ellis contributed.

5   le Huray (1978, p. 312) observes that an alto part may be missing. Wulstan (in Gibbons, 1978) makes the same suggestion and amends the anthem accordingly. See also Phillips, 1991, pp. 118-119.

its shortcomings *Deliver us, O Lord* bears the marks of Gibbons's authorship. Typical of his habits is the scalar descent of an octave, split between the upper parts, and again between the lower parts, at the words 'and gather us from among the heathen' (Ex. 30).

Ex. 30. Orlando Gibbons, *Deliver us, O Lord*, bars 12-15

The influence of both Weelkes and Byrd may be visible in the spirited anthem *Hosanna to the Son of David*. Its ABA form may reflect knowledge of Weelkes's more restrained six-part setting of a similar text,[6] but it is also related by its form, and by its key and the voices required, to Byrd's *Exalt thyself, O God*, a possibly Jacobean setting of another celebratory text.[7] *Exalt thyself* is itself related to Byrd's *Sing joyfully*, which emphasizes references to 'the God of Jacob', and perhaps marked some event in the reign of King James.[8] *Hosanna to the Son of David* may have had a similar purpose. Its text has every appearance of being assembled to honour James. The words 'Blessed be the kingdom' are in fact read as 'Blessed be the King' in some sources, though these do not include the Chapel Royal word-books.[9]

[6]   Stephens (1975) draws attention to Weelkes's use of the same form in other anthems. He does not specify these, but presumably means *Alleluia, I heard a voice* and *Gloria in excelsis Deo*.

[7]   James, 1998.

[8]   Harley, 1997, p. 300.

[9]   The confusion over 'kingdom' and 'King' may be due to the occurrence of the

The anthem's original nature is uncertain, since it includes verse-like sections which create doubt about whether it started life as a full anthem. In the first half of the seventeenth century it seems to have been sung in some places as a verse anthem. Sets of part-books disagree within themselves and with each other,[10] although the bass voice is always omitted from passages where the tenors are divided.[11] Reduced forces sing 'Hosanna to the Son of David' and 'Hosanna in the highest heavens', but the second cry is triumphantly taken up by the full choir at the end.

Whatever its nature or genesis, *Hosanna to the Son of David* provides a demonstration of Gibbons's abilities, such as might have been demanded by a special occasion. It is consistently contrapuntal, and embodies a variety of technical devices: imitation, inversion, retrogression, and the combination of different motives. All are well integrated, and the whole grows from just a few ideas. The first verse-like section embodies a point based on a single phrase which ascends an octave, and subsequently expands to a ninth; then, before the verse is repeated in a modified form, the point gives rise to a tonally more adventurous intermediate section for the full choir.[12]

A contrast to *Hosanna to the Son of David* is provided by Gibbons's least ostentatious full anthem, the compact and accomplished *Almighty and everlasting God*. It is a setting of the Collect for the third Sunday after Epiphany. In a manuscript which may have been copied by John Stephens (who in 1625 was the Chapel Royal's 'Recorder of Songes' and in 1626/7 was elected Clerk of the Cheque) it is described as the 'Anthem to Mr Gibons Short Servis'.[13] There is good reason to accept this. Both works are in F and for the same four voices, and the anthem is written in a lucid counterpoint that is not at odds with the predominantly homophonic style of the Short Service. Furthermore,

different words in otherwise similar passages from Mark and Luke (the text is a conflation of Matthew xxi.9, Mark xi.10 and Luke xix.38). The different readings are detailed in Gibbons, 1978, p. 200. The word-books are BL MS Harleian 6346 and Bodleian Library MS Rawlinson Poet. 23.

10   See Gibbons, 1978, pp. 199-200. Morehen (1995(b), p. 207) refers to local practices in rearranging compositions for more convenient scorings when the occasion demanded.

11   And, briefly, from one passage where they are not divided: bars 53-57 in Gibbons, 1978. The sources indicate 'Full' in this passage.

12   The piece is analysed by Ellis and Pilgrim, 1984.

13   Index to St John's College, Oxford, MS 180; Morehen, 1969, pp. 391-407; Cheque Book, ff. 7ᵛ, 71ʳ; Rimbault, 1872, pp. 12, 156. The practice of associating an anthem with a particular Service is discussed by Morehen, 1995(b), pp. 211-212.

Almighty and everlasting God shows the keen sense of tonality present in the Service.[14] The entries of the initial point begin on F and B flat, and although there is a strong cadence on C at the word 'infirmities', a tendency to the subdominant is stressed by the flattening of the seventh degree on either side of the cadence. The tendency is counterbalanced by emphasis on the dominant during the remaining two-thirds of the piece, but recurs in the final plagal cadence.

The circumstances surrounding the composition of *Lift up your heads* and *O Lord, in thy wrath* are unknown. Gibbons's authorship is clear in both, but the form and details of each are dictated by his reading of the text. It is often Gibbons's texts which enable him to impose his own personality on pieces embodying traditional methods of composition, for many of them encourage his expressionistic inclinations.

The six-part penitential anthem *O Lord, in thy wrath* is a case in point. It is among the shorter of Gibbons's full anthems, but it is one of his most masterly.[15] The fluent counterpoint contains little genuine imitation and little in the way of elaboration, but it is supported by a strong harmonic framework, and all the elements are brought adeptly together in a concentrated whole. Accomplishment may not, however, imply late composition in the case of a musician as gifted as Gibbons. *O Lord, in thy wrath* in fact opens with a device reminiscent of the one which begins Gibbons's song *O that the learned poets*, published in 1612. But in the song two points are so combined that a voice which has sung one continues with the other;[16] in the anthem it is only the first treble and the bass that continue thus. The initial four entries begin on the same note, and at once start to generate the suspensions which offset an underlying chordal tendency, and give the anthem a peculiar intensity of feeling (Ex. 31 on p. 166).

Lift up your heads is another six-part anthem, for the same forces as *Hosanna to the Son of David*. It is clearly sectionalized, and though Gibbons ends each section with a cadence on the tonic he achieves tonal variety within sections. There is variety, too, in the musical motives distinguishing the verbal phrases, and the forms they assume. The flow of ideas and their rapid modification, indeed, recalls Gibbons's later keyboard fantasias. Many motives are formed from rising notes, in response to the thought conveyed by the words, and combined in a highly imitative manner to create a fabric of constantly changing density.

---

14   See p. 215.

15   Fellowes's opinion was that it 'ranks as one of the most perfect penitential anthems in the whole range of polyphonic music' (TCM, 1948, p. 19.)

16   See p. 146, Ex. 27.

Ex. 31. Orlando Gibbons, *O Lord, in thy wrath*

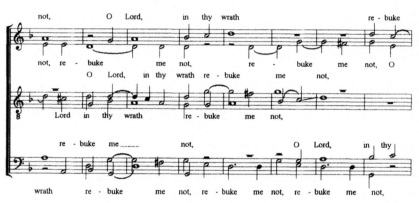

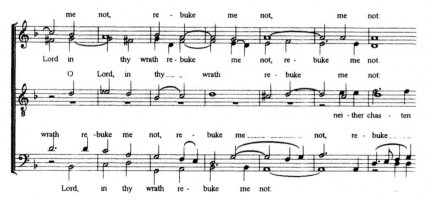

Dates can be suggested tentatively for two full anthems, and less tentatively for a third. *I am the resurrection* appears in a source compiled after 1614,[17] but since the piece is a setting of words from the Order for the Burial of the Dead there is a possibility that it was composed for the funeral of Prince Henry in 1612.[18] *O Lord, in thee is all my trust* may belong to the years 1611-19, like the verse anthems which it follows in Christ Church MS Mus. 21. *O clap your hands* is reported to have been performed in 1622, though the question of whether this is the date of composition is discussed below.

I am the resurrection certainly conveys the sense of deep sorrow which Prince Henry's death engendered, and the ability it demonstrates matches Gibbons's skill in pieces he is known to have composed about that time. Although two parts must be reconstructed editorially, there is no doubt about the anthem's excellence.[19] Gibbons's melodic invention, and his sense of proportion and balance, are shown at their best in the flowing lines of the first dozen bars, where the idea of resurrection is illustrated by rises of a sixth and then a seventh in the treble part, of a sixth in the extant inner part, and of a ninth in the bass. Long melodic phrases persist throughout, and perfect cadences are well spaced.

O Lord, in thee is all my trust sets *The Lamentation*, a popular text appended to the metrical psalms of Sternhold and Hopkins.[20] Its somewhat austere aspect may, as Wulstan suggests, be attributable to 'the evident survival into Gibbons's lifetime of a puritan tradition of ascetic musical treatment of some of the more penitential psalm texts', and a custom of setting the words 'in a restrained and sometimes

17   The piece occurs anonymously in BL Additional MS 29427, an alto part-book, partly in the hand of Thomas Myriell and including pieces from Leighton's *Teares or Lamentacions* of 1614. The anthem is ascribed to Gibbons, and pitched a fifth lower, in an incomplete set of part-books apparently copied by Alfonso Ferrabosco (Additional MSS 29366-8).

18   See pp. 39-41. *I am the resurrection* is too accomplished to support the suggestion of Monson (1982, p. 7), that it may date from Gibbons's days at King's College.

19   Headings in the part-books show that the anthem was for five voices. A reconstruction is included in Gibbons, 1978. The suspicions of Vining (1973) regarding the authenticity of the piece can be set aside.

20   The words are attributed to John Marckant (Markant) in Fellowes, 1967, p. 706, but they are not so attributed in the editions of *The Whole Booke of Psalmes* of Sternhold and Hopkins inspected for the purposes of this chapter, and no author is named in connection with other settings which have been examined. *The Whole Booke of Psalmes* credits Marckant with different verses headed *The Lamentation of a Sinner*, and beginning 'O Lord, turn not away thy face'.

severely declamatory manner'.[21] This, rather than composition early in Gibbons's career, may be the reason for certain archaic features in the piece.[22] In fact, the possibility of late composition is suggested by its association in Christ Church MS Mus. 21 with a group of anthems bearing inscriptions indicating that they were written in the last decade of Gibbons's life. The anthem's austerity is in any case more of the spirit than the musical fabric. The harmonies are generally rich, varied and interesting, and in spite of several passages of homophonic or almost homophonic writing, Gibbons's long melodic lines are much in evidence. Such melodic expansiveness means that the fitting of the text to the music demands considerable verbal repetition.

Gibbons is said to have composed *O clap your hands* to help his friend William Heyther, who in 1622 needed a piece of music for submission as a doctoral degree exercise.[23] But, while the story may essentially be true, details are open to question. Is a reference to Jacob in the words (Psalm 47) intended as a compliment to King James?

> For the Lord is high, and to be feared: he is the great King upon all the earth ... He shall choose out an heritage for us: even the worship of Jacob, whom he loved.

Was the anthem first written to celebrate some event in James's reign? And, having fulfilled its initial purpose, was it recycled to assist Heyther? Or, alternatively, was it originally written (but never used) in connection with Gibbons's own supplication for a degree?[24] A reference to the King need not preclude that possibility. The anthem is one which would have been particularly suitable to the occasion, since it is a demonstration piece for eight voices, and so would have complied with

21   Gibbons, 1978, p. ix. Settings of the same words in Thomas Ravenscroft's publications must have been among the most widely circulated. In *Pammelia* (1609) the text is set as a canon in unison. Two four-part settings are included in *The Whole Booke of Psalmes: with the Hymnes ... Newly corrected and enlarged by Thomas Ravenscroft* (1621). The tenor part of the first is the tune given by Sternhold and Hopkins. Gibbons's setting is independent of this familiar tune.

22   Phillips (1991, p. 119) draws attention to 'the kind of mean-leading which was common in Tallis's music'. Quoting an example that occurs at the words 'But when in heart they shall repent', he says: 'it is a device which does not occur elsewhere in Gibbons, not even in his 'short' writing. Phillips's statement on p. 118 that *O Lord, in thee is all my trust* is attributed to Byrd as well as Gibbons should be corrected; it evidently results from a misreading of Gibbons, 1978, p. ix.

23   See pp. 64-66.

24   Ibid.

the statutes of the University of Oxford.[25] Without resorting overmuch to precise imitation, Gibbons deploys a battery of contrapuntal devices. Despite the number of voices and the artifice in the anthem's construction, the result is almost madrigal-like in its lightness of touch.[26]

O clap your hands is the longest of Gibbons's full anthems, and is divided into two main sections, the first and shorter of which ends with — and thus emphasizes — the reference to Jacob. Gibbons sets the text phrase by phrase, and links the phrases by means of musical motives whose relationship it is usually easy to perceive. The most readily recognized element in them is the pair of repeated crotchets which crops up in almost every motive in both parts of the anthem.

Although each voice is rested briefly, all eight sing for most of the first main section. In the second main section, which sets words conveying ideas separable from those of the first, Gibbons adopts a different approach. He employs the voices antiphonally, combining them in differently constituted groups to produce an effect of greater colour and spaciousness. The difference between the two sections has raised the question of whether *O clap your hands*, though transmitted in complete form by each of the two sources, could 'possibly be a marriage of two originally independent compositions'.[27] The similarity of motives in each section nevertheless makes this unlikely.

It is an interesting question whether, had the approximate date of *O clap your hands* been unknown, we should recognize it as probably the last of Gibbons's full anthems, and one which may well have been written some years after *Hosanna to the Son of David* and *Lift up your heads*, whose vitality it shares. There are two things that make it difficult to date Gibbons's anthems on the basis of style alone. One is the early age at which he reached maturity as a composer. The other is his ability to approach afresh each new text and each new occasion for an anthem. He had the gift of producing individualised works whose chronological relationship is not always easily apparent.

25   The Laudian Code of 1636 formalized earlier requirements for the submission by a doctoral candidate (who had to be a Bachelor of Music of five years' standing) of a composition in six or eight parts (Oxford University, 1888; Clark, 1887-88, ii, p. 145). Prior to that date the requirements have to be deduced from entries concerning individual candidates in the University's Registers of Convocation and Congregation. Nathaniel Giles, for example, had to submit a composition in eight parts (Clark, ii, p. 146).

26   Harper (1983, p. 767) refers to the 'persistent use of canzona rhythms (especially at the opening of each main section), of clearly delineated ensemble textures and successive, boldly articulated figures characterized by their rhythmic drive and crisp interchange'.

27   Morehen, 1995(b), p. 204.

9

VERSE ANTHEMS

The popularity of verse anthems in Gibbons's lifetime can be put down to a number of factors. Those listed by le Huray include their colourfulness, compared with full anthems, and the practical consideration of placing the main burden of performance on the ablest singers.[1] It might be added that the congregation of the Chapel Royal, for which most, if not all, of Gibbons's verse anthems must have been written, would probably have recognized in the genre something of the spirit which pervaded courtly entertainments. Through a mental association with the drama of the masque, the verse anthem added an extra dimension to the drama of the Anglican ritual. The opposition of solo voice or voices and chorus is often intensely theatrical.[2] So is the way in which the verse anthem lends itself to dramatic narrative, as in *This is the record of John* and *See, see, the word is incarnate*.

It may be claimed that Gibbons's verse anthems are among his greatest achievements. This is the judgement of the second half of the twentieth century, but it was not that of the first half. In 1925 Fellowes wrote: 'Passing [from the full anthems] to the verse anthems it must be frankly admitted we find ourselves on a decidedly lower level'. He added that much of the music in the verse anthems must 'inevitably be placed no higher than the second class'.[3] This opinion was echoed in the preface to volume 4 of *Tudor Church Music*, though Fellowes later retracted it.[4] As late as 1954 Reese, doubtless relying on Fellowes's

1 le Huray, 1978, p. 225.

2 Verse anthems cannot, of course, be compared exactly with the songs for masques, because of the dances often interspersed between the passages which are sung in the latter. But consider by way of example the alternating treble and tenor voices and the succeeding chorus in Jonson's *The Masque of Beautie* (1608), and the song 'by two Faies' in his *Oberon* (1611), after which there shortly follows 'a full song ... by all the voyces'. Some, at least, of the music for these masques was by Alfonso Ferrabosco.

3 Fellowes, 1951, pp. 61-62; first published in 1925. Fellowes was, however, giving voice to a long-held opinion. Boyce printed none of Gibbons's works in the verse style in his collection of 1760-73, and Burney showed no interest in them in his *General History* (1769-89). The sole verse anthem by Gibbons in Barnard's collection is *Behold, thou hast made my days*.

4 Writing of what was said in TCM 4 (1925), Fellowes observed that 'In making their estimate of the value of Gibbons's Church Music, the editors seem, in the light of later experience, to have laid too much stress on the works of an admittedly experimental

initial judgement and the introduction to the *Tudor Church Music* edition, observed: 'Often in Gibbons' verse anthems ... the solo passages are marred by a too "busy" accompaniment, and even in the full sections of the works a decline in style is noticeable'.[5] A change of opinion had however become apparent shortly before, in an enthusiastic but perceptive article by Howard, who wrote of Gibbons's verse anthems: 'in this manner of composition, despite the adverse view that many have felt it fashionable to express, I would contend that he is inferior to none'.[6] Palmer gave a similar assessment in the year which saw the publication of Reese's criticisms.[7] Nearly fifty years on, it is not difficult to accept that, in his verse anthems, Gibbons proved himself an inventive, original and worthy successor to his great forerunners in the Chapel Royal.

The verse style allowed Gibbons the freedom to use a large number of compositional elements, and to do so in ways which he found most congenial. It further permitted him to vary and combine these elements into patterns which were never repeated. In consequence, Gibbons's verse anthems display the full scope of his musical imagination and the technical skills which give it form. The endless number of designs which could be created was hinted at by Charles Butler, who asserted that 'a solemn Antem, wer*e*in a sweet*e* Melodious Treble, or Countertenor, sing*eth* single, and *th*e ful Qir*e* answer*eth*, (muc*h* mor*e* w*h*en 2 suc*h* single voices, and 2 ful Qir*e*s enterchangeably repli*e* on*e* to an o*th*er, and at *th*e last cloz*e* all toge*th*er) ... mak*eth* suc*h* a heavenly Harmoni, as is pleasing unto God and Man'.[8]

General layout of Gibbons's verse anthems

Verse anthems are typically divided into sections, each of which is begun by a soloist or small ensemble of singers and completed by the full choir. However, specimens of the genre furnished by Gibbons's predecessors, such as Thomas Morley's three surviving verse anthems, differ enough from one another to have suggested a range of possible developments to Gibbons, who experimented widely and pursued no

nature as contrasted with those written in the traditional polyphonic style' (TCM, 1948, p. 19).

5   Reese, 1954, p. 814.

6   Howard, 1951. Recognition of the quality and forward-looking nature of Gibbons's verse anthems is also clear in Walker, 1952, containing revisions completed by J. A. Westrup in 1951.

7   Palmer, 1954.

8   Butler, 1636, p. 41.

single line of progress. It is easier to trace his musical growth in his abstract fantasias than in his series of verse anthems. Their plans bear no apparent relation to the chronology of composition, since (as noted with regard to Gibbons's full anthems) each anthem is an individual response to a particular text and set of circumstances, quite possibly resulting from a specific requirement.

A simple example of Gibbons's method of dividing his material occurs in *Great King of Gods*,[9] where each section is a setting of one of the four rhyming triplets which make up the text. Another occurs in *Glorious and powerful God*. Here each section sets a stanza of the poem. The division of prose texts hinges on the separable ideas which they express (which may match verses of the Bible).

Longe-range considerations of tonality play little part in the definition of sections. Virtually every chorus closes with a cadence on the tonic.[10] So do most verses, though a very few end with a cadence on the fifth above.[11] As elsewhere in Gibbons's music, however, considerable tonal and harmonic variety occurs locally, and is often connected with fluctuations in emotional intensity (Ex. 32).

It is usual in Gibbons's verse anthems for all or some of the words forming part of a verse to be reiterated in the succeeding chorus, often giving emphasis to a significant phrase. In a number of cases the music of the choruses draws, to a greater or lesser extent, on the vocal parts of the preceding verses. In some instances the organ accompaniment of verses may also provide material for the choruses. So too may untexted passages, which (in sources that contain them) occur in the vocal parts before or between passages setting the words.[12] But Gibbons's procedure in creating relationships between verses, choruses and accompaniments is never straightforward. At the risk of being tedious, the examination of

9   Printed in Gibbons, 1964(b) with words by H. R. Bramley beginning 'Great Lord of Lords'. These first appeared in F. A. G. Ouseley's edition of Gibbons's church music (1873).

10   In *O God, the King of Glory*, which is in d, the first chorus ends on C. In *See, see, the word is incarnate* (in g), the short chorus 'a glorious ascension' ends on F. Of the latter anthem, le Huray (1978, p. 315) remarks that there are only three emphatic cadences in the entire piece, and that this and the general lack of word repetition contribute to its forward drive.

11   In *O God, the King of Glory* the short verse interjection 'and the Holy Ghost', before the final choral passage, ends with a bare octave a minor third above the tonic.

12   The untexted passages in any anthem are generally closely related to the organ part. Their origin and purpose is open to debate, and is discussed below (pp. 197-205).

Ex. 32. Orlando Gibbons, *Blessed are all they that fear the Lord*, bars 41-48

his verse anthems one by one will illustrate his capacity for constantly novel invention. (This examination will need to be refined later, by a less superficial exploration of a few selected anthems.)[13] Although he was occasionally reluctant to expend unnecessary effort on some aspects of composition, he strove perpetually to create musical forms suited to

13   See pp. 186-196. The anthems examined later are not considered here: *Behold, thou hast made my days*, *This is the record of John*, and *Grant, O holy Trinity*.

his texts, exploring the possibilities of the medium afresh in each new piece.

In the first chorus of *Almighty God, who by thy Son*, the treble part repeats (with small alterations) the treble part of the quartet from the preceding verse, the second alto part repeats what was previously sung by the first alto, and the other voices have new parts.[14] The second chorus repeats the words of the second verse, but only fragments of the music.

Half of the alto solo that begins *Blessed are all they that fear the Lord* provides the second alto part of the first chorus; the other choral parts are taken from the preceding organ part (or untexted parts). The second verse requires six voices, but the chorus which follows it incorporates a solo section of the verse. The third verse is sung by different combinations of voices; the succeeding chorus repeats neither the words nor music of that verse, although it includes references to earlier musical material.

The alto solo from the first verse of *Glorious and powerful God* reappears as part of the first chorus. In the same way, the bass part of the second verse is repeated in the second chorus, and the bass part of the third verse in the third chorus. All the choruses draw additionally on the organ part (or untexted parts) of the verses, and the exultant last chorus ends by expanding and developing earlier material. This is capped by a largely independent 'Amen', which breathtakingly demonstrates Gibbons's ability to transport the listener, in the space of three bars, beyond exultation almost to a mystical region.

Gibbons's settings of 'Amen' may derive from Byrd, for whom the words 'Amen' and 'Alleluia' were often a cue for a freely decorative conclusion. Half of Gibbons's more or less complete full anthems end with an 'Amen', though the only setting of any length concludes *Deliver us, O Lord*.[15] (*Hosanna to the Son of David* has a lengthy 'Hosanna' instead.) About the same proportion of his verse anthems ends with 'Amen', though it is usually more substantial than in the full anthems. (Copies of *If ye be risen again with Christ* replace 'Amen' with 'So be it'.) One factor in determining whether an anthem should end with an 'Amen' is the nature of the text. But the feature has a particular purpose in the verse anthems, which helps to explain why it is usually longer there (though its length may in part reflect the fact that the verse anthems were often written later in Gibbons's career than the full

14   The vocal parts of the verses are incomplete, but the first quartet is intact.

15   On Gibbons's settings of 'Amen' generally, see Howard, 1951, p. 164 (where the unidentified quotation 'It is proportion that beautifies everything' comes from the dedication of *The First Set of Madrigals and Mottets*).

anthems). It provides a solution to a problem Gibbons also faced in terminating his fantasias,[16] by creating a satisfying ending to a series of sections which might, if the text were longer, be extended indefinitely.

The first two choruses of *Great King of Gods* borrow only words from the verses that precede them. This may be because the sustained vocal lines of these verses make them unsuitable for Gibbons's purpose in the choruses which follow them. Gibbons however links the third chorus closely to its verse by words and music, before embarking on one of his most striking settings of the word 'Amen'.[17] In *Sing unto the Lord* it is the middle chorus which draws upon the words and music of the preceding verse, while the other choruses are free of repetition. By contrast, the first and last choruses of *We praise thee, O Father* draw (inexactly) upon the verses that precede them. *Lord grant grace* has a comparable pattern. The choruses do not borrow from the music of the verses, but the first chorus repeats words sung by two voices in the preceding verse ('Holy, holy, holy, Lord God of hosts'). The words of the second verse, sung by eight voices, are not repeated, and the chorus simply continues from the point where the verse ends.

The choruses of *O God, the King of Glory* repeat words already sung in the verses. While there is no literal repetition of the music, some material from the verses does recur in the choruses, as demonstrated by Ex. 33 (on pp. 176-177) — which incidentally provides an illustration of Gibbons's penchant for using the rising scale as a basis of composition.

The choruses of *If ye be risen again with Christ* and *Behold, I bring you glad tidings* take their words from the verses, but the musical material (including that embodied in the organ accompaniment) is often developed in so complex a manner that, in spite of a recurrence of ideas, straightforward repetition can hardly be said to take place. The most obvious recurrence in the vocal parts of *Behold, I bring you glad tidings* arises in the setting of 'Glory be to God on high', where Gibbons finds an opportunity to repeat the rising scale of which he was so fond.

O all true faithful hearts[18] is the only one of Gibbons's fully extant verse anthems to have a choral refrain, which follows each of the three

16   See p. 125.

17   Phillips (1991, p. 132) notes that this Amen has been 'customarily sung in recent years by itself as the "three-fold amen", a tradition which apparentlty started in 1902 with an arrangement in Novello's *Parish Choir Book*'.

18   Printed in Gibbons, 1964(b), with words by H. R. Bramley beginning 'O thou, the central orb', first published in F.A.G. Ouseley's edition of Gibbons's church music (1873). 'O all true British hearts' is given in the Chapel Royal word-books (BL MS Harleian 6346; Bodleian Library MS Rawlinson Poetical 23). Vining (1973) and Brett (1981, p. 226) draw attention to seventeenth-century adaptations.

Ex. 33. Orlando Gibbons, *O God, the King of glory*

continued

Ex. 33 *continued*

verses. The form is plainly connected with the purpose of the piece, for it was composed (almost certainly in 1619) as 'A thanks Giving for the Kings happie recoverie from a great dangerous sicknes',[19] and the recurring refrain functions both as praise of God for his mercy, and as flattery of the King himself. The incomplete anthem *Thou God of wisdom* (a prayer for the preservation of the King, Queen and Prince of Wales) is also equipped with a refrain. So are two incomplete anthems whose authenticity is open to question: *Praise the Lord, O my soul* and *Unto thee, O Lord*.[20] The last in fact has two refrains.

See, see, the word is incarnate has a unique structure. The longer than usual prose text traces Christ's history from birth to resurrection, and in order to keep the length of the anthem within bounds and maintain the speed of the narrative Gibbons repeats neither the words nor the music of the verses in the choruses, although musical ideas recur throughout the piece in both the vocal parts and the organ part (or untexted parts). Ex. 34 is taken from the version with untexted passages in Christ Church MS Mus. 21; while the organ part given in other sources is not shown, it includes all the untexted phrases cited. The example illustrates how a phrase in the untexted tenor of bar 6 is related to groups of notes in the solo alto and untexted bass parts of bars 6-7, and how the untexted bass of bar 7 reappears in the chorus as the bass of bar 13. These groups of notes are echoed in quasi-imitation between the untexted parts and the solo alto of bars 54-57. (Other recurrences may also be seen, such as that of the rising phrase in the bass of bars 5-6 and the second alto of bars 54-55.) In the final extract, the alto parts' phrases in bars 13 and 15 ('Glory be to God') are expanded by the untexted first alto part of bars 98-99.

Choruses

Gibbons always thought aurally in setting words. He clearly relished the sound of a choir, and the opportunities afforded him by a body of different voices. *O God, the King of Glory* contains one of many choruses in which this is conspicuous (bars 27-40). The phrase 'Which has exalted thine only Son Jesus Christ our Lord' rises with growing intensity through the voices from the bass to the treble, and is repeated,

19   Annotation in Christ Church MS Mus. 21. See pp. 55-56 on the King's illness.
20   Both are included in Gibbons, 1925, and Gibbons, 1978. Vining (1974) questions the authenticity of *Praise the Lord* and rejects *Unto thee, O Lord* as spurious. The style of the second, at least, seems to confirm his opinion. Only the words survive of *This is the day wherein the Lord hath wrought* (BL, Harleian MS 6346, f. 58ᵛ), but the couplets which follow the stanzas may have been sung to the same music.

Ex. 34. Orlando Gibbons, *See, see, the word is incarnate*

continued

Ex. 34 *continued*

before the exultant conclusion 'with great triumph unto thy kingdom in heav'n'. But each of Gibbons's verse anthems has its special qualities, and his choral writing utilizes the whole array of voice combinations, styles and techniques at his disposal.

Gibbons's choruses, in his verse anthems as in his full anthems, usually have one or two treble parts, one or two alto parts, and single tenor and bass parts.[21] The five-part chorus of *If ye be risen again with*

21   The eight-part full anthem *O clap your hands* is an exception; the tenor and bass

Christ has two treble parts and only one alto part, because Gibbons wishes to maintain the two treble lines used in the verses. Sometimes, as in *Blessed are all they that fear the Lord* (at the words 'and ever shall be, world without end'), voices are combined in different groups to produce differences of choral texture.

The choruses of *Blessed are all they that fear the Lord* begin with a brief passage of homophony, and continue contrapuntally. Only the last introduces imitation, which — as is generally the case with Gibbons, in both his vocal and instrumental music — quickly gives way to free counterpoint. The choruses of *Sing unto the Lord*, by contrast, all start imitatively, though imitation is thereafter fragmentary at best. The choral refrain of *O all true faithful hearts* is almost entirely homphonic, but the anthem ends with a contrapuntally elaborate and highly imitative 'Amen'. While one of Gibbons's intentions is undoubtedly to create variety for its own sake, his intention is also to use it as a means of rendering his text easily intelligible and so to emphasize its message. All the choruses of *This is the record of John* fall unmistakeably into polyphonic and homophonic sections, though the third begins with only a short homophonic passage:

(1) (*Homophonic*) And he confessed, and denied not, (*polyphonic*) and said plainly, I am not the Christ.

(2) (*Polyphonic*) And they asked him, What art thou then? Art thou Elias? And he said, I am not. (*Homophonic*) Art thou the prophet? And he answered, No.

(3) (*Homophonic*) And he said, (*polyphonic*) I am the voice of him that crieth in the wilderness, Make straight the way of the Lord.

In each case the distinction between homophony and polyphony serves a particular purpose: in the first chorus, to break the text into two complementary parts; in the second, to separate the first passage from the second, which is essentially a repetition; and in the third, to give prominence to John's message.

Because of Gibbons's regard for the special demands of each text, the scale of his choruses varies greatly, both within individual anthems and from one anthem to another. No single principle governs the length of choruses, either in relation to verses or to one another. The fact that, within almost half the anthems, the choruses increase progressively in length seems to be of no general significance.

voices, as well as the higher voices, each have two parts.

Verses

The disposition of voices in Gibbons's verses is extremely varied.[22] The verses of *Behold, thou hast made my days*, *This is the record of John*, and *Grant, O Holy Trinity* are all sung by a single voice.[23] Those of *Glorious and powerful God* take the form of duets between an alto and a bass. *Sing unto the Lord* gives the verses in turn to two basses, two altos, and an alto and a bass. The verses of *Great King of Gods* include duets, but involve three singers. *If ye be risen again with Christ* employs two trebles in its outer verses, and supplements them with an alto in the middle verse. The verses of *O God, the King of Glory* use singers in groups of two, three or four. An alto soloist sings the first and last verses of *See, see, the word is incarnate*, but the three middle verses make use of five singers in all.

The verses of the remaining complete anthems form more intricate patterns, and their plans are best clarified by tabulation.

Scoring of verses in six anthems

---

tr: *treble* a: *alto* t: *tenor* b: *bass*

Almighty God, who by thy Son: (1) a II,[24] then tr, a I, t, b, (2) tr, a I and II; followed by b I and II.

Behold, I bring you glad tidings: (1) tr and a I,[25] (2) tr I and II, a I and II, with b replacing a I; then a I followed by a II.

continued

---

22   Tables of the scoring are given by Palmer, 1954, pp. 112-113, and le Huray, 1978, p. 316.

23   Peterhouse MS 44 transposes the alto solos of *This is the record of John* up an octave, perhaps the result of a local practice of giving them to a particular singer, but Gibbons probably intended that they should lie in the middle of a five-part texture. The vocal part of the verses of *Grant, O Holy Trinity* is lost, but can be reconstructed with some accuracy from the organ score; the reconstructions printed in Gibbons, 1925, and Gibbons, 1964(b), are often in agreement, though the latter (which transposes the anthem up a minor third) assigns the solos to a treble instead of an alto.

24   Contratenor (alto) II part lost from extant copies.

25   The chorus dividing the first and second verses is only two bars long.

Scoring of verses in six anthems *continued*

Blessed are all they that fear the Lord: (1) a II, (2) solos and various combinations: a II; tr I and II, first with a I and then with a II; a I, t, b; a II, (3) tr I and II and t; a II, t, b; tr I alternating with tr II, a I alternating with a II, t, b; tr II, a I and II, t, b.

Lord, grant grace: (1) tr, alternating with a II, (2) eight voices variously combined: tr I, a II, b I; a I, t I, b II; tr II, a II, b I; tr I, a I, t I, b II; tr II, a II, t II, b II, overlapping with the other four voices; tr II, a II, t II, b I; tr I, a I, t II, b II; tr II, a II, t II, b I.

O all true faithful hearts: (1) a II, (2) tr I, a II, (3) tr I and II, at first as a duet, then mingling with a I and II, t and b.

We praise thee, O Father: (1) tr, a I, b, (2) t I and II, (3) a I and II, alternating with tr I and II, (4) tr I, a II, t I, alternating with tr II, a I, t II; concluding with tr I and II, a I, t I and II.

The multiplicity of voice combinations is not simply the result of a desire to create different vocal colours. Closer scrutiny of four of the anthems in the above table will make clear that, in each case, Gibbons's plan is related to the nature of his text.

The principle underlying *O all true faithful hearts* is a simple one: that of countering the static tendency induced by the recurring refrain. This is achieved by increasing the number of voices and the complexity of the writing in each succeeding verse.

The prose text of *Blessed are all they that fear the Lord* is divided into sections, which form the verses. (With the exception of the last chorus, which is a setting of the doxology, the choruses repeat words from the preceding verses.) The second and third verses are subdivided further, and each subdivision is scored separately. The allocation of particular voices to particular passages thus becomes a means of presenting the text in easily assimilable phrases:

[Verse 2]

(a II) Thy wife shall be as the fruitful vine upon the walls of thine house, (tr I and II, a I) thy children like olive branches (tr I and II, a II) round about thy table (a I, t, b) round about thy table.

(a II) Lo, thus shall the man be blessed that feareth the Lord.

The ideas expressed by *We praise thee, O Father* are again separated from one another in the interests of clarity. But, in contrast to the didactic text of *Blessed are all they that fear the Lord*, the text of *We praise thee, O Father* is a song of glorification and gratitude, and this is reflected in the scoring. The first verse, 'We praise thee, O Father, for the glorious resurrection of thy Son Jesus Christ, our Lord', is a trio for treble, alto and bass. It is the bass which begins (and which introduces the idea of resurrection with a series of rising notes),[26] but Gibbons may have intended that, in a small compass, the three kinds of voice should represent all mankind. The second verse, 'for he is the very Paschal Lamb, which was offered up for us, and hath taken away the sins of the world', explains why praise is due. The semi-canonic setting for two tenors accords with the intellectual quality of this expository portion of the text. The third verse carries the explanation further, and this too is sung more or less canonically. Each of its three distinct and significant ideas is stated by a pair of altos and reiterated by a pair of trebles:

(a I and II) who by his death hath destroyed death, (tr I and II) who by his death hath destroyed death,

(a I and II) and by his rising to life again, (tr I and II) and by his rising to life again

(a I and II) hath restored to us everlasting life, (tr I and II) hath restored to us everlasting life.

The fourth verse is the culmination of the song of praise, and gains an extra intensity from being sung by groups of three voices, perhaps representing humankind, and the angels and archangels mentioned in the text.

The distribution of the text among several groups of voices not only serves to clarify and emphasize particular passages, but is an aspect of the theatricality of Gibbons's verse anthems. The duet which begins *Lord, grant grace* is a prayer, leading into another chorus of praise, this time by mankind, angels and saints. The second verse continues the

26   In this anthem, as elsewhere, Gibbons is sparing in his use of word-painting, and in the succeeding chorus the word 'resurrection' is illustrated only on its last occurrence, when it is sung by the tenor and bass. However, all the solo voices make an octave leap in singing 'And by his rising to life'.

praise of God, with each verbal phrase sung twice, by alternate groups of voices (angels and saints). This gives way to another chorus, in which 'everything that hath breath' joins in praising God.

As well as governing the layout of Gibbons's anthems, his texts govern the nature of the vocal lines in the verses. The verse beginning at bar 58 of *Glorious and powerful God* begins with illustrative descending notes setting the words 'O down on us', and though such patent word-painting is not pursued,[27] the verse continues with a series of distinct musical phrases setting successive verbal phrases. The last couplet ('Founder and foundation Of endless habitation') forms the most strongly characterized phrase of all.

The movement of the solo voice in *See, see, the word is incarnate* changes to match the changing ideas expressed by the words. A change of motion emphasizes 'The earth quakes, the sun is darkened', much as verbal phrases are often emphasized in Gibbons's songs. Indeed, it might be said that his skill in this direction is frequently greater than it is in his songs. His conception of melody changed over the years, as well. While *Sing unto the Lord* may not be a particularly late anthem, it is easier to connect its opening solos with the music of Purcell than with the solo songs of Byrd — or, for that matter, of the youthful Gibbons. Another solo with a strongly Purcellian character opens *Glorious and powerful God*.

One reason why these solos are so suggestive of a later time is Gibbons's ability to convey the meaning of his texts by emotional means that strike us as modern, as well as by the structural means outlined earlier. This is partly a matter of matching the character of a passage in the text to the type of voice by which it is sung. Gibbons was not wholly consistent, but he seems frequently to have chosen a voice or voices suited to the meaning and emotional content of the words. His fondness for two voices working together, often in imitation, has been pointed out by several writers.[28] In *We praise thee, O Father*, two tenors sing the meditative 'for he is the very Paschal Lamb' — described by Howard as 'fraught with an intensity and passion that is reminiscent of Monteverdi'.[29] Did Gibbons actually feel like that about the subject of his text? To ask the question is as irrelevant as to ask whether an opera

27   The word 'Arise', however, rises through all the voices of the chorus in bars 86-87.

28   e.g. Howard, 1951, p. 164; Palmer, 1954, p. 110.

29   Wulstan (in Gibbons, 1964(b), p. vii) notes how rarely Gibbons allocates verses to the tenor voice, and remarks on the relative lack of esteem in which it was held. 'Bass Verses occur more often and the dramatic qualities of the low voice were evidently appreciated'.

composer shares the anguish of his characters; what matters is that he knew how to evoke emotional fervour when it was required. The less intense third verse is sung by pairs of altos alternating with pairs of trebles, until its last joyful phrase, 'hath restored to us everlasting life', is sung by two trebles and then by all four voices together.

Three anthems with solo verses

In looking in greater detail at some of Gibbons's verse anthems, it will be convenient to examine three in which the verses are given throughout to a single alto soloist.[30] This will make it easier to discuss the essential function which the organ (or untexted) parts perform in the totality of Gibbons's musical structures.

The solos of *This is the record of John* proclaim the influence of the declamatory song being developed by Gibbons's contemporaries. The decorated vocal line of the cadence at the end of the first verse seems to come from a court air. It is not hard to find points of comparison between Gibbons's anthem and a song like *Bring away this sacred tree* by Nicholas Lanier, who performed it in Campion's 'masque of squires' presented for the wedding of the Earl of Somerset in 1613 (Ex. 35).[31]

Ex. 35

(a) Nicholas Lanier: *Bring away this sacred tree* (final bars)

*Bass original, other parts editorial

continued

30   See note 23 on p. 182 on the substitution of the treble voice in *Grant, O Holy Trinity* and *This is the record of John.*

31   See p. 50. For the song, see Spink, 1971, no. 1 (with words beginning 'Weep no more'); Spink, 1974, pp. 44-45 ('the earliest ayre that is clearly of the same type as that which was to flourish over the next 30 years'); and Sabol, 1978, pp. 76-77, 553-554.

Ex. 35 *continued*

(b) Orlando Gibbons: *This is the record of John* (bars 11-17)

The text of *This is the record of John* differs from the texts of most
of Gibbons's other anthems. Whereas they are expressions of penitence
or joy, *This is the record of John* is a narrative. The anthem's solo voice
accordingly moves smoothly phrase by phrase, with cadences carefully
placed so as 'to match the verbal punctuation with its appropriate
musical equivalents'.[32] The verses include few repetitions of complete

32   le Huray, 1978, p. 317. An analysis of *This is the record of John* is included in
Ellis and Pilgrim, 1984.

musical phrases, and the choruses do not repeat straightforwardly the music of the verses. There is nevertheless much repetition of smaller groups of notes, in the organ and untexted parts as well as in the vocal parts, as Ex. 36 shows. (The version from Christ Church MS Mus. 21 is given, with untexted passages and without organ accompaniment.) The function these small groups perform in bonding all the parts together is apparent from the outset. A group of three ascending notes (2), which is part of the very first phrase (1), appears throughout the piece in reversed form (3), or both reversed and inverted (4). It appears as group 5 in the penultimate bar, reversed and augmented. The method is related to the one developed by Gibbons in his mature keyboard fantasias, such as the *Fantazia of foure parts* (MB 20/12),[33] from which *This is the record of John* may not be far removed in date of composition.

Ex. 36. Orlando Gibbons, *This is the record of John*

continued

33   See p. 101.

Ex. 36 *continued*

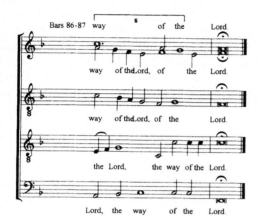

A similar process of linking is apparent between the texted parts and the organ part or untexted parts of *Behold, thou hast made my days* (the recurrent phrase to which 'verily' is sung in the first verse is the same as the phrase numbered 3 in Ex. 36 from *This is the record of John*, although the two anthems may have been written several years apart). In this anthem, however, a plainer connection exists between the verses and choruses. The first chorus takes its words, and the last few notes of the treble part, from the preceding alto solo. References to earlier music are made by the other parts of the first chorus, and the bass draws entirely upon the lowest organ or untexted line of the verse. The anthem's other choruses contain comparable verbal repetitions and musical references.

The solemnity of *Behold, thou hast made my days*, said to have been composed for Dr Anthony Maxey in 1618 when he was on his deathbed,[34] is intensified by recitative-like elements in the solo part (another indication of the influence upon Gibbons of developments in the field of secular song). Gibbons compensates for some lack of lyricism by giving the verses a varied tonality. The first contains cadences on E, C, and the tonic (A). The second explores more widely, and emphasizes D, E and A. The third roams fairly freely, but is centred on A and C. At the same time, the solo part gains in range and flexibility as the anthem progresses. Sequences are more frequent, and phrases of the melody start to suggest an instrumental origin, so that the verse leads naturally into the third chorus, which bears a close resemblance to the third strain

34   See p. 161. le Huray (1978, p. 317) is slightly misleading in describing Psalm 39, from which the text is taken, as 'one of the two psalms said or sung at the funeral service'. The psalm was not introduced into the Prayer Book until 1662.

of one of Gibbons's keyboard pavans (MB 20/17, probably written before 1612).[35] The beginning of the chorus (Ex. 37b) borrows from the passage in the pavan marked with an asterisk in Ex. 37a. The anthem's reputed circumstances of composition seem to be verified by this quotation from a pavan which in turn quotes from Dowland's *Lachrymae* (see Ex. 2a on p. 88). Dowland's piece was undoubtedly in Gibbons's mind, for in the second verse and chorus of the anthem (bars 33-36 and 40-43) the words 'truly, my hope is even in thee' are sung to its famous motive.

Ex. 37.

(a) Orlando Gibbons, pavan MB 20/17, third strain

continued

35   The relationship between *Behold, thou hast made my days* and the pavan is remarked by Wulstan (in Gibbons, 1964(b), p. 216). Wulstan, and Rose (1968, p. 166), both mention a resemblance between the third chorus of *Behold, thou hast made my days* and Thomas Tomkins's verse anthem *Hear my prayer*. Each sets the words 'O spare me a little, that I may recover my strength before I go hence and be no more seen'. Resemblances between Tomkins's *Praise the Lord, O my soul* and Gibbons's now incomplete setting of the same text are noted by Vining (1974, p. 74).

Ex. 37 *continued*

(b) Orlando Gibbons, *Behold, thou hast made my days*, bars 69-80

continued

Ex. 37b *continued*

The verses of *Grant, O Holy Trinity* have to be reconstructed, but (assuming a valid conclusion can be drawn from the surviving organ part)[36] it is apparent that, although the choruses repeat words from the verses, they do not in any elementary sense repeat the melodies. Much of the anthem is nevertheless generated by the notes to which the solo voice should probably sing 'O Holy Trinity' in the first verse, and the related phrases which follow ('thy servant Charles our King', 'may evermore rejoice'). This is illustrated in Ex. 38, where the phrases marked 1a and 2a in the first chorus are all variants of phrases 1 and 2 in the first verse, and 3 is a retrograde form of 1.

Grant, O Holy Trinity provides other illustrations of Gibbons's thematic resourcefulness. The second verse, as reconstructed, sets the words 'Give him many happy years on earth' to an expansion of a phrase from the first verse (Ex. 39a on p. 195). It repeats them to a phrase that sounds like an inversion of the expanded phrase, but is also related to a phrase in the first chorus, to which the treble sings 'may evermore rejoice' (Ex. 39b). All these phrases seem to originate in one that occurs

---

36   Bodleian Library, Tenbury MS 791; Christ Church, Oxford, MS Mus. 1001; Durham, Cathedral Library, MS A4. See le Huray, 1960, on these sources. The reconstructions in Gibbons, 1925, and Gibbons, 1964(b), on which the remarks here are based, are largely in agreement.

in the organ introduction and accompaniment to the first verse (Ex. 38, bars 1-4). The phrase's successive appearances in the accompaniment of the first verse (Ex. 38, bars 6-7) create a rising scale which may have suggested the scalar passages that begin the organ part of the second verse (Ex. 39c). There is always a risk of being over-enthusiastic in the pursuit of thematic links of this kind, but — whether they result from intention or instinct — there is no doubt that they abound in Gibbons's verse anthems.

Ex. 38. Orlando Gibbons, *Grant, O Holy Trinity*, first verse and chorus

continued

Ex. 38 *continued*

Ex. 39. Passages from Orlando Gibbons, *Grant, O Holy Trinity*

Gibbons's skill in the development of his material informs the whole piece, and the 'Amen' swiftly reviews all that has gone before (Ex. 40).

Ex. 40. Orlando Gibbons, *Grant, O Holy Trinity*, bars 63-69

continued

Ex. 40 *continued*

Fragmentary verse anthems

Nine of Gibbons's verse anthems are known mainly from organ scores, or from texts without music. These are listed in the catalogue of Gibbons's works (see p. 298). Some have been completed by their most recent editor,[37] but do not suggest any modification of conclusions reached from an examination of the anthems which survive in a complete or nearly complete form.

The instrumental parts of Gibbons's verse anthems

Organ parts exist for all Gibbons's complete or nearly complete verse anthems. They are preserved in separate organ books, while the singing parts are generally contained in vocal part-books, one for each part. Some verse anthems exist in copies which present the vocal parts in score, but there are no vocal scores which include an organ part written out separately on two staves.

The organ books provide both a basis for the accompaniment which is an essential constituent of a verse anthem, and 'a conductor's copy shewing for rehearsal purposes the main points of entry'.[38] To fulfill the

37   Gibbons, 1978. See also Gibbons, 1925, pp. 325-346; Gibbons, 1964(b), p. 225.
38   Gibbons, 1964(b), p. viii. There are also organ parts for most of Gibbons's full

latter purpose, an organ part must follow the vocal parts closely. But this does not mean simply duplicating them. Without being a thorough bass, the organ part may incorporate a bass line that is not present in the vocal parts;[39] or it may thicken the texture, by adding inner notes that are absent in the choral parts. In these respects the role of the organ is analogous to its role in the instrumental consorts of Coprario, in which Gibbons played the keyboard part.[40] Very often, particularly in accompanying a solo voice, or in providing an introduction or interlude when all the voices are silent, the organ is given its own material. This may anticipate and trigger events in the vocal parts. The organ leads off *Behold, I bring you glad tidings* with an introduction, five semibreves in length, embodying a point of imitation which prefigures the vocal duet of the anthem's first verse.[41] Just before the first, very brief, chorus ('glad tidings of great joy'), the organ plays a group of four rising crotchets which is almost immediately inverted by the first alto. The group recurs in the accompaniment to the third verse, and then — usually, but not always, modified and inverted — reappears in all the parts of the third chorus ('unto us a Son is given'). It makes another appearance, often in an extended form, in the final chorus. The frequency with which the organ and vocal parts are integrated in Gibbons's verse anthems suggests that the former must be derived in some way from his original manuscripts.

Christ Church MS Mus. 21 poses the question of whether Gibbons's verse anthems were ever performed with an accompaniment provided by instruments other than an organ. This occurs because the manuscript contains copies in which untexted passages are entered on the same staves as the vocal parts, before or between the passages to which words are set, and continuous with them (see Ex. 36 on p. 188, and Ex. 41 on p. 198).[42] The untexted parts are closely related to the organ parts preserved in other sources. It is unlikely that the manuscript was made

anthems, but they were almost certainly intended for use only in rehearsal.

39   See Ex. 48 on p. 223.

40   See pp. 59, 62.

41   Field (1988, pp. 218-219) makes a striking comparison (with examples) between the beginnings of *Behold, I bring you glad tidings* and a fantasia-suite by John Coprario, and makes the point that the instrumental piece aspires 'to deliver persuasive musical utterance in the manner of the more oratorical types of song, such as verse anthem or passionate lute air'.

42   Gibbons's verse anthems included in Mus. MS 21 are: *Behold, thou hast made my days*, *Blessed are all they that fear the Lord*, *Great King of Gods*, *Glorious and powerful God*, *Lord, grant grace*, *O all true faithful hearts*, *See, see, the word is incarnate*, *Sing unto the Lord*, *This is the record of John*, and *We praise thee O Father*.

Ex. 41.   Orlando Gibbons, *Behold, thou hast made my days*. The untexted
           parts (from Christ Church MS Mus. 21) and the organ part (from
           Durham Cathedral Library MS A1) are presented together for
           purposes of comparison; there is no suggestion that they should be
           played at the same time.

continued

Ex. 41 *continued*

continued

Ex. 41 *continued*

for practical use (which would have demanded part-books, or a book laid out so that it could be used by performers gathered round a table), but there are several other possible explanations of its origin. It may be a score whose scribe compiled it from personal interest or for the purpose of study, condensing on to one set of staves parts that were originally written separately for voices and an organ or other instruments. Alternatively, it may record adaptations made from an organ book, perhaps with a view to eventual performances involving instruments, such as might have taken place domestically with a consort of viols (though the untexted passages are at times independent of any surviving organ book). Or it may reflect Gibbons's method of writing his music before handing it to a copyist to prepare the vocal and organ parts needed for performance. This notion is supported by signs of the manuscript's close connection with Gibbons, whose music was among the first to be entered, and the interesting variant versions it contains of several of his pieces.[43]

Untexted passages occur on the same staves as texted passages in other sources of verse anthems by various composers, including Gibbons. Perhaps that is the way pieces combining voices and

---

43   See Harper, 1983, and Appendix II to Gibbons, 1964(b). The manuscript may contain some of Gibbons's late amendments, e.g. the expanded and improved endings of *Blessed are all they that fear the Lord* and *See, see, the word is incarnate*. It may at one time have been owned by a member of the family which included Gibbons's patron Sir Christopher Hatton (Wainwright, 1997, pp. 187-189).

instruments were usually composed, presenting a general conception permitting various modes of performance. Thomas Myriell copied untexted parts for Gibbons's *See, see, the word is incarnate* into the part-books of the private collection he entitled *Tristitiae Remedium*,[44] and that anthem also occurs, again with untexted parts, in another set of part-books (Christ Church MSS Mus. 56-60).[45] Untexted passages are included, too, in the surviving part-books of Gibbons's song *Do not repine, fair sun*, a secular counterpart of the verse anthem *Great king of Gods*.[46] Like his other secular songs, this may have been performed with viols, though neither here nor in the anthems is it made clear whether a solo voice should be doubled by an instrument, or whether the whole consort should play or remain silent during choruses.[47]

Although there is no sold evidence to support the conjecture, there is little difficulty in believing that some of Gibbons's verse anthems were composed, or may from time to time have been arranged, as consort songs with choruses. A number of them have words suggesting a non-liturgical intention, while words of Biblical origin were included in various published collections described as 'apt for instruments and voices' or 'apt for viols and voices'.[48] Furthermore, transfers from anthem to song and vice versa undoubtedly took place over a long period. Byrd's anthem *Alack, when I look back* probably started as a consort song; and his *Christ rising again*, published as a song in 1589, occurs in comparatively early sources as a verse anthem.

Although unambiguous testimony about the domestic performance of Gibbons's anthems would be welcome, there is at least a justification for experimentation with viol accompaniment. But what about performances in church? While there is some evidence of the occasional participation of instruments other than the organ in English church music in Gibbons's time, our sources of information are sadly reticent about the

---

44   BL, Additional MSS 29372-7. For a possible link with the Hatton collection, see Wainwright, 1997, pp. 64-66

45   Christ Church MSS Mus. 56-60 have a Hatton association. They were originally connected with the Fanshawe family, which included Alice, the wife of Gibbons's patron, Sir Christopher Hatton (Wainwright, 1997, p. 189).

46   *Do not repine* is in New York Public Library, Drexel MSS 4180-5. Short untexted passages also occur in copies of Gibbons's *Almighty God, who by thy Son* (Lambeth Palace MS 764, a bass part) and *Behold, I bring you glad tidings* (Pembroke College, Cambridge, MS 4, a medius part).

47   See Gibbons, 1964(b), notes to *See, see, the word is incarnate*, *Sing unto the Lord*, and *We praise thee O Father*.

48   For example, Richard Alison's *An Howres Recreation in Musicke* (1606), and Michael East's *The Fourth Set of Bookes* (1618).

precise manner in which they took part. It may be guessed that the nature of performance depended upon place, time and the available resources. No attempt has ever been made comprehensively to survey the surviving evidence, and the following does not pretend to be complete.[49]

The author of an anonymous tract on church music, probably written before the Civil War, seems to have been familiar with the use of instruments:

> Organs and instruments were appointed to be used in the Churche to praise God withall, but also for divers other good consideracons, one was to sett out the melodye of the songes the same being added to the singinge.[50]

The author wrote further of 'ye Organs or instruments' being 'added to the songe', but he expatiates only on the role of the organ, and it is possible that 'to sett out the melodye' refers to an organ providing support for congregational singing. Henry Peacham likewise wrote unspecifically in *The Compleat Gentleman* (1622) of 'our practise of singing and playing with Instruments in his Majesties Chapell, and our Cathedral Churches'.[51]

Cornetts and sackbuts are however mentioned in several documents as taking part in performances which are likely to have been primarily vocal. At Westminster Abbey, Orlando Gibbons's Chapel Royal colleague Edmund Hooper was paid 13s 4d for 'the cornet*tes* and Sagbot*tes* upon the Queenes daye' in 1599,[52] while the records of Trinity College, Cambridge, show that wind instruments were employed in the chapel at various times from the 1590s onwards.[53] At Greenwich Palace, on 1 May 1605, when the young Princess Mary was baptized,

> then began an Antheme, shewinge the Dedication of the Royall Infant unto allmighty God by Baptisme (the Chorus whereof was filled wth the help of Musicall Instrumentes)...[54]

At Exeter, in 1609, it was recorded that Edward Gibbons's assistant, Peter Chambers, was a performer on the 'doble Sackbutte' and 'single

---

49   Parrott, 1978, is a brief survey of the subject.

50   BL, Royal MS 18.B.XIX, f. 12^r.

51   Peacham, 1622, p. 97.

52   Westminster Abbey, WAM 33653, f. 4

53   References to a sackbut occur in the Senior Bursar's Accounts (Nelson, 1989, *passim*; Payne, 1993, p. 146).

54   Cheque Book, f. 32^r; Rimbault, 1872, p. 168.

Sackbutte'.[55] 'Organs, and other wind Instruments' were played as Prince Henry's body rested at St James's Palace in 1612.[56] Westminster Abbey's accounts for 1625-26 include payments 'To the Musicõns for playinge on the Cornettes and Sagbuttes'.[57]

All the above passages are tantalizingly vague, but some imply the participation of only one or two instruments, and none intimates that instruments had any function beyond reinforcing one or more of the vocal lines or substituting for absent singers, as apparently happened at Princess Mary's christening.[58] Other sources are open to the interpretation that instruments were introduced chiefly on special occasions. John Hawarde wrote the following description of the Garter ceremony at Whitehall on 23 April 1597:

> Firste morning Sarvice in the Chappell wth solemne musike & voyces, Doc. Boole [Bull] then playing, the Lordes of the order then presente ... after there severall Congees, there is shorte service, the Clergie all in there riche Copes, wth the princely musike of voyces, organes, Cornettes & sackbuttes; & in like order her Matie goes one procession & so returnes, & shee & the reste of the order offer at the highe altar, & so service endes, & shee departes: then goes many princely services, at the firste soundes many trumpettes, after playes 2 drommes & the fyfe ...[59]

Anthony à Wood unearthed the information that at Oxford, on 27 August 1605, when the King, Queen and Prince of Wales visited the cathedral (the chapel of Christ Church), they heard a 'service mixt with instrumental and vocal musick'.[60] A parallel account says that 'The Service was very solemn, the Quire full, & excellent voices, mixt with Instruments'.[61] The description of another ceremony says:

---

55   Exeter Cathedral Archives, D&C 3553, ff. 11[r], 13[r].

56   See p. 40.

57   Westminster Abbey, WAM 33682, f. 43[v]. The musicians were paid £16 in 1625 and again in 1626.

58   See p. 252 for the need for instruments to strengthen choirs after the Restoration.

59   Hawarde, 1894, pp. 74-75. Hawarde's manuscript formed part of the Morrison collection (described in the ninth report of the Historical Manuscripts Commission, part III, appendix, p. 406ff). It was item 3098 in Sotheby's sale of the collection in May 1919, and was bought by G. D. Smith. Attempts to discover its present whereabouts have been unsuccessful.

60   Wood, 1792-96, ii, p. 285.

61   BL, Harleian MS 7044 (olim Baker XVII), pp. 206-207; Nichols, 1828, i, pp. 546-547.

Thursday the 2. of January 1622[/3]. a new built Church ... within Algate, was consecrated ... by the name of Saint *James* Church, and there the Quire of Saint *Paules*, with sundry Instruments of Musique, with great solemnity, sung *Te Deum*, and diverse Antheams ...'[62]

In the years after Gibbons's death, Charles I's wind musicians were divided into two groups of six, serving in alternate weeks (later into two groups of seven, serving in alternate months), and playing in the Chapel Royal and at the King's table. All these musicians, with three others, were detailed to serve on the principal feast days and collar-days.[63] There is nothing to indicate that this practice prevailed any earlier than 1633, but there must be a suspicion that, by that date, anthems were sometimes performed in the Chapel Royal, if nowhere else, in a more colourful way than is often supposed. The records do not specify the particular kinds of instruments used in the Chapel, but members of the group are referred to in other connections as performing on the recorder, the cornett and the sackbut, and most of them were proficient on more than one instrument. The participation of wind musicians was revived when Charles II was restored to the throne after the Commonwealth. Edward Chamberlayne, in describing the work of the organists of the Chapel Royal soon after the Restoration, was quite definite about this, but failed to say when the practice began:

> Three other of the said Clerks are chosen to be the *Organists*, to whom are joyned upon *Sundays, Collar* dayes, and other *Holy-dayes*, the *Sick-buts* and *Cornets* belonging to the Kings Private Musick, to make the Chappell Musick more full and compleat.[64]

Butler (1636) maintained that 'becaus *Entata* [stringed instruments] ar often out of tune ... in our *Chyrch* solemnities onely *the* Wind*e* instruments (*w*hose Not*e*s ar constant) bee in us*e*'.[65] The records of places of worship nevertheless include references to stringed instruments, though it is uncertain what they imply. At Westminster Abbey the Treasurer's accounts list a payment of five shillings to

---

62   Stowe, 1631, pp. 1034-1035.

63   PRO, LC5/132, p. 345 (4 December 1633), LC5/134, p. 221 (22 December 1637); Ashbee, 1986-96, iii, pp. 74, 94-95. A collar-day is one on which knights wear the collar of their order. In 1634 twelve surplices were provided for the wind musicians serving in the Chapel Royal (Ashbee, iii, p. 81).

64   Chamberlayne, 1669, p. 236. This has clear implications for the performance of Christopher Gibbons's anthems.

65   Butler, 1636, p. 103.

Edmund Hooper 'for Strynges for the viall*es*'.[66] The Abbey's viols may however have been played by choristers as part of their musical education, or during concerts in the Jerusalem Chamber, not during services.[67] It is not clear whether a reference (1635) by Lieutenant Hammond to Exeter cathedral's 'Vialls, and other sweet Instruments' means that he heard them during a service.[68] Nor is it evident whether familiarity with the participation of viols in church led John Barnard, who was a minor canon of St Paul's, to place on the title-page of *The First Book of Selected Church Musick* (1641) a quotation from Psalm 150: 'Praise him with stringed Instruments and Organs'.

If any conclusion can be drawn from all this, it is only that no firm conclusion can be drawn. Anthems may at times have been performed recreationally with viols, but though church musicians seem often to have been viol players, pre-Restoration evidence for the use of stringed instruments in church during services is very slender. Sackbuts and cornetts were used in church on special occasions in Gibbons's lifetime, but the manner of their use is far from clear. A sizeable body of wind instruments seems to have been used in the Chapel Royal, but the earliest evidence dates from eight years after Gibbons's death. In short, there is nothing to challenge the belief that Gibbons's verse anthems were usually accompanied only by an organ. On the other hand, it is not entirely out of the question that they should, on occasion, receive more colourful performances than those customarily accorded them.

66   Westminster Abbey, WAM 33653, f. 4^r.

67   Henry Machyn, in diary entries for 16 June 1561 and 11 May 1562, mentions the children of Westminster Abbey playing on viols, but not during services (BL, Cotton MS Vitellius F. V; Machyn, 1848). The children of St Paul's also played viols during the mid-sixteenth century (Holinshed, 1807-8, iv, p. 7, referring to September 1553; Essex Record Office, D/DP A8, referring to Thomasine Petre's wedding in February 1559/60). At Canterbury, where there was a chest of 'viols for the choristers' school', the cathedral spent £7 on a second chest in 1615, to be maintained by certain of the lay clerks (Bowers, 1995, p. 442). During the 1590s Trinity College, Cambridge, made several payments for viol strings, and once (1596-97) for lute strings (Nelson, 1989, *passim*), but there is no evidence that stringed instruments were ever used during services in the college chapel.

68   Hammond, 1936, p. 74.

10

LITURGICAL MUSIC

Gibbons's liturgical music comprises two settings of the preces (the opening versicles and responses in the Anglican offices: that is to say, short petitions sung as verse and response), with which are associated settings of proper psalms specified in *The Book of Common Prayer*, and two services (settings of words from the unchanging parts of the daily Anglican rite).

Preces

The numbering usually given to Gibbons's sets of preces may be arbitrary. It derives from John Barnard's printed collection of 1641, *The First Book of Selected Church Musick*. Echoes of earlier composers suggest that Gibbons's 'Second' Preces are his first, as indeed they are described in part-books formerly at Peterhouse, Cambridge.[1] It may be that, like Byrd's so-called First Preces, which were probably written after his Second Preces, Gibbons's 'first' set results from the composer's reconsideration of an earlier work.

By Gibbons's time the practice of making settings of the preces and the proper psalms (the latter often associated with particular settings of the preces) was long-established. Gibbons was undoubtedly familiar with a body of settings by his predecessors and contemporaries. Passages in his Second Preces are very like passages in Byrd's First Preces (Ex. 42 on pp. 208-209). It is difficult to say whether the younger composer deliberately copied the work of the older, or simply found himself recalling a familiar setting. In either case, Gibbons was following a time-honoured tradition, for Byrd's Second Preces are indebted to Tallis's First Preces, which in turn incorporate part of the relevant chant from John Merbecke's *The Booke of Common Prayer Noted* (1550).

Gibbons's two sets of preces are in different keys. The 'first', and possibly later, is in G, while the 'second', and possibly earlier, is in F. To avoid confusion they should preferably be identified by key. Apart from their keys, the sets have much in common. Each is for Gibbons's standard choir of five voices. Their bass-lines are frequently identical, and they differ little in their harmonies and in the rhythms and the lengths of the notes to which the words are set. Each shows a slightly

---

1   Peterhouse music MSS, deposited at Cambridge University Library. The key to the part-books is provided by Hughes (1953, p. 20), who adopts Barnard's numbering.

greater rhythmic complexity at the words 'to help us', 'Holy Ghost', and 'is now ... Amen. Praise ye the Lord' (Ex. 43 on pp. 210-211).

Attached to the Preces in G is a setting of verses 15-21 of Psalm 145, *The eyes of all wait upon thee*. This is a psalm specified in the *Book of Common Prayer* for Evensong on Whit Sunday. Two sources add a further setting, *Awake up my glory—Open to me the gates*, combining verses from Psalms 57 and 118. These are respectively for Matins and Evensong on Easter Day, though the heading 'for Easterday at Evensonge' appears in the part-books.[2] The Preces in F are associated with only one psalm, a setting of verses 1-14 of Psalm 145 (*I will magnify thee, O God my King*). The notion that Barnard reversed the order of the preces is strengthened by the attachment to the 'second' set of the first half of Psalm 145, while the second half of the psalm is coupled with the 'first' set.

If sources compiled after Gibbons's death are to be relied upon, the alternation of versicles and responses in the Preces in F is matched, in the psalm attached to them, by alternation between the decani and cantoris sides of the choir. (There is a need for care in making assumptions about Gibbons's intentions, however, for copyists and editors seem sometimes to have imposed their own ideas about alternation between the two sides of the choir.[3] This caveat applies whenever the subject occurs below.) The alternation of versicles and responses is matched, in the psalms attached to the Preces in G, by the alternation of verse sections and fully choral sections. Since Gibbons increasingly turned to the verse style in his sacred music, this may be a further indication that the 'First' Preces and their psalms are later than the 'Second' Preces and the psalm associated with them.[4]

The partition of *The eyes of all* into verse and choral sections reflects natural divisions in the text. The sections are linked one to another by correspondences between them. For example, the verse setting of 'thou givest them their meat in due season' is paralleled by the choral setting of 'thou openest thine hand and fillest all things living with plenteousness'. That in turn is paralleled by a choral setting of 'The Lord is nigh unto all them that call upon him'. The psalm concludes with

2   The Peterhouse set and another at Durham Cathedral. For details of sources, see Gibbons, 1925, pp. xxviii-xxix.

3   Morehen, 1995, pp. 208-211.

4   It may be that Gibbons sought to link the psalms to the preces by key, as well as style. The 'first' setting of the preces and its first psalm are in G with no flat in the signature; the second psalm is in a 'minor' version of the key (G with one flat). The 'second' setting (in F) has a psalm in d with a flat in the signature (in modern terms, the relative minor).

Ex. 42.

(a) William Byrd, First Preces

continued

Ex. 42 *continued*

(b) Orlando Gibbons, Preces in F

Ex. 43.

(a) Orlando Gibbons, Preces in F

continued

Ex. 43 *continued*

(b) Orlando Gibbons, Preces in G

the last echo of these phrases, in the setting of the words 'and ever shall
be, world without end'. Because melody is a principal tool in forging
such links, Gibbons has to repeat words in order to meet his musical
needs.

Each of the psalms supplying the words of *Awake up my glory*
expresses short, separable ideas, so no sense of awkwardness is created
by joining them, and Gibbons tackles them as a single text. The only
section to end with a cadence on any note but the tonic (G) occurs well

after the join, when a cadence is formed on D. The setting begins and ends with verse and choral sections, but in the inner sections (if we can accept that Gibbons's intention is represented by posthumous sources)[5] the text's piecemeal thought process is matched by the alternation of the cantoris and decani sides of the choir. Once again Gibbons relies heavily on melody, and where necessary extends his text by repetition. Many of the melodic shapes occurring throughout the piece are inspired by a rising motive in the first verse section, which is inverted in the second.

I will magnify thee begins and ends with a section for full choir, but sources present it throughout the remainder of its length as alternating short sections for the cantoris and decani sides. The writing is economical, with little word repetition, and all sections (except the brief opening passage for full choir) are closely similar.

The Short Service

The titles 'Short Service' and 'Second Service', by which Gibbons's two Services are customarily known, are once again those printed by John Barnard in *The First Book of Selected Church Musick* (1641).[6] The Short Service is fully choral, but the Second Service is in the verse style, and is more descriptively known as the Verse Service.

The Short Service provides music for Matins (Venite, Te Deum[7] and Benedictus), for Communion (Kyrie and Creed), and for Evensong (Magnificat and Nunc Dimittis).[8] It is essential to view these settings in their liturgical context: not as forming a unified composition, but as a series of movements separated by spoken passages from *The Book of*

5   See the caveat on p. 207.

6   The Short Service is also found in a now incomplete set of part-books (Royal College of Music MSS 1045-1051), dated 1625, the year in which Gibbons died. It is the earliest surviving set to contain any of Gibbons's music for the liturgy. It also includes some of his anthems. It belonged to Barnard, and material from it might have been intended for a second printed collection.

7   Peterhouse Music MSS 35-37, 42-45, deposited at Cambridge University Library, contain a Latin adaptation of the Te Deum. Hughes (1953, p. 21) is in error in ascribing to Gibbons another Latin Te Deum, of which the tenor part occurs in MS 35; it is in fact an adaptation of the Te Deum from Byrd's Great Service. The error is repeated in Daniel and le Huray, 1972, ii, p. 107, and in le Huray's list of Gibbons's works in Grove, 1980. The piece is correctly identified by Kerman, 1981, p. 29.

8   An additional Sanctus is adapted from the Te Deum. It was printed by Boyce (1760-73, iii, p. 299), but the earliest source is a copy, in a hand attributed by Fellowes to William Child, inserted into part-books at St George's Chapel, Windsor (Gibbons, 1925, p. xxix). The manuscript was not available for examination at the time of writing.

Common Prayer. It is nevertheless probable that Gibbons had some idea of unifying the movements by means of head-motives.[9] Resemblances can be pointed out between the initial notes of the treble part in the Venite, Benedictus, Te Deum, Kyrie and Magnificat. The Creed and Nunc Dimittis do not rise so quickly to c", but the family resemblance is not entirely lacking (Ex. 44 on p. 214).

The popularity of the Short Service in its own century can be measured by its survival in a remarkably large number of early manuscripts, besides Barnard's printed collection, and this popularity has endured.[10] Burney, in spite of particular criticisms which he consigned to a footnote, waxed lyrical over the Short Service:

> The harmony of Gibbons's service in F, printed by Dr. Boyce, is pure, clear, and grateful; and the melody more accented and flowing than I have found in any choral Music of equal antiquity.[11]

Like other settings of a similar nature, Gibbons's Service is 'short' in the sense of being succinct. It is in a tradition formed in the early years of the Anglican church. The requirement that the words should be presented in an easily comprehensible fashion meant that musical settings had to be plain and clear. Gibbons's work, though remarkably tuneful, is restrained and concise. Any temptation to expand the shorter movements is resisted. In the common manner of such services, the scoring is restricted to four voices, words are not repeated for purely musical reasons, and the writing is largely homophonic with each syllable sung to one note.[12] Relief is provided by passages of discreet counterpoint. Imitation is in general sustained only briefly, though the end of the Nunc Dimittis incorporates a canon at the fourth between the two highest voices.[13]

9   Similar groups of notes appearing at the beginnings of movements, and establishing a relationship between them. Use of the technique by English composers can be traced back to the fifteenth century. It occurs, for example, in the *Sine nomine* mass of Taverner, the four-part mass of Tallis, and in Byrd's Great Service and masses.

10   The sources are listed in Gibbons, 1925, p. xxix.

11   Burney, 1776-89, iii, p. 329 (1935, ii, p. 265). More recently Howard (1951) has described the Short Service as 'perhaps the finest setting of the Anglican Office that has ever been written for Cathedral use', and Phillips (1991, p. 410) calls it 'much the most interesting of its kind'.

12   Despite this, copyists frequently found difficulty in underlaying the words of the inner parts. See le Huray, 1978, pp. 107, 311. Some of Gibbons's anthems, too, suggest that he was less than careful in fitting words to the music of the inner parts.

13   This was particularly praised by Burney, who wrote: 'The *two parts in one*, of

Ex. 44. Orlando Gibbons, Short Service

Venite

O   come,   let   us   sing   un - to   the   Lord

Te Deum

We praise thee, O   God,   we   know - edge   thee

Benedictus

Bless - ed   be   the   Lord   God   of   Is - ra - el

Kyrie

Lord,   have   mer - cy up - on   us,   and   in - cline   our   hearts

Creed

The   Fa - ther Al - might - y,   ma - ker of heaven and earth, and of all things vi - si ble

Magnificat

My   soul   doth mag - ni - fy   the Lord,   and   my spirit   re - joic - eth

Nunc Dimittis

Lord, now let - test thou thy   ser - vant   de - part   in peace, ac - cord- ing to thy word

the GLORIA PATRI, though they may be the cause of some confusion in the words, discover no restraint or stiffness in the melody, which continues to move with the same freedom, as if no *canon* had existence' (Burney, 1776-89, iii, pp. 329-330; 1935, ii, p. 265).

Gibbons's debt to his predecessors shows itself in details, as well as in his general approach. The prominent central cadence on A in his Te Deum, at the words 'Thou art the King of Glory, O Christ', reflects the continued structural influence of pre-Reformation plainsong.[14] But despite working within a traditional framework, Gibbons displays great skill in coping with the constraints of the short service style. He confers vitality on the chordal writing by simple expedients, such as allowing one or two voices to get momentarily out of step with the others.[15] He also shows independence of mind. This appears from a comparison of his Short Service with Byrd's. Subject to the caveat entered on p. 207, both composers lend variety to a limited medium by giving passages to the decani and cantoris sides of the choir as well as to the full choir, but Gibbons often differs from Byrd in the allocation of such passages.[16] He eschews any gesture like Byrd's six-part opening of the Creed, choosing rather to relax his severity in that movement by permitting individual voices to sing short passages in crotchets, and by briefly contrasting different combinations of voices (at 'and was crucified', for example). In the Magnificat, where Byrd sets 'he hath scattered the proud in the imagination of their hearts' in rigid homophony, Gibbons scatters illustrative crotchets.

Yet there can be little doubt that Gibbons knew Byrd's Short Service, both as a performer and as a student of composition. Gibbons's Benedictus may owe something to Byrd's in the first few notes of the treble part and in the rising crotchets of the final passage for full chorus ('Glory to the Father and to the Son'). The beginning of Gibbons's Nunc Dimittis may perhaps recall Byrd's, as well.[17] A deeper debt is apparent in Gibbons's awareness of tonality. In setting the Venite, Byrd chooses five different notes on which to form cadences at the ends of sections, using four of the notes several times. Gibbons also forms cadences on five notes, but as he divides his text into longer sections and places relatively greater emphasis on the part-writing, he uses only three of the

14   Aplin, 1979, pp.274-275.
15   Phillips (1991, pp. 410-411) draws attention to the passage in the Magnificat, at the words 'He remembering his mercy hath holpen his servant Israel', where 'a tight dislocation of rhythm is caused by the entry of the tenor, who repeatedly accents the offbeats against the other parts'.
16   It should however be noted that Gibbons follows Byrd in giving to the full choir the whole of his Nunc Dimittis, and most of his Magnificat. Monson (in Byrd, 1980, pp. x-xi) draws attention to the probability that Byrd, like Tallis before him, did not intend alternatim performance of these movements.
17   See p. 216, concerning a possible recollection of Byrd's Nunc Dimittis in Gibbons's Second Service.

notes frequently.[18] Near the beginning of each piece, its composer has a cadence which occurs only once: Byrd a minor third above the tonic ('salvation'), and Gibbons a major third above the tonic ('above all gods'). A little more than halfway through the movement, as if momentarily to break out of the narrower limits he has set, Gibbons has another cadence that occurs just once, on the fourth ('wilderness').

The Second, or Verse Service

Gibbons's Second Service provides music for Matins and Evensong: Te Deum and Jubilate (an optional alternative to the Benedictus),[19] and Magnificat and Nunc Dimittis. A good deal of editorial work is unfortunately required before any of the movements (particularly those for Matins) can be performed. One of the chief difficulties lies in discrepancies between the extant organ and vocal parts.[20] The work can nevertheless be seen as a masterpiece in the verse style, and — quite as much as Gibbons's verse anthems — it contains elements of theatricality which heighten the drama of the religious ritual. The Second Service covers an extraordinarily wide range, from the Te Deum, with its anguished cries of 'O Lord' and the greater confidence of 'O Lord, in thee have I trusted', to the Jubilate's tripping spirit and the solemnity, humility and culminating richness of the Nunc Dimittis.

The Second Service looks back no further than William Byrd, whose own Second Service, though setting only the movements for Evensong, was highly influential, and is the earliest in the verse style to survive intact.[21] There may, as Turbet suggests, be a recollection of the opening of Byrd's Nunc Dimittis at the start of Gibbons's setting of the same text,[22] though there is also a connection with the head-motives of

18   Philips (1991, p. 410) notes that 'Gibbons was concerned to restrict the type and frequency of the cadences by throwing the musical interest onto part-writing'. He adds: 'The Evening Canticles are an extreme example of this, since they only cadence on the dominant and tonic'.

19   Barnard (1641) says in the index to his collection that among those pieces 'many times, Sung in stead of Anthems' was 'The Jubilate in Mr. *Gibbons* Service'.

20   The editors of Gibbons, 1925, published a reconstruction of all four movements, omitting stretches of the organ part. An edition by Fellowes (Gibbons, 1936) includes only the Magnificat and Nunc Dimittis. Unpublished editions for recordings have been made by Thurston Dart (Argo ZRG 5151) and Edward Higginbottom (CRD 3451). An unattributed edition prepared for a recording (ASV CD GAU 123) takes account of the possible inaccuracy mentioned in note 22 below.

21   It may be no later than the 1570s.

22   Turbet, 1988, p. 489, where attention is drawn to a second treble part at the

Gibbons's Short Service. Gibbons seems in any case to have been influenced as much by the verse service of another of his predecessors in the Chapel Royal, Thomas Morley, as by Byrd's work. Morley's setting provides music for the liturgy throughout the day, though verse treatment is accorded only to the Te Deum, Benedictus, and (more particularly) the Magnificat and Nunc Dimittis.[23]

The choral sections of Gibbons's Second Service are set for five voices, which are occasionally divided. The writing is often semi-homophonic, with imitation kept to a minimum. The most striking use of imitation is saved for the ends of sections, where it is clear that Gibbons admired the manner in which Byrd often set the words 'Amen' and 'Alleluia'. There are however contrasts, both within movements and between one movement and another. For instance, long stretches of five-part counterpoint are admitted into the Te Deum, whereas in the Magnificat such passages occupy considerably less space.

Gibbons's verse sections are seldom for a solo voice, but often for two, three or more singers. This, and the possibility of allocating parts to singers from either side or both sides of the choir, allows him to separate fully choral passages by verses of varied colour, texture and orientation. On occasion he gradually increases the size of the group singing the verse, so that the transition to the following choral section is less sharply marked (Ex. 45 on p. 218). Though Byrd had done much the same thing in his Great Service, his setting is on a larger scale, and Gibbons's debt may be to the less expansive setting by Morley.[24]

beginning of Gibbons's Nunc Dimittis, entering a semibreve later than the first. This may be an accretion, lacking the composer's authority.

23   Morley probably died about the beginning of October 1602, shortly before Gibbons joined the Chapel Royal. Some of Gibbons's contemporaries in the Chapel Royal wrote verse services, but whether they did so before or after Gibbons is uncertain. Those most likely to have done so at about the same time are his senior colleagues Edmund Hooper and Nathaniel Giles. Thomas Weelkes, who also wrote verse services, was described on the title-page of his *Ayeres or Phantasticke Spirites* (1608) as both 'Organest of the Cathedral Church of Chichester' and a 'Gentleman of his Majesties Chapell' — perhaps meaning a Gentleman Extraordinary, since his name does not appear in the court records. His verse services were probably written over several years, though he may have found composing difficult by 1609, when he was first charged with neglecting his duties.

24   Hooper's verse service, too, consistently uses ensemble verse sections with varied scoring, but although Hooper is quite as radical in his way as Gibbons's, he creates quite a different effect. Virtually the only examination of Hooper's music is Gant, 1999.

Ex. 45. Orlando Gibbons, Second Service, Te Deum (organ omitted)

continued

Ex. 45 *continued*

Gibbons's verse sections contain writing of sundry kinds. The solos of the Jubilate resemble the solo vocal parts of his consort songs, with rests between the phrases, and words repeated to meet the dictates of the melody (Ex. 46a). The resemblance is emphasized by the contrapuntal accompaniment. In a verse of the Te Deum, by contrast, several voices proceed in canon (Ex. 46b).

Ex.46. Orlando Gibbons, Second Service

(a) Jubilate

continued

Ex. 46 *continued*

(b) Te Deum (organ omitted)

Verses may be linked to the choral passages that follow them in a variety of ways. Frequently Gibbons creates the link by melodic means, as at the start of the Te Deum, where the continuation into the chorus of the upper line of the verse is visible in the gradually rising melodic peaks (Ex. 47). Later in the Te Deum, the words 'O Lord, save thy people' are set as a versicle sung by two voices, while the words which follow ('and bless thine heritage') are set as a choral response. The passage continues in like manner, and it is by such methods that Gibbons not only links the verses and choruses, but habitually emphasizes the sense of the words.

Ex. 47. Orlando Gibbons, Second Service, Te Deum (organ omitted)

On a few occasions the division of a movement is achieved by changes of time. The Jubilate is governed by the proportional sign C3,[25] until the words 'come before his presence with a song', after which there is a change to ₵ for the song itself. Closely adjacent changes of sign in the Nunc Dimittis divide the movement into two roughly equal portions, and mark out the words 'To be a light to lighten the gentiles, and to be the glory of thy people Israel'. In other cases the meaning of the words

25   Sometimes C in the sources.

may be pointed up by changes of rhythm without any change of proportional sign. Dotted crotchets in the Jubilate give added life to the words 'O go your way into his gates with thanksgiving, and into his courts with praise: be thankful unto him, and speak good of his name'.

Long as the Second Service is, almost all the sections into which it is divided end with a cadence on D (the tonic) or A. In a work where long-range melodic repetition is not used as a unifying element, repeated cadences on just two notes provide the listener with a means of orientation. But Gibbons's tonal scheme is not quite as limited as this suggests. Intermediate cadences may occur on other notes, such as that on F, midway through the first full chorus of the Te Deum. Later in the Te Deum the notion that 'thou shalt come to be our judge' is marked out as significant by a cadence formed exceptionally on C. This cadence serves the further purpose of dividing a very long movement a little after its central point.

Gibbons shows particular skill in investing melodically similar material with a variety of harmonies. It is here that the organ accompaniment often performs an essential function, as it does in the verse section of the Jubilate beginning 'O go your way into his gates'. Two vocal parts sketch the harmonies, which are realized by the organ in a manner that recalls Gibbons's keyboard fantasias. Frequently, indeed, the organ part shows, by condensing the vocal parts, how close the Second Service sometimes approaches to Gibbons's instrumental style: compare Ex. 48 opposite, from the Magnificat of the Second Service, with Exx. 8-11 on p. 100-104. Gibbons's music, for every medium, though constantly inventive, is extraordinarily consistent.

Ex. 48. Orlando Gibbons, Second Service, Magnificat

11

ORLANDO GIBBONS'S DEATH

On 31 May 1625 King Charles set out from London to meet his wife, a girl of fifteen.[1] John Chamberlain reported that her entourage was 'a little armie of <u>4000</u> at least'.[2] The King's party was less numerous, but included a large group of musicians. Payment was later made 'To Henry Martin Serjaunt Trumpetto[r]: and xvj[en] others of his fellowes upon the Councell*es* warraunte dated xxj° Junii <u>1625</u> being Cõmaunded to wayte uppon his Matie: at Canterbury, and Dover, and alsoe in fetching of the Queenes Matie: out of ffraunce by the space of xxviij[t] dayes ended xvj[to] Junii <u>1625</u>'.[3] There were also Jerome Lanier, Anthony Bassano and other musicians who played wind instruments.[4] It is likely that a band of string players accompanied them, since Adam Vallet received payment for himself 'and xj[en] other of his fellowe Musicõns' who travelled from Whitehall to Canterbury and back again.[5] Nathaniel Giles, who held a post at St George's Chapel, Windsor, in addition to his post as Master of the Children of the Chapel Royal, was given twenty days' leave by the Windsor Chapter to go to Canterbury. It is evident from the Chapter's resolution that the whole of the Chapel Royal accompanied the King.[6] This naturally included the Chapel's senior organist, Orlando Gibbons.

1 For an account of the King's journey, see Toynbee, 1955.

2 PRO, SP16/3 no. 60; CSPD, 1858(c), p. 43; Chamberlain, 1939, ii, p. 622. For another contemporary account see CSPV, 1913, pp. 81-82, 87-88.

3 PRO, E351/544, m. 192[r]; Ashbee, iii, p. 134.

4 PC2/33, f. 81[r]; Privy Council, England, 1934, p. 116; Ashbee, 1986-96, viii, p. 91. Lanier, Bassano and eleven other wind musicians are mentioned, but the group may have consisted of twelve in all (see the next note).

5 PRO, E351/544, m. 193[r]; Ashbee, 1986-96, iii, p. 134. A signet warrant of May 1625 authorized two payments to Vallet: one of £20 for himself, and another of £24 to be divided among twenty-four musicians who travelled to Dover (PRO, SO3/8; Ashbee, iii, p. 6). The numbers are rather confusing, but it appears that, apart from the trumpeters and the musicians of the Chapel Royal, the King was accompanied by twelve wind musicians and twelve string players.

6 St George's Chapel, Windsor, Chapter Acts 2, f. 125[r], entry dated 20 May 1625 (not available for consultation at the time of writing); Shaw, 1991, p. 344; Fellowes, 1979, p. 41. The entry in the Chapter Acts, as quoted by Fellowes, says that Giles was to go to Canterbury 'cum tota regia capella quando rex noster Carolus obviam ibat reginae suae ex Gallia transfretanti'.

The citizens of Canterbury added to the musical celebrations. The King completed his journey in less than a day, and the city council afterwards paid 'the Musitians for theire Musicke, at his Mat^{es} entrance into this Citty: by appoyntm^t of Mr Maior'. The accounts record another payment 'to the waites of the Citty for theire Musicke at the king*es* being heere, and at ye ffrench Embasserds whoe came in May last'; and 'Fees due to the kings servants at his being here in Can*terbury* June 1625' include those to trumpeters, drummers and a fifer, while another entry reads: 'To the king*es* Musitions the auncient fee — x^s'.[7]

The cathedral authorities, too, made special preparations for the royal visit. An entry in the Treasurer's accounts under the heading 'Expensae Necessariae' records a payment of twenty shillings, 'pro emendacione organoru*m* in adventu*s* Regis'. Another seems to mean that payment was made in respect of two occasions — possibly, though it is only a guess, on the King's arrival and again after he had met the Queen at Dover and returned with her to the city — on which a canopy supported by gilded posts was set up, presumably over a throne ('pro auratura baculoru*m* de le canopie Regis ad duas vices xlvi^s').[8]

After first reaching Canterbury the King stayed only two days before setting off for Dover. As his bride was delayed, he returned on Wednesday 8 June. Henrietta Maria eventually reached England on the evening of Sunday 12 June, and was accommodated at Dover Castle. Early the next morning the King departed once more for Dover, where he arrived at about ten o'clock. Later that day the royal couple travelled to Canterbury by coach, and remained there until Wednesday 15 June. They journeyed to London on 16 June.

Gibbons is said to have composed an anthem for the royal marriage,[9] but the tale may be no more than part of a traditional belief that an

---

7 Canterbury Cathedral Archives, CC/FA/23, ff. 250^v, 247^r, 249^r.

8 Canterbury Cathedral Archives, DCc/TA33.

9 In editing a collection of anthems, Rimbault (1846, p. 1) mentioned 'Part-books formerly in the possession of the celebrated John Evelyn, and now forming one of the many musical rarities in the library of the Editor ... the last composition entered being an Ode composed by Orlando Gibbons for the marriage of that king [Charles I] with the Princess Henrietta Maria'. The reference is apparently to Drexel MSS 4180-5, but these end with a collection of fantasias by Gibbons. (For a list of the contents see Monson, 1982, pp. 149-153.) The 'ode' Rimbault had in mind must be *Do not repine fair sun*, which occurs much earlier in the manuscripts, and was in any case written for King James's Scottish journey. It is true, as Fellowes observed (1951, p. 44), that Gibbons's anthem *Grant, O Holy Trinity* would have been suitable for performance in the cathedral on 12 June, which was Trinity Sunday, but there is nothing to suggest that any of Gibbons's music was performed.

Anglican wedding service took place on 13 June. It was current by the Restoration, for *The Life and Death of that Matchless Mirrour of Magnanimity, and Heroick Vertues Henrietta Maria de Bourbon* (1669) says: 'At *Canterbury, June* $^{14}_{24}$ 1625, they were personally married'.[10] This appears to be without foundation, as the treaty of marriage imposed the condition that there should be no other religious ceremony than the one which took place outside Notre Dame.[11] The story was nevertheless developed in Agnes Strickland's statement that 'The king and queen were married, according to the rites of the church of England, in the great hall of St. Augustine, at Canterbury. No particulars of the ceremony have been preserved, excepting that the great English composer, Orlando Gibbons, performed on the organ at the royal nuptials'.[12] But Gibbons died while the King was at Dover on Whit Sunday 5 June. The only record of music at this particular time is a payment to drummers 'for theire service 2 daies at the kings coming from Dov^r wth his Queene and at his depting from this Citty'.[13]

John Meade, writing to Sir Martin Stuteville, said that 'Orlando Gibbon, the Kings Organist coming on Saturday [*sic*] from service at Christ Church [the cathedral] fell downe dead'.[14] The entry in the Cheque Book does little to convey the stir this caused:

> Mr Orlando Gibbons Organist died the vth of June being then Whitsonday at Canterbury wher the Kinge was then to receave Queene Mary who was then to com out of ffraunce, and Thomas Warwick was sworne in his place Organist the first daie of July followinge & to receave the pay of the Pistoler.[15]

In fact, Gibbons's death bred great alarm, for the plague was then rampant in London. Gibbons's home parish of St Margaret's,

---

10   The statement occurs on p. 12. The book was reissued in 1671 as *Memoires of the life and death of ... Henrietta Maria de Bourbon*. The date 'June $^{14}_{24}$' reflects a difference of ten days between the old and new calendars.

11   Toynbee, 1955, p. 87, where the history of the legend is reviewed.

12   Strickland, 1885, v, pp. 212-213. Strickland compounds the error by adding in a footnote: 'The fact is recorded on his tomb in Canterbury cathedral'.

13   Canterbury Cathedral Archives, CC/FA/23, f. 246^r.

14   BL, Harleian MS 389, f. 458^r. Meade was a Fellow of Christ's College, Cambridge; Stuteville lived at Dalham in Suffolk.

15   Cheque Book, f. 7^r; Rimbault, 1872, p. 11. The duplicate cheque book reads: 'Orlando Gibbons died the vth of June, & Thomas warrick sworne in his place the first of July & to Receave the paye of Pistler' (Bodleian Library, Rawlinson D.318, f. 31v; Ashbee, 1986-96, viii, p. 324).

Westminster, kept a special record: 'The Accompte ... for the releife and ordering of persons infected with the Plague in the most lamentable yeare of Contagion 1625'. The entries include 'M^{ris}. Gibbons ij^s. ij^d '.[16] The citizens of Canterbury were so worried that they made a payment 'to one ... to inquire about one Mrs Hayward whoe was thought to be dead at London of the sicknes'.[17] Her belongings had been returned to Canterbury, and it was feared that there was a danger of contagion from them.

The day after Gibbons's death Sir Albertus Morton wrote to Lord Conway that he had delayed his departure from Canterbury until the cause was certified by physicians.[18] The certificate he enclosed was signed by Drs Leonard Poe[19] and Jacob Domingo.[20]

Wee whose names are heere underwrytten: having beene called to give o^r counsailes to Mr Orlando Gibbons: in the tyme of his late & suddaine sicknes, wch wee found to be in the beginning, lethargicall, or a profound sleep: out of w^{ch}, wee could never recover him, neyther by inward nor outward medicines, & then instantly he fell in most strong, & sharp convulsions: wch did wring his mouth up to his eares, & his eyes were distorted, as though they would have beene thrust out of his head & then suddenly he lost both speach, sight, & hearing, & so grew apoplecticall & lost the whole motion of every part of his body, & so died. Then here upon (his death being so suddaine) rumors were cast out y^t he did dye of ye plague,

16   Westminster Archives.

17   Canterbury Cathedral Archives, CC/FA/23, f. 247^r.

18   PRO, SP16/3, no. 37-37i; CSPD, 1858(c), p. 39; Ashbee, 1986-96, viii, p. 89. Morton and Conway were Secretaries of State. The city's Burghmote minutes for the years 1603-1629, which may have contained information about the action taken by the Mayor following Gibbons's death, have been lost.

19   Poe is listed a number of times in records of the royal household, e.g. PRO, E351/544, m. 121^r, of 1620. He had aristocratic patrons, through whom he secured a licence to practice. Chamberlain wrote on 5 October 1606 that 'Po got great credit in my L. of Salisburies last sicknes, and there is order for his grace in both the universities, to passe out doctor presently' (PRO, SP14/23, no. 32, manuscript numbering; Chamberlain, 1939, i, p. 232; CSPD, 1857, p. 332, calendars Chamberlain's letter, but omits the reference to Poe). Poe was made one of the King's Physicians in Ordinary in January 1608/9, and was present at Salisbury's death in 1612.

20   When, in 1605, Domingo was cited before the College of Physicians for practising in London, he produced letters testimonial as an Extra Licentiate. He was examined and approved by the Censors' board, and admitted a Licentiate on 1 October 1606 (Munk, 1861, p. 118). Domingo's name does not appear among those of the medical men at King James's funeral, although Poe is listed (PRO, LC2, f. 37^r).

whereupon wee together wth M^r. Maiors appoyntment, caused his body to be searched, by certayne woemen that were sworne to deliver the truth, who did affirme y^t they never saw a fayrer course.[21] Yet nothwithstanding wee to give full satisfaction to all, did cause the skull to be opened in o^r presence & wee carefully viewed the bodye, wch wee also found to be very cleene wth out any show or spott, of any contagious matter. In the braine wee found the whole, & sole cause of his sicknes namely a great admirable blacknes & syderation in the outside of the braine, wth in ye braine (being opened) there did issue out abundance of water intermixed wth blood & this wee affirme to be the only cause of his suddaine death.

    Poe.

    Domingo.

The medical examination must have been conducted hastily, for Gibbons's body was buried the day after his death. The *Register booke of Christninges, Marriages and Buriall within the precinct of the Cathedrall and Metropoliticall Church of Christe of Canterburie* contains the simple entry: '1625: Orlando Gibbins buried June: 6: 1625:'[22]

In spite of the careful examination made of Gibbons's body, the fear still lingered that he died of the plague. A week afterwards John Chamberlain wrote: 'that wch makes us the more afraid is that the sickness increaseth so fast ... Orlando Gibbon the organist of the chappell (that had the best hand in england) died the last weeke at Caunterburie not wth out suspicion of the sicknes'.[23]

Besides succeeding to Orlando Gibbons's place as organist in the Chapel Royal, Warwick received his other posts at court. Warrants were issued for the payment to him for life of annuities of forty-six and forty pounds in respect of 'two severall places of his Ma^{tes} musicians in ordinary, In such man*ner* as Orlando Gibbons deceased late had & enjoyed during his life'.[24] Although Warwick had earlier attracted lines addressed by John Davies of Hereford '*To my deere friend, countryman,*

21   Meade wrote that Gibbons had 'no signe of plague on him, but is thought to have died of wind' (BL, Harleian MS 389, f. 458^r).

22   Canterbury Cathedral Archives, U3/100/P17/5/16; Hovenden, 1878, p. 115.

23   PRO, SP16/3, no. 60; CSPD 1858(c), p. 43; Chamberlain, 1939, ii, p. 622; Ashbee, 1986-96, viii, p. 90.

24   PRO, SO3/8 (June 1625); Ashbee, 1986-96, iii, p. 7. Also SP38/13 (25 June 1625); Ashbee, viii, p. 90; CSPD, 1858(c), p. 541. The declared accounts record: 'And to Thomas warwicke succeeding the said Orlando Gibbons aswell in the said pay of xlvi^{li} per ann, as likewise succeeding him in one other place of one of his Ma^{tes}: ordenary Musicōns at xl^{li} per ann*um*...' (PRO, E351/544 m. 182^v; Ashbee, iii, p. 133).

and expert Master in the liberall Science of Musick',[25] his appointment may have owed more to his social connections than to his musicial abilities, for in 1629/30 the Dean forbade him to play verses because of his 'insufficiency'.[26]

Elizabeth Gibbons arranged for a monument to be erected to her husband in the cathedral. 'In 1626', wrote Nicholas Stone, the King's master mason, 'I sett up a monument at Canterbury for Erlando Gebons the Kings organest for the which his wyf paid 32[li]'.[27] The monument includes a bust of Gibbons, and the words:

ORLANDO GIBBONIO CANTABRIGIAE INTER MUSAS ET MUSICAE NATO
SACRAE R CAPELLAE ORGANISTAE SPHAERARUMQ HARMONIAE
DIGITORUM PULSU AEMULO
CANTIONUM COMPLURIUM QUAEQ EUM NON CANUNT MINUS
QUAM CANUNTUR CONDITORI
VIRO INTEGERRIMO ET CUIUS VITA CUM ARTE SUAVISSIMUS MORIBUS
CONCORDISSIME CERTAVIT
AD NUPT C R CUM M B DOROBERN ACCITO ICTUQ HEU SANGUINIS
CRUDO ET CRUDELI FATO EXTINCTO CHOROQ COELESTI TRANSCRIPTO
DIE PENTECOSTES A D N MDCXXV
ELIZABETHA CONIUX SEPTEMQ EX EO LIBERORUM PARENS
TANTI VIX DOLORIS SUPERSTES MERENTISS[O] MOERENTISS[A] P
VIXIT A M D[28]

25   Davies, 1611, p. 203: 'One Citty brought us forth, and brought us up ...' Davies supplied the words for Thomas Weelkes's madrigal *Death hath deprived me of my dearest friend*, written in memory of Thomas Morley.

26   Cheque Book, f. 40[v]; Rimbault, 1872, p. 78. Warwick nevertheless tried his hand at composition; for example, his verse anthem *I lift my heart unto the hills* occurs in John Browne's manuscript part-books (BL Additional MSS 29366-8), into which it was probably copied by the younger Alfonso Ferrabosco. For a note on Warwick see Harley, 1997, p. 380.

27   Sir John Soane's Museum, notebook of Nicholas Stone; Spiers, 1919, p. 63. Stone lived 1586-1647.

28   An extremely inaccurate translation of the inscription was published by Dart (1726, p. 52); this was copied by Boyce (1760-63, i, p. viii), and so gained wide currency. The following translation is given by Boyd, 1962, p. 87: 'To Orlando Gibbons born at Cambridge amidst the Muses and for music, organist of the Royal Chapel and rivaling by the stroke of his fingers the harmony of the spheres, composer of many anthems which sing his praises as often as they themselves are sung, a man of most upright character, whose personality vied (though most harmoniously) with his musicianship in charm, summoned to the marriage [festivities] of King Charles and Marie of Bourbon at Dover and deprived of life by a lamentable rush of blood and the

The Dean and Chapter of Westminster granted Gibbons's widow administration of his goods on 13 July 1626. The entry in the Act Book is endorsed 1627.[29] A parallel entry appears in the records of the Prerogative Court of Canterbury.[30] Events however ran ahead of the legal process, for Elizabeth Gibbons died about the middle of 1626, and was buried at St Margaret's, Westminster, on 2 July.[31] Gibbons's home in the Woolstaple was listed as that of 'Widdowe Gibbons' in the parish books for 1625-26 and 1626-27, but her name did not appear in the following year.[32] Fellowes reported that Fuller Maitland, whose article on Gibbons in the *Dictionary of National Biography* states that Elizabeth's will was proved on 30 July 1626, could not recollect the source of his information, and if there was a will it has not been found.[33]

The administration of Gibbons's affairs and the custody of his children during their minority were now made the responsibility of his brother Edward. A grant of administration by the Prerogative Court of Canterbury is dated 27 October 1628, but perhaps that was the date when an arrangement which had existed since Elizabeth's death was formalized.[34] Wood's garbled account is that Orlando Gibbons's son Christopher was 'bred up from a Child to Musick under his Uncle *Ellis Gibbons*, Organist of *Bristow*', though Ellis Gibbons had died in 1603, and neither Ellis nor Edward Gibbons was organist of Bristol.[35] The fact may be that some of Orlando's children lived with Edward in Exeter. The youngest, also Orlando, was to die there, probably shortly before August 1650 when the administration of his affairs was granted to his sisters Elizabeth (whose married name was Greenslade) and Mary (whose married name was Soper).[36] It is however possible that Christopher Gibbons was educated in London, as will be shown in the next chapter.

cruel hand of fate and translated to the choir of heaven on Whitsunday in the year of our Lord's birth 1625 — Elizabeth his wife and mother of his seven children, barely surviving her most admirable husband in her extreme grief and wretchedness, has erected this. He lived   years   months   days'. Elizabeth Gibbons evidently believed her husband to have been born at Cambridge. The blanks in the last line were never filled in.

29   Westminster Archives, Act Book III, f. 104^v.

30   PRO, Prob. 6/11, f. 171^v (manuscript numbering).

31   Westminster Abbey Muniment Room, register of St Margaret's; Burke, 1914.

32   Westminster Archives, Overseers' books, St Margaret's parish.

33   Fellowes, 1951, p. 48. The editors of Gibbons, 1925, said (p. xix) they had 'searched for the will in vain'.

34   PRO, Prob. 6/13, f. 52^r (manuscript numbering).

35   See note 91 on p. 16.

36   PRO, Prob. 6/25, f. 125^r (manuscript numbering).

PART III

12

CHRISTOPHER GIBBONS

Christopher, the first of Orlando Gibbons's sons to survive infancy, was about ten years old when his father died in 1625. On his mother's death, in the following year, he probably became a ward of his uncle Edward.[1] The possibility that he nevertheless remained in London, maybe as a chorister of the Chapel Royal, is suggested by a letter of 2 July 1663, written by King Charles II to the University of Oxford. This states that 'Christopher Gibbons, one of y^e. Organists of Our Chapple Royal hath from his youth, served Our Royal Father and Our selfe'.[2] The court certainly took an interest in the boy's welfare. A note in a Signet Office docquet book records the despatch of 'A letter to Sr Robert Dallington kt, Governor of Suttons Hospitall in the Charterhouse, for Christopher Gibbons, Sonne of Orlando Gibbons deceased, to be admitted into a schollers place wch shall first happen to be void there. ρcured by Mr Secretary Coke. dated 20. Jan: 1626' (i.e. 1626/7).[3] The entry is marginally annotated 'gratis'. The Governors of Charterhouse approved Christopher's election on 21 June 1627,[4] but records of admissions are lost, so there is no confirmation that he attended the school.

Wood's remarks about Christopher Gibbons's education may be partly the result of guesswork. He says that Christopher was 'bred up from a Child to Musick under his Uncle *Ellis Gibbons*', but this cannot be wholly accurate, and obviously reflects the confusion between Ellis and Edward evident in Wood's other passages concerning the Gibbons family.[5] It is however possible that Christopher received instruction from Edward after a schooling at Charterhouse, and this idea is supported by evidence that for a time he may have lived with Edward in Exeter. On 15 October 1633 the will of John Chapple, an Exeter merchant, was

---

1 See p. 230.

2 PRO, SP44/12, p. 24; CSPD, 1862, p. 191; Ashbee, 1986-96, viii, p. 159. Burney and Hawkins both say Gibbons served in the Chapel Royal, but their statements are probably based on Wood, who summarized the letter printed on p. 262 below (Wood, 1691-92, ii, col. 833 (1813-20, *Fasti*, ii, col. 277); Burney, 1776-89, iii, p. 461 (1935, ii, p. 362); Hawkins, 1776, iv, p. 412 (1963, ii, p. 713)).

3 PRO, SO3/8; Ashbee, 1986-96, iii, p. 23.

4 Marsh and Crisp, 1913, p. 8.

5 Wood, 1691-92, ii, col. 833; 1813-20, *Fasti*, ii, col. 277. Wood's statement is repeated by Boyce, 1760-63, i, p. viii; Burney, 1776-89, iii, p. 461 (1935, ii, p. 362); and Hawkins, 1776, iv, pp. 412-413 (1963, p. 713).

witnessed by a Christopher Gibbons, though he is not identified as the musician.[6]

There can be no doubt that Christopher showed exceptional promise, and retained the interest of the court, for the next that is heard of him is an entry of 23 June 1638 in the diary of John Young, Dean of Winchester: 'My L. Chamberlains letter was reade in the behalfe of Mr. Gibbons to be our organist'.[7] On 25 June Young wrote:

> I admitted Jo: Silver Mr of the Queresters and singing man, and Ch: Gibbons organist and singing man. His plase is to be made him worth 30 lib. per An. at my L. Chamberlain's comand, and because the Mr. of the Quiristers is allowed 40 lib. whereof Gibbons hathe 10 lib. We addet to Jo. Silver the uther singing man's place to make his oup'.[8]

The formal admission of Gibbons and Silver to their posts took place at a Chapter meeting on 26 June.[9]

Opposition to the rule of Charles I came to a head in the next few years, and he and the Queen left London in January 1621/2. The ensuing Civil War was to affect Christopher Gibbons directly. According to the royalist propaganda sheet *Mercurius Rusticus*, Parliamentary soldiers entered Winchester Cathedral in December 1642, carrying the altar to an alehouse where they set it on fire, 'and in that fire burnt the Books of Common-prayer, and all the Singing-books belonging to the Quire: They throw down the Organ, and breake the stories of the Old and New Testament, curiously cut in carved work, beautified with Colours, and set round about the top of the Stalls of the Quire ...'[10] A post-Commonwealth document quoted in full below states that Christopher Gibbons 'was constrayned with the reverend Deane and Prebends to flye into his late ma[ties]: Garrisons where he tooke upp Armes and faithfully served his late Ma[tie]: during all the warr'.[11]

---

6   Chapple's will was destroyed in the Second World War, and survives only in the form of a copy made by Miss Olive Moger, which is at the Exeter Central Library.

7   Young, 1928, p. 140.

8   Ibid., p. 141. The accounts of Winchester Cathedral for 1640 show that Silver received £35 and Gibbons £30; see Shaw, 1991, p. 296.

9   Winchester Cathedral, Chapter Acts 1622-45, f. 56r; Shaw, 1991, p. 296.

10   *Mercurius Rusticus*, 1643-44, 'XX. Week. *Febr.* 24. 1643[/4] ... The Countries Complaint of the Sacriledges ... on the Cathedrall Churches of this Kingdome'. The pamphlets published under the title *Mercurius Rusticus* were edited by Bruno Ryves, a chaplain to Charles II who became Dean of Windsor at the Restoration.

11   PRO, SP29/31, no. 66 (printed folio no. 130). A belief in Gibbons's soldiering appears first to have been given currency by Rimbault (1866, p. 182), who clearly knew

The Chapter records of Winchester Cathedral were discontinued in 1645, at about the time that the city surrendered to Cromwell,[12] and were not resumed until the Restoration. Gibbons's association with the Cathedral does not seem formally to have been severed, however. In 1646, when he married, he was still described as 'of Winchester', although the ceremony took place in London, at the church of St Bartholomew the Less, on 23 September.[13] Gibbons's wife was Mary, a daughter of Dr Robert Kercher, Prebendary of Winchester and of St Paul's Cathedral. The couple are not known to have had any children, and she must have died at some time before 1655, for Gibbons remarried in that year.[14]

Gibbons's connection with Winchester Cathedral continued in being for some years. On 2 June 1648, the Committee for Sequestrations considered 'ye Peticõn of χfer Gibbons late organist of Winchester', and 'ordered that the Co: of Hamptshire doe call the Trẽr before them & allowe the Pet^r. w^t shall appr to bee due to him of his stipend & arrears of the Lands & Revenues chargeable therewith'.[15] On 24 November 1655, the Trustees for the Maintenance of Ministers granted him five pounds.[16] He received nothing when a further distribution to Winchester

of the document quoted here, since he says: 'When the dean and prebends fled, he accompanied them and served in one of the garrisons' (repeated in Rimbault, 1872, p. 219). He did not divulge his source, and later writers have either adopted the notion as a cautious hypothesis (e.g. Scholes, 1934, pp. 241, 288; Shaw, 1991, p. 297), or embraced it uncritically (Rayner and Rayner, 1970, p. 153). In 1642, about the time that Christopher Gibbons may have left Winchester, St John's College 'Payed to Gibbons the Organist for his q*uate*ridge —— 4^l–10^s–0' (St John's College, Rental Book SB4.5, f. 226^v). Although there is no other evidence that Gibbons was in Cambridge, it is not impossible that he spent a short time in the town where he probably had relatives. Another possibility is that the organist was Richard Gibbons, who composed two fantasies for four viols, which occur in Marsh's Library, Dublin, MSS Z3.4 1-6 and Bodleian Library, Oxford, MSS Mus. Sch. c.64-69 (inscribed 'George Stratford 1641').

12 The surrender took place on 28 September 1645 (Bailey, 1856, p. 148).

13 St Bartholomew's Hospital Archives, register of St Bartholomew the Less.

14 Chester, 1876, p. 156, and Fellowes, 1951, p. 50, mistakenly identify her with the Mary Gibbons who was buried 15 April 1662 in the North Cloister, Westminster Abbey. The Precentor's book describes that Mary as a widow (Westminster Abbey MS 61228A, f. 147^r).

15 PRO, SP20/5, f. 52^r; Matthews, 1948, p. 17.

16 PRO, SP28/290 ('The Accompt of Lawrence Steele Esq: Treasurer', s.v. Southampton, recording a payment to 'M^r. Xρõfer Gibbons one of the Late Quiremen of the Cathedrall of Winton by Order of the 16:th of October 1655'); Matthews, 1948, p. 17.

Cathedral staff was made in 1657, although he reappeared in the cathedral's Chapter Books in 1660. An entry for Midsummer 1661 has 'resignavit' written against his name.[17]

Commonwealth London

In the face of looming defeat, King Charles I surrendered to the Scots in May 1646. Oxford, where the court had been established, fell to the Parliamentary forces in June 1646. Gibbons's activities may soon have become centred on London, where (as noted above) he was shortly married, and where a teacher and free-lance musician might make a reasonable living. In 1651, the year which saw the defeat and escape to the Continent of Charles II, who had succeeded to the throne on his father's execution in January 1648/9, Gibbons's name was included among those of the 'many excellent and able Masters' of London recommended to anyone desiring a teacher 'For the Organ or Virginall'.[18] A glimpse of his other activities is given by the journal of Lodewijck Huygens:[19]

[10 March 1652] In the afternoon at about four o'clock we visited Sir John Danvers' son,[20] with Mons[r]. Rosin, who had been his tutor. First we heard a famous organist named Gibbons play on a chamber organ[21] that stood there, which was pumped by foot. After him we heard a young gentleman sing some English songs while the aforesaid organist played the bass.

[25 March 1652] We went on [from the Tower] to our destination, that is, M[r] [Davis] Mell's,[22] in order to hear some music played. So we did. When

17   Winchester Catherdal, Chapter Books, November 1660, and Midsummer 1661; Shaw, 1991, p. 297.

18   *A Musicall Banquet, set forth in three choice varieties of musick* (1651), printed for John Benson and John Playford.

19   BL, Egerton MS 1997, ff. 68[r-v], 83[v]-84[r]; translation from the Dutch based on Huygens, 1982, pp. 92, 105. Lodewijck Huygens was the brother of Christian Huygens (1629-95), the mathematician and physicist. Their father was Constantin Huygens (1596-1687), Heer van Zuylichem, statesman, humanist, poet and composer.

20   Sir John Danvers (1588?-1655) had several children by his second wife, whom he married in 1628.

21   The Dutch original has 'positif'.

22   Mell lived in the parish of St Olave, Hart Street, not far from the Tower (Bannerman, 1916). The Mell family was prominent among court musicians before and after the Commonwealth (see Ashbee, 1986-96, i, iii, v, viii, *passim*). Davis (or David) Mell was one of the signatories of a petition sent to the Council for the Advancement of

we entered they were playing a concerto for organ, that Gibbons played, bass viol and two violins,[23] one of which was played by the master of the house, who played admirably well. After that they played another concerto for harpsichord, lute, theorbo, bass viol and violin.[24] The harpsichord was played by Rogers,[25] whose compositions were being performed, while his brother played the lute.[26] At about seven o'clock we left ...

Gibbons's consort music

Gibbons's surviving consort pieces were evidently written for performances of the kind described by Huygens, and later by Pepys.[27] They include four suites for a single treble instrument, bass and organ, and six suites for two trebles, bass and organ, each consisting of a fantasia, almain and galliard.[28] In addition there are three extended fantasias, which include subsidiary movements, and eighteen single dances, all for two trebles, bass and organ. Four of the latter can be combined with one of the fantasias to form another suite. There are a further sixteen two-part airs, and three four-part fantasias.

Although it seems probable that Gibbons began composing consort music when he settled in London, he appears never to have been a prolific composer, and there is at present little information to indicate whether he went on writing consort music throughout his life. None of

Musick on 19 February 1656/7 (PRO, SP18/153, f. 123ʳ, printed folio no. 253ʳ; CSPD, 1883, p. 285). He may have been one of five unnamed masters of music to whom, on 29 February 1655/6, Cromwell ordered payment to be made from the monument money at Westminster (PRO, SP25/59, f. 120ᵛ; SP25/76, page numbered variously 572, 577 and 121 (the last in pencil); CSPD, 1882, p. 204). 'Monument money' was derived from fees paid by those erecting a monument: Westminster Abbey Precentor's Book 61228A contains many pages where such payments are listed.

23   'hant violin' in the original.

24   'hant viool'.

25   Benjamin Rogers (1614-1698) had a varied career, at St George's Chapel, Windsor; Christ Church Cathedral, Dublin); Eton College; and Magdalen College, Oxford. In 1653 he received a MusB from Cambridge University on the recommendation of Cromwell. See Shaw, 1991, as indexed.

26   John Rogers (d. 1676) was one of the leading lutenists of his day. See Grove, 1980, s.v. 'Rogers, John'; Ashbee, 1986-96, i, v, viii, *passim*.

27   For Pepys, see pp. 258-259. A few pieces exist in autograph copies (see Dodd, 1980-89).

28   See Holman, 1993, pp. 267-272, on the adoption of the violin as the treble instrument of choice; and Holman, 1996 (especially p. 370), on the role of the organ in consort music.

the sources is likely to have been copied much before the Restoration. Despite the work embodied in several theses,[29] much remains to be done before sound judgements can be made about the development of Gibbons's consort music from pieces of the kind played by 'Coprarios musique' before the Civil War,[30] and about its relationship to the music of Gibbons's contemporaries.

Roger North, who knew some of Gibbons's consort music, thought that it was bold, solid, and strong, but tended to be disconnected and rough.[31] This opinion has been echoed more recently by Meyer, who applies to Gibbons's consort music the phrases 'personal and almost ecstatic', and 'grimly passionate'.[32] It may be added that a great deal of it is tuneful, attractive, and worthy of more attention than it has received since the composer's death. The dissonances, false relations and unresolved suspensions to which Meyer points may, perhaps, indicate that Gibbons tended to think in terms that came naturally to a keyboard player. They also indicate that he lived in a new era. His fondness for agile phrases, often leaping from note to note, or rising or falling over a wide interval, seems to result from the manner of violin playing introduced by Thomas Baltzar.[33] The age to which Gibbons belonged is evident, too, in the key system underlying his compositions. Unlike his father's music, which in great part retained characteristics of the sixteenth-century modes, the younger Gibbons's music reflects a general transition to the major and minor scales. It was not until 1688 that Thomas Salmon wrote: 'As much as I can observe from the compositions of the most Eminent Masters for these last Twenty years, this interval constitution of an Octave is but twofold: either with a greater Third, Sixth, and Seventh: or a Lesser Third, Sixth and Seventh'.[34] Christopher Gibbons's music of all periods is nevertheless well on the way towards this condition. An almain from a fantasia suite for two violins, bass viol and organ, illustrates something of Gibbons's style (Ex. 49).[35]

29   Rayner, 1963; Field, 1970; Johnson, 1971.

30   See pp. 61-62.

31   BL, Additional MS 32533, f. 17ʳ (c.1726); North, 1959, p. 299. 'D.ʳ Chr. Gibbons a great master in yᵉ *ecclesiastica*ˡˡ stile, amd also in consort musick, of whom I have had setts of fancys, & some Ayres, the latter in a lute style but yᵉ others ve*ry* bold, solid, & strong but Desultory & not without a litle of yᵉ Barbaresque'.

32   Meyer, 1982.

33   See Holman, 1993, pp. 268-271.

34   Salmon, 1688.

35   Bodleian Library MS Mus. Sch. c.102a-b, ff. 3ᵛ, 23ᵛ, 43ᵛ (Almain 23 in Dodd, 1980-89). The bass part is written on paper with an oblong format, which suggests that it was intended for the use of the organist; this is confirmed by the inscription 'Organ part'

Ex. 49. Christopher Gibbons, almain in d (Dodd 23)

continued

was intended for the use of the organist; this is confirmed by the inscription 'Organ part' on f. 48ʳ. There is no fully written out organ part.

Ex. 49 *continued*

Cupid and Death

Cupid and Death is one of the theatrical productions which mark a transition from the Stuart court masque to Restoration opera. The printer's preface to the first edition of the libretto by the dramatist James Shirley, published in 1653, states: 'This Masque was born without ambition of more, than to make good a privat entertainment, though it found, without any address or design of the Author, an honorable acceptation from his Excellency, the Embassadour of *Portugal*, to whom it was presented by Mr. *Luke Channen*, &c'.[36] It therefore seems that by the time the masque was printed there had been two performances, one given privately, and another given before the Ambassador.[37] According to Wood, Shirley was a schoolmaster during the interregnum, 'mostly in the *White Fryers*',[38] so it is possible that the masque was first performed by pupils of his school, at some time before 26 March 1653, the date which the title-page gives for the performance before the Ambassador. Channen, the presenter, can be identified as the person mentioned by Pepys on 24 September 1660, in connection with 'a dancing-meeting in Broadstreet, at the house that was formerly the Glasse house (Luke Channell Maister of the Schoole)'.[39]

36   *Cupid and Death* is placed in its historical context by Dent, 1928, and White, 1983. The former (pp. 81-88) gives an extended account of the work. James Shirley (1596-1666) had already collaborated in other musical entertainments: *The Triumph of Peace* (set by William Lawes and Simon Ives, and staged at Whitehall by the Inns of Court in February 1633/4), and the school masque *The Triumph of Beautie* (set at least partly by William Lawes, and published in 1646).

37   The Ambassador was the Condé de Penaguião, who negotiated the Treaty of Peace and Alliance between King John and Olver Cromwell, signed in 1654.

38   Wood, 1691-92, ii, cols. 260-265; 1813-20, iii, cols. 737-744.

39   Pepys, 1970-83, i, p. 253. Channell is mentioned as a dancing-master elsewhere, e.g. in *Roscius Anglicanus* (1708) by John Downes.

It is not known whether Gibbons wrote music for the initial productions, but a complete score was prepared by Matthew Locke of the music which he and Gibbons provided for a production in 1659, at the Military Ground in Leicester Fields.[40] Locke carefully initialled his own contributions, forming the major part of the music, and added Gibbons's name to his colleague's instrumental airs and three songs. Gibbons was some years older than Locke, but it is possible that the two composers had become acquainted at Exeter, where in the years before the Civil War Locke grew up as a chorister and secondary of the Cathedral. It is, however, necessary to treat with scepticism statements that Locke received his training from Gibbons's uncle Edward, since Edward Gibbons's regime at Exeter was notably lax in the years (from about 1630) when Locke was there.[41]

Gibbons's pieces for *Cupid and Death* consist of some instrumental airs, and two solo songs and a duet, each with a four-part chorus.[42] The instrumental airs are similar to those which Gibbons composed for consort, and — judging by the band that played for *The Siege of Rhodes*[43] — are likely to have been written for similar forces. (Locke's manuscript sets them out on one or two treble staves and a bass stave.) Two of the songs, *Victorious men of earth* and *Change, O change your fatal bows*, are in the style of the declamatory songs developed for pre-war Stuart masques, while the attractive duet *Open bless'd Elysium grove* is in the vein of melodious masque songs. The elegiac *Take pity, Gods* (Ex. 50 on p. 242) serves, in its ingenuous way, to close the fourth entry of the masque as choruses of lamentation were later to conclude Blow's *Venus and Adonis* and Purcell's *Dido and Aeneas*.[44]

40 BL, Additional MS 17799.

41 An entry in Wood's manuscript notes reads: 'Lock (Matthew) was bred a chorister in the Cathedral Church of Exeter ... while William Wake was Master of the choristers there ...' (Bodleian Library, MS Wood D 19(9), f. 86ᵛ). Wake was in fact a lay vicar and deputy organist of Exeter Cathedral, 1635-42; he became Master of the Choristers in 1671 (Shaw, 1991, pp. 108-109). It was presumably the same William Wake who was sworn into the next place to be vacant in the Chapel Royal in 1663 (Cheque Book, f.44ᵛ; Rimbault, 1872, pp. 49-50), though it is not clear whether he actually served in the Chapel. For evidence that Christopher Gibbons may have been in Exeter when Locke was there, see pp. 233-234.

42 All printed in Locke and Gibbons, 1965.

43 See p. 246.

44 The mood is anticipated in the possibly choral conclusion of Orlando Gibbons's *Nay let me weep*.

Ex. 50. Christopher Gibbons, *Take pity, Gods*

Gibbons's organ music

On 12 July 1654, during a tour of Oxford, John Evelyn found Gibbons at Magdalen College:

> there was still the double *Organ*, which abominations (as now esteem'd) were almost universaly demolish'd: Mr, *Gibbon* that famous *Musitian*, giving us a taste of his skill & Talent on that Instrument ...[45]

The organ was presumably one that was later moved to Hampton Court. An inventory of goods at the palace, dated 18 June 1659, includes (among the items 'In the Greate Hall') 'One large Organ and a Chaire Organ which was brought from Maudlin College in Oxford'. A marginal note says: 'Val*ue* about 300ˡⁱ'.[46] The organ must have been the cause of Gibbons's visit to the college, but his presence in Oxford is less easily explained. Had he been one of the musicians who met regularly in the

45   Evelyn, 1959, p. 341.

46   PRO, SP18/203, f. 89ᵛ (printed folio no. 74ᵛ). Double organ: an instrument with two manuals, 'great' and 'chair'.

city, the fact would surely have been recorded by Anthony à Wood. It could be that he was paying a visit to his father's birthplace, where he may still have had relations, or to musical friends there. It could, alternatively, be that he was friendly with Arthur Phillips, whose father is said by Wood to have come from Winchester.[47] Phillips had been *informator* at Magdalen before the Civil War, and may have remained in Oxford at least until his successor as Professor of Music, John Wilson, was appointed in 1656.[48]

Evelyn offers no clue to what he heard Gibbons play. Since Gibbons apparently wrote little for keyboard instruments, it must be assumed that his reputation as a performer reflected his powers as an improviser and continuo player. Most, and probably all, the dances attributed to Gibbons in keyboard sources are versions of pieces composed for strings. His seven pieces bearing the title 'verse' or 'voluntary' all spring from the tradition of contrapuntal compositions for organ established in Tudor times. There is nothing to show when they were written, unless 'verse' can be held to indicate composition after the Restoration, for the re-established services of the Church of England.[49] The sources are, however, inconsistent in the titles they give these pieces, when they give any at all.

Three of Christopher Gibbons's keyboard pieces, according to the sources, are for double organ (numbered 1694, 1697 and 1698 by Brookes).[50] Two of them (nos. 1694 and 1697) exist in different versions. The shorter version of each probably resembles Gibbons's original composition. There is good reason for thinking that the extended endings (two in the case of Brookes 1697) are not by Gibbons.[51] For one thing, the endings contain much that is in a distinctly later style than that of the compositions to which they are attached. It may also be that instructions for the use of the two manuals do not derive directly from the composer, though in the most reliable source (Christ Church MS Mus. 47) the registration shows variety and imagination.[52]

The character which must have pervaded Gibbons's organ playing can easily be perceived in his written voluntaries. He divides each piece into sections, based on different points of imitation, in the manner of his Elizabethan and Jacobean predecessors, and while his voluntaries are not as tightly constructed as those of Byrd or Orlando Gibbons, they include

47   Bodleian Library MS Wood 19 D(4) 106, f. 99ʳ.
48   Shaw, 1991, p. 381.
49   See Cox, 1984, i, pp. 8-10, on the organ's part in services.
50   Brookes, 1996.
51   Cox, 1984, i, pp. 81-90.
52   Ibid., pp. 213-214.

some material that might easily be mistaken for the work of an older composer. In this respect no. 1697 appears a little more old-fashioned than no. 1694. But they also exhibit a type of writing in which the leaping, often arpeggiated figures breathe an entirely new spirit, not dissimilar to that of the composer's consort music. He carries further the agility present in the part-writing of his father's later keyboard fantasias (compare Ex. 51 with Ex. 12 and 13 on pp. 105-106).

Ex. 51. Christopher Gibbons, voluntary for double organ (Brookes 1694)

While some figures clearly derive from Bull, they quickly give way to others that are new and individual (Ex. 52).

Ex. 52. Christopher Gibbons, voluntary for double organ (Brookes 1694)

continued

Ex. 52 *continued*

Second marriage

In April 1655 Gibbons married his second wife, a widow named Elizabeth Filbridge (*née* Ball).[53] The fact was recorded twice: in the register of St Mary at Hill, and in the register of the bride's parish, St Clement Danes.[54] Why the marriage was recorded at St Mary at Hill is hard to say, for it was not Gibbons's home parish; the register of St Clement Danes describes him as dwelling in the parish of St Giles Cripplegate.

Christopher and Elizabeth lived at first near St Clement Danes, and are listed in the 'Temple Barr' section of a rate book for the year ending on Lady Day 1659.[55] Their five children were baptized in the church between 1655/6 and 1660. The parish register does not actually refer to the children's father as the musician, but there can be little doubt of his identity. The eldest child was named Orlando, after the grandfather he never knew; the twins who followed were named after their parents. Mary, the elder of two subsequent daughters, eventually went abroad and had not returned by 1682; her sister Ann was apprenticed, but to whom and in what capacity is unknown.[56]

In 1664 the Gibbons family was living in New Street, Westminster.[57] This is affirmed by an advertisement in the *London Gazette*:

53   The register of St Mary Somerset records the marriage of an Elizabeth Ball and 'Thomas Fallbridge' on 15 September 1644. Elizabeth's relations are mentioned in her will: see pp. 277-281.

54   Register of St Mary at Hill (Guildhall Library MS 4546): 'Christopher Gibbons and Elizabeth Phelbridge were married the 16th of April 1655'. Register of St Clement Danes (Westminster Archives), 22 April 1655.

55   Westminster Archives, MS B25.

56   Elizabeth Gibbons's will. See p. 278.

57   A statement by Zimmerman (1983, p. 42), that Gibbons 'occupied the house in Great Almonry South in which the Purcells had lived up to the time of the death of Henry the elder in 1664', is inaccurate. The overseers' accounts for the parish of St Margaret's show that in 1664 'Hen. Peirshall' lived in 'Greate Almnory', where in 1663

C Hristopher Gibbons Doctor in Musick, and principal Organist to His Majesty in private and publick, had stoln out of his house, which is in New street, betwixt the [Almonry] and Orchard street in Westminster, the 26th of June, between 9 and 12 in the Morning, a Silver Tankard, to the value of near Seven pounds, with the marks of $^{G}_{C\;E}$ on the handle: the reward for any that can give tidings of the same to the said Mr. Gibbons is Two pounds.[58]

The house in New Street is probably the one described in an affidavit of 1682 as being in Orchard Street.[59]

On 23 May 1656, a year or so after Gibbons's second marriage, he took part in another stage work, The Siege of Rhodes. This — so the title page of Davenant's libretto tells us — was performed 'At the back part of Rutland-House in the upper end of Aldersgate-Street, London'.[60] At the end of the book are lists of the composers, the singers, and — in some copies, but not all — 'The Instrumental Musick'.[61] The latter consisted of Christopher Gibbons, who presumably provided a keyboard continuo, William Webb,[62] Humphrey Madge,[63] 'Thomas Balser, A German',[64] Thomas Bates,[65] and John Banister.[66]

he was listed between Mr Babington and Mrs Swettenham (who evidently moved into the house occupied by Henry Lawes in 1661). Gibbons is listed as living in New Street, where his name appears between those of Solomon Holmes and John Spicer (Westminster Archives, MS E177).

58   London Gazette, no. 588, 3-6 July 1671; 'Almonry' (sometimes spelled 'almnory' or 'almry') is printed as 'Ambry'. See the map on p. 34 for the streets.

59   See p. 281.

60   William Davenant, The Siege of Rhodes (London, 1656).

61   The instrumental music was composed by Charles Coleman and George Hudson, and the vocal music by Henry Cooke, Henry Lawes and Matthew Locke. The singers were Cooke, Locke, Gregory Thorndell, Edward Coleman, John Harding, Henry Purcell the elder, and Catherine Coleman (Edward Coleman's wife).

62   Webb, a former Gentleman of the Chapel Royal, sang and played the lute in Shirley's The Triumph of Peace (1634).

63   Madge was appointed as one of the King's violinists in 1660.

64   Baltzar, the celebrated violinist, was born in Lübeck. He served at the Swedish court, and arrived in England c.1655.

65   Bates was listed by John Playford as a teacher 'For the Voyce or Viole' (A Musicall Banquet, 1651). He was appointed to a court post in 1660.

66   Banister, a violinist, joined the King's musicians in 1660, and in 1662 became the leader of a select band of string players. He is noted for his part in establishing commercial concerts in the 1670s.

The Restoration

With the restoration of the monarchy in 1660, Gibbons found himself at the centre of English musical life. King Charles entered London on 29 May, and it was not long before Gibbons procured the posts at court and at Westminster Abbey which had once been held by his father.

A step towards Gibbons's appointment as a court musician, in the private music, was taken on 19 June, when (as Pepys noted)[67] the King went to supper at Baynard's Castle, in Thames Street:

> Mr Gybbons approved of by ye King at Baynards Castle, and an organ to be made for him./ for ye verginalls in ye Presence in Mr. Warwicks place.[68]

Thomas Warwick, who had succeeded to Orlando Gibbons's places in 1625, had died during the interregnum, and confirmation of Christopher Gibbons's appointment as 'one of ye Virginall players' was given on 25 June.[69] The Cheque Book of the Chapel Royal, and court establishment lists (the earliest of which was probably compiled about 1661), reveal that Gibbons also became an organist in the Chapel Royal.[70] He further appears in subsidy lists for the royal household; but the King's servants enjoyed privileges granted in earlier reigns, and were discharged from the payment of subsidies.[71] The accounts of the Treasurer of the Chamber record much delayed payments to Gibbons for 'exerciseing two places' in 1665, though these had been amalgamated in 1625.[72] The combined annual value of the posts was still eighty-six pounds.

67   Pepys, 1970-83, i, p. 78.

68   PRO, LC3/2; Ashbee, 1986-96, i, p. 3. In the memorandum quoted, 'verginalls' replaces the deleted word 'organs'.

69   PRO, LC3/2 and LC3/3. LC5/137, p. 245-246 (Ashbee, 1986-96, i, p. 7), is a warrant of 9 November 1660 to prepare a bill concerning the appointment for the King's signature, 'the first payment to commence from the feast of St John Baptist last past ...' Establishment lists for 1660-68 include Gibbons as a virginalist: LC 3/73, p. 102; LC3/25 (Ashbee, i, p. 220). Giles Tomkins was appointed as a virginalist at the same time (LC3/25, p. 54).

70   Cheque Book, f. 44^r (Rimbault, 1872, p. 128); PRO, LC9/388 and LC3/25, p. 56 (Ashbee, 1986-96, i, p. 226).

71   PRO, LC5/138, pp. 380-381, 385; E179/266/22; T51/5, p. 14 (Ashbee, 1986-96, i, p. 50-51; v, p. 45; viii, p. 165; *Calendar of Treasury Books*, 1904, p. 565). The documents date from 1663, though Parliament had granted the subsidies some time earlier. A copy of a discharge, possibly of the same date, appears in the Cheque Book of the Chapel Royal, f. 48^v (Rimbault, 1872, pp. 93-95).

72   PRO, E351/548, f. 3^v; E351/549, f. 5^r (Ashbee, 1986-96, v, pp. 124, 127). See

Gibbons not only held posts at court, but until the middle of 1661 (as noted above) was still organist of Winchester Cathedral.[73] This is confirmed by two documents of February 1660/1, connected with a petition submitted by Gibbons about property in Freefolk, near Winchester, to which he had a claim by virtue of his first marriage.[74] One document, a covering minute, reads:

To the Kings most Excellent Ma[tie]:
The humble petition of Christopher Gibbons one of your
Ma[ties]: servants in ordinary

Humbly sheweth

That your pet[r] by meanes of the Marriage with Mary one of the Daughters of Docto[r] Kercher deceased late Prebend of your Ma[ties]: Cathedrall Church of the holy Trinity of Winton, hath an equitable tythe or clayme of Tenant*es* right to a certeyne Copyhold Tenement in ffreefolke, late Masons within the Mannor of Whitechurch and parcell of the possessions belonging to the said Cathedrall Church and now in the possession of one John Campian, who hath noe other tythe thereunto then by possession obteyned in the tyme of the Warr

May it therefore please your sacred Ma[tie]: to vouchsafe your Ma[ties]: most gracious letters recomendatory to the Deane and Chapter of your Ma[ties]: said Church on your pet[s] behalfe.

And your pet[r] shall
ever pray &c

p. 60-61 concerning the places which had been held by Orlando Gibbons. The following documents record payments, often long overdue, to Christopher Gibbons in respect of the period 1671-1673: E351/546, f. 5[r], f. 18[r], f. 32[v]; E351/547, f. 4[r]; E351/548, f. 3[v]; E351/549, f. 5[r]; AO1/397/90, f. 5[r]; AO1/398/94, f. 4[v]; AO1/398/95, f. 4[v]; AO1/399/97; AO1/399/100; AO1/401/106 (Ashbee, 1986-96, v, pp. 108, 112, 115, 122, 124, 127, 130, 133, 137, 140, 143, 150). In undated establishment lists of the 1660s Christopher Gibbons is described as one of the 'Private Musick For lutes and voyces Theorboes & virginalls', and as both a virginalist and a member of the Private Musick (PRO, LC3/25, pp. 52, 58; Ashbee, 1986-96, i, pp. 225, 227). In E36/231, f. 117[v] and SP29/76, no. 67 (Ashbee, viii, p. 167) he appears as a musician in ordinary.

73   See p. 236.

74   PRO, SP29/31, nos. 65-66 (printed folio nos. 129-130); CSPD, 1860, p. 518; Ashbee, 1986-96, viii, p. 142.

The other document, a copy of a submission signed by an array of dignitaries, reads:

Whereas Christopher Gibbons is one of his Maties Musicians in ordinary and his Maties Organest in the Chappell, and also is Organest in the Cathedrall Church of the holy Trinity in Winchester, Which said last mencõned Organest place, the said Christopher exercised for many yeares before the late unhappy warr untill in the tyme of the violent prosecucõn of the Church he was constrayned with the reverend Deane and Prebends to flye into his late Maties: Garrisons where he tooke upp Armes and faithfully served his late Matie: during all the warr, And having marryed one of the daughters of Docto^r Robert Kercher deceased late one of the Prebends of the said Church, who in his life tyme about the beginning of the late warr had Contracted with the then Deane and Chapiter amongst other things for an Estate of Two Lives in Revercõn of one life then in being and since deceased in a Copyhold Tenement held of the Mannor of Whitchurch then in the possession of [blank] Mason to be graunted to such persons as the said Docto^r Kercher should nominate and had a warrant from the then Deane and Chapiter directed to the Steward of the said Mannor for the passing of the Estates Accordingly, wch was prevented by the warrs and the death of the said Docto^r Kercher Now therefore we desire yo^w to examine the premises and to graunt a warrant for the said Copyhold Tenement being now voyd and in your possession upon a Moderate ffyne unto the said Christopher Gibbons and his assignes for such three lives as he or they shall nominate and appointe According to the usuall Course and Custome in like Cases, ffor wch we shall remayne

Yo^r loving freinds

Dat: Vet. ffebruary

1660. Ac: Ebor
Jo: Duresme
Geo: Worcest^r Br: Winton
Jo: Earles Joh: Exon[75]

The petition was evidently successful, for when Gibbons died the copyhold passed to his second wife, Elizabeth, who bequeathed it to her daughter Elizabeth.[76]

75 The signatories were: Dr Accepted Frewen, Archbishop of York; John Cosin, Bishop of Durham; Brian Duppa, Bishop of Winchester; John Gauden, Bishop of Exeter; George Morley, Bishop of Worcester; and John Earle (or Earles), Dean of Westminster.
76 See pp. 277-278.

The Chapel Royal and Westminster Abbey

Gibbons was one of three organists in the Chapel Royal.[77] The others were Edward Lowe and William Child. Two of them were required to be on duty at any time, one playing the organ and the other in his surplice in the choir. 'At solemne times', reads the Cheque Book of the Chapel Royal, 'they shall all three attend; the auncientist organist shall serve and play ye service on the ye eve and Dayes of ye solemne feastes viz: Christmas, Easter, St George, and Whitsontide; The second organist shall serve the second day. And the third the third day. Other dayes they shall wait according to their monthes'.[78]

Gibbons seems to have taken up the additional post of organist at the Abbey towards the end of 1660, since the accounts for Michaelmas 1661 record his receipt as organist of a year's salary of ten pounds.[79] His appointment was apparently unaffected by a resolution of the Chapter of the Chapel Royal, made on 19 December 1663, that 'No man shalbe admitted a Gentleman of his Majesties Chappell Royall but shall first quit all interest in other quires, and those that relate at present to other churches besides the Chappell, shall declare their choice either to fix at their churches, or to the Chappell ... his Majestie not permitting them to belong to both'.[80] Indeed, the close relationship between the musicians of the Chapel and Westminster Abbey which had existed in the time of James I and Charles I continued under Charles II. Like the Abbey's other musicians, Gibbons's salary was augmented by a variety of supplementary payments. He was given 7s 4d for playing at the funeral of the Princess Royal on 29 December 1660, and for various other funerals (at the improved rate of 7s 10d). He received a dividend from the Abbey's farm rents, and regularly had a share of fees paid by those permitted to erect monuments.[81] He received a payment in connection with the tuning of the Abbey organs in 1661 (though George Dallam was

---

77   Cheque Book, f. 44^r (Rimbault, 1872, p. 128); PRO, LC9/388 and LC3/25, p. 56 (Ashbee, 1986-96, i, p. 226). There is no need to consider whether Gibbons was Charles II's organist who befriended Froberger during the latter's visit to England. The impossibility of the visit occurring under the circumstances described by Johann Mattheson, and accepted elsewhere (e.g. by the Rayners), is satisfactorily demonstrated by George J. Buelow (Mattheson, 1740, pp. 88-89; Rayner and Rayner, 1970, p. 156; Grove, 1980, s.v. 'Froberger, Johann Jacob').

78   Cheque Book, f. 46^r; Rimbault, 1872, p. 83.

79   Westminster Abbey, WAM 33695.

80   Cheque Book, f. 45^v; Rimbault, 1872, p. 81.

81   Westminster Abbey, Precentor's Book, 61228A (funeral of Princess Royal: f. 4^v; farm rents, 27 April 1661: f. 15^r; monuments: ff. 21^v-56^v).

paid for the same duty for a whole year), and 'for Organ Bookes' in 1662.[82] When the post of Master of the Choristers became vacant, with the death in May 1664 of the elder Henry Purcell, Gibbons temporarily held that as well. There is no specific record of his appointment, but the Abbey's accounts for 1665 show that he received two separate payments of ten pounds as organist and as Master of the Choristers, and payment for part of the year for the maintenance of ten choristers.[83]

In collaboration with Henry Cooke, the Master of the Children of the Chapel Royal, and the elder Henry Purcell at the Abbey, Gibbons must have played a leading part in re-establishing the music of the two institutions. His work as a composer for the Chapel, and probably the Abbey, is represented by a dozen anthems. The words of two — *Above the stars* and *How long wilt thou forget me?* — were printed in the second edition of James Clifford's *Divine Services and Anthems* (1664). It is not certain whether their omission from the first edition of 1663 means that they were recent works. *How long wilt thou forget me?* was among four of Gibbons's pieces published by John Playford in *Cantica Sacra* (1674),[84] and it was added to the books of the Chapel Royal in the late 1670s.[85] Judging by the number of other sources in which it is preserved, it enjoyed considerable popularity.

All Gibbons's anthems are of the verse type, with continuo accompaniment.[86] They are usually for one or two trebles with or without a bass voice, and a chorus in three or four parts. The extracts below from *How long wilt thou forget me?* are typical (Ex. 53). Different versions are sometimes given by different sources, however, perhaps due to adaptation to meet local needs.[87] The verses often resemble songs of the mid-century, and both verses and choruses have a kinship with Gibbons's contributions to *Cupid and Death*. Their

82   Westminster Abbey, WAM 33695, f. 4^v; 33696, f. 5^v.

83   WAM 33698, f. 2^r. Gibbons received £33 6s 8d for the choristers out of a whole year's sum of £60 6s 8d. He gave up both posts in 1666: see p. 263.

84   The others were *Celbrate Dominum*, *Sing unto the Lord*, and *Teach me, O Lord*.

85   PRO, LC5/141 p. 431-3; Ashbee, 1986-96, i, p. 163. *How long wilt thou forget me?* was added to the books of the Chapel Royal between 12 February 1676/7 and 25 December 1680, along with *Teach me, O Lord* (PRO, LC5/144, p. 40; LC5/121; Ashbee, 1986-96, i, p. 193).

86   See Holman, 1993, pp. 393-414, on the peformance of anthems by the Restoration Chapel Royal, which may on occasion have been more complex than is indicated by existing manuscripts. See also the quotation from Edward Chamberlayne's *Angliae Notitia* on p. 207 above.

87   Spink (1995, pp. 33-34) prints part of another version of *How long?* (from Fitzwilliam Museum MS 117). The verse differs slightly, and the chorus is in four parts.

simplicity probably reflects the poor state of choirs in the early years of the Restoration.[88] According to Matthew Locke, reliance was placed on 'Cornets and Mens feigned Voices' to perform treble parts, because there was 'not one Lad ... capable of singing his Part readily'.[89]

Ex. 53. Christopher Gibbons, *How long wilt thou forget me?*, part of first verse and final chorus

continued

88   Spink (1995, pp. 292-293), refers to the suggestion by Cheverton (1985) that Gibbons's anthems may not have been intended for liturgical use. He notes that, although some were in the repertoires of cathedrals, on the whole they did not circulate widely. This, and the observation that their style is early, leads him to speculate that they may have been for private devotional use, perhaps before the Restoration. Although this is not impossible, there are no pre-Restoration sources to support the theory. An alternative hypothesis is that they were composed when church music was being re-established (as suggested by the sources quoted above), and that, having no recent anthems on which to model his own, Gibbons wrote them in the style he had cultivated during the Commonwealth.

89   Locke, 1673. Westminster Abbey appears to have employed a regular cornettist after the Restoration, and payments were made 'To John Hill for playing on the Cornet in the Church' in 1661 and 1662 (Westminster Abbey: WAM 33695, f. 4^v, a payment of £2 10s in 1661; WAM 33696, f. 5^r, £4 in 1662).

Ex. 53 *continued*

continued

Ex. 53 *continued*

high-est, Yea, I will praise the name of the Lord most high-est, most high-est.

high-est, Yea, I will praise the name of the Lord most high-est, most......... high-est.

high-est, Yea, I will praise the name of the Lord most high-est, most... high-est.

Gibbons's anthems were largely forgotten after his death. Many copies are now incomplete, and a modern edition is much needed. Burney was aware of them (though he appears not to have known of Gibbons's consort and keyboard music), but wrote:

> The compositions of this master, which were not numerous, seem never to have enjoyed a great degree of favour; and though some of them are preserved in the Museum Collection, they have long ceased to be performed in our cathedrals.[90]

Thomas Tudway offered an explanation of this, which — while it has the flavour of gossip, and is manifestly not accurate in every detail — reflects a truth about the replacement of the musicians of Gibbons's generation by the likes of Blow and Purcell:

> His Majesty [Charles II] who was a brisk, & airy Prince, comeing to y[e] Crown in y[e] Flow'r, & vigour of his Age, was soon, if I may so say tyr'd wth y[e] Grave & Solemn way, And Order'd y[e] Composers of his Chappell, to add Symphonys &c wth Instruments to their Anthems; and ther upon Establis'd a select number of his private Music, to play y[e] Symphonys, & Retornello, w[ch] he had appointed ... The old Masters of Music viz: D[r] Child, D[r] Gibbons, M[r] Law,[91] the Organists to his Majesty, hardly knew how, to comport themselves, wth these new fangl'd ways, but proceeded in their Compositions, according to y[e] old Style, & therfore, there are only some Services, & full Anthems of theirs to be found.[92]

90   Burney, 1776-89, iii, p. 461 (1935, ii, p. 362).
91   Edward Lowe.
92   BL, Harleian MS 7338, f. 2v (dated 1715). The story is reminiscent of one recounted by Pepys (20 November 1660), that 'the King did put a great affront upon

In addition to his anthems, Gibbons is credited with a chant setting of *O come, let us sing*.[93] He seems also to have written a Magnificat and Nunc Dimittis, for 'Dr Gibbons evening Service wth verses' was copied into the Chapel Royal's music books in the late 1670s. However, this appears to have been lost.[94]

Gibbons made four settings of Latin words: *Gloria Patri, Laudate Dominum, O bone Jesu*, and *Celebrate Dominum*. It is possible that *Celebrate Dominum* (Ex. 54 on p. 256), which much resembles his English anthems, was written for the Catholic chapel of Queen Catherine of Braganza,[95] as it was published in *Cantica Sacra* (1674) with pieces by Matthew Locke, who was the Queen's organist from 1662 until his death in 1677, and by Richard Dering, who was the organist of the Queen Mother, the Catholic Henrietta Maria, during her early years in England (probably from 1626 until his death in 1630). However, since *Gloria Patri* and *Laudate Dominum* are known to have been performed in 1664 in connection with the award of Gibbons's doctorate, when their Latin texts would have lent a suitably scholarly character to the proceedings, it may be that all four Latin pieces were written with that occasion in mind.[96] Other works performed as part of the degree exercise were the anthem *Not unto us O Lord*, and 'Act songs with ye symphonyes' (two of which were from *Cupid and Death*).[97]

Singleton's Musique, he bidding them stop and bade the French Musique play' (Pepys, 1970-83, i, pp. 297-298).

93   British Library Additional MS 37027. *O come, let us sing* is one of a group of chants written on paper of the first half of the eighteenth century. A pencilled note in a later hand ascribes the first chant to Christopher Gibbons; other chant settings of the same words are ascribed to William Turner, Henry Purcell (presumably the elder), and others.

94   Works copied are listed in PRO, LC5/141 p. 432; LC5/144, p. 40 (= f. 28^v); Ashbee, 1986-96, i, pp. 163, 193.

95   At St James's 1662-71, and afterwards at Somerset House.

96   The printed version of *Celebrate Dominum* apart, the four pieces are found only in manuscripts with Oxford associations, at Christ Church and the Bodleian Library.

97   Bodleian Library MSS Mus. Sch. c.138 and Mus. Sch. c.139. The latter includes the inscription 'Thes thinges followinge are Dr Gibbons. & were performed at his Act. to bringe in his songes. 11 Jully: 1664'.

Ex. 54. Christopher Gibbons, *Celebrate Dominum*, first verse and final chorus

continued

Ex. 54 *continued*

Musical life in London

Soon after the Restoration, the King's musicians sought to recover the powers by virtue of which their predecessors had claimed to control professional musicians everywhere except in Cheshire.[98] It was claimed also that the powers originated in a charter granted by Edward IV to his minstrels in 1469. Attempts to exercise them in the 1630s had led to a serious conflict between the royal musicians and those of the City of London. It was never satisfactorily resolved, and the royal musicians' reconstitution of the 'Corporacõn for Regulateing the Art and Science of Musique' brought about renewed antagonism. Matters were not settled until essentially mediaeval attitudes towards professional organization were swept away by the commercial presentation of concerts and operas.[99]

The Corporation met at a house in Durham Yard, in the Strand, with Nicholas Lanier, the Master of the King's Music, as Marshall and Henry Cooke as Deputy Marshall.[100] John Hingston and George Hudson were chosen as Wardens for the first year. On 28 October 1662 Christopher Gibbons was among those granted the powers of an Assistant of the Corporation.[101] On 13 January 1663/4, the Marshall, Wardens and Assistants ordered that Christopher Gibbons, Matthew Locke, Charles Coleman and William Gregory were 'to come to the Chamber at Durham yeard on Tewsday next at too of the Clock in the Afternoone and to bring each of them tenn poundes or to shew Cause to the Contrary'.[102] Later minutes contain no indication that Gibbons ever played a leading role in the Corporation's affairs.

Gibbons's participation in musical life beyond the court is attested by Pepys. At the Earl of Sandwich's, on 19 May 1661, 'Captain Cooke, Mr. Gibbons, and others of the King's Musique were come to present my Lord with some songs and Symphonys which were performed very finely'.[103] There was a similar occasion on 13 June 1662, when Pepys

98   On the situation in Cheshire, see Woodfill, 1953, pp. 118-119.

99   Events are summarized in Harley, 1968, pp. 16-19. See also documents transcribed in Ashbee, 1986-96, v, pp. 245-253.

100   The Corporation's minute book is BL Harleian MS 1911. The earliest extant minutes are those of 'the 22th of October 1661'. The book's contents are transcribed in Ashbee, 1986-96, v, pp. 254-269.

101   BL, Harleian MS 1911, f. 1[v].

102   Ibid., f. 3[v].

103   Pepys, 1970-83, ii, p. 103. Sir Edward Montagu (1625-72), who was the son of Sir Sidney Montagu and Paulina, the daughter of John Pepys of Cottenham, was created Earl of Sandwich in July 1660. Samuel Pepys was his secretary, and customarily wrote

was entertained by the Countess of Sandwich: 'Mr. Loxton, Gibbons, and Goodgroome with us, and after dinner some Musique'.[104] The entry Pepys made in his diary on Sunday 21 December 1662 reads:

Walked to White-hall and there to Chappell; and from thence upstairs and up and down the house and galleries on the King's and Queen's side; and so through the garden to my Lord's lodging, where there was Mr. Gibbons, Madge, and Mallard and Pagett, and by and by came in my Lord Sandwich, and so we had great store of good Musique.[105]

Again, on 27 May 1663, he wrote:

So walked to little Chelsy, where I found my Lord Sandwich with Mr. Becke, the maister of the house, and Mr. Creed at dinner. And I sat down with them, and very merry. After dinner (Mr. Gibbons being come in also before dinner done) to Musique; they played a good Fancy, to which my Lord is fallen again and says he cannot endure a merry tune — which is a strange turn of his humour, after he hath for two or three years flung off the practice of Fancies and played only fiddlers' tunes ...[106]

It was no doubt with some sadness that, in July 1672, Gibbons received eight yards of black cloth to make a mourning livery for Sandwich's funeral. The Earl had died in the Dutch war which was a major cause of the King's parlous financial position.[107]

---

of him as 'my Lord'.

104   Ibid., iii, p. 108. Loxton: perhaps Laxton, Sandwich's apothecary. Goodgroome: perhaps John (c.1630?-1704), singer, composer, and Gentleman of the Chapel Royal, rather than Theodore, Pepys's singing-master.

105   Ibid., iii, p. 287. Paget: lawyer and amateur musician. Mallard (Tom Mallard on 18 December 1664): perhaps Thomas Mallard, an Italian lutemaker (see Ashbee, 1986-96, viii, p. 114); he played Pepys's viol and set a tune for him. Humphrey Madge: see note 63 on p. 246.

106   Ibid., iv, p. 160. Sandwich lodged at Becke's house. John Creed: Deputy Treasurer to the Fleet (1660), Secretary to the Commissioners for Tangier (1662), married a niece of Lord Sandwich (1668).

107   LC5/140, p. 521 (printed folio no. 265ʳ); the entry in Ashbee, 1986-96, i, p. 116, should not be read as indicating that Gibbons received cloth for other musicians. Sandwich died in action against the Dutch in Southwold Bay, 28 May 1672, and was buried in Westminster Abbey on 3 July.

The Worcester organ

In 1662 Christopher Gibbons was consulted by the authorities of Worcester Cathedral, in his capacity as organist of Westminster Abbey.[108] This may have been because the cathedral's own organist, Richard Browne, was growing old (he died in August 1664).[109] The story of the Worcester organ is a long one, and not altogether happy. The organ built by Thomas Dallam in 1613 was rebuilt by George Dallam in 1661-62. The cathedral authorities afterwards entered into discussions with William Hathaway, who was invited to set up a chair organ, on the understanding that this might lead to a contract for a great organ.[110] On 12 March 1662/3 the Dean of Worcester, Dr Thomas Warmestry, wrote to Hathaway, putting a stop to further work. His letter was addressed: 'ffor Mr Hathaway Organ maker/ these in London./ leave this with Mr Gibbons Organist of Westminster/ to be sent with speed as Directed'. On 30 March the letter was followed by another to the same effect.[111]

'A particular of such materialls as are now remaining in the house of Mr Harthaway, towards ye making up of a Great Organ for ye Cathedrall of Worcester' was drawn up on 26 April 1663.[112] It was costed, and included the losses said to have been sustained by Hathaway, who himself signed an account of the money he had spent on the carriage of materials and in setting up the chair organ.[113]

A few weeks later Gibbons wrote to the Dean as follows:[114]

Reverend S^r

as I have formerly p^{r}sented M^r. Hathaway an Organ-maker to you, soe you may be confident thatt he is a very honest man; & fitt for thatt purpose. if

---

108 The documents concerning this episode are principally those gathered in Bodleian Library MS Add. C.304^a, ff. 124^r-144^v. Further information is provided by Bodleian Library MS Tanner 45, f. 19^r.

109 Shaw, 1991, p. 307.

110 Hathaway was active as an organ-builder before the Civil War. See, for example, the churchwardens' accounts of St Martin-in-the-Fields for 1637 (Freeman, 1921, p. 4).

111 Copies of letters in Add. C.304^a, f. 124^r.

112 Add. C.304^a, f. 125^r, 129^r.

113 Add. C.304^a, f. 127^r.

114 Add. C.304^a, f. 143^r (autograph letter).

security be required; I and M^r. Locke ye Queenes-Organist wilbe bound for him

Thus I take leave & rest

London, June 22th. 1663

Yo^r most obliged &
humble serv^t.
Christo: Gibbons

assoone as ye Anthems wch. I promised you are faire & well-prickt you shalbe certaine of them.

In June and November 1663 Hathaway was paid £35 for his journey and 'towards ye new organ'.[115] In April 1665, however, he put in a bill for the chair organ and material purchased for the great organ. The Dean's strong reponse detailed complaints about Hathaway's workmanship, and a document of 8 May 1665 reads:

We whose names are here subscribed ... attest, & upon o^r oathes are ready to affirme; That ye Chaire organ made by m^r Hathaway, is altogether insufficient, & not at all fit for any Cathedrall; for that it hath neither shape nor Modell of a double organ; besides three of ye stops of ye sd organ are altogeth^r useless ...[116]

Thomas Harrison found 'neither forme order or good materialls nor workmanlike' in the chair organ, and said the pitch was wrong.[117]

Testimony given by Nathaniel Tomkins, in a document of 22 May 1665, includes the suggestion that Hathaway had paid Gibbons 'to procure ye work of ye Organ at Worcest^r'.[118] A note at the end says:

Mr Dallam beeinge prest by Mr Sayor What hee knew Concerninge any Contract made beetweene D^r. Gibbons & Mr Hathaway ... answ^d to this purpose y^t hee did not think it would have come to this but y^t others Could say more in it then hee & beeinge asked who? hee sd hee might ask Mr Hinckston (who is Imployed in ye tuninge of ye Kings Instrm^{ts}.

115 Worcester Cathedral Library, Treasurer's Accounts, A LXXIII.

116 Add. C.304^a, f. 135, signed by the organist Richard Davis and seventeen others.

117 Add. C.304^a, ff. 139^r. Tanner 45, f. 19^r, refers to 'M^r. Harrison (who was old Dallams Servant and maried his daughter)'.

118 Add. C.304^a, ff. 131$^{r.v}$. Nathaniel Tomkins was a son of Thomas Tomkins. Writing to the Archbishop of Canterbury, the Bishop of Worcester said: 'I rely very much upon M^r. Tomkins skill, bread in his cradle, and all his life among Organs who is an excellent organist' (Tanner 45, f. 19^r).

On 5 August 1665 the Bishop of Worcester (Robert Skinner) wrote a letter to the Archbishop of Canterbury (Gilbert Sheldon), covering papers relating to 'M^r. Deane of Worcesters defense agt M^r. Hathawayes p^{r}tenses and allegōns about ye Chaire Organ made, and fixt, and the great Organ to be made but now bargained for'.[119] He suggested that Gibbons and Hathaway took advantage of the Dean, knowing his 'utter ignorance in Re musica' and that he 'had no more skill in an Organ then a beast that hath no understanding'. Of Hathaway's claim in connection with the proposed great organ, he said: 'And for ye Materialls pvided ... tis no way pbable that ... they were for this Organ, when soone after he had made ye Chaire Organ he was forbidden to pceede anie farther'.

Gibbons's Oxford doctorate

On 2 July 1663 the King recommended that Gibbons should receive a doctorate from the University of Oxford:

> Trusty and wellbeloved wee greet you well Whereas the bearer Christopher Gibbons one of y^e. Organists of Our Chapple Royal hath from his youth, served Our Royall Father & Our selfe & hath soe well improved himselfe in Musicke as well in Our owne Judgem^t, as y^e. Judgements of all men wellskilld in y^t science as y^t hee may worthily receive ye hono^r & degree of Doct^r therein wee in consideration of his merit & fittness thereunto, have thought fit by these Our Lr̄es to recommend him unto you & to signify Our gracious Pleasure to you that hee be forthwth admitted & created D^r in Musick he performing his Exercise, & paying all his due ffees any Statute or Custome w^{t}hever to ye contrary not wthstanding And for &c:[120]

Wood describes the University's acquiescence:

> *July* 7. *Christoph. Gibbons* one of the Organists of his Majesties Chap. was then licensed to proceed Doctor of Musick: which degree was completed in an *Act* celebrated in S. *Maries* Church on the eleventh of the said month ... He was licensed by vertue of his Majesties Letters, written in his behalf ...[121]

Wood's slightly inaccurate account (Gibbons was never organist to Charles I) contains the only verbal portrait of Gibbons which we have:

---

119   Tanner 45, f. 19^r.

120   PRO, SP44/12, pp. 23-24; CSPD, 1862, p. 191; Ashbee, 1986-96, viii, p. 159.

121   Wood, 1691-92, i, col. 833 (followed by Burney, 1776-89, iii, p. 461; Hawkins, 1776, iv, pp. 412-413; Boyce, 1760-63, i, p. viii); Clark, 1887-88, i, pp. 148-149. For the music performed on the occasion, see p. 255.

Convocation, wherein the king's letters were read for Christopher Gibbons, organist to king Charles I and II, to be admitted Dr. of Mus., paying his fees and doing his exercises; but what prevented him from comming I know not. A person most excellent in his faculty, but a grand debauchee. He would sleep at Morning Prayer when he was to play on the organ.[122]

Some of Wood's information came from the University's Register of Convocation, which contains a copy of the King's letter and a record of Gibbons's supplication.[123] Wood may also have known a note added to one of Gibbons's pieces in Christ Church MS Mus. 1142A, thought to be an autograph copy.[124] It reads: 'drunke from the Catherne Wheele'.

Gibbons's later life

Gibbons held his two posts at Westminster Abbey until 25 March 1666, when he was succeeded by Albertus Bryne as organist, and Thomas Blagrave as Master of the Choristers.[125] His continued presence in the Chapel Royal is indicated by Pepys's diary entry for 23 December 1666: 'I to the Chapel to find Dr. Gibbons; and from him to the Harp and Ball to transcribe the Treble which I would have him set a bass to'.[126] Whether he continued to play an active part in the private music is uncertain. An entry in an establishment list on 7 January 1667/8 records authorization for Christopher Preston to fill Gibbons's post in the private music, without pay, and to enjoy both the place and the pay upon Gibbons's death. Warrants to give effect to this were prepared.[127]

It is possible (though there is no record to prove it) that, in his fifties, Gibbons was permitted to reduce his workload, while retaining his full pay. Such generous treatment of royal servants had a long history, though at this time its practical effects may have been negligible, because

122   Wood, 1891-1900, ii, p. 5. The convocation was on 10 February 1664.

123   Oxford University Archives, NEP/Supra, Reg Ta, p. 180.

124   'A verse for the Organ' in F (Brookes, 1996, no. 1695). The name 'Christ. Gibbons' appended to the piece seems likely to have been written by the composer.

125   Westminster Abbey, WAM 33699, f. 2ʳ. Payments of £10 for each post are expressed as '$\chi\rho°$ Gibbons ½ Albert Bryne ½' and '$\chi\rho°$ Gibbons ½ Thomas Blagrave ½'. See also the Precentor's book, 61228A, 29 June 1666.

126   Pepys, 1970-83, vii, p. 418. Gibbons's name appears in an undated list of members of Chapel musicians which may cover this period (PRO, LC3/25, p. 56; Ashbee, 1986-96, i, p. 226).

127   PRO, LC 3/73, f. 58ᵛ (= p. 102); LC5/139, p. 6; SO3/16, p. 166 (Ashbee, 1986-96, i, p. 220, 81; v, p. 57). Preston contributed a suite of four pieces and two hornpipes to Locke's *Melothesia* (1673).

the salaries of members of the royal household were often long overdue. On 19 December 1666 John Hingston told Pepys that 'many of the Musique are ready to starve, they being five years behind hand for their wages ... He says all must come to ruin at this rate, and I believe him'.[128] It is no surprise to find that on 14 May 1672 Edmund Waters entered a petition against Gibbons for 'a certaine sum of money', to answer for which 'M[r] Gibbins so appeared upon Wednesday morning'.[129]

Retrenchment was the watchword, but Gibbons was exempted from its effects both by name and as a musician of the Chapel Royal:

These are to Certifie that whereas by an Order of his Ma[te] Concerning the Retrenchm[t]. of his Ma[tes] Musick Dated the One & twentieth day of ffeb 1668[/9] His Ma[te] was pleased among others to exempt out of the said Retrenchm[t] his Musick of the Chappell ...[130]

Whether or not fewer demands were made upon Gibbons by his royal master, he continued to be active outside the court. He and Pepys went 'to see an Organ at the Deane of Westminster's lodgings at the Abby' on 24 February 1667/8; and on 3 August 1668 he promised to provide Pepys with 'some things for two flagelettes'.[131] Writing many years later to Dr Arthur Charlett, the Master of University College, Oxford, Pepys was proud to recall his acquaintance with Gibbons.[132]

An entry in the vestry minutes of St Martin-in-the-Fields, the royal parish church, shows that in 1674 Gibbons was the church's organist.

Consideration being taken of an Annuall salery for Dr Gibbon y[e] Organest for playing on y[e] Organs It is ordered that the sum of Twenty pounds p annum be paid him quarterly by the Churchwardens for the time being that is to say five pounds each Quarter. The first quarterly payment to be made at o[r] Lady day 1675 One thousand Six hundred Seventy and five The s[d] Doctr Gibbon to pay y[e] bellows blower.[133]

The appointment may have been prompted by the church's acquisition of a new organ, originally built for St George's Chapel, Windsor.[134]

128 Pepys, 1970-83, vii, p. 414.

129 PRO, LC5/189, f. 24[v]; Ashbee, 1986-96, i, p. 115.

130 PRO, LC5/12, pp. 231 (quoted above), 239 (list of names); Ashbee, 1986-96, i, pp. 89, 91.

131 Pepys, 1970-83, ix, pp. 89, 271.

132 Pepys, 1932, pp. 243, 320 (4 August 1694 and 5 November 1700).

133 Westminster Archives, MS F2004 (16 December 1674); Freeman, 1921, p. 6.

134 Freeman, 1921, pp. 7-8, 13. The organ was erected at Windsor by Ralph Dallam

Gibbons did not occupy his post at St Martin-in-the-Fields for long. His death was thus recorded in the Cheque Book of the Chapel Royal:

Dr. χⁱᵒpher Gibbons Organist, of his Ma:ᵗⁱᵉˢ Chappell Royall departed this Life the 20th. day of October 1676. in who's place was sworne mʳ John Chrissostome du sharroll, the 26. day of the same month. 1676.[135]

He was buried in the cloisters of Westminster Abbey on 24 October.[136]

More than three hundred years after Gibbons's death, it is extremely difficult to form a just opinion of him as a composer. Perhaps because his surviving keyboard works are few in number, and require only one performer, they have been collected in a modern edition.[137] The survival of Locke's score of *Cupid and Death* is a piece of exceptional good fortune, which has led to another modern edition. The remainder of Gibbons's music presents a different picture. A few of his vocal pieces were printed during his lifetime, but none seems to have been published in its original form, and none has been printed since his death. Scarcely any of Gibbons's numerous pieces for strings and continuo have been published in modern editions, and many of the extant manuscript copies are in the form of parts rather than scores. A formidable task awaits editors, publishers and performers. The regard in which he was held in his own time suggests that it may prove worthwhile. Henry Hall, the organist of Hereford Cathedral, wrote of 'happy artfull *Gibbons*'.[138] A cryptic memorandum in the Lord Chamberlain's papers sums him up as 'a rare man'.[139]

Gibbons's place as organist of the Chapel Royal was taken by John Blow, a former child of the Chapel who was sworn in as a Gentleman in March 1673, and became Master of the Children in July 1674.[140] A few

in 1660; how it came to be moved to St Martin-in-the-Fields is not entirely clear.

135 Cheque Book, f. 9ʳ; Rimbault, 1872, p. 16.

136 Chester, 1876, p. 189.

137 See p. 302. A few pieces have been printed singly or in anthologies.

138 'To the *Memory of my Dear Friend Mr.* Henry Purcell', prefacing Henry Purcell, *Orpheus Britannicus* (1698).

139 PRO, LC3/2, f. 3ʳ, probably dating from 1660. In full, the note reads:'Christ: Gibbons Organist by Mʳ Brome: a rare man', perhaps meaning that Gibbons's appointment at the Restoration was sponsored by Brome.

140 PRO, RG8/110, pp. 17-18f, reads: 'Dʳ Gibbons Organist dye'd October the 20th 1676. In whose Place came Mʳ John Blow Master of the Children; in his place was sworn in Ordinary Monsieur [Sharoll]' (name partly illegible). Also Cheque Book, ff. 8ᵛ; Rimbault, 1872, pp. 15-16. Blow succeeded Giles Tomkins as a virginalist in the private music in January 1668/9 (PRO, LC3/25, p. 52; Ashbee, 1986-96, i, p. 225).

days later Christopher Preston was admitted to Gibbons's place in the private music, in accordance with the agreement reached in 1667/8.[141]

Burney and Hawkins each refer to Blow as one of Gibbons's pupils,[142] which information they may have gathered from Blow's memorial in Westminster Abbey. There is little evidence concerning Gibbons's other pupils, and references to them seem for the most part to be based on the assumption that he instructed boys, such as Henry Purcell, who were choristers in the Chapel Royal.[143]

Gibbons left no written will, but expressed the wish that his wife should be his executor.[144] In her own will she acknowledged the help she received from John Thacham of the Middle Temple, who had previously assisted her husband.[145] In view of the arrears of wages owing to Gibbons, he not suprisingly left some debts.[146] Creditors were the vintner John Johnson and the fruiterer Margaret Nye, to whom Gibbons owed £6 15s 0d and £2 11s 0d respectively.[147]

Elizabeth Gibbons outlived her husband by some six years, making her will on 19 March 1677/8, and amending it on 26 March 1680.[148] In her last illness she was nursed for upwards of two years by Jane Stock, the wife of a bricklayer.[149] She was buried (as 'Elizabeth Bull', a variant of her maiden name, Ball) on 27 December 1682 in the Cloisters, Westminster Abbey.[150]

---

141 PRO, LC5/141, p. 473; Ashbee, 1986-96, i, p. 165. Preston himself must have died by 1 January 1689/90, when his widow appointed her cousin, Allan Chambers of the Middle Temple, to receive money due to him (PRO, LC9/342; Ashbee, 1986-96, ii, p. 30).

142 Burney, 1776-89, iii, p. 461 (1935, ii, p. 362); Hawkins, 1776, iv, p. 486 (1963, ii, p. 740).

143 Wood's manuscript notes refer to Purcell as 'originally one of the Children in the King's Chapel. Bred under D^r. Chr. Gibbons, I think ...' (Bodleian Library, MS Wood 19 D(4) 106, f. 104^r).

144 See p. 277.

145 See pp. 280. A set of accounts for 1678-79 (PRO, AO1/401/109; Ashbee, 1986-96, v, p. 153) records the receipt by Thacham, as Elizabeth Gibbons's attorney, of a quarter's wages of £21 10s 0d due to Christopher Gibbons in 1673.

146 Elizabeth Gibbons's will refers to 'Two hundred seaventy nine poundes and Tenn shillings or thereabouts Arreares of my said Husbands Sallaryes remaining yett unpaid in the Office of his Maties Treasury Chamber'.

147 PRO, LC5/141, p. 512; Ashbee, 1986-96, i, p. 168.

148 See pp. 280-281.

149 Ibid.

150 The identification was first made by Chester, 1876, p. 206.

APPENDICES · LISTS OF WORKS

BIBLIOGRAPHY · INDEXES

APPENDIX A

RICHARD GIBBONS'S DESCENDANTS

Unless otherwise noted, the following information is drawn from parish registers held in local archives collections[1] or the family wills printed in Appendix B.

(i)

Richard Gibbons; married Alice (children listed at ii below); died at Oxford, probably in 1577 (see p. 14).

(ii)

Unknown son of Richard Gibbons (see p. 5); he may have had a daughter named Elizabeth.[2]

William Gibbons, son of Richard, born c.1540, buried 26 October 1595 at Holy Trinity, Cambridge. His wife Mary was buried at Holy Trinity 19 April 1603. Their children were:

Richard, buried at St Mary the Great, Cambridge, 11 July 1566 (see p. 7).

Edward, baptized 21 March 1567/8 at St Mary the Great, Cambridge; died c.1650 (see p. 23). *See also* iii *below.*

Ellis, baptized 30 November 1573 at Holy Trinity, Cambridge. Married Joan. Died 1603, apparently in the parish of St Benet Paul's Wharf, London.

Mary, baptized 27 February 1578/9 at Holy Trinity, Cambridge. Married Christopher Edmunds 20 July 1602 at St Botolph's, Cambridge.

Jane, baptized 5 April 1580 at Holy Trinity, Cambridge. Unmarried in 1603.

Ferdinando, born 1581 or 1582? (see p. 17).

Orlando, baptized 25 December 1583 at St Martin's, Oxford. Died at Canterbury, 5 June 1625. *See also* iii *below.*

continued

---

1 For printed editions see: Brooke and Hallen, 1886 (St Mary Woolchurch); Burke, 1914 (St Margaret's, Westminster); Chester, 1876 (Westminster Abbey); Reynell-Upham and Tapley-Soper, 1910 (Exeter Cathedral); Tapley-Soper, 1933 (St Paul's, Exeter).

2 An Elizabeth Gibbons is mentioned in the will of Mary Gibbons, the wife of William Gibbons, as her niece (see p. 274).

Susan, buried 3 December 1576 at St Mary the Great, Cambridge.
Thomasine (dates unknown). *See also* iii *below.*
Elizabeth (dates unknown). *See also* iii *below.*

(iii)

Edward Gibbons (see ii above) married:

(1) Jane, buried 7 April 1628 at Exeter Cathedral. Their children were:

Robert, baptized 1 July 1597 at Holy Trinity, Cambridge.[3]
Mary, baptized 11 April 1599 at Holy Trinity, Cambridge; married
    Greenwood Randall 4 May 1626 at Exeter Cathedral.[4]
Jane, married Thomas Gale 4 May 1626 at Exeter Cathedral.[5]
Joan, buried 19 June 1627 at Exeter Cathedral.
William, baptized 24 October 1607 at Exeter Cathedral.
Murrey, buried 28 February 1636 at Exeter Cathedral. Married
    Mary; their son Edward was baptized 22 August 1632 at Exeter
    Cathedral, and buried there 13 May 1637. Mary married James
    Lake 29 January 1641.

(2) Mary Bluet, buried 9 January 1664 at Exeter Cathedral.

Thomasine Gibbons (see ii above) married Thomas Hopper 1 May 1598
at Holy Trinity, Cambridge. Their children were:

Mary, baptized 25 March 1599 at Holy Trinity, Cambridge.
Agnes, baptized 22 December 1600 at Holy Trinity, Cambridge.

Elizabeth Gibbons (see ii above) married James Dyer 13 November 1600
at Holy Trinity, Cambridge. Their only known child was:

Ann, baptized 22 November 1601 at Holy Trinity, Cambridge.

---

3   Possibly the Robert Gibbons buried at Holy Trinity on 5 July 1597, although that
may have been an older person. A Robert Gibbons married Elizabeth Lyng at Holy
Trinity on 20 October 1617; their son John was baptized at Holy Trinity on 13
September 1618, and their daughter Mary on 14 May 1620. A Robert Gibbons was
named as an innkeeper and musician in 1625-27 (Cambridge University Library,
University Archives, V.C. Ct. I.11, ff. 29^v, 74^r-76^r); it is not impossible that he was
Edward's son.

4   Evidently a double wedding, since Jane Gibbons was married on the same day.
Greenwood Randall's son Orlando was baptized at the cathedral on 14 September 1627.

5   Entry duplicated in the registers of the parish of St Paul, Exeter. Jane must have
died before 14 July 1639, when Thomas Gale married Mary Mayne.

Orlando Gibbons (see ii above) married Elizabeth Patten 17 February 1605/6 at St Mary Woolchurch Haw. Their children were:

James, baptized 2 June 1607, buried 4 June 1607, at St Margaret's, Westminster.

Alice, baptized 5 August 1613 at St Margaret's, Westminster.

Christopher, baptized 22 August 1615 at St Margaret's, Westminster; died 20 October 1676, buried in the Cloisters, Westminster Abbey, 24 October 1676. *See also* iv *below.*

Ann, baptized 6 October 1618 at St Margaret's, Westminster.[6]

Mary, baptized 9 April 1621 at St Margaret's, Westminster.[7]

Elizabeth, baptized 16 March 1621/2 at St Margaret's, Westminster.[8]

Orlando, baptized 29 August 1623 at St Margaret's, Westminster; probably died at Exeter c.1650.[9]

(iv)

Christopher Gibbons (see iii above) married:

(1) Mary Kercher, 23 September 1646 at St Bartholomew the Less; she died before April 1655.

(2) Elizabeth Filbridge (*née* Ball, widow of the parish of St Clement's), 22 April 1655 at St Clement Danes; she was buried (as 'Elizabeth Bull') 27 December 1682 in the Cloisters, Westminster Abbey.[10] Their children were:

Orlando, born 20 February 1655/6; baptized 26 February 1655/6, buried 11 December 1657, at St Clement Danes.

Christopher and Elizabeth (twins), born 28 July 1657; baptized 4 August 1657 at St Clement Danes.

Mary, born 13 September 1658; baptized 29 September 1658 at St Clement Danes.

Anne, baptized 7 June 1660 at St Clement Danes.

---

6   An Anne Gibbons married William Stocke at St Margaret's on 20 December 1647.

7   Married Soper (PRO, Prob. 6/25, f. 125[r], manuscript numbering).

8   Married Greenslade (PRO, Prob. 6/25, f. 125[r], manuscript numbering).

9   See p. 230.

10   The identification was first made by Chester, 1876, p. 206.

People named Gibbons resident in Cambridge, whose relationship, if any, to the descendants of Richard Gibbons of Oxford is unknown

Annis Gibbons, married Edward Syssen 25 January 1572/3 at St Mary the Less.

Henry Gibbons, baptized 23 October 1576 at St Benedict's.

Elizabeth Gibbons, baptized 1 April 1580 at St Benedict's.[11]

William Gibbons, baptized 12 May 1584 at St Benedict's.

William Gibbons, buried 4 October 1625 at Holy Trinity.

Francis, daughter of Francis Gibbons, baptized 21 March 1584/5 at All Saints.

Richard Gibbons, buried 8 November 1588 at St Mary the Less,.

Richard, son of Richard Gibbons, baptized 13 March 1585/6 at St Mary the Less; married Margaret Nowell 27 September 1608 at St Mary the Less.

George Gibbons, baptized 31 March 1588 at St Mary the Less,.

Ann, daughter of Robert Gibbons, baptized 20 July 1617 at St Mary the Great.

Allis, daughter of Robert Gibbons, baptized 12 September 1624 at All Saints.

Thomas Gibbon, married Anna Holmes 5 May 1625 at Holy Trinity, by licence.

Rebecca, daughter of Robert Gibbons, baptized 18 December 1625 at All Saints.

Ann Gibbons, married Robert Paynter 25 July 1627 at Holy Trinity.

Mary Gibbons, married Ralph Hattley 28 October 1629 at Holy Trinity.

11   See note 2 on p. 269.

APPENDIX B

WILLS

The will of William Gibbons, Orlando Gibbons's father[1]

In the name of God Amen In the moneth of October In the yeare of our Lord god 1595 Willm̄ Gibbon of Cambridge in the Countie of Cambridge musitian being sicke in body but of a good & perfect minde and memorie made and declared his last will and testament nūcupative[2] in manner and forme followinge viz ffirst he gave & com̄ended his soule to almightie god and his bodye he comended to χρstian buriall And as touchinge his worldlie goodes wherewᵗʰ god had blessed him he disposed as followeth viz he willed that marie Gibbon his wiffe shoulde have all his goods whatsoevʳ to dispose amongst his children as she should thincke convenient and at her discretion Wittnesseˢ hereof Humfrye Tredwaye Mʳ of Arts[3] and Edward Gibbon Batchelour of Musicke.

(Proved 13 November 1595 by Marie Gibbon the relict.)

The will of Mary Gibbons, Orlando Gibbons's mother[4]

In nomine dei Amen The seaventeenth day of March in yᵉ yeere of oʳ Lord 1602 I Mary Gybbons of Cambridge in the county of Camb: widowe; though sicke in body yet whole in mynd and memory doe institute and ordeyne this my last will and testament in manner and forme following. ffirst I bequeath my soule to god, who gave it me assuredly beleeving and trusting in Jhesu Christ and in him only to be saved, and my body to yᵉ earth from whence it came to lye as neere my deceased husband as conveniently I may. Itm̄ I give and bequeath to yᵉ poore of Trinity parish in Cambr: twenty shillings Itm̄ I give & bequeath to Elyzabeth Deyer my daughter sixe and twenty poundes xiijˢ iiijᵈ of

1 Cambridgeshire County Record Office, will register of Ely Archdeaconry Court, v, f. 183ʳ·ᵛ.

2 Nuncupative: declared orally.

3 Tredwaye (1568/9-1641) came from Easton-on-the-Hill, Northamptonshire. He was educated at Eton and King's College, obtaining an MA in 1592 (Venn and Venn, 1922-27, iv, p. 262).

4 Cambridgeshire County Record Office. The original will is transcribed here. The probate copy, which differs in some details (e.g. it reads 'in the yeare of oʳ Lord god 1602') is in the will register of Ely Archdeaconry Court, vi, ff. 152ᵛ-153ᵛ.

good and lawfull mony of England to be payed her w^thin ij monethes next after my death. Itm̃ I gyve unto Jane Gibbons my daughter twenty sixe pounds xiij^s iiij^d of lawfull english mony to be payd her w^thin one yeere next after my death Itm̃ I gyve more unto my sayd daughter Jane Gibbons a mourning gowne yf she be p^{re}sent at my funerall. Itm̃ I gyve to fferdinando Gibbons my sonne twenty six poundesxiij^s iiij^d to be payd him when he shalbe 23 yeers of age. Itm̃ I gyve to Orlando Gibbons my sonne twenty sixe poundes xiij^s iiij^d to be payd him when he shalbe one and twenty yeeres of age. Itm̃ I freely acquitt Thomasin Hopper my daughter of that vj^{li} for wch her husband standeth endebted unto me, reserving to my executor the 20^s wch he hath in his handes, the debt amounting (as I take it) to vij^{li} x^s. Itm̃ I gyve my sonne Edward Gibbons and his wyfe each of them a mourning gowne. Itm̃ I give my sonne Dyer and his wife each of them a mourning gowne. Itm̃ I give my two sonnes fferdenando and Orlando each of them a mourning cloake. Itm̃ I give my sonne in lawe Christoph Edmunds a mourning cloake and his wyfe Mary a mourning gowne. Itm̃ I gyve my daughter Joane Gibbons the wyfe of my sonne Ellis Gibbons a mourning gowne Allways provyded yf they be present at my buryall. Itm̃ I give to Mary Gibbons the daughter of my sonne Edward a peece of silver plate to ye full value of fyve poundes And to his daughter Joane a peece of silver plate to ye value of forty shillings to be payed them and eyther of them w^thin one yeare next after my death. Itm̃ I give Elizabeth Gibbons my neice⁵ fyve poundes of lawfull English mony when she shalbe sixe and twenty yeeres of age. Itm̃ I give to Mr Tredway⁶ a ringe of twenty shillinges price w^thin 2 moneths after my death. Itm̃ I gyve and bequeath to my sonne Ellis Gibbons all ye rest of my goods and chattells whatsoev^r moveable or immoveable, my debte*s* and funeralls first discharged, whome (being fully resolved of his zeale to god, and dewtifull affection to me) I make full and sole executo^r of this my last will and testament. In witnesse wherof I have sett my hand and seale to these p̃snts the day and yeere above written in ye yeare of her ma^{tes} Reyne 45

Sealed & subscribed in the p̃sente*s*
of James Deyer   the m̃ke ✝ of Mary
   Orlando Gibbons⁷   Gibbons

After ye making of this my last will and testament I thought it convenient uppon speciall causes me thereunto moving to bestowe more uppon my

5   An Elizabeth Gibbons was baptized at St Benedict's, Cambridge, on 1 April 1580.
6   Several words following have been deleted: 'whom I ... my last will'.
7   Signed by Dyer and Gibbons.

daughter Hopper my best gowne and silck Apron. And whereas I bequeathed unto Mary Gibbons and Joane Gibbons the daughters of my sonne Edward two peeces of plate, I ordeyne that my silver beaker shalbe one for the eldest, and the little guilt cuppe for ye younger w^{ch} (were my estate greater) should have bene of more value. And in regard that my sonne fferdenando standeth endebted unto me in the summe of x^{li} my will is it should be deducted owt of his former porcōn. And to this being in ᵱfect memory I subscribe the xi of Aprill 1603

The marke of Mary Gibbons[8]
Itm̄ I gyve unto[9]

(Proved by Ellis Gibbons, 21 April 1603.)

The will of Ellis Gibbons, Orlando Gibbons's brother[10]

In nōie dei Amen. I Ellys Gibbons weake in boddye, but whole in mynde, Doe give and Bequeath my soule to the protection of the Allmightie and my bodye to be buried as it shall please my Executo^r./ Item I give unto my welbeloved wief, my ffee simple in Cambridge duringe her lief, and the Lease in Paules churcheyard duringe her lief, and after, to come to my Executo^r./ Item I give unto my brother dyers childe xx^{li}./ Item I give my Brother fferdinando xx^{li}./ Item I give my Brother Orlando xx^{li}./ Item I give and Bequeath all my other good*es* and Chattells to my Brother Edward Gibbons of Acton, whome I make my full executo^r./ In Wittnes whereof I have hereto sett my hand this xiiijth of May 1603/

By me Ellis Gibbons

In the p^{r}sence of us
Jane ffleetewood
Theophila Parsons
James Dyer &
Elizabeth Dyer./

(Proved by Edward Gibbons, 18 May 1603.)

8   A mark added with extreme difficulty.
9   Incomplete.
10   PRO, Prob. 10/216, which although in the form of, and filed as, an original will is apparently a copy; PRO, Prob. 11/101, f. 252^r, is a probate copy. The copies differ in spelling, capitalization and punctuation. See p. 16 concerning the note providing evidence that Ellis Gibbons died in the parish of St Benet Paul's Wharf.

The will of John Patten, Orlando Gibbons's father-in-law.[11]

In the name of God, Amen. The five and Twentieth daie of ffebruarie Anno dñi 1622, And in the twentieth yeere of the raigne of our soveraigne Lord James by the grace of God Kinge of England ffrance and Ireland defender of the faith &c and of Scotland the sixe and fiftie. I John Patten of Westminster gent being sometimes visitted with sicknes moving me to feare suddaine death doe therefore now being in perfect health and memorie, thankes be to God make and ordaine this my last will and testament in manner followinge by vertue whereof I doe revoke repeale and frustrate all and everie my former wills, to all intentes constructions and purposes that is to say ffirst and before all things herein I doe render and bequeath my soule unto Almightie God that gave it, hoping in the onely and alone sacrifice of our Lord and saviour Jesus Christ to obtaine remission of all my sinnes and everlasting life, who hath loved me, and gave himselfe for me. And for my bodie I leave the same to the disposition of mine Exectuor for the manner and place of burriall thereof. Item I give and bequeath unto the children of Orlando Gibbons and my daughter his wife the summe of two hundreth pounds of lawfull money of England Item I give unto my sonne Richard Patten[12] one hundreth and fiftie pounds to be paide him within six moneths after my decease. Item I give unto Olyver Patten the sonne of Rich: Patten one hundreth pounds to be putt forth for his best use by my Executor untill he come unto yeares of discrecion. Item I give unto Sir William Walter and Henrie Plumpton to each of them fortie shillings apeece to make either of them a ringe making them two Overseers of this my last will and testament. Item I give and bequeath unto my Godsonnes John Flower, Henry Plumpton and Robert Lane fortie shillings a peece. Item I give unto Rich: Goulding my man five pounds. Item I give to the Children of Christs Hospitall fiftie shillings And to the poore where I am buried fiftie shillings. All the rest of my goods householdstuffe, plate, debts readie money and things whatsoever not given by this my will I give and bequeath unto Orlando Gibbons my sonne in lawe whom I make the sole Executor of this my last will and testament. Had, made, declared and given under my hand and seale the daie and yeere abovewritten in the presence of us whose names are subscribed. John

11   PRO, Prob. 10/404, which although in the form of, and filed as, an original will is a copy; Westminster Archives, Camden, f. 13[r-v], and PRO, Prob. 11/142, ff. 194[r-v], are probate copies. The copies differ in spelling, capitalization and punctuation.

12   The wills of Richard and Oliver are in the Westminster Archives: see Burke, 1913.

Patten. Cromwell Walter. Richard Gouldinge. Peregrin Tomkyns. Thomas Garnett.

(Proved by Orlando Gibbons, 17 September 1623.)

The will of Christopher Gibbons, Orlando Gibbons's son[13]

Memorandum That Christopher Gibbons late of the Parish of S^t. Margaret Westminster D^r. of Musick Deceased upon or about the seaventeenth day of October in the yeare of our Lord one Thousand six Hundred and seaventy six being of perfect mind and memory, and asked who should bee his Executor wth an intent to declare his last Will and Testament Nuncupative Declared that his Wife meaneing Elizabeth Gibbons his Relict should bee his Executrix and shee being then p^{r}sent hee desired shee would take his Estate and dispose of it for the maintenance of herselfe and children or to that effect In the p^{r}sence and heareing of credible Witnesses Elizabeth Rabliss the marke of Ann Ball.

(Proved by Elizabeth Gibbons, 6 November 1676.)

The will of Elizabeth Gibbons, the wife of Christopher Gibbons[14]

In the name of God Amen I Elizabeth Gibbons of the Citty of Westm^r widdow Relict and Executrix of the last will and testament nuncupative of my late Husband Christopher Gibbons late of Westm^r aforesaid Docto^r of Musicke and one of his Maties Musitians in ordinary deceased, being sicke and weake in body, but of perfect minde and memory praised bee Almighty God therefore, doe hereby Revoke all former wills by me made, And doe make and ordaine this my last Will and Testam^t in manner and forme following, First and principally I Humbly recommend my Soule into the hands of my Lord and Saviour Jesus Christ by the merritts of whose bitter passion I hope I shall bee saved, And for my body my Will is that it bee decently buryed as neere my late Husband as may bee according to the discretion of my Executo^r hereafter named And as touching the worldly goods wherewith It hath pleased God to blesse me, I dispose thereof as followeth, First in regard from and after my decease the Coppyhold Messuage or Tenem^t and Lands wth their appurtenances in Freefolke[15] in the County of South$\tilde{}$on which I now hold

---

13   PRO, Prob. 11/352, ff. 239^v-240^r.

14   Original will: PRO, Prob. 10/1136; probate copy, differing in spelling, capialization and punctuation: PRO, Prob. 11/372, ff. 29^v-31^r.

15   See p. 248.

for Terme of my naturall life according to the Custome of the Mannor will come and remaine unto my Daughter Elizabeth for the Terme of her naturall life; [16] < Therefore I give unto her my said Daughter Elizabeth onely fifty poundes of lawfull money of England to bee paid unto her at the expiracōn of her apprenticeshipp and not before by my said Executo[r] hereafter named and of the Two hundred seaventy nine poundes and Tenn shillings or thereabouts Arreares of my said Husbands Sallaryes remaining yett unpaid in the Office of his Ma[ties] Treasury Chamber if the same Arreares shall bee by my said Executo[r] hereafter named then received but if not then received then the said fifty poundes to bee paid unto my said Daughter Elizabeth assoone after as the said Arreares shall be [by][17] my said Executo[r] hereafter named received Item I give and bequeath unto my Daughter Ann One hundred poundes of like lawfull money being due and owing to me from Thomas Marsh Esqr by Bond heretofore taken in the name of my Cozen Henry Sherborne of Bedfont[18] to bee paid by my said Execu[r] hereafter named unto her my said Daughter Ann > att the expiracōn of her Apprenteshipp if shee bee then of the Age of one and twenty yeares and if shee bee not of that Age att the expiracōn of her apprentishipp then the said one hundred poundes to be paid unto her when shee shall attaine to that Age and in the meane time the interest thereof to bee received and then afterwards paid every six monethes by my Execu[r] hereafter named unto my said Daughter Ann for her necessary apparrell during her apprentishipp Item I give and bequeath unto my said Daughter Ann the further sume of One hundred poundes more like lawfull money to be paid unto her after the expiracōn of her said Apprentishipp if shee be then of the Age of One and Twenty yeares as aforesaid by my said Executo[r] hereafter named out of the aforesaid Arreares of my said late Husbands Sallaryes in the Office of his Ma[ties] Treasury Chamber if the said Arreares shall bee by my said Executo[r] hereafter named then received but if not received then my Will and minde is that the said One Hundred poundes last mencōed shall bee paid by my said Execu[r] hereafter named unto my said Daughter Ann assoone as the said Arreares of my late Husbands Sallaryes shall be by him received and not otherwise Item I give and bequeath unto my Daughter Mary if shee shall ever hereafter returne into England the sume of Twenty poundes of like lawfull money to bee paid unto her within One yeare next after her Returne by my said Execu[r] hereafter named out

16   The words enclosed here by editorial angle brackets are scored through in the original; they are likewise scored through in the probate copy, and marginally annotated 'sic orig'.

17   Omitted from original will.

18   In Middlesex.

of the aforesaid Arreares of my said late Husbands Sallaryes in the Office of his Ma[ties] Treasury Chamber if the same Arreares bee by my said Execu[r] hereafter named then received otherwise as soone after as the same Arreares shall bee by him received as aforesaid and not otherwise And if any or either of [19]<them> my said Three Daughters Elizabeth, Mary and Ann shall happen to dye before such time as her or theire particular Legacy or Legacyes aforemencõed shall become due and payable to them or any or either of them in such manner as aforesaid then the Legacy or Legacyes of her or them soe dying shall come remaine and bee paid by my said Executo[r] hereafter named unto and amongst the Survivo[r] and survivo[r]s of them my said Three Daughters share and share alike, Item I give and bequeath unto my Sister Ann Ball the sume of five and Twenty poundes of like lawfull money to bee paid unto her by my said Execu[r] hereafter named out of by and with the first moneyes that hee shall or may receive of the said Arreares of my said late Husbands Sallaryes as aforesaid, Item I give unto my Brother Leonard [20]<Ball Tenne poundes of like lawfull money to bee paid unto him in the second place after my said Sister Annes aforesaid Twenty five pounds out of by and wth the moneyes that he my said Executo[r] hereafter named shall or may receive of the aforesaid Arreares of my said late Husbands Sallaryes as aforesaid Item I give and bequeath unto my late Husbands Godsonn and my Nephew Orlando Ball the like sume of Tenne poundes like money And unto my Nephew Willm Ball my said Brother Leonards other sonne the sume of five poundes like money to bee paid unto them respectively att theire respective Ages of One and Twenty yeares by my said Executo[r] hereafter named out of and by and with the aforesaid Arreares of my said late Husbands Sallaryes as aforesaid, if then received or assoone after as the same shall bee received And if any or either of them the said Leonard Orlando or William shall happen to dye before such time as his or theire said Legacy shall become due and payable as aforesaid then the Legacy and Legacyes of him or them soe dying shall come remaine and bee paid unto the survivo[r] and survivo[r]s of them the said Leonard Orlando and William in such manner as aforesaid> Item I give and bequeath unto my said Two Daughters Elizabeth and Ann and unto my sister Ann Ball and [21]<unto my Sister in Law Ann Heath> widdow and unto my Cozen Mary Davis [22]<and to

---

19   Scored through.

20   The words within angle brackets are scored through. In the probate copy they are scored through and marginally annotated 'sic orig'.

21   The words that follow are scored through.

22   Scored through.

my good ————se[23] Elizabeth Rablis > Thirty poundes[24] amongst them
to bee equally divided (That is to say) five poundes apeice to bee laid out
in Mournings for themselves respectively to bee worne att my funerall,
Item I give unto my loveing friends M[rs] Gavill of Milford Lane and unto
M[rs] Sarah Warner of S[t] Martins Lane to each of them A Gold Ring of
Thirty shillings price to weare in remembrance of me Item my minde
and will is that my said Sister Ann Ball shall have such parte of my
wearing Apparrell as is most fitt for her wearing And that my said Two
Daughters Elizabeth and Ann shall have the rest of my said wearing
Apparrell to bee equally divided betweene them at the discrecõn of my
said Execu[r] hereafter named And whereas I did heretofore intrust my
reall friend John Thacham of the Middle Temple London Gent with the
putting forth of the sume of One Hundred poundes of lawfull money of
England for mee att interest And knowing his ability and distrusting the
security upon which hee lent out that money I chose rather to accept of
his owne Bonds of Two hundred poundes to secure the repaym[t] thereof
which he gave me accordingly then thother security upon which the
money was lent as aforesaid, And whereas the said John Thacham about
seaventeene yeares since became bound with and for my late Husband
and for his proper debt in One Bond of One Hundred poundes for paym[t]
of fifty poundes with interest for the same which now amounts unto One
Hundred poundes or thereabouts In consideracõn whereof And for the
said Mr Thachams indempnity and satisfaccõn I doe hereby give and
bequeath remise and release unto my said Trusty and reall ffriend the
said Mr Thacham the said Bond of Two Hundred poundes wherein he
stands bound for paym[t] of One Hundred as aforesaid And all and every
sume and sumes of money whatsoever thereupon due and owing or
which att the time of my death shall bee thereupon due and owing And I
doe hereby make ordaine and appoint the said M[r] John Thacham sole
Executo[r] of this my last will and Testam[t] conteyning Two sheetes of
paper affixed together att the topp thereof unto every of which said
sheetes I have sett my hand and Seale the Nineteenth day of March in the
Thirtyeth yeare of the Reigne of our most gracious Sovereigne Lord
Charles the second by the grace of God of England Scotland Fraunce and
Ireland King Defender of the ffaith &c Annoq Dñi 1677. And I doe
hereby earnestly desire my said Execu[r] to take especiall care (as I trust
hee will) of my said Children during theire minorityes that they may not
bee deceived or defrauded of that small livelyhood and fortune which
belongs unto them./ And which I have in and by this my last Will and

23   Illegible. Not in probate copy.

24   End of page, signed and sealed. The seal, evidently made with a ring, shows a
heart pierced diagonally by crossed arrows.

Testam^t given unto them in such manner as aforesaid And for an Addition to my said Two daughters Elizabeth and Ann their aforemencõed Legacyes my further Will and minde is That after all my owne and my late Husbands just debts and all the particular Legacyes herein and hereby before particularly mencõed and bequeathed and all my funerall charges and expences and all other incident Charges shall be fully satisfyed paid and discharged by my said Executo^r All the rest and residue of my said Estate (if any) not herein and hereby before bequeathed shall bee divided betweene my said Two Daughters Elizabeth and Ann whereof my said Daughter Elizabeth to have Two thirds thereof And my said Daughter Ann the other third thereof

Elizabeth Gibbons[25]

Signed, Sealed, published and declared
to bee the last will of the above
named Elizabeth Gibbons by her
the said Elizabeth in the
p^rsence of us
Robert Mille
Elizabeth Rabliss
George Meriam.

(Proved by John Thacham, 22 January 1683.)

Two affidavits, dated 30 December 1682, are enclosed with the above will. The first is initialled by the testator's sister Anne Ball, who is described as a spinster of fifty-one years living in Westminster. It says

... That about halfe a yeare next before the death of the said dec^d (shee dying on the 26th day of March last was two yeares) this Dep^t being with her at her house in Orchard Streete[26] in West^r shee ye said dec^d desired her to bring a little trunck to her wch this Dep^t did which shee unlocked and thereout shee tooke the will hereunto annexed and called for a pen and ink which being delivered to her by Jane Stock her Nurse then psent the said dec^d declared that shee would scratch her Brother Ball (meaning Leonard Ball her Brother) and his Children and Mary Davie out of her will, and shee then with a pen struck out

---

25   The signature appears to have been written with great difficulty. A seal is again added.

26   This may be the house in New Street, between Orchard Street and the Almonry, where the Gibbons family lived in 1671. See p. 246.

and obliterated the sev^{r}all lines in ye will ex*hibi*ted in manner as now appeareth and having soe done shee folded up her will againe and put it into the foresaid trunck and locked the same ... at which time ye said dec̃d was sitting in her Chaire in her Chamber and was of p̃fect mind and memory and discoursed sensibly and well And this Dep^t alsoe saith that she sev^{r}all times heard the said dec̃d ... not long before her death say, that her daughter Elizabeth Gibbons should have nothing but her copyhold [Estate][27] which would come to her after her death.

The second affidavit, to the same effect, is signed with the mark of 'Jane Stock wife of William Stock of the City of Westm^r Bricklayer aged 55 yeares or thereabouts', who had nursed Elizabeth Gibbons for upwards of two years.

27   Conjectural reading.

APPENDIX C

FANTAZIES OF III. PARTS

The first printed edition of the *Fantazies* seems, for reasons given above, to have appeared in 1619 or 1620.[1] It exists in three conditions, which may represent three issues. It could be contended that there were only two issues, of which the second exists in two states or includes copies that are now incomplete, but the conjectural publishing history outlined below argues against this. There is no reason to think that there was any more than one printing, although the engraved plate of the first page was altered after a few copies forming the first issue had been run off.

All the surving copies are printed from the same plates, which are almost certainly the work of William Hole.[2] The first engraved page, in its original state, reads:

FANTAZIES OF III. PARTS.

To the patterne of virtue & my ho^ble freind Mr Edward Wraye one of ye Groomes of his Ma^ts bedChamber.

Sir: It is not ye worthines of the worke but my affection which I unfainedlie present: And having no other meanes to expresse it, I heartily intreat you to accept of this untill I shall finde a better way to discover ye same so shall I rest one of those y^t shall most honor you.

Orlando Gibbons

The second issue has the imprint 'LONDON At the *Bell* in St P*auls* Church-yard' added in the left-hand corner below the dedication. The Bell was the sign of Thomas Adams and, from his death in 1620 until 1625, of his widow Elizabeth.[3] One surviving copy of the *Fantazies* in which the imprint is present differs from other copies containing it, in having an additional title-page printed from movable type, and putatively represents a third issue. The new title-page may have been modelled partly on the title-page of *The First Set of Madrigals and Mottets*, and reads:

1 See p. 62.

2 See pp. 46, 62.

3 Wheatley, 1908, p. 82. Adams was a warden of the Stationers' Company from 1610 to 1618. On 30 October 1609 the Company determined the right of Adams and William Barley to print music books (Jackson, 1957, p. 39).

FANTASIES OF THREE PARTS. COMPOSED BY *Orlando Gibbons* Batchelour of Musick, And Late Organist of His MAIESTIES Chappell Royall in ordinary. Cut in Copper, the like not heretofore extant. *LONDON*, At the *Bell* in S^t. *Pauls* Church-yard'.[4]

The above remarks are based on the four known copies of the *Fantazies*:

A Short-title Catalogue (STC), 1976-86, no. 11823; Hind, 1952-64, ii, p. 339.[5] Copies at:

(1) Christ Church, Oxford. Altus and Basso parts only, bound separately. The Altus part has the page carrying the title and dedication. The binding preserves grey paper covers inscribed 'Altus [etc.]/ Orl:/ Gibbons his/ 3 parts'.

(2) Euing Collection, Glasgow University Library, bound as one in the order: dedication, Altus I-IX, Tenore I-IX, Basso I-IX.[6]

STC, no. 11824; Hind, ii, p. 339. Copy at Royal College of Music, bound as one in the order: dedication, Basso I-IX, Tenore I-IX, Altus I-IX.[7] Otherwise identical with the above copies, except for the imprint in the lower left corner of the first page. It is uncertain whether this copy once had the additional title-page possessed by the British Library copy described below.

STC, no. 11825; Hind, ii, p. 339. Copy at British Library, bound in one volume in the order: dedication, Altus I-IX, Tenore I-IX, Basso I-IX.[8] Otherwise identical with STC 11824, but with a leaf forming an additional preliminary title-page printed from moveable type. The leaf is printed on paper which is different from that of other pages.

4   The additional title-page's phrase 'Cut in copper, the like not heretofore extant' cannot truthfully refer to the printing of music from engraved plates, since *Parthenia* (not to mention foreign publications) had appeared several years earlier. Probably the printer was ill-informed or not fussy about this. If, on the other hand, the phrase has another meaning, it must refer to the publication of part-books for stringed instruments, or to 'the style, instrumentation and purpose of the music' (Dart, 1956, p. 349).

5   Hind misreads the dedication, giving 'ho^{ble}' as 'noble'.

6   The title-page is inscribed 'Richard Clark Lay Clerk of West^r Abbey Sepr. 1834'. A portrait of Gibbons taken from Hawkins, 1776, is glued in as a frontispiece. Manuscript bar-lines and other annotations have been added to some pieces.

7   There are some manuscript additions.

8   The altus part of the first fantasia has been altered in manuscript, mainly by the addition of bar-lines.

It can be surmised that Gibbons distributed presentation copies of the *Fantazies* before the imprint was added to the dedication page. If, as appears to be the case, William Hole added the imprint to the plates he had engraved, the alteration was made before his death in the first half of 1624. Indeed, it would not be surprising if it was made immediately the number of sheets required for presentation copies had been printed, so that the printer's task suffered little interruption, and so that Gibbons could place his *Fantazies* on public sale as soon as possible. The title-page set in movable type, however, seems to have been printed after Gibbons's death on 5 June 1625, for it describes him as 'late organist of his Majesties Chappell Royall'.[9] It is possible that Elizabeth Adams did not give up her business until the end of 1625, and that before the business closed down she or Gibbons's widow wished to dispose of unsold copies of the *Fantazies*, and offered them for sale as a third issue with an additional new title-page. The British Library copy shows no signs of having been printed from plates that were noticeably worn, so it is unlikely that they were used for printing more than the initial, probably very small, batch of copies.

It is not the purpose of this appendix to provide a bibliographical analysis of the *Fantazies*, but a few observations may be in place. The publication is printed only on one side of each leaf. Krummel says it is 'assembled in three gatherings of nine leaves each, each gathering to be used by one of the performers', and that it is 'Quarto format, with one plate used to print two pages'.[10] But, in the absence of more detailed study, these statements cannot be accepted without qualification. Some pages in the British Library copy indeed bear an impression either at the top or the bottom, as though printed from half a plate, but this seems not to be true of all pages in all copies. Some pages of the copies at Christ Church and the Royal College of Music seem to bear the impression of a single plate. It is, moreover, hard to see how sheets uniformly printed from two-page plates could have been folded and cut to give upper-page and lower-page impressions in the order in which they appear in the British Library copy. But since all copies are tightly bound, the make-up

---

9   Dart (1956, p. 343) contended that the words 'late organist' mean that Gibbons's duties as organist of the Chapel Royal ceased when he was appointed to the Privy Chamber (which Dart evidently supposed to be the King's Privy Chamber), but Gibbons never ceased to be an organist of the Chapel Royal, even when he was appointed to other court posts and to the post of organist of Westminster Abbey. Dart's argument that Thomas Tomkins was organist of the Chapel towards the end of Gibbons's lifetime would have force only if there had been one organist at a time in the Chapel Royal, but there were two, of whom Gibbons remained one to the end of his life.

10   Krummel, 1975, pp. 146, 149.

of any copy cannot readily be ascertained, and it is not easy to discern how the printer dealt with the problem of producing three nine-leaf part-books plus a preliminary leaf bearing the title and dedication, or how his solution has been disguised by the binders of the extant copies. It may well be that the publication exhibits peculiarities of sheet cutting, printing and folding similar to those of *Parthenia In-Violata*.[11] A detailed examination of watermarks and plate positions in all copies will be required before any valid conclusions can be reached, but the copy at Glasgow University Library may offer a partial clue. As the leaves for Tenore II and Tenore IX are noticeably stiffer than other leaves, it is possible that they are the halves of one fold.

The contents of the *Fantazies* were reprinted from movable type and introducing bar-lines in:

XX. Konincklycke FANTASIEN, *om op* 3 *Fioolen de Gamba en ander Speel-tuigh to gebruycken*. Gestelt door de Konstige Engelse Speel-meesters, T. LUPO. I. COPRARIO. W. DAMAN. En noch IX. FANTASIEN, *Om met* 3 *Fioolen de Gamba en ander Speel-tuygh te gebruycken*. Door ORLANDO GIBBONS, Organist en Zang-meester, van de Koninck van Engeland. HOOGHSTE-GELUIT.[12] EERSTE DEEL. t'AMSTERDAM, By *Paulus Matthysz*. inde Stoof-steegh, in't Muzyk-boek, gedrukt. 1648.[13]

This edition includes a separate title-page preceding Gibbons's fantasias:

IX FANTASIEN, *met 3. Fioolen, Gestelt door* ORLANDO GIBBENS, Organist en Zangh-meester, van de Kapel van den Koninck van Engelandt. HOOGHSTE-GELUIT.[14] t'AMSTERDAM, By *Paulus Matthysz*. inde Stoof-steegh, in't Muzyk-boek, gedrukt. 1648.

11   See the bibliographical note by Richard J. Wolfe in the facsimile edition of *Parthenia In-Violata* (New York, 1961), and his article in the *Bulletin* of the New York Public Library, lxv, 1961, pp. 347-64.

12   The part-books are described as 'hooghste-', 'middelste-' or 'laeghste-' as appropriate.

13   See Rasch, 1972, for the background to this edition, but see also p. 65 above.

14   'hooghste-', 'middelste-' or 'laeghste-'.

APPENDIX D

PORTRAITS

Orlando Gibbons

John Hingston's will, made on 12 December 1683, five days before his death, says: 'I give and bequeath unto the use of the musickschool in Oxford the Picture of my ever hono^rd. Master m^r. Orlando Gibbon'.[1] It seems impossible to discover whether the picture now in the library of the Faculty of Music at Oxford, showing Gibbons in three-quarter view and clothed in what may be the 'rich cope' of a Gentleman of the Chapel Royal,[2] is the one bequeathed by Hingston. The portrait is not included among those listed by Thomas Forde, the Chaplain of Christ Church, as hanging in the Music School at Oxford about 1720.[3] The picture seems in fact to have gone undocumented until 1904, when it was included as no. 131 in an exhibition in the Examination Schools.[4]

Poole may or may not have been right in saying that the portraits owned by the Faculty of Music 'fall into two classes — those that were given to the school actually by the subjects themselves or by persons closely connected with them, and those that were bought by Dr. Philip Hayes about 1770 with the object of completing the series and filling up gaps in it'.[5] But there seems to be no evidence for her statement, which has been repeated subsequently, that the portrait of Gibbons was 'Given to the Music School by Dr. Philip Hayes before 1795'.[6] However, the

1 PRO, Prob. 10/1146; probate copy: Prob. 11/375, ff. 134^r-135^r; proved 16 February 1683/4. Hingston's will refers to other portraits he owned: those of Elizabeth, Countess of Burlington and Cork; her grandfather, Francis, Earl of Cumberland, to whom Hingston was apprenticed in 1621 (Hulse, 1983, p. 25); her father, Henry, Earl of Cumberland; her brother-in-law, Edward, Earl of Sandwich; and her husband, Richard, Earl of Burlington and Cork.

2 There is nothing to support statements that the painting represents Gibbons in academic dress. There was no prescribed academic dress for those holding music degrees at Oxford and Cambridge in the early seventeenth century (Hargreaves-Mawdsley, 1963, pp. 77-78, 87, 119, 126).

3 Bodleian Library MS Mus.e.17, f. iii^r.

4 Several statements about the portrait made by Poole (1911-26 and 1912-13) are based on the exhibition catalogue (Oxford University, 1904), which Mr and Mrs R. L. Poole assisted in preparing.

5 Poole, 1912-13, p. 145.

6 Poole, 1911-26, i, p. 151.

truth of Poole's further statement, that the portrait is a copy, is borne out by the poor quality of the painting itself, and is supported by a handwritten label on the back of the frame, which says: 'Orlando Gibbons Music Doctor from the original in possession of Mr Fussell'.[7] The writing could well be Victorian, and this is consonant with a printed label, which is also attached to the back of the frame. The printing on the label is partly obscured, but reads: 'To Her Majesty the Queen ... RYM... Co'. Presumably the portrait was reframed during the late nineteenth century by the Oxford firm founded by James Ryman, carver and gilder.[8] These facts appear to mean either that, when reframing took place, somebody knew of the existence of the original picture, or more likely — since the whereabouts of the original picture were unknown at the beginning of the twentieth century — that the label mentioning Fussell was copied from an earlier source (perhaps a label on the old frame). The label's testimony to the existence of an original portrait of Gibbons is the only thing, apart from tradition and a vague resemblance to the monumental bust, which supports the notion that it is he who is represented in the Oxford painting.

It is possible that, in fashioning Gibbons's monument, Stone based his bust of Gibbons on a painted portrait, though this is conjecture.[9] The earliest illustration of the monument is the poor engraving, probably by James Cole, in Dart's *History and antiquities of the cathedral church of Canterbury* (1726).[10] The engraved 'portrait' by Charles Grignion (1717-1810) in Hawkins's *A general history of the science and practice of music* (1776) may may owe something to the monument, or may have its origin in another source.[11]

7   Poole says 'apparently a copy made for the purpose', i.e. for donation by Hayes. No evidence has been found to support the quite reasonable supposition that Fussell was a member of the family who were musicians at Winchester Cathedral. The family is first known to have been connected with Winchester Cathedral in 1706, when a boy named Fussell became a chorister (Matthews, 1975, p. 25). Mr Paul Vining and the present author have tried separately to trace the original portrait through people named Fussell, but without success.

8   The firm, which appears in directories of Oxfordshire throughout Queen Victoria's reign, adopted the name 'Ryman and Co'. about 1880. Its address was 24 (later 24 and 25), High Street, Oxford. The date of the firm's royal appointment has not been discovered.

9   For comments on the bust, and the likelihood that it was based at least in part upon a painted portrait, see Vining, 1977.

10   Dart, 1726, pp. 51, where it appears next to an illustration of the monument of Adriani Saravia.

11   The engraving shows Gibbons full face; there is no reason to suppose that any

The Canterbury bust was probably the model for Henry Hugh Armstead's figure of Gibbons on the Albert Memorial.[12] A copy of the bust, made by Arthur George Walker, was given to Westminster Abbey by a former Master of the Worshipful Company of Musicians, C. T. D. Crews. It was unveiled at the commemoration held in the Abbey on 5 June 1907. The original bust featured in the tercentenary service held at Canterbury in 1925.[13]

Christopher Gibbons

At some stage a portrait of Christopher Gibbons was acquired for the Music School at Oxford, where it was hanging on the east wall about 1720.[14] There seems to be no documentary evidence to support the traditional belief that it was presented by Gibbons himself. The notion that it shows Gibbons in his doctoral robes appears to be unfounded. It is more likely that he is wearing the dress of a Gentleman of the Chapel Royal. He is shown holding a rolled sheet of music, no doubt one of his own compositions. In 1905 the portrait was included as no. 116 in the exhibition of portraits held at the Examination Schools, Oxford.[15] It now hangs in the Faculty of Music building at Oxford.

authority attaches to it, or that it can be taken as evidence of academic dress. It is among several cut from Hawkins in Bodleian Library MS Top. Oxon. c. 16 (nos. 98, 99 and 101 are of Orlando Gibbons, William Child and William Croft respectively.)

12   The memorial was begun in 1864 and the public was admitted on 3 July 1872. The statue of Prince Albert was not erected until 1876. The figure of Gibbons is among those of musicians in the marble frieze around the base on the south side.

13   Canterbury Cathedral Archives, U3/100/5/16. See Turbet, 2000.

14   Bodleian Library MS Mus.e.17, f. iii^r. Although Poole states that the portrait is inscribed 'A. V. DYCK FECIT', no signature is now readily apparent. The painter is in any case most unlikely to have been Sir Anthony Van Dyck, who died in 1641, and it has been said that the artist is 'known only in connexion with this portrait' (Oxford University, 1905, p. 102). The back of the portrait bears Ryman's label, like the portrait of Orlando Gibbons. The engraving by James Caldwall printed by Hawkins (1776, iv, p. 412) is apparently based on the painting.

15   Several statements about the portrait made by Poole (1911-26) are based on the exhibition catalogue (Oxford University, 1905).

LIST OF ORLANDO GIBBONS'S WORKS

For the sources of Gibbons's works see the modern editions listed below. For recordings, see the bibliography (p. 314) under Greenhalgh, 1999.

A. MODERN EDITIONS

Brett, Philip, ed. *Consort songs ... Second, revised edition*. London, Stainer and Bell, 1974. *Musica Britannica*, 22. (Contains Gibbons's *The cries of London*.)

Gibbons, Orlando. *Consort music, transcribed and edited by John Harper*. London, Stainer and Bell, 1982. *Musica Britannica*, 48.

Gibbons, Orlando. *Do not repine, fair sun. A welcome song composed in 1617 ... Edited by Philip Brett*. London, Stainer and Bell, 1961.

Gibbons, Orlando. *... First set of madrigals & motets (1612). Edited by Edmund H. Fellowes, revised by Thurston Dart*. London, Stainer and Bell, 1964. *The English Madrigalists*, 5.

Gibbons, Orlando. *Full anthems, hymns and fragmentary verse anthems, transcribed and edited by David Wulstan*. London, Stainer and Bell, 1978. *Early English Church Music*, 21.

Gibbons, Orlando. *Keyboard music, transcribed and edited by Gerald Hendrie. Second, revised edition*. London, Stainer and Bell, 1967. *Musica Britannica*, 20.

Gibbons, Orlando. *Orlando Gibbons 1583-1625*. London, Oxford University Press, 1925. *Tudor Church Music*, 4. (Editorial Committee: P. C. Buck, E. H. Fellowes, A. Ramsbotham, S. Townsend Warner. Contains Gibbons's Services, Preces and psalms, hymns and anthems. Noted in the following catalogue only when it contains pieces not included in a more recent edition.)

Gibbons, Orlando. *Second evening Service. Edited by Edmund H. Fellowes ...* London, Oxford University Press, 1936. *Tudor Church Music, Second series*, 85. (Magnificat and Nunc Dimittis only.)

Gibbons, Orlando. *Verse anthems, transcribed and edited by David Wulstan*. London, Stainer and Bell, 1964. *Early English Church Music*, 3.

Leighton, Sir William. *The tears or lamentations of a sorrowful soul, transcribed and edited by Cecil Hill*. London, Stainer and Bell, 1970. *Early English Church Music*, 11.

Parthenia: William Byrd, John Bull, Orlando Gibbons. Transcribed and edited by Thurston Dart ... Second, revised edition. London, Stainer and Bell, 1962.

Tudor church music. Appendix. With supplementary notes by Edmund H. Fellowes ... London, Oxford University Press, 1948. (Gibbons: pp. 19-20.)

B. PIECES PRINTED DURING GIBBONS'S LIFETIME

THE *FIRST SET* OF MADRIGALS AND MOTTETS of 5. Parts: apt for Viols and Voyces. *NEWLY COMPOSED* by *Orlando Gibbons*, Batcheler of Musicke, and Organist of his Maiesties Honourable Chappell *in Ordinarie. London*: Printed by Thomas Snodham, the Assigne of *W. Barley*. 1612.

Dedication: Sir Christopher Hatton.[1]

1	The silver swan[2]		captived are – 'Mongst
2	O that the learned poets[3]		thousands good[6]
3-6	I weigh not fortune's	12	Now each flowery bank[2]
	frown – I tremble not at	13	Lais now old[2]
	noise of war – I see	14	What is our life?[7]
	ambition never pleased –	15	Ah dear heart[2]
	I feign not friendship [4]	16	Fair is the rose
7-8	How art thou thralled –	17-19	Nay let me weep – Ne'er
	Farewell all joys		let the sun – Yet if that
9	Dainty fine bird[5]		age
10-11	Fair ladies that to love	20	Trust not too much[8]

PARTHENIA or THE MAYDENHEAD of the first musicke that *euer was printed for the VIRGINALLS. COMPOSED By three famous Masters: William Byrd, D^r: John Bull, & Orlando Gibbons, Gentilmen of his Maties: most Illustrious Chappell. Ingrauen by William Hole. Lond: print: for M^{ris}. Dor: Euans. Cum priuilegio. Are to be sould by G: Lowe print^r in Loathberry* [No date.][9]

Dedication: Frederick, Elector Palatine, and Princess Elizabeth. [*continued*

---

1 The copy presented to Hatton by Gibbons may be the one at Christ Church, Oxford (see p. 38).

2 For the origin of the words see note 11 on p. 135.

3 Words by Nicholas Breton.

4 Words by Joshua Sylvester.

5 An anonymous translation of 'O come se' gentile' from Battista Guarini, *Rime*, 1598, f. 83ᵛ. See Fellowes, 1967, p. 691.

6 Edmund Spenser, *The Faerie Queene*, III, i, 49.

7 Sir Walter Raleigh? (See Raleigh, 1951, pp. 143-145.)

8 Expanded from the second of Virgil's *Eclogues*, lines 17-18.

9 The initial printing must have taken place before 14 February 1612/3 (see p. 44).

Parthenia, continued]

Contributions by Gibbons are numbered XVI-XXI.

16	Galliard MB 20/25	19	Galliard [to the pavan]
17	Fantasia of four parts		MB 20/19
	MB 20/12	20	The Queen's command
18	The Lord of Salisbury his		MB 20/28
	pavan MB 20/18	21	Prelude MB 20/2

THE TEARES OR LAMENTACIONS OF A SORROWFVLL SOVLE: Composed with Musicall Ayres and Songs, both for Voyces and diuers Instruments. *Set foorth by Sir* William Leighton *Knight, one of his Maiesties Honourable Band of Gentlemen Pensioners*. And all Psalmes that consist of so many feete as the fiftieth Psalme, will goe to the foure partes for Consort. *LONDON* Printed by *William Stansby*. 1614.

Dedication: Prince Charles.

Each of Gibbons's contributions is numbered 6 in the section in which it appears.

O Lord, how do my woes increase   O Lord, I lift my heart to thee *a* 5
a 4 EECM 11/24   EECM 11/34

FANTAZIES OF III. PARTS ... [No date].[10]

Dedication: Edward Wraye.

See Appendix C for an account of the different states of the Fantazies.

1	g (flat) MB 48/7	6	d MB 48/12
2	g (flat) MB 48/8	7	d MB 48/13
3	g (flat) MB 48/9	8	d MB 48/14
4	d MB 48/10	9	d MB 48/15
5	d MB 48/11		

10   The initial printing must have occurred during the period from July 1618 to February 1621/2 (see p. 62). Among numerous post-publication copies, eight of these fantasias occur in keyboard manuscripts: see Brookes, 1996, nos. 1719, 1725-1731.

THE HYMNES AND SONGS OF THE CHURCH. *Divided into two Parts ... Translated, and Composed* BY G. W. LONDON, Printed by the Assignes of GEORGE WITHER. 1623. *Cum Privilegio Regis Regali.* Dedication: King James.[11]

Gibbons contributed tunes with basses to the following (included with the original numbering in EECM 21):

1	Now shall the praises of the Lord be sung	20	Lord, I will sing to thee
3	Sing praises, Israel, to the Lord	22	O Lord of hosts
		24	How sad and solitary
4	Now in the Lord my heart doth pleasure	31	Lord, thy answer I did hear
5	Thy beauty, Israel, is gone	34	Thus angels sung[12]
9	Come kiss me with those lips	41	O all you creatures[13]
13	O my love, how comely	44	Come Holy Ghost[14]
14	Arise, thou north wind	46	As on the night before this blessed morn[15]
18	Who's this, that leaning on her friend	47	A song of joy unto the Lord[16]
		67	When one among the twelve there was[17]

C. PIECES NOT PRINTED DURING GIBBONS'S LIFETIME

Arrangements by others of Gibbons's music are not included

Services

Short (First) Service (Venite – Te Deum – Benedictus – Kyrie – Creed – Magnificat – Nunc Dimittis)[18] TCM 4

11 For different editions and their relationships, see *Short-title catalogue,* 1976-86, nos. 25908-25910a.7, and Wulstan, 1978, pp. x-xii and 204-206.

12 The tune is a shortened version (by Wither?) of 9.

13 Not in all editions.

14 The tune is an expansion (by Wither?) of 9.

15 The tune, adapted (by Wither?) from 47, is in only one edition.

16 The tune is not in the edition containing 46.

17 The tune (by Gibbons?) had appeared in Edmund Prys's *Llyfr y Psalmau* (Llundain, 1621).

18 The Te Deum also exists (1) in a Latin adaptation (Cambridge University Library, Peterhouse Music MSS 35-37, 42-45), (2) adapted as a Sanctus (see note 8 on p. 212).

Verse (Second) Service (Te Deum – Jubliate – Magnificat – Nunc Dimittis) TCM 4

First Preces, and Psalms: (1) cxlv.15-21 (The eyes of all wait upon thee),[19] and (2) lvii.9-12 – cxviii.19-24 (Awake up, my glory – Open to me the gates)[20] TCM 4

Second Preces, and Psalm cxlv.1-14 (I will magnify thee, O God my king)[21] TCM 4

Full anthems

Almighty and everlasting God[22] a 4 EECM 21/1

Deliver us, O Lord[23] a 5 EECM 21/2

Hosanna to the Son of David[24] a 7 EECM 21/3

I am the resurrection[25] a 5 EECM 21/4

Lift up your heads[26] a 6 EECM 21/5

O clap your hands[27] a 8 EECM 21/6

O Lord, in thee is all my trust[28] a 5 EECM 21/7

O Lord, in thy wrath[29] a 6 EECM 21/8

Verse anthems

Almighty God, who by thy Son[30] EECM 3/1

Behold, I bring you glad tidings[31] EECM 3/2

19   For Whit Sunday Evensong.

20   Combines psalms for Easter Day Matins and Evensong. The passage from Psalm lvii is verses 9-12 in the Bishops' Bible, but verses 8-11 in the Authorized Version.

21   For Whit Sunday Evensong.

22   Collect for third Sunday after Epiphany.

23   Psalm cvi.47-48.

24   Combines Matthew xxi.9 (Gospel, first Sunday in Advent), Mark xi.10 and Luke xix.38 (tenth Sunday after Trinity).

25   John xi.25-26 (the Order for the Burial of the Dead).

26   Psalm 24.7-8, 10.

27   Psalm 47.

28   Anonymous words from *The Whole Booke of Psalmes* compiled by Thomas Sternhold and John Hopkins (see p. 167).

29   Psalm vi.1-4.

30   Collect for St Peter's Day.

31   Luke ii.10-11, 14.

Behold, thou hast made my days[32]
  EECM 21/3

Blessed are all they that fear the
  Lord[33] EECM 3/4

Glorious and powerful God[34]
  EECM 3/5

Grant, O Holy Trinity EECM 3/6[35]

Great King of Gods EECM 3/7[36]

If ye be risen again with Christ[37]
  EECM 3/8

Lord, grant grace[38] EECM 3/9

O all true faithful hearts
  EECM 3/11[39]

O God, the king of glory[40]
  EECM 3/10

See, see, the word is incarnate[41]
  EECM 3/12

Sing unto the Lord[42] EECM 3/13

This is the record of John[43]
  EECM 3/15

We praise thee, O Father[44]
  EECM 3/16

Consort songs

Do not repine, fair sun[45]

The cries of London MB 22/67

Viol fantasias of two parts

F *a* 2 MB 48/1
F *a* 2 MB 48/2
C *a* 2 MB 48/3

d *a* 2 MB 48/4
G *a* 2 MB 48/5
d (flat) *a* 2 MB 48/6

32   Psalm xxxix.6-8, 13-15 (Bishops' Bible verse numbers; Authorized Version 5-7, 12-13).

33   Psalm cxxviii. 1-4, for the marriage service.

34   'An Anthem for the Consecration of a Church or Chappel' (Clifford, 1664).

35   The Chapel Royal word-books (Bodleian Library MS Rawlinson Poet. 23; BL MS Additional 6346) give the readings 'Grant O Holy Trinity' for the opening verse and 'Grant Holy Trinity' for the chorus.

36   Printed in EECM 3 with words by H. R. Bramley beginning 'Great Lord of Lords', substituted in F. A. G. Ouseley's edition of Gibbons's church music (1873).

37   Colossians iii.1-4 (Epistle for Easter Day).

38   Modelled on Collect for All Saints' Day?

39   Printed in EECM 3 with words by Bramley beginning 'O thou the central orb', substituted in Ouseley's edition (1873).

40   Collect for the Sunday after Ascension Day.

41   'The words were made by Doctor Goodman De: of Rochester' (Christ Church, Oxford, MS Mus. 21).

42   Psalm xxx.4-10.

43   John i.19-23 (fourth Sunday of Advent).

44   Based on Easter season Collects?

45   Words attributed to Joseph Hall.

Viol fantasias with double bass

g (flat) *a* 3 MB 48/16	d *a* 3 MB 48/19
g (flat) *a* 3 MB 48/17	C *a* 4 MB 48/24
d *a* 3 MB 48/18	C *a* 4 MB 48/25

Viol fantasias of six parts (See also: D. Incomplete and lost works)

g (flat) *a* 6 MB 48/31	d *a* 6 MB 48/34
g (flat) *a* 6 MB 48/32	a *a* 6 MB 48/35
d *a* 6 MB 48/33	a *a* 6 MB 48/36

Viol In Nomines

d (flat) *a* 4 MB 48/26	g (flat) *a* 5 MB 48/28
d (flat) *a* 5 MB 48/27	g (flat) *a* 5 MB 48/29

Other pieces for viols

Galliard in G *a* 6 MB 48/42
Pavan (De le roye) in a and e *(a* 5?) MB 48/30[46]
Pavan in G *a* 6 MB 48/41
Go from my window *a* 6 MB 48/40

Keyboard fantasias[47]

C MB 20/13	d (flat) MB 20/8
C MB 20/14	g (flat) MB 20/9
C MB 20/49[48]	a MB 20/10
d MB 20/6	a MB 20/11
d (for a double organ) MB 20/7	

Keyboard pavans and galliards

Pavan in d MB 20/15[49]   Pavan in g (two flats) MB 20/16

---

46   Ascribed to 'Mr Gibbons' in BL Additional MSS 30826-8 (incomplete).
47   Fantasias may be called 'fancy' or 'voluntary' in the sources. See the discussion on p. 94 concerning the lack of distinction between a prelude and a fantasia.
48   Entered without title or composer in Christ Church, Oxford, MS Mus. 1142A, as the third of four fantasias, the other three of which are by Gibbons.
49   Mistitled 'Almain' in BL MS R.M. 23.1.4.

Pavan in a MB 20/17[50]
Galliard in d MB 20/21
Galliard in d MB 20/22
Galliard in d MB 20/23

Galliard in d (*Lady Hatton*)
MB 20/20
Galliard in a MB 20/24[51]

Other keyboard pieces

French air MB 20/32
Almain in C MB 20/35
Almain in d MB 20/33
Almain in d (*French*) MB 20/41[52]
Almain in G (*The King's Jewel*)
MB 20/36
Almain in G MB 20/37
Almain in a MB 20/34[53]
Coranto in d (*French*) MB 20/38
Coranto in d (flat) MB 20/39[54]

Coranto in a MB 20/40[55]
The fairest nymph MB 20/43[56]
Ground in C (*Italian*) MB 20/27[57]
Ground in a MB 20/26
The hunt's up (*Peascod time*)
MB 20/30
Lincoln's Inn mask MB 20/44[58]
A mask MB 20/45[59]
Prelude in a MB 20/1[60]
Prelude in d (flat) MB 20/5[61]

50   Mistitled 'fantasia' in editions by J. E. West and Margaret Glyn.
51   Wrongly ascribed to Thomas Tomkins in New York Public Library MS Drexel 5612.
52   'A mask' or 'Nan's mask' in some sources. For the sources of this and other alternative titles given below see the textual commentary to MB 20.
53   'A toy' or 'An air' in some sources.
54   'A mask'. A version of this piece (in a) is ascribed to Christopher Gibbons in New York Public Library MS Drexel 5611, and is included in Rayner, 1967. A similar version (in d) is attributed to Orlando Gibbons in Farrenc, 1863.
55   'A toy'.
56   'Gray's Inn mask'.
57   'Almain' in some sources.
58   'Tap up all your strong beer', and 'The Prince's mask'.
59   'The Temple Mask'.
60   'Fantasia' or 'A running fantasia' in some sources.
61   Classed as a fantasia by Hendrie (in Gibbons, 1967).

Prelude in d MB 20/3[62]

Verse in a MB 20/4[63]

Whoop, do me no harm MB 20/31

Welcome home MB 20/42[64]

The woods so wild MB 20/29

D. INCOMPLETE AND LOST WORKS

Verse anthems

Almighty, God which hast given[65]
    EECM 21/1[66]

Lord, we beseech thee[67] EECM
    21/2

O glorious God[68] EECM 21/8

Praise the Lord, O my soul
    EECM 21/3[69]

So God loved the world[70]
    EECM 21/4

Teach us by his example
    EECM 21/7

This is the day[71] EECM 21/9

Thou God of wisdom EECM 21/5

Unto thee, O Lord EECM 21/6[72]

Pieces surviving in versions for string consort

g (flat) *a* 6 MB 48/39

g (two flats) *a* 6 MB 48/37

g (flat) *a* 6 MB 48/38

E. FALSE AND DOUBTFUL ATTRIBUTIONS

Church music[73]

Arise, O Lord God[74]

Behold, the hour cometh[75]

62   'A fancy' or 'A voluntary' in some sources.

63   Classed as a prelude by Hendrie (in Gibbons, 1967).

64   'Almain', 'The welcome', 'A mask', and 'Mrs Judith Brown's delight'.

65   Based on Second Communion Collect and Proper Preface for Christmas Day.

66   Fragmentary verse anthems have a separate numerical sequence in EECM 21.

67   Attributed to 'Mr Gib' in the table inside the front cover of Christ Church MS Mus. 1001; anonymous on ff. 39ᵛ-41ᵛ ('for yᵉ Annuntiation of ye Virgin Mary').

68   Only the words survive.

69   Authenticity questioned by Vining, 1974.

70   'Anthem for Whitsunday' (Bodleian Library, Tenbury MS 791).

71   Only the words survive.

72   Possibly spurious; rejected by Vining, 1974.

73   For attributions of spurious anthems see Gibbons, 1964, p. 225; le Huray, 1978, pp. 312-314.

74   By Leonard Woodeson.

75   By Thomas Tomkins.

Gloria[76]

Have mercy upon me, O God
TCM 4[77]

Have pity TCM 4[78]

O Lord, increase our faith TCM 4[79]

Out of the deep EECM 21/9[80]

Sing we merrily TCM 4[81]

Te Deum[82]

The secret sins EECM 3/14[83]

Why art thou so heavy TCM 4[84]

Keyboard

Air in d MB 20/53[85]

Almain in d[86]

Coranto in d MB 20/54[87]

Coranto in d MB 20/55

Coranto in d MB 20/56[88]

Coranto in d MB 20/57[89]

76   Attributed to Gibbons by Zimmerman (1983, p. 396), but in fact from John Blow's Service in G. See Shaw, 1962, p. 265.

77   In William Byrd's *Psalmes, songs, and sonnets* (1611).

78   By Christopher Gibbons.

79   By Henry Loosemore. See Morehen, 1971.

80   Almost certainly by William Byrd (see note 7 on p. 158).

81   Sometimes attributed to Christopher Gibbons; in fact an adaptation of Palestrina's five-part *Exulte Deo*.

82   Cambridge University Library, Peterhouse Music MS 35. Ascribed to Gibbons by Hughes (1953, p. 21), and by Daniel and le Huray (1972, ii, p. 107); in fact an adaptation with Latin text of the Te Deum from Byrd's Great Service.

83   Probably by William Mundy. See le Huray, 1978, pp. 313-314.

84   By Henry Loosemore. See Morehen, 1971.

85   Ascribed to Gibbons in National Library of Scotland MS 9449 (Lady Jean Campbell's book), but plainly in a later style.

86   Not in MB 20. Attributed to 'M^r: Gibbons' in BL Additional MS 63852, f. 5^r; anonymous or attributed to Robert Johnson in other sources.

87   Ascribed to Gibbons in Thomas Heardson's unreliable manuscript (New York Public Library Drexel 5611), but to Treasure in Bibliothèque Nationale MS Paris Conservatoire Rés. 1185 (copied by Cosyn) and to La Barre in Christ Church MS Mus. 1236.

88   MB 20/55-56 are ascribed to Gibbons in Heardson's manuscript, which is the only source.

89   Ascribed to Gibbons by Heardson, anonymous elsewhere.

Courante in d[90]

Fantasia in a MB 20/51[91]

Fantasia in a MB 20/48[92]

Fantasia in G MB 20/58[93]

Fantasia in G MB 20/59[94]

Galliard in a MB 20/50[95]

Prelude in G MB 20/46[96]

Prelude in G MB 20/47[97]

Saraband in C MB 20/52[98]

Voluntary in a[99]

90 Attributed to Orlando Gibbons in Farrenc, 1863. See note 54 on p. 297.

91 'Dorick musique' in Paris Conservatioire MS Rés. 1185, followed by Christ Church MS Mus. 1113. In both manuscripts it is succeeded by another 'Dorick' piece ascribed to Bull. The pieces are printed as nos. 57-58 in MB 14: *John Bull. Keyboard music: I*, edited by John Steele and Francis Cameron (1960),

92 'A voluntary', 'Kiri Eleyson', and 'In nomine' (incorrectly). Ascribed to Gibbons in manuscripts compiled by Benjamin Cosyn (BL R.L. 23.1.4) and William Ellis (Christ Church MS Mus. 1113). Thomas Tomkins lists it in his table of contents with John Bull's In Nomines (Bibliothèque Nationale MS Paris Conservatoire Rés. 1122).

93 Ascribed to Gibbons in Christ Church MS Mus. 1113, but it is in an archaic cantus firmus style and contains no hint of the mature Gibbons.

94 Ascribed to 'Or: Gibbons' in Christ Church MS Mus. 1113, p. 159. Hendrie (in Gibbons, 1967, p. 104) suggests that it may be an arrangement of a three-part string fantasia, perhaps by Christopher Gibbons.

95 Ascribed to Gibbons by Cosyn (BL R.L. 23.1.4), but charcteristic of Cosyn's own keyboard style.

96 'A touch', 'A voluntary'. See the next note.

97 Both the preludes in G are ascribed to Gibbons in Bibliothèque Nationale MS Paris Conservatoire Rés. 1185. This was probably compiled by the elder Robert Creighton in the 1630s. In New York Public Library MS Drexel 5609, which Sir John Hawkins drew in part from Creighton's manuscript, the preludes are again attributed to Gibbons. They bear the name 'Mr Bird' in a section of BL Additional MS 31403, which may have been compiled in the 1630s by Elway Bevin.

98 Ascribed to Gibbons in two sources, but clearly in a later style. The composer is given as Richard Portman in Christ Church MS Mus. 1177. Portman was a chorister under Gibbons at Westminster Abbey, where he became organist on Gibbons's death.

99 By Christopher Gibbons, but attributed by implication to Orlando Gibbons in *Ten select voluntaries for the organ. Composed by Orlando Gibbons, Blow, Purcell, Doctr Green, Doctr Boyce, Mr Jams Martin Smith ... & J. Stafford Smith ...* (Book III of *A collection of voluntaries, for the organ or harpsicord*, c. 1775-80.)

Viol consort

Galliard in g (flat) *a* 3 MB 48/23
Fantasia in d *a* 3 MB 48/20 (double
    bass)[100]
Fantasia in d *a* 3 MB 48/22 (double
    bass)
Fantasia in a *a* 3 MB 48/21 (double
    bass)

100   MB 48/20-22 probably by John Coprario (see p. 131).

LIST OF CHRISTOPHER GIBBONS'S WORKS

A. MODERN EDITIONS

Cox, Geoffrey. *Organ music in Restoration England: a study of sources, styles, and influences*. New York, Garland, 1989. 2 vols. *Outstanding Dissertations in Music from British Universities*. (Volume 2 contains seven keyboard pieces by Gibbons.)

Gibbons, Christopher. *Fantasias à 4: no. 1 in G minor, no. 2 in A minor (VdGS Air nos. 81 and 82). Edited by Christopher D. S. Field*. Viola da Gamba Society of Great Britain, Supplementary Publication, 142.

Gibbons, Christopher. *Keyboard compositions. Edited by Clare G. Rayner*. Second, revised edition by John Caldwell. Neuhausen-Stuggart, Hänssler-Verlag for the American institute of Musicology, 1989. *Corpus of Early Keyboard Music*, 18.

Locke, Matthew, and Gibbons, Christopher. *Cupid and Death ... edited by Edward J. Dent. Second, revised edition*. London, Stainer and Bell, 1965. *Musica Britannica*, 2.

Sources of Gibbons's music are listed in:

Brookes, Virginia. *British keyboard music to c.1660. Sources and thematic index*. Oxford, 1996.

Daniel, Ralph T. and le Huray, Peter. 1972. *The sources of English church music 1549-1660*. London. *Early English Church Music*, Supplementary volume 1, parts I and II.

Dodd, G. *The Viola da Gamba Society of Great Britain thematic index of music for viols*. London, 1980-89.

B. PIECES PRINTED IN GIBBONS'S LIFETIME OR SOON AFTER

Cantica Sacra: Containing Hymns and Anthems FOR *TWO VOICES* to the *ORGAN*, both *Latine* and *English*. COMPOSED By Mr. *Richard Dering*. Dr. *Benjamin Rogers*. Dr. *Christoph: Gibbons*. Mr. *Matth: Locke*, and Others. THE SECOND SETT. London, Printed by *W. Godbid*, for *John Playford*, 1674.

Contains the following by Gibbons:[1]

Celebrate Dominum	Sing unto the Lord
How long wilt thou forget me?	Teach me, O Lord, the way

---

1   Manuscript sources give different versions.

CHOICE AYRES and SONGS TO SING TO THE Theorbo-Lute, or Bass-Viol: BEING Most of the Newest *Ayres* and *Songs* sung at COURT, And at the Publick THEATRES. *Composed by several Gentlemen of His Majesty's* Musick, *and others*. THE THIRD BOOK. *LONDON*, Printed by *A. Godbid* and *J. Playford* Junior, and are Sold by *John Playford*, at his Shop near the *Temple* Church; and *John Carr*, at his Shop at the *Middle Temple-Gate*, 1681.

Contains the following by Gibbons, from *Cupid and Death:*

Change, O change, your fatal bows (with chorus Take pity, Gods)

Victorious men of earth (with chorus He hath at will)

C. PIECES NOT PRINTED DURING GIBBONS'S LIFETIME

Cupid and Death

The text by James Shirley was printed twice:

CUPID *AND* DEATH. *A MASQUE.* As it was Presented before his Excellencie, The Embassadour of PORTUGAL, Upon the 26. of *March*, 1653. *Written by J. S.* LONDON, Printed according to the Authors own Copy, by *T. W.* for *J. Crook*, & *J. Baker*, at the Sign of the Ship in St. *Pauls* Church-yard, 1653.

CUPID AND DEATH, A Private Entertainment, represented with SCENES & MUSICK, VOCALL & INSTRUMENTALL. Writen by *J. S.* LONDON, Printed for *John Crooke & John Playford*, and are to be sold at their Shops in St. *Paul's* Church-yard and in the Inner Temple. 1659.

The music for the 1659 production, by Matthew Locke and Christopher Gibbons, survives in a score written by Locke (BL Additional MS 17799). The numbers ascribed to Gibbons are:

Instrumental airs[2]
Change, O change, your fatal bows (with chorus Take pity, Gods)

Open bless'd Elysium grove (with chorus If this place be not heaven)
Victorious men of Earth (with chorus He hath at will)

2   Versions appear also in manuscripts of consort music (see music for string consort, listed below).

Verse service

Magnificat and Nunc Dimittis (Lost)[3]

Verse anthems

Above the stars[4]   O praise the Lord, all ye heathen[7]
Ah, my soul   Sing unto the Lord, O ye saints[8]
God be merciful unto us[5]   Teach me, O Lord[8]
How long wilt thou forget me?[6]   The Lord said unto my lord
Not unto us, O Lord

The following survive incompletely:

Have pity upon me[9]   Lord, I am not high-minded
Help me, O Lord

Chant

O come let us sing

Latin vocal works

Celebrate Dominum[10]   Laudate Dominum
Gloria Patri   O bone Jesu

---

3   See p. 255.

4   Another *Above the stars* is credited to Gibbons in Christ Church MS Mus. 92, and is listed by Brookes, 1996, as no. 1693. The ascription to 'Christo Gibbons' is apparently not in the hand of the original scribe.

5   Attributed to Gibbons in Christ Church MS Mus. 14, but to Locke in Fitzwilliam Museum MS 117.

6   See *Cantica Sacra* (1674), above. Additional source, not listed by Daniel and le Huray: Durham Cathedral Library MS B1 (see Crosby, 1986).

7   Additional source, not listed by Daniel and le Huray: Durham Cathedral Library MS B1 (see Crosby, 1986).

8   See *Cantica Sacra* (1674), above.

9   Erroneously attributed to Orlando Gibbons in Gibbons, 1925.

10   See *Cantica Sacra* (1674), above.

Keyboard verses or voluntaries

The sources apply the terms 'verse' and 'voluntary' arbitrarily, when they give titles at all. Pieces are identified here by numbers allocated to them in Brookes, 1996, and Dodd, 1980-89.

Verse in d (Brookes 1696)
Verse or voluntary in d (Brookes 1694)
Verse in F (Brookes 1695)
[Verse] in a (Brookes 1692)

[Voluntary] in C (Brookes 1690)
Voluntary in C (Brookes 1698)
Voluntary in a (Brookes 1697)[11]
[Fragment] (Brookes 247)[12]

The following pieces for consort appear in keyboard sources:

Almain (Brookes 2391, Dodd 66)
[Galliard] (Brookes 2392, Dodd 67)
[Saraband] (Brookes 2393, Dodd 68)
Almain (Brookes 2394, Dodd 64)

[Corant] (Brookes 2395, Dodd 65)
[Almain] (Brookes 2396, Dodd 69)
[Corant] (Brookes 2397, Dodd 71)
[Saraband] (Brookes 2398, Dodd 72)

The following appears only in a keyboard manuscript, but may originally have been for consort:

[Saraband] in F (Brookes 1691)

String consort

Pieces are identified by numbers allocated to them in Dodd, 1980-89

Sets for treble, bass and organ, each consisting of fantasy, almain and galliard:

d (Dodd 1-3)
d (Dodd 4-6)

D (Dodd 7-9)
D (Dodd 10-12)

---

11   There are different versions: see Gibbons, 1989. The piece is erroneously attributed by implication to Orlando Gibbons in *Ten select voluntaries for the organ. Composed by Orlando Gibbons, Blow, Purcell, Doctr Green, Doctr Boyce, Mr Jams Martin Smith ... & J. Stafford Smith ...* (Book III of *A collection of voluntaries, for the organ or harpsicord*, c. 1775-80.)

12   In Christ Church MS Mus. 1142A, f. 9^v-10^r, and perhaps entered by the hand (which may have been the composer's) that wrote Brookes 1695 in the same source.

Sets for two trebles, bass and organ, each consisting of fantasy, almain and galliard:

a (Dodd 13-15)	d (Dodd 22-24)
a (Dodd 16-18)	D (Dodd 25-27)
d (Dodd 19-21)	D (Dodd 28-30)

Additional pieces for two trebles, bass and organ:

Air in g (Dodd 43)	Corant in g (Dodd 48)
Air in g (Dodd 45)	Fantasy in d (Dodd 39)[14]
Almain in d (Dodd 31)[13]	Fantasy in d (Dodd 40)[15]
Almain in d (Dodd 33)	Fantasy in d (Dodd 41)[16]
Almain in F (Dodd 36)	Galliard in D (Dodd 53)
Almain in g (Dodd 42)	Galliard in d (Dodd 34)
Almain in g (Dodd 51)	[Galliard] in g (Dodd 52)
Corant in d (Dodd 32)	[Pavan] in F (Dodd 35)
Corant in F (Dodd 37)	Saraband in g (Dodd 49)
Corant in g (Dodd 44)	[Saraband] in F (Dodd 38)
Corant in g (Dodd 46)	

Almain in g (Dodd 47)[17]
Saraband in g (Dodd 50)

Two-part airs

Almain in d (Dodd 61)	Saraband in d (Dodd 63)
Almain in d (Dodd 64)	[Saraband] in g (Dodd 68)
Almain in d (Dodd 66)	[Saraband] in d (Dodd 75)
Corant in d (Dodd 62)	
[Corant] in d (Dodd 65)	[Almain] in G (Dodd 69)[18]
Corant in G (Dodd 71)	[Brotch] in G (Dodd 73)
[Galliard] in g (Dodd 67)	[Corant] in G (Dodd 70)
[Galliard] in d (Dodd 74)	Saraband in G (Dodd 72)

13   When Dodd 31-34 are combined with the fantasy Dodd 22, they form an alternative set to Dodd 22-24.

14   Extended fantasy, including subsidiary corant and other, untitled, movements.

15   Extended fantasy, including subsidiary almain and other, untitled, movements.

16   Extended fantasy, including untitled subsidiary movements.

17   Dodd 47 and 50 are from *Cupid and Death*

18   Dodd 69, 70, 72 and 73 are from *Cupid and Death*.

Four-part fantasies

g (Dodd 81)   a (Dodd 82)[20]
g (Dodd 83)[19]

D. FALSE AND DOUBTFUL ATTRIBUTIONS

[Corant] in a (Brookes 1689)[21]
Fantasia in G (MB 20/59)[22]
Let thy merciful ears[23]
The Lord is my shepherd[24]
Sing we merrily[25]
Voluntary in d[26]

19   Not attributed to Christopher Gibbons in the source, but almost certainly his work. See Dodd, 1980-89.

20   Not attributed to Christopher Gibbons in the source, but partly in his hand and almost certainly his work. See Dodd, 1980-89.

21   Originally set by Orlando Gibbons (MB 20/39), in d. While it is possible that Christopher Gibbons made a simplified version of a tune previously arranged by his father, a misattribution seems more likely. See note 54 on p. 297.

22   Ascribed to 'Or: Gibbons' in Christ Church MS Mus. 1113, p. 159, Hendrie (in Gibbons, 1967, p. 104) suggests that it may be an arrangement of a three-part string fantasia, perhaps by Christopher Gibbons.

23   Listed by Arkwright, 1915-23, as possibly by Christopher Gibbons, but certainly not by him.

24   Attributed to 'Dr. Gibbons or Mr. Wise', but probably by the latter.

25   An adaptation of *Exultate Deo* by Palestrina.

26   Included as an appendix in the first (1967) edition of Christopher Gibbons's *Keyboard compositions*, edited by Clare G. Rayner; in fact from Orlando Gibbons's *Fantazies of III. Parts*.

BIBLIOGRAPHY

Annual Byrd Newsletter. 1995- . (Annual supplement to *Early Music Review*, first issued with no. 11, June 1995.)

Aplin, John. 1979. 'The survival of plainsong in Anglican music: some early English Te-Deum settings', *Journal of the American Musicological Society*, xxxii, pp. 247-275.

Arkwright, G. E. P. 1915-23. *Catalogue of music in the library of Christ Church Oxford ...* London. 2 vols.

Ashbee, Andrew. 1986-96. *Records of English court music*. Snodland (later Aldershot). 9 vols.

———— 1992. *The harmonious musick of John Jenkins. Volume one: the fantasias for viols*. [Surbiton.]

———— ed. 1998. *William Lawes (1602-1645): essays on his life, times and work ...* Aldershot.

———— and Holman, Peter, eds. 1996. *John Jenkins and his time: studies in English consort music*. Oxford.

———— and Lasocki, David. 1998. *A biographical dictionary of English Court musicians 1485-1714, compiled by Andrew Ashbee and David Lasocki assisted by Peter Holman and Fiona Kisby*. Aldershot. 2 vols.

Aston, Peter. 1980. 'Orlando Gibbons and the English musical tradition', *Music Teacher*, lix, pp. 17-18.

Bailey, Charles. 1856. *Transcripts from the municipal archives of Winchester ...* London.

Baines, Francis. 1968. [Letter.] *Viola da Gamba Society, Bulletin*, xxviii, p. 25.

———— 1970. 'Fantasias for the great dooble base', *Chelys*, 2, pp. 37-38.

———— 1978. 'The consort music of Orlando Gibbons', *Early Music*, vi, pp. 540-543.

Baldwin, David. 1990. *The Chapel Royal ancient and modern*. London.

Banks, Chris, et al, eds. 1995. *Sundry sorts of music books: essays on the British Library collections. Presented to O. W. Neighbour ...* London. (Joint editors: Malcolm Turner and Arthur Searle.)

Bannerman, W. Bruce, ed. 1916. *The registers of St. Olave, Hart Street, London. 1563-1700 ...* London. *Harleian Society Publications, Registers*, 46.

Barber, Richard, ed. 1988. *The worlds of John Aubrey ...* London.

Barlow, William. 1604. *The summe and substance of the conference, which, it pleased his excellent Majestie to have with the Lords, Bishops, and other of his clergie ... at Hampton Court. January 14. 1603 ...* London.

Barnard, John. 1683. *Theologa-historicus, or the true life of the most reverend divine, and excellent historian Peter Heylyn D.D. Sub-dean of Westminster ...* London.

——— 1641. *The first book, of selected church musick, consisting of services and anthems, such as are now used in the cathedrall, and collegiat churches of this kingdome.* London.

Bent, Ian, ed. 1981. *Source materials and the interpretation of music: a memorial volume to Thurston Dart.* London.

Beschreibung der Reiss. 1613. *Beschreibung der Reiss ... Volbringung des Heyraths: und glücklicher Heimführung ... des ... Herrn Friederichen dess Fünften ... mit der ... Princessin Elizabethen ... Jacobi dess Ersten Königs in Gross Britannien Eingen Tochter ...* [Heidelberg.]

Blayney, Peter W. M. 1990. *The bookshops in Paul's Cross churchyard.* London. *Occasional papers of the Bibliographical Society*, 5.

Bowers, Roger. 1995. 'The liturgy of the cathedral and its music, c.1075-1642'. In Collinson, 1995, pp. 408-450.

Boyce, William, ed. 1760-73. *Cathedral music: being a collection in score of the most valuable and useful compositions for that service, by the several English masters of the last two hundred years.* London. 3 vols.

Boyd, Morrison Comegys. 1962. *Elizabethan music and musical criticism ... Second edition.* Philadelphia, Pa.

Breton, Nicholas. 1952. *Poems by Nicholas Breton (not hitherto reprinted) edited ... by Jean Robertson.* Liverpool.

Brett, Philip, ed. 1974. *Consort songs ... Second, revised edition.* London. *Musica Britannica*, 22.

——— 1981. 'English music for the Scottish progress of 1617'. In Bent, 1981, pp. 209-226.

Bridge, Frederick. 1919-20. 'The musical cries of London in Shakespeare's time', *Proceedings of the Musical Association*, xlvi, pp. 13-20.

Bridge, Joseph C. 1913. 'The organists of Chester Cathedral', *Journal of the Architectural, Archaeological, and Historic Society for the County and City of Chester and North Wales, New Series*, xix, pp. 63-124.

Brooke, J. M. S. and Hallen, A. W. C., eds. 1886. *The transcript of the registers of the united parishes of S. Mary Woolnoth and S. Mary Woolchurch Haw ... 1538 to 1760 ...* London.

Brookes, Virginia. 1996. *British keyboard music to c.1660. Sources and thematic index.* Oxford.

Bull, John. 1967. *John Bull. Keyboard music: I, edited by John Steele and Francis Cameron, with introductory material by Thurston Dart. Second, revised edition.* London. *Musica Britannica*, 14.

Bullough, Geoffrey, ed. 1962. *Narrative and dramatic sources of Shakespeare ... Volume IV, Later English history plays ...* London.

Burke, Arthur Meredith, ed. 1913. *Indexes to the ancient testamentary records of Westminster ...* London.

——— 1914. *Memorials of St Margaret's church, Westminster. The parish registers, 1539-1661.* London.

Burney, Charles. 1776-89. *A general history of music from the earliest ages to the present period*. London. 4 vols. (With critical and historical notes by Frank Mercer, London, 1935. 2 vols.)

Butler, Charles. 1636. *The principles of musik*. London.

Byrd, William. 1980. *The English services edited from manuscript and printed sources by Craig Monson*. London. *The Byrd Edition*, 10a.

———— 1983. *The English anthems edited from printed and manuscript sources by Craig Monson*. London. *The Byrd Edition*, 11.

Calderwood, David. 1678. *The true history of the Church of Scotland, from the beginning of the Reformation, unto the end of the reigne of King James VI* ... [Rotterdam].

Calendar of state papers and manuscripts, relating to English affairs, existing in the archives and collections of Venice:

———— 1913. ... *Vol. XIX. 1625-1626. Edited by Allen B. Hinds* ... London.

Calendar of state papers, domestic series:

———— 1857. ... *of the reign of James I. 1603-16 ... Edited by Mary Anne Everett Green* ... London.

———— 1858(a). ... *of the reign of James I. 1611-1618 ... Edited by Mary Anne Everett Green* ... London.

———— 1858(b). ... *of the reign of James I. 1619-1623 ... Edited by Mary Anne Everett Green* ... London.

———— 1858(c). ... *of the reign of Charles I. 1625, 1626 ... Edited by John Bruce* ... London.

———— 1859. ... *of the reign of James I. 1623-1625 ... Edited by Mary Anne Everett Green* ... London.

———— 1860. ... *of the reign of Charles II. 1660-1661 ... Edited by Mary Anne Everett Green* ... London.

———— 1862. ... *of the reign of Charles II. 1663-1664 ... Edited by Mary Anne Everett Green* ... London.

———— 1863. ... *of the reign of Charles I. 1633-1634 ... Edited by John Bruce* ... London.

———— 1867. ... *of the reign of Charles I. 1636-1637 ... Edited by John Bruce* ... London.

———— 1882. ... *1655-6 ... Edited by Mary Anne Everett Green* ... London.

———— 1883. ... *1656-7 ... Edited by Mary Anne Everett Green* ... London.

———— 1891. ... *of the reign of Charles I. 1645-1647 ... Edited by William Douglas Hamilton* ... London.

Calendar of Treasury Books. 1904. *Calendar of Treasury books, 1660-1667 ... Prepared by William A. Shaw* ... London.

Camden, William. 1691. *V. Cl. Gulielmi Camdeni, et illustrium virorum ad G. Camdenum epistolae ... Praemittitur G. Camdeni vita. Scriptore Thome Smitho* ... London.

Carpenter, Nan Cooke. 1958. *Music in medieval and Renaissance universities.* Norman, Okla.

Challis, C. E., ed. 1992. *A new history of the Royal Mint.* Cambridge.

Chamberlain, John. 1939. *The letters ... edited ... by Norman Egbert McClure.* Philadelphia, Pa. 2 vols. *American Philosophical Society, Memoirs,* 12/1-2.

Chamberlayne, Edward. 1669. *Angliae Notitia, or the present state of England ...* London.

—— 1673. *Angliae Notitia; or the present state of England: the first part ... The seventh edition ...* London.

Chambers, E. K. 1923. *The Elizabethan stage.* Oxford. 4 vols.

Charteris, Richard. 1977. *John Coprario: a thematic catalogue of his music; with a biographical introduction.* New York.

—— 1982. 'A postscript to 'John Coprario: a thematic catalogue of his music with a biographical introduction (New York, 1977)', *Chelys,* 11, pp. 13-19.

Chester, Joseph Lemuel, ed. 1876. *The marriage, baptismal, and burial registers of the collegiate church or abbey of St. Peter, Westminster ...* London.

Chettle, G. H. 1980. *Kirby Hall, Northamptonshire ... Revised and expanded by Peter Leach ... [3rd edition].* London

Cheverton, Ian. 1985. 'English church music of the Restoration period, 1660-c.1676.' (Dissertation, University of Wales.)

[*Civitates orbis terrarum.* 1575.] *De praecipuis, totius urbibus, liber secundus.* Antwerp.

Clark, Andrew, ed. 1887-88. *Register of the University of Oxford ... (1571-1622) ...* Oxford. 3 vols. *Oxford Historical Society,* 10-12.

Clifford, James, ed. 1663. *The divine services and anthems usually sung in the cathedrals and collegiate choirs in the Church of England.* London.

—— ed. 1664. *The divine services and anthems usually sung in his Majesties chappell, and in all cathedrals and collegiate choires in England and Ireland. The second edition, with large additions.* London.

Clopper, Lawrence M., ed. 1979. *Records of early English drama. Chester ...* Manchester.

Collinson, Patrick, et al., eds. 1995. *A history of Canterbury Cathedral.* Oxford. (Joint editors: Nigel Ramsay and Margaret Sparks.)

Committee for Advancement of Money. 1888. *Calendar of proceedings of the Committee for Advancement of Money, 1642-1656 ... Edited by Mary Anne Everett Green ...* London.

Cooper, Barry. 1974. 'English solo keyboard music of the middle and late Baroque.' (Dissertation, University of Oxford. Revised version published New York, 1989, in series *Outstanding Dissertations in Music from British Universities.*)

Cooper, Charles Henry. 1842-1908. *Annals of Cambridge ...* Cambridge. 5 vols. (Volume 5 edited by John William Cooper.)

Cornwallis, Sir Charles. 1751. *An account of the baptism, life, death and funeral, of ... Prince Frederick Henry, Prince of Wales ...* London. (Contains *The life and death of our late most incomparable and heroic Prince Henry, Prince of Wales ... 1641. Written by Sir Charles Cornwallis ... in a letter to a friend*; the remainder consists of two anonymous tracts occasioned by the death of Prince Henry.)

Corser, Thomas. 1867. *Collectanea Anglo-poetica: or, a bibliographical and descriptive catalogue of a portion of a collection of early English poetry ... Part III.* [Manchester.] *Chetham Society, Remains*, 71.

Cox, Geoffrey. 1984. 'Organ music in Restoration England. A study of sources, styles, and influences.' (Dissertation, University of Oxford. Revised version published New York, 1989, in series *Outstanding Dissertations in Music from British Universities*. 2 vols.)

Crosby, Brian. 1986. *A catalogue of Durham Cathedral music manuscripts.* [Oxford].

Crosfield, Thomas. 1935. *The diary of Thomas Crosfield M. A., B. D. Fellow of Queen's College, Oxford ... edited ... by Frederick S. Boas ...* London.

Crossley, Alan, ed. 1979. *A history of the County of Oxford ... Volume IV: the City of Oxford.* London. *Victoria History of the Counties of England.*

CSPD. See *Calendar of state papers, domestic series.*

CSPV. See *Calendar of state papers and manuscripts, relating to English affairs, existing in the archives and collections of Venice.*

Cuneo, Anne. 1995. 'Francis Tregian the younger: musician, collector and humanist?' *Music & Letters*, lxxvi, pp. 398-404.

Cunningham, Walker. 1984. *The keyboard music of John Bull.* Ann Arbor, Mich. *Studies in Musicology*, 1.

Daniel, Ralph T. and le Huray, Peter. 1972. *The sources of English church music 1549-1660.* London. *Early English Church Music*, Supplementary volume 1, parts I and II.

Dart, J. 1726. *The history and antiquities of the cathedral church of Canterbury ...* London.

Dart, Thurston. 1956. 'The printed fantasies of Orlando Gibbons', *Music & Letters*, xxxvii, pp. 342-349.

———— 1970. 'Two English musicians at Heidelberg in 1613', *Musical Times*, cxi, pp. 29-32.

———— and Coates, William, eds. 1955. *Jacobean consort music.* London. *Musica Britannica*, 9.

———— and Donington, Robert. 1949. 'The origin of the In Nomine', *Music & Letters*, xxx, pp. 101-106.

Davies, C. S. L. and Garnett, Jane, eds. 1994. *Wadham College.* Oxford.

Davies, John. 1611. *The scourge of folly.* London.

Dent, Edward J. 1928. *Foundations of English opera: a study of musical drama in England during the seventeenth century.* Cambridge.

Deutsch, Otto Erich. 1959. 'Cecilia and Parthenia', *Musical Times*, c, 1959, pp. 591-592.

Devon, Frederick. 1836. *Issues of the Exchequer ... during the reign of King James I ...* London.

Dodd, G. 1980-89. *The Viola da Gamba Society of Great Britain thematic index of music for viols.* London.

Dublin Virginal Manuscript. 1983. *The Dublin virginal manuscript. New edition with an introduction and commentary by John Ward.* London.

Duffin, Ross W. 1993. 'Princely pastimes, *or* A courtly catch, being the history of another musical fragment at Case Western Reserve University', *Notes*, xlix, pp. 911-924.

Ellis, Mark, and Pilgrim, Jack. 1984. *Gibbons: anthems (i) This is the record of John (ii) Hosanna to the son of David.* Leeds. *Mayflower Study Guides*, 6.

Evelyn, John. 1959. *The diary of John Evelyn edited by E. S. de Beer.* London. *Oxford Standard Authors.*

Farrenc, A., ed. 1863. *Pièces pour le clavecin composées par divers auteurs anglais des XVIᵉ˙ et XVIIᵉ˙ siècles. (Iᵉʳ receuile).* Paris. *Le trésor des pianistes.* (Reprinted New York, 1977.)

Fellowes, Edmund H. 1951. *Orlando Gibbons and his family: the last of the Tudor school of musicians ... Second edition.* London.

—— ed. 1967. *English madrigal verse 1588-1632. Revised and enlarged by Frederick W. Sternfeld and David Greer. Third edition.* Oxford.

—— 1979. *Organists and masters of the choristers of St. George's Chapel in Windsor Castle ... Second edition ...* Windsor.

Ferguson, Howard, ed. 1974. *Anne Cromwell's virginal book, 1638 ...* London.

Field, Christopher D. S. 1970. 'The English consort suite of the seventeenth century.' (Dissertation, University of Oxford.)

—— 1998. 'Formality and rhetoric in English fantasia-suites'. In Ashbee, 1998, pp. 197-249.

Foster, Joseph. 1891-92. *Alumni Oxonienses ... 1500-1714 ...* Oxford. 4 vols.

Foster, J. E., ed. 1905. *Churchwardens' accounts of St Mary the Great Cambridge from 1504 to 1635 ...* Cambridge. *Cambridge Antiquarian Society, Publications, Octavo series*, 35.

Freeman, Andrew. 1921. 'The organs and organists of St. Martin-in-the-Fields, London', *The Organ*, i, pp. 1-19.

Gant, Andrew. 1999. 'A neglected genius', *Church Music Quarterly*, no. 144, pp. 32-33.

Gerardy, Theo. 1963. 'Die Papiermühle Arensburg und ihre Nesselblatt-Wasserzeichen 1604-1650', *Papiergeschichte*, xiii, pp. 25-30.

Gibbons. 1925. *Orlando Gibbons 1583-1625.* London. *Tudor church music*, 4. (Editorial Committee: P. C. Buck, E. H. Fellowes, A. Ramsbotham, S. Townsend Warner.) See also below: Tudor. 1948.

—— 1936. [*Orlando Gibbons*]. *Second evening Service. Edited by Edmund H. Fellowes* ... London. *Tudor Church Music, Second series*, 85. (Magnificat and Nunc Dimittis only.)

—— 1964(a). *Orlando Gibbons. First set of madrigals & motets (1612). Edited by Edmund H. Fellowes, revised by Thurston Dart.* London. *The English Madrigalists*, 5.

—— 1964(b). *Orlando Gibbons: verse anthems, transcribed and edited by David Wulstan.* London. *Early English Church Music*, 3.

—— 1967. *Orlando Gibbons. Keyboard music, transcribed and edited by Gerald Hendrie. Second, revised edition.* London. *Musica Britannica*, 20.

—— 1978. *Orlando Gibbons: II. Full anthems, hymns and fragmentary verse anthems, transcribed and edited by David Wulstan.* London. *Early English Church Music*, 21.

—— 1982. *Orlando Gibbons. Consort music, transcribed and edited by John Harper.* London. *Musica Britannica*, 48.

—— 1989. *Christopher Gibbons. Keyboard compositions. Edited by Clare G. Rayner. Second, revised edition by John Caldwell.* [n. p.] *Corpus of Early Keyboard Music*, 18.

Godt, Irving. 1982. 'Prince Henry as Absolom in David's Lamentations', *Music & Letters*, lxii, pp. 318-333.

Göhler, Albert. 1902. *Verzeichnis der in den Frankfurter und Leipziger Messkatalogen der Jahre 1564 bis 1759 angezeigten Musikalien* ... Leipzig.

Greenhalgh, Michael. 1999. 'A Gibbons discography', *Brio*, xxxvi, nos. 1 ('Introduction and instrumental music') and 2 ('Vocal music').

Greg, W. W. 1956. *Some aspects and problems of London publishing between 1550 and 1650.* Oxford.

—— 1967. *A companion to Arber* ... Oxford.

Grieve, Hilda E. P. 1954. *Examples of English handwriting 1150-1750* ... [Chelmsford]. *Essex Record Office Publications*, 21.

Grove. 1980. *The new Grove dictionary of music and musicians, edited by Stanley Sadie.* London. 20 vols.

Hacket, John. 1692. *Scrinia reserata: a memorial offer'd to the great deliverings of John Williams, D.D.* ... London.

Hall, Joseph. 1949. *The collected poems of Joseph Hall* ... *Edited by A. Davenport.* Liverpool.

[Hammond.] 1936. *A relation of a short survey of the western counties made by a Lieutenant of the Military Company in Norwich in 1635. Edited* ... *by L. G. Wickham Legg* ... *Camden Miscellany vol. XVI.* London. *Camden Third Series*, 52.

Hargreaves-Mawdsley, W. N. 1963. *A history of academical dress in Europe until the end of the eighteenth century* ... Oxford.

Harley, John. 1992-94. *British harpsichord music.* Aldershot. 2 vols.

—— 1997. *William Byrd: Gentleman of the Chapel Royal.* Aldershot.

—— 1998. 'New light on William Byrd', *Music & Letters*, lxxix, pp. 475-488.

Harper, John. 1983(a). 'The distribution of the consort music of Orlando Gibbons', *Chelys*, 12, pp. 3-18.

—— 1983(b).'Orlando Gibbons: the domestic context of his music and Christ Church MS21', *Musical Times*, cxxiv, pp. 767-770.

Hawarde, John. 1894. *Les reportes del cases in Camera Stellata 1593 to 1609 from the original MS. of John Hawarde ... Edited by William Paley Baildon* ... London.

Hawkins, Sir John. 1776. *A general history of the science and practice of music* ... London. 5 vols. (With a new introduction by Charles Cudworth, New York, 1963. 2 vols.)

Hendrie, Gerald. 1962-63. 'The keyboard music of Orlando Gibbons (1583-1625)', *Proceedings of the Royal Musical Association*, lxxxix, pp. 1-15.

Hind, A. M. 1905. *List of the works of native and foreign line-engravers in England* ... London.

—— 1952-64. *Engraving in England in the sixteenth and seventeenth centuries* ... London. 3 vols.

Holinshed, Raphael. 1807-8. *Holinshed's chronicles of England, Scotland and Ireland*. London. 6 vols.

Holman, Peter. 1973-74. 'George Jeffries and the 'great dooble base'', *Chelys*, 5, pp. 79-81.

—— 1993. *Four and twenty fiddlers: the violin at the English court 1540-1690*. Oxford. *Oxford Monographs on Music*.

—— 1996. '"Evenly, softly, and sweetly acchording to all": the organ accompaniment of English consort music'. In Ashbee and Holman, 1996, pp. 353-382.

Hovenden, Robert, ed. 1878. *The register booke of christnings, marriages, and burialls within the precinct of the cathedrall and metropoliticall Church of Christ of Canterburie ....* London. *Harleian Society, Publications. Registers*, 2.

Howard, Michael. 1951. 'Orlando Gibbons', *Musical Times*, xcii, pp. 160-164.

Hughes, Anselm. 1953. *Catalogue of the musical manuscripts at Peterhouse Cambridge* ... Cambridge.

Hulse, Lynn. 1983. 'John Hingeston', *Chelys*, xii, pp. 23-42.

—— 1996. 'Musical apprenticeship in noble households'. In Ashbee and Holman, 1996, pp. 75-88.

Huygens, Lodewijck. 1982. *The English journal 1651-1652, edited and translated by A. G. H. Bachrach and R. G. Collmer*. Leiden. *Publications of the Sir Thomas Browne Institute, New Series*, 1.

Jackson, William A., ed. 1957. *Records of the Court of the Stationers' Company 1602 to 1640*. London.

Jacquot, Jean. 1954. 'Lyrisme et sentiment tragique dans les madrigaux d'Orlando Gibbons'. In Centre National de la Recherche Scientifique, *Musique et poésie au XVIe siècle*, Paris, 1954, pp. 139-151.

────── ed. 1955. *La musique instrumentale de la renaissance*. Paris. *Journées internationales d'études sur la musique instrumentale de la Renaissance* [*1954*].

James, Peter. 1988. '"Exalt thyself, O God": the rediscovery of Byrd's festive anthem', *Annual Byrd Newsletter*, no. 4, pp. 9-10.

Jocquet, D. 1613. *Les triomphes, entrées, cartels, tournois, cérémonies, et aultrer magnificences, faites en Angleterre et au Palatinat pour le mariage et reception de ... Frédéric V ... at de Madame Élisabeth ...* Heidelberg.

Johnson, J. 1971. 'The English fantasia-suite c.1620-60.' (Dissertation, University of California at Berkeley.)

Johnson, Rose Marie. 1972. 'A comparison of "The cries of London" by Gibbons and Weelkes', *Journal of the Viola da Gamba Society of America*, ix, pp. 38-43.

Jonson, Ben. 1925-52. *Ben Jonson edited by C. H. Herford and Percy Simpson ...* Oxford. 11 vols.

Kerman, Joseph. 1962. *The Elizabethan madrigal: a comparative study*. New York. *American Musicological society, Studies and Documents*, 4.

Knights, Francis. 1990. 'A Restoration version of Gibbons' Short Service'. *Organists' Review*, lxxvi, pp. 97-100.

Krummel, Donald W. 1975. *English music printing 1553-1700*. London.

Laud, William. 1695. *The history of the troubles and tryal of ... William Laud, Lord Arch-Bishop of Canterbury. Wrote by himself ...* London.

Lawes, William. 1991. *William Lawes. Fantasia suites, transcribed and edited by David Pinto*. London. *Musica Britannica*, 60.

le Huray, Peter. 1960. 'Towards a definitive study of pre-Restoration Anglican service music', *Musica Disciplina*, xiv, pp. 167-195.

────── 1978. *Music and the Reformation in England 1549-1660*. Cambridge.

Leighton, Sir William. 1970. *The tears or lamentations of a sorrowful soul, transcribed and edited by Cecil Hill*. London. *Early English Church Music*, 11.

Letters and papers. 1896. *Letters and papers, foreign and domestic, of the reign of Henry VIII ... Arranged and catalogued by James Gairdner ... and R. Brodie ... Vol. XV*. London.

Locke, Matthew. 1673. *The Present Practice of Musick Vindicated*. London.

────── and Gibbons, Christopher. 1965. *Cupid and Death ... edited by Edward J. Dent. Second, revised edition*. London. *Musica Britannica*, 2.

Machyn, Henry. 1848. *The diary of Henry Machyn, citizen and Merchant-Taylor of London, from A.D. 1550 to A.D. 1563. Edited by John Gough Nichols*. London.

The Magnificent Entertainments. 1613. *The magnificent princely, and most royall entertainments given to the high and mighty Prince and Princesse ... with a true relation of all the gifts, presentations, showes, pageants, fire-workes, and other sumptuous triumphs in every place where the said Princes were lodged and received, after landing upon the coast of Germany.* London.

The Mariage of Prince Fredericke. 1613. *The mariage of Prince Fredericke and the Kings daughter, the Lady Elizabeth, upon Shrovesunday last ...* London.

Mark, Jeffrey. 1925. 'The Orlando Gibbons tercentenary: some virginal manuscripts in the Music Division', *Bulletin of the New York Public Library*, xxix, pp. 847, 860.

Marsh, Bower, and Crisp, Frederick Arthur, eds. 1913. *Alumni Carthusiani: a record of the foundation scholars of Charterhouse, 1614-1872.* London.

Mattheson, Johann. 1740. *Grundlage einer Ehren-Pforte ...* Hamburg.

Matthews, A. G. 1948. *Walker revised: being a revision of John Walker's Sufferings of the Clergy during the Grand Rebellion 1642-60.* Oxford.

Matthews, Betty. 1975. *The organs and organists of Winchester Cathedral.* [2nd revised edition]. Winchester.

McConica, James, ed., 1986. *The history of the University of Oxford ... Volume III: the collegiate university ...* Oxford.

McGuiness, David. 1995. 'Gibbons's solo songs reconsidered', *Chelys*, xxiv, pp. 19-33.

McKerrow, R. B., et al. 1910. *A dictionary of printers and booksellers in England ... 1557-1640 ...* London.

Mellers, Wilfred. 1954. 'La Mélancholie au début du XVIIe siècle et le madrigal anglais'. In Centre National de la Recherche Scientifique, *Musique et poésie au XVIe siècle*, Paris, 1954, pp. 153-168.

Mercurius Rusticus. 1643-44. *The first weeke [-XXI. Week]. Mercurius Rusticus, or the countries complaint of the murthers, robberies, plundrings, and other outrages, committed, by the rebells. on His Majesties faithfull subjects ... May 20. 1643 [-March. 16. 1643].* (Edited by Bruno Ryve.)

Meyer, Ernst Hermann. 1982. *Early English chamber music from the middle ages to Purcell ... Second, revised, edition edited by the author and Diana Poulton.* London.

Monson, Craig. 1982. *Voices and viols in England, 1600-1650: the sources and the music.* Ann Arbor, Mich.

Morehen, John. 1969. 'The sources of English cathedral music c.1617-1644.' (Dissertation, University of Cambridge.)

——— 1971. 'The Gibbons-Loosemore mystery', *Musical Times*, cxii, pp. 959-960.

——— 1978. 'The English consort and verse anthems', *Early music*, vi, pp. 381-385.

——— ed. 1995(a) *English choral practice 1400-1650.* Cambridge. *Cambridge Studies in Performance Practice.*

———— 1995(b) 'The "burden of proof": the editor as detective'. In Morehen, 1995(a), pp. 200-220.

Morley, Thomas, 1597. *A plaine and easie introduction to practicall musicke.* London. (Edited by R. Alec Harman, London, 1952.)

Munk, William. 1861. *The roll of the Royal College of Physicians of London* ... London.

Musicians' Company. 1909. *An illustrated catalogue of the music loan exhibition held ... by the Worshipful Company of Musicians at Fishmongers' Hall June and July 1904.* London.

Nelson, Alan H., ed. 1989. *Records of early English drama. Cambridge ...* Toronto.

Nichols, John. 1828. *The progresses, processions, and magnificent festivities of King James I.* London. 3 vols. in 4.

Noble, Jeremy. 1955. 'La répertoire instrumental anglais (1550-1585)'. In Jacquot, 1955, pp. 91-114.

North, Roger. 1959. *Roger North on music, being a selection from his essays written during the years c.1695-1728 ... edited by John Wilson.* London.

Oxford University. 1888. *Statutes of the University of Oxford codified in the year 1636 under the authority of Archbishop Laud ... edited by ... John Griffiths ...* Oxford.

———— 1904. *Catalogue of a loan collection of portraits of English historical personages who died prior to the year 1625 exhibited in the Examination Schools, Oxford ... April and May, MDCCCCIIII.* Oxford.

———— 1905. *Catalogue of a loan collection of portraits of English historical personages who died between 1625 and 1714 exhibited in the Examination Schools, Oxford April and May, MDCCCCV.* Oxford.

Page, William, ed. 1912. *The Victoria history of the county of Hertford ... Volume three.* London. *Victoria History of the Counties of England.*

Palmer, William. 1954. 'Gibbons's verse anthems', *Music & Letters*, xxxv, pp. 107-113.

Parrott, Andrew. 1978. 'Grett and solompne singing: instruments in English church music before the Civil War', *Early Music*, vi, pp. 182-187.

Parthenia in-violata. 1961. *Parthenia in-violata ... Facsimile of the unique copy in the New York Public Library. Historical introduction by Thurston Dart, bibliographical note by Richard J. Wolfe, foreword by Sydney Beck.* New York.

Payne, Ian. 1988. 'British Library Add. MSS 30826-28: a set of part-books from Trinity College, Cambridge?', *Chelys*, 17, pp. 3-15.

———— 1989. 'Instrumental music at Trinity College, Cambridge, c.1594-c.1615: archival and biographical evidence', *Music & Letters*, lxviii, pp. 128-140.

———— 1991. 'The provision and practice of sacred music at Cambridge colleges and selected cathedrals c.1547-c.1646. A comparative study of the archival evidence.' (Dissertation, University of Cambridge. Published New York, 1993, in series *Outstanding Dissertations in Music from British Universities*.)

Peacham, Henry. 1622. *The compleat gentleman*. London.

Pepys, Samuel. 1932. *Letters and the second diary of Samuel Pepys. Edited ... by R. G. Howarth ...* London.

────── 1970-83. *The diary of Samuel Pepys ... edited by Robert Latham and William Matthews ...* London. 11 vols.

Phillips, Peter. 1991. *English sacred music 1549-1649*. Oxford.

Pinto, David. 1990. 'The music of the Hattons', *Royal Musical Association Research Chronicle*, 23, pp. 79-108.

────── 1993. 'Walter Earle and his successors', *The Consort*, xlix, pp. 13-16.

────── 1996. 'Gibbons in the bedchamber'. In Ashbee and Holman, 1996, pp. 89-109.

Playford, John. 1651. *The English dancing master: or plaine and easie rules for the dancing of country dances, with the tune to each dance*. London.

────── 1683. *An introduction to the skill of musick ... The tenth edition, corrected and enlarged ...* London.

Poole, Rachael. 1912-13. 'The Oxford music school and the collection of portraits formerly housed there', *Musical Antiquary*, iv, pp. 143-159.

────── [as Mrs Reginald Lane Poole]. 1911-26. *Catalogue of portraits in the possession of the university, colleges, city, and county of Oxford ...* Oxford. 3 vols. *Oxford Historical Society*, 57, 81, 82.

Poulton, Diana. 1982. *John Dowland. [Second edition]*. London.

Powell, W. R., ed. 1966. *A history of the county of Essex ... Volume V.* London. *Victoria History of the Counties of England.*

Privy Council, England. 1934. *Acts of the Privy Council of England. 1625-1626 ...* London.

Privy Council, Scotland. 1894. *The register of the Privy Council of Scotland edited ... by David Masson ... Vol. XI A.D. 1616-1619 ...* Edinburgh.

Purser, John. 1992. *Scotland's music: a history of the traditional and classical music of Scotland ...* Edinburgh.

Puttenham, George. 1936. *The arte of English poesie ... Edited by Gladys Doidge Willcock and Alice Walker*. Cambridge.

Raleigh, Sir Walter. 1951. *The poems of Sir Walter Ralegh edited with an introduction by Agnes C. Latham*. London. *The Muses Library.*

Rasch, Rudi A. 1972. 'Seventeenth-century Dutch editions of English instrumental music', *Music & Letters*, liii, pp. 270-273.

Rayner, Clare G. 1963. 'A little-known 17th-century composer, Christopher Gibbons (1615-1676).' (Dissertation, University of Indiana.)

────── and Rayner, Sheila Finch. 1970. 'Christopher Gibbons: "That famous musitian"', *Musica Disciplina*, xxiv, pp. 151-172.

Reese, Gustave. 1949. 'The origins of the English In Nomine', *Journal of the American Musicological Society*, ii, pp. 7-22.

—— 1954. *Music in the Renaissance*. New York. (Second edition 1959.)

Reynell-Upham, W. U. and Tapley-Soper, H., eds. 1910. *The registers of baptisms, marriages and burials of the City of Exeter. Volume 1. The registers of the cathedral* ... Exeter. *Devon and Cornwall Record Society, Publications.*

Rimbault, Edward F., ed. 1846. *A collection of anthems, for voices and instruments, by composers of the madrigalian era, scored from a set of ancient M.S. part books formerly in the Evelyn collection* ... London. (Title-page undated; preface dated Christmas Eve, 1845.)

—— 1866. 'The organs and organists of Westminster Abbey', *Notes and Queries*, series III, x, p. 182.

—— ed. 1872. *The old cheque-book or book of remembrance of the Chapel Royal from 1561 to 1744*. London. (Reprinted, with an introduction by Elwyn A. Wienandt, New York, 1966.)

Robson, Thomas. 1830. *The British herald, or cabinet of armorial bearings of the nobility & gentry of Great Britain & Ireland*. Sunderland. 3 vols.

Rose, Bernard, ed. 1968. *Thomas Tomkins: Musica Deo sacra: II* ... London. *Early English Church Music*, 9.

Royal Commission on Historical Manuscripts. 1874. *Fourth report* ... *Pt. I. Report and appendix* ... London.

—— 1888. *Twelfth report, appendix, part I. The manuscripts of the Earl Cowper, K. G.* ... *Vol. I* ... London.

—— 1940. *Report on the manuscripts of the Marquess of Downshire* ... *Volume four Papers of William Trumbull the elder January 1613 - August 1614 Edited by A. B. Hinds* ... London. *Historical Manuscripts Commission*, 75.

—— 1970. *Calendar of the manuscripts of* ... *the Marquess of Salisbury* ... *at Hatfield House* ... *Part XXI (1609-1612). Edited* ... *by G. Dyfnallt Owen* ... London. *Historical Manuscripts Commission*, 9.

Rye, Walter, ed. 1891. *The visitacion of Norffolk, made and taken by William Hervey, Clarencieux King of Arms, anno 1563, enlarged with another visitacion made by Clarenceux Cooke* ... *and also the visitation made by John Raven, Richmond, anno 1613*. London. *Harleian Society, Publications*, 32.

Sabol, Andrew J., ed. 1978. *Four hundred songs and dances from the Stuart masque*. Providence, R.I.

Salmon, Thomas. 1688. *A Proposal to Perform Musick, in Perfect and Mathematical Proportions*. London.

Salter, H. E., ed. 1926. *Oxford city properties*. Oxford. *Oxford Historical Society*, 83.

—— ed. 1928. *Oxford council acts 1583-1626* ... Oxford. *Oxford Historical Society*, 87.

Salter, Lionel. 1979. 'Gibbons: keyboard pieces', *Music Teacher*, lviii, pp. 17-18.

Scholes, Percy A. 1934. *The Puritans and music in England and New England: a contribution to the cultural history of two nations*. London.

Scot, Stefan. 1997. 'The Prayer Book in practice: textual anomalies and their implications in Tudor musical settings of the first Book of Common Prayer', *Brio*, xxxiv, 1997, pp. 81-89.

Shaw, Watkins. 1961.'A Cambridge manuscript from the Chapel Royal', *Music & Letters*, xlii, pp. 263-267.

—— 1991. *The succession of organists of the Chapel Royal and the cathedrals of England and Wales from c.1538* ... Oxford.

Short-title catalogue. 1976-86. *A short-title catalogue of books printed in England, Scotland, & Ireland and of English books printed abroad 1475-1640. First compiled by A. W. Pollard & G. R. Redgrave. Second edition* ... London. 2 vols.

Skeat, Walter W. 1901. *The place-names of Cambridgeshire* ... Cambridge. *Cambridge Antiquarian Society, Publications, Octavo Series*, 36.

Smith, John Edward. 1900. *A catalogue of Westminster records* ... *in the custody of the vestry of St. Margaret & St. John* ... London.

Smith, S. A. 1901. *Index of wills proved in the Prerogative Court of Canterbury. 1584-1604. Vol. IV* ... *edited by Edward Alexander Fry*. London. *British Record Society*, 25. (*The Index Library*.)

Society of Antiquaries. 1790. *A collection of ordinances and regulations for the government of the royal household, made in divers reigns* ... London.

Spencer, Terence John Bew, and Wells, Stanley, eds. 1967. *A book of masques in honour of Allardyce Nicoll*. Cambridge.

Spiers, Walter Lewis, ed. 1919. *The note-book and account book of Nicholas Stone Master Mason to James I and Charles II* ... Oxford. *Walpole Society*, 7.

Spink, Ian, ed. 1971. *English songs 1625-1660* ... London. *Musica Britannica*, 32.

—— 1974. *English song: Dowland to Purcell*. London.

—— 1995. *Restoration cathedral music 1660-1714*. Oxford.

Spottiswoode, John. 1847-51. *The history of the Church of Scotland* [*edited by M. Russell and Mark Napier*] ... Edinburgh. 3 vols.

Stephens, Howard. 1975. 'Orlando Gibbons: "Hosanna to the Son of David"', *Music Teacher*, liv, pp. 14-15.

Stevenson, W. H. and Salter, H. E. 1939. *The early history of St. John's College, Oxford* ... Oxford. *Oxford Historical Society, New Series*, 1.

Stowe, John. 1631. *Annales, or, a generall chronicle of England. Begun by John Stow: continued and augmented ... unto the end of this present yeere, 1631. By Edmund Howes* ... London.

Strickland, Agnes. 1885. *Lives of the Queens of England* ... Vol. V. London.

Strong, Roy C. 1959. 'Queen Elizabeth I as Oriana', *Studies in the Renaissance*, 6, pp. 251-260.

Sylvester, Joshua. 1880. *The complete works ... edited ... by ... Alexander B. Grosart* ... Printed for private circulation. *Chertsey Worthies Library.* 2 vols.

Tapley-Soper, H., ed. 1933. *The registers of baptisms, marriages & burials of the City of Exeter. Volume II. The parishes of Allhallows, Goldsmith Street, St. Pancras, St. Paul* ... Exeter. *Devon and Cornwall Record Society, Publications.*

TCM. See *Tudor Church Music.*

Thewlis, George A. 1940. 'Oxford and the Gibbons family', *Music & Letters*, xxi, pp. 31-33.

Thompson, Ruby Reid. 1992. 'The 'Tregian' manuscripts: a study of their compilation', *British Library Journal*, xviii, pp. 202-204.

Thurley, Simon. 1998. *The lost palace of Whitehall.* London. (The publication of the same author's *Whitehall Palace* (New Haven, Conn., 1999) is anticipated at the time of writing.)

Toynbee, Margaret. 1955. 'The wedding journey of King Charles I', *Archaeologia Cantiana*, xlix, pp. 75-89.

Tudor Church Music. 1948. *Tudor church music. Appendix. With supplementary notes by Edmund H. Fellowes* ... London.

Turbet, Richard. 1988. 'Homage to Byrd in Tudor verse services', *Musical Times*, cxxix, pp. 485-490.

——— 2000. 'The music of Orlando Gibbons in printed editions 1625-1925'. [Publication anticipated in *Fontes Artis Musicae*, xlvii.]

Turner, William H. 1880. *Selections from the records of the city of Oxford* ... Oxford.

Venn, John and Venn, J. A. 1913. *The book of matriculations and degrees: a catalogue of those who have been matriculated or admitted to any degree in the University of Cambridge from 1544 to 1659* ... Cambridge.

——— 1922-27. *Alumni Cantabrigienses ... Part I: from the earliest times* ... Cambridge. 4 vols.

Vining, Paul, 1974. 'Orlando Gibbons: the incomplete verse anthems', *Music & Letters*, lv, pp. 70-76.

——— 1975. 'Orlando Gibbons: an index to the full and verse anthems', *Early Music*, iii, pp. 379-381.

——— 1977. 'Orlando Gibbons: the portraits', *Music & Letters*, lviii, pp. 415-429.

———— 1979. 'Wither and Gibbons: a prelude to the first English hymn book', *Musical Times*, cxx, pp. 245-246.

———— 1983. 'Gibbons and his patrons', *Musical Times*, cxxiv, pp. 707-709.

Wainwright, Jonathan P. 1997. *Musical patronage in seventeenth-century England: Christopher, first Baron Hatton (1605-1670)*. Aldershot.

Walcott, E. C. Mackenzie. 1849. *Westminster ...* London.

Walker, Ernest. 1952. *A history of music in England ...Third edition revised and enlarged by J. A. Westrup*. Oxford.

Walker, John. 1714. *An attempt towards recovering an account of the numbers and sufferings of the clergy of the Church of England ...* London.

Ward, A. W. and Waller, A. R., eds. 1910. *The Cambridge history of English literature. Volume V.* Cambridge.

Webb, E. A. 1921. *The records of St. Bartholomew's Priory and of the church and parish of St. Bartholomew the Great West Smithfield ...* London. 2 vols.

Wess, Joan. 1986. 'Musica Transalpina, parody, and the emerging Jacobean viol fantasia', *Chelys*, 15, pp. 3-25.

West, J. E. 1910-11. 'Old English organ music', *Proceedings of the Musical Association*, xxxvii, pp. 1-16.

Wheatley, H. B. 1908. 'Signs of booksellers in St. Paul's churchyard', *Transactions of the Bibliographical Society*, 9, pp. 67-106.

White, Eric Walter. 1983. *A history of English opera*. London.

Willetts, Pamela. 1972. 'The identity of Thomas Myriell', *Music & Letters*, liii, pp. 431-433.

———— 'Benjamin Cosyn: sources and circumstance'. In Banks, et al, 1995.

Williams, C. F. Abdy. [1893.] *A short historical account of the degrees in music at Oxford and Cambridge ...* London.

Wilson, David Harris. 1956. *King James VI and I*. London.

Wood, Anthony à. 1691-92. *Athenae Oxonienses. An exact history of all the writers and bishops who have had their education in the most ancient and famous University of Oxford ...* London. 2 vols. (*Fasti* appended as separate sections to each volume. The complete work reprinted in 4 vols. as *Athenae Oxoniensis ... to which are added the Fasti, or annals of the said university ... A new edition, with additions ... by Philip Bliss*, London, 1813-20. *Fasti* appended as separate sections to volumes 3 and 4.)

———— 1792-96. *The history and antiquities of the University of Oxford ...* Now first published in English ... by John Gutch. Oxford. 2 vols. in 3.

———— 1891-1900. *The life and times of Anthony Wood, antiquary, of Oxford, 1632-1695, described by himself. Collected from his diaries and other papers by Andrew Clark ...* Oxford. 5 vols. *Oxford Historical Society*, 19, 21, 26, 30, 40.

Woodfill, Walter L. 1953. *Musicians in English society from Elizabeth to Charles I.* Princeton, N. J.

Young, John. 1928. *The diary of John Young S.T.P. Dean of Winchester ... edited by Florence Remington Goodman*. London.

Zimmerman, Franklin B. 1983. *Henry Purcell, 1659-1695: his life and times. Second, revised edition*. Philadelphia.

INDEX OF WORKS BY ORLANDO GIBBONS

This index includes only a few works of doubtful authenticity; a list of pieces attributed to Gibbons mistakenly or on inadequate grounds is given on pp. 298-301. Many of Gibbons's keyboard works appear under different titles in different sources; alternative titles are given in footnotes on pp. 296-298.

continued

NAME AND SUBJECT INDEX

continued